INSTITUTES

POLITICAL AND MILITARY

INSTITUTES

POLITICAL AND MILITARY;

WRITTEN ORIGINALLY

IN THE MOGUL LANGUAGE;

BY THE GREAT

TIMOUR, IMPROPERLY CALLED TAMERLANE

MAJOR DAVY,

JOSEPH WHITE, B. D.

GYAN

Published by

Gyan Publishing House
5, Ansari Road
Daryaganj, New Delhi-110002
Phone: 011-47034999, 9811692060
E-mail: books@gyanbooks.com

Distribution Network
gyanbooks.com
India, USA, Canada, UK, Australia, France

ISBN : 978-81-212-9747-9 (PB)
First Published, 1773

2nd Impression 2023

Printed at: Gyan Press, Delhi.

INSTITUTES POLITICAL AND MILITARY
Author: MAJOR DAVY; JOSEPH WHITE

TIMOUR.

From an Original in the Bodleian Library

INSTITUTES
POLITICAL AND MILITARY,
WRITTEN ORIGINALLY
IN THE MOGUL LANGUAGE,
BY THE GREAT
TIMOUR, IMPROPERLY CALLED TAMERLANE;

First translated into PERSIAN by ABU TAULIB ALHUSSEINI; and thence into ENGLISH, with Marginal Notes,

BY MAJOR DAVY,
PERSIAN SECRETARY TO THE COMMANDER IN CHIEF OF THE BENGAL FORCES
From the Year MDCCLXX to MDCCLXXIII.
AND NOW PERSIAN SECR. TO THE GOVERNOR GENERAL OF BENGAL.

The Original PERSIAN transcribed from a MS. in the Possession of Dr. WILLIAM HUNTER, PHYSICIAN EXTRAORDINARY to the QUEEN, F. R. & A. S. and of the ROYAL ACADEMY of SCIENCES at PARIS; and the WHOLE WORK published with a Preface, Indexes, Geographical Notes, &c. &c.

BY JOSEPH WHITE, B. D.
FELLOW of WADHAM COLLEGE, and LAUDIAN PROFESSOR of ARABIC IN THE UNIVERSITY OF OXFORD.

TO

WILLIAM DEVAYNES, ESQ.

CHAIRMAN,

AND THE OTHER DIRECTORS

OF THE

HONOURABLE THE EAST INDIA COMPANY

IN THE YEAR 1780;

THIS WORK,

WHICH THEIR MUNIFICENCE

HAS CAUSED TO BE PUBLISHED,

FOR THE INSTRUCTION OF THE COMPANY'S SERVANTS

IN THE LANGUAGE OF THEIR SETTLEMENTS IN THE EAST,

IS WITH MUCH RESPECT AND GRATITUDE INSCRIBED

BY

W. DAVY AND J. WHITE.

PREFACE.

THE illustrious Name of TIMOUR was first made known to Europe by tradition: and his heroic actions are still celebrated by many who have never seen the history written by Ali Yezdi, nor perused the accounts of D'Herbelot and Voltaire. I am therefore happily unencumbered with the embarrassments of an author who labours to combat general prejudices, or to introduce a new character to the world.

THE life of this great conqueror was written, in obedience to the command of his grandson, by Ali Yezdi, a native of Persia. That work, which has been translated into French by Petis de la Croix (and from his translation into English) is valuable, not so much for the flowery phrases with which it abounds, as for the authenticity of its materials: it was collected from the journals regularly kept by the Emperor's secretaries, in which were recorded every event and transaction of his reign.

In the thirty sixth year after the death of Timour, his life was again written, in Arabic, by Ahmed Ibn Arabshah, a Syrian. That author possessed, like the former, a lively and descriptive pen: but what he gains in elegance, he loses in truth and candour; for in every page of his work may be discerned the hatred of a conquered enemy, and those national prejudices which are disgraceful to an historian.

Other histories of Timour's life and actions have been written, and some of them are now preserved in European cabinets. One of them which has eclipsed the rest, and which alone deserves to be the object of our particular notice, was written under the conqueror's inspection, if not by his own hand. The superior value of this history is at once perceived: for it was drawn not only from those authentic sources to which Ali Yezdi found access, but also from a personal recollection of those transactions whose motives and objects were perhaps known only to himself. It has not yet found its way into Europe: but I have been informed by Mr. Davy, who has read it in the East, that it is a minute and faithful narrative of an interesting and eventful period. I therefore hope my friend, who will spare no search or expence to procure it, will bring it with him when he returns from his public station abroad, and translate for the information and entertainment of his country, a larger and more certain account of Timour's conquests than we now possess. To this history, some who have no other wish than to lessen its estimation, have objected, that it must certainly be partial, and that its imperial author must have studiously concealed his vices from the reader's eye, and reflected upon his virtues more light than they will bear. But these harsh opinions can be pronounced or credited by those only who are unacquainted with his writings, and the praise which his enemies have given him, that he was a lover of veraciy, who hated, detected, and punished falsehood, with sincerity, penetration and constancy. That he might pursue his great objects by the light of truth, he made use of every friend and every foe: and in his Institutes he does not blush to acknowledge his errors and misfortunes, but glories that he has profited by them. Ambition, the infirmity of noble minds, was perhaps his only fault. The desire of conquest is a principle which the liberty of modern times has justly reprobated. But TIMOUR's conquests were in a great measure produced by other causes; by the manners of the age and country in which he lived, and by the treachery of kings, who whilst they envied his greatness, professed themselves his friends. It is needless to speak of his valour; for who has not heard of his successful wars, his perseverance and resolution in distress, and his serene and temperate conduct after victory? That he possessed the humane and liberal virtues cannot be doubted, when we read that he forbore to take revenge when it could not interfere with his interest, and that he extended the rights of subjects and citizens to nations who were willing to be slaves. When he had seen his vast empire rising, like the infant world, out of anarchy under his victorious hands, he dispensed order through every part of the dominion he had created, and governed it with wisdom, justice and benevolence. There is therefore less reason to blame his ambition, than to admire the amiable moderation by which it was restrained.

If

If the reader of this preface has not perused any history of TIMOUR's actions, he will think these praises laboured, perhaps will call them extravagant; if he has, he will consider them as the free tribute which honest admiration and a feeling heart pays to the virtues of an exalted character. There is, however, another reason which has induced me to speak so largely in this place of TIMOUR's character, and of the History written by himself: for from that History he selected those Designs and Institutes which I have the honour of presenting in this volume to the public.

THERE is ever a solemnity and a kind of sacred authority in the instructions which a dying parent delivers to his offspring. When the Lord of the East laid down his sceptre, which he had long and well supported, he did not leave to his successor a verbal injunction, a short lesson of morality, which might soon be forgotten amidst the cares and pleasures of a court; but bestowed with his empire a gift more valuable, the art to preserve it. In the leisure of his declining years, he had thrown a retrospective eye over the scenes of a long and various life, and thence he committed to writing for the perpetual instruction of his imperial descendants, those rules of government and those measures of policy which himself had invariably followed: and from his History he collected, without regard to chronological order, the several plans he had formed, and their success. To these he added his OMENS, which are omitted in this publication, because, however consistent they might have been, when they were written, with the manners and religion of the East, and whatever political purposes they

might

might then have tended to promote, the present age wisely disregards such superstitions.

THE MS. of which I now present a translation to the public, is to be found in that inestimable repository of literary treasures, Dr. WILLIAM HUNTER's Museum. *

---

* This Museum is universally known as one of the most august monuments of a love of science now existing in the world, and is become much too illustrious an object of curiosity not to merit a more exact description than has yet been given of it to the public. My reader therefore will, I am persuaded, readily forgive me, if I embrace this opportunity of acquainting him in a more detailed manner, with the great extent and variety of those obligations which its generous possessor has already conferred, and is likely to confer in a still higher degree upon the learned world.

IN saying that the Museum stands unrivalled in the number, usefulness, and neatness of the ANATOMICAL PREPARATIONS, I say no no more than what every person is prepared to expect. No man could approach Dr. HUNTER's Museum without a conviction that no exertion of art, no expence would be wanting to illustrate and embellish a science which his own studies have carried to a degree of excellence, that has made our Metropolis the first school of anatomy in the world.

THE collection of MEDALS acquired at an immense expence, defies the competition of any Royal Cabinet in Europe, that of his most Christian Majesty only excepted. The latter, which before the establishment of Dr. HUNTER's was without a rival, can hardly claim a decided superiority; in many respects is confessedly its inferior. The Doctor, who is not more distinguished by his possession than by his knowledge of these treasures, is at present employed, with the learned and ingenious Mr. COMBE, in publishing a part of them in three divisions; one containing the Greek cities, another the Persian, Phenician, Samaritan, Palmyrene, Punic &c. and the third the Greek Kings.

Of this MS. I published in 1780 a translated Specimen. The attention with which that experiment of the public favour and opinion was received, gave birth to the present work,

---

The work will be executed not only with elegance and splendor, but with a degree of accuracy and fidelity totally unusual in publications of this sort.

The Library comprehends most of the early printed books of the xv. century, the rare editions of the classics, the expensive works of natural history, of general history, and antiquities; and particularly all the curious and valuable books in medicine. And in addition to this collection of printed books, there is a considerable collection of MSS. in all the languages that are cultivated by men of erudition.

The collection of natural history is enriched with specimens of the most beautiful productions in every class. The class of fossils, and likewise that of corals, and of Birds possess many specimens that are peculiar to this cabinet. The class of shells is ample and elegant; the same character is applicable to that of insects. And there is a numerous catalogue of miscellaneous curiosities not reducible to any particular arrangement.

This Museum, thus splendidly and scientifically established, has been the laborious and expensive acquisition of a Gentleman, to whose love of science the academies of our own and other countries have borne the most honourable testimonies.

The public must be anxious to know the final destination of such treasures; it is largely interested in their fate, and would have abundant reason to lament their dispersion. But, happily for the world, their proprietor is actuated by much higher motives than those of mere personal gratification; a selfish, solitary love of letters was not the primary inducement that influenced his mind; and in proportion as his treasures become more important, he feels more strongly the obligation of devoting them to the use of the public. Such an act of munificence, as, I hear, He intends to perform in bequeathing his collection to the public

which I immediately determined to execute. As I proceeded in the tranſlation, I found difficulties in the ſequel, which had not occurred in the ſpecimen: and I obſerved in the courſe of the work ſo many terms of the Military Art, which my ſtudies had never led me to examine, and ſo many idioms of the Tartar Language which no lexicon in Europe has explained, that I choſe to decline the firſt honours of the preſent publication, and deſired to devolve the whole taſk of tranſlation on Mr. DAVY. His knowledge of that art and language pointed him out as one peculiarly qualified to undertake it; and his ready compliance with my requeſt has added an obligation of a public nature to many inſtances of private friendſhip. The tranſlation was fortunately completed, when Mr. DAVY was called to India by an honourable appointment under LORD MACARTNEY. The ſubordinate duties of an Editor, therefore, reverted to me: and I hope that by my accuracy in ſuperintending the impreſſion of the Original, and my diligence in compiling the Indexes, I ſhall give ſatisfaction to my friendly aſſociate as well as to the public. That I may not however loſe any aſſiſtance which a colleague ſo ingenious and intelligent can contribute, I have ſubjoined to this preface a Letter on the Authenticity of the Inſtitutes, with

---

public, is all that is wanting to perpetuate the gratitude of the learned world, and to place the name of HUNTER on a footing of equality, in the eſtimation of future ages, with the SLOANES, the MAFFEIS, and other illuſtrious benefactors of mankind.

IT was to the Doctor's library that this publication was indebted for the original MS; and it was ſtill further aſſiſted by a donation of three plates, and a very liberal encouragement of ſubſcription.

which

which I was favoured in anſwer to my earneſt requeſt, and which has received the praiſe and aſſent of all who have read it.

THIS is all, concerning the Author and the Edition, that I think neceſſary to be obſerved to the general readers of TIMOUR's Inſtitutes; a work, which if I am not miſled by the prepoſſeſſions of an editor, will be eſteemed curious and valuable by men of various profeſſions. The ſcholar is ever delighted with a larger knowledge of illuſtrious characters, with their remains reſcued from long oblivion, and all that tends to throw additional light on the hiſtory of mankind. He who ſtudies and profeſſes the military art, will ſurvey with pleaſure modes of marſhalling and encamping armies, and the ſtratagems of a great conqueror, judiciouſly and ſucceſsfully formed, though different from his own. The politician muſt be intereſted in the peruſal of meaſures, by which diſtant nations were united under the ſame government, and which baffled all the dangerous intrigues of powerful courts and deſigning men.

BUT the moſt immediate and evident advantage that can be derived from the preſent publication, remains yet to be told. The ſuperiority which a knowledge of the Perſian language confers on its poſſeſſors in our Eaſt India ſettlements is allowed by all whoſe civil or military ſtations have obliged them to reſide in thoſe countries. To thoſe readers who have not received this perſonal conviction, I recommend an attentive conſideration of Mr. DAVY's letter upon the ſubject, which I have added for their peruſal at the end of this volume,

volume, and by which every doubt that remains will be removed. To facilitate the attainment of this beautiful language, a Dictionary, and a Grammar, have been published by two Gentlemen, whom I have the honour to call my friends. The first of these performances is distinguished by immense labour and accuracy, the other by that propriety of arrangement which is peculiar to an elegant mind. But a language is neither learnt nor studied in a grammar or a dictionary. It can only be acquired by the help of books, or oral converse: and it has often been lamented by gentlemen intending to enter into the company's service abroad, and therefore desirous of learning the Persian language, that in England where it cannot be acquired by colloquial methods of instruction, the secondary advantages of printed Persian volumes should be wanting.

THAT this deficiency may no longer be the occasion of difficulties and a reason of complaint, the Institutes of TIMOUR are now published in a faithful English version, and the Persian from which it is translated. Nothing can be more happily calculated for the purpose of teaching a language than a work like the present, abounding with that simple grandeur which is peculiar to Eastern compositions, and which has been so often admired in the scriptures of the Hebrew testament.

GRATITUDE will not suffer me to conclude these prefatory remarks, without expressing acknowledgements to C. W. BOUGHTON ROUSE, Esq; for favours which he has conferred with a friendly politeness on the work and its editor; for the use of a valuable Persian MS. which containing a considerable portion of the original work, has enabled me to collate and correct

many

many faulty passages; and for the communication of several curious Persian papers, by the help of which my pupils in that language have derived such advantages from my lectures as could not be supplied by the single assistance of the printed volume.

I ALSO desire the same ingenious Gentleman to accept my public thanks for the translation of the Brahminic Prayer, * with which he has favoured me, and which, in compliance

---

* Notwithstanding Mr. DOWE's assertion to the contrary, there is reason to believe that various translations of Shanscrit books have been composed in the Persian language; and that the theology and philosophy of the Hindoos have been a subject of enquiry amongst men of rank in Indostan, when letters were much cultivated. In a curious and valuable work composed about two centuries ago by the command of the Emperor Akbar, we find a large account of the astronomy, philosophy, religious principles and customs of this very singular nation. This is not the only Persian work that illustrates the history of a people so little known. A translation has been made into the same language of the famous Shanscrit poem, called Mahbarit (or the great war) said to contain a hundred and twenty thousand stanzas. We find likewise that Dara Shekoo, one of the sons of the Emperor Shah Jehan, paid such attention, and gave such encouragement to the professors of the Hindoo Religion, that he was treated as an infidel by his younger brother Aurengzebe, who made this partiality a plea for exciting all the Mahommedans against him, and preventing his succession to the empire of his father. This learned prince was the author of many works, the most valuable of which, perhaps, is his summary of the Four Bedes (or sacred books) of the Hindoos, containing very curious and abstract discussions of their metaphysics and religious principles, *upon the nature and existence of the world — of the supreme Being — of the human mind and its faculties — of the worship due to the supreme Being, as sole Creator of the world* &c. &c.

Some translated fragments of this work, as well as the original Persian, having been shewn me by Mr. ROUSE, I was highly struck with the sublimity and beauty of many of the passages; and judging that a specimen would be extremely acceptable to the readers of this volume, I requested leave to insert at the end of it *One of the Prayers directed by the Brahmins to be offered up to the Supreme Being.*

with my wishes he has given me permission to publish. I have therefore inserted it, annexed to the specimen of *Eusoof* and *Zoolleikha*, in the present publication: not merely for the sake of that beauty of thought and expression, of which there is much in both to be admired; but because, like the work of TIMOUR, it serves to prove that a knowledge of the Persian displays to the European scholar not only whatever is valuable in its native compositions, but also the yet undiscovered treasures of the Shanscrit, the Mogul, and other remote languages of the East.

WADH. COLL.
Oct. 15. 1782.

J. WHITE.

The knowledge of the particulars contained in this note I owe to my conversations on the subject with Mr. ROUSE, from whose general acquaintance with the literature of India I have derived much curious and useful information.

Mr. DAVY's Letter on the Authenticity of the Inſtitutes.

Glouceſter, Oct. 24. 1779.

"MY GOOD FRIEND,

I HAVE received your favour of the 20th inſtant, and wiſh moſt heartily that my ability to comply with your requeſt was equal to my inclination.

"YOU apply to me for *external* evidence to eſtabliſh the Authenticity of TIMOUR's Inſtitutes: it is by no means an eaſy taſk which you impoſe on me; ſuch reaſons, however, as have led me to believe them genuine, I ſhall freely communicate. How far they may tend to remove the doubts of unbelieving Critics, I cannot pretend to ſay; poſſibly, in the opinions of ſuch Gentlemen, they may only ſerve to eſtabliſh my own credulity: be that as it may, I ſhall ſet out with declaring to you, that I cannot produce any *hiſtorical* proofs of the Authenticity of theſe Inſtitutes.

"THE only Hiſtories of TIMOUR, which I have read (that written by himſelf excepted,) are thoſe of *Shurruf u'deen Alli Yezzudi* and *Mirkhond:* the latter is in the *Rouzut ul Suffau.* True it is that neither of theſe authors, to the beſt of my remembrance, take any notice of the Inſtitutes, or of the Hiſtory (or Commentaries) of TIMOUR, ſaid to be written by himſelf. *Alli Yezzudi* ſays, that TIMOUR was always attended by ſeveral learned and able men, whoſe ſole employment was to keep a ſort of hiſtorical Journals of all Tranſactions as they occurred, both military and civil; that they were directed to adhere

adhere minutely to the truth in their relations of the most trifling facts, and that they were still more particularly enjoined to observe the strictest impartiality in their narratives of the conduct and actions of the Emperor himself. These historical Journals, if they may be so called, were, from time to time, read in his presence, in the presence of his Ministers and Officers, and of the learned: they were compared with, and corrected by, each other, by the Emperor himself, and by such of his people as had a personal knowledge of the Transactions therein related. It must be allowed, that this was no bad way of collecting authentic materials for the history of a mighty Emperor, governing a mighty Empire; if he took care to enforce his commands by proving himself superior to flattery, and by an encouragement of that truth and impartiality, which he so strictly enjoined. From these materials, some of which were in prose, some in verse, some in the Turki (or Mogul) language, some in the Persian, *Alli Yezzudi*, afterwards compiled the History of the Reign and Conquests of Timour, as he himself declares: and with the assistance of these very materials, it is concluded that TIMOUR wrote that voluminous and valuable History of his own Life, to which he added his Institutes. How it came to pass that that History and those Institutes were not taken notice of either by *Alli Yezzudi*, or *Mirkhond*, it is impossible, at this distance of time, to tell; but though the cause cannot with certainty be pointed out, there is room for many plausible conjectures. The historical Journals before mentioned were numerous, and they were public also; the great and the learned had free access to them; many copies of them were taken, and, with the originals, handed down to posterity: the Life of TIMOUR, and his Institutes, on the contrary, was a private work, composed by himself, with the assistance which those materials afforded him. This work the Conqueror was led to engage in from motives to us unknown: amusement or ambition, or both, might urge him to the arduous undertaking. Whether it was written with his own hand,

hand, or by a favourite and trusty amanuensis, is uncertain; but which ever was the case, it is most probable, that one copy only existed during his life-time, and possibly for many years afterwards: what became of that copy, during the confusions that followed his death, is equally uncertain and open to conjecture. But after all, it is no unreasonable supposition, that such a work in manuscript might have existed, though *Alli Yezzudi* and *Mirkhond* knew nothing of the matter. That they were not acquainted with it, is evident: for if they had, and thought it authentic, they would have bestowed upon it all the applause which is due to the intrinsic merit of the work; if they had known and thought it spurious, they would have refuted its authenticity. But they have done neither; they are totally silent on the subject: from whence we may conclude, that they were strangers to the work. But it by no means follows, that such a work could not exist, because they, or even cotemporary authors, knew nothing about it.

"THE History of TIMOUR, written by himself, carries with it the strongest proofs that he wrote for posterity only; and that he could not, in prudence, or in policy, make his work public during his life: for it contains not only the same accurate detail of the Facts and Occurrences of his reign, as are found in other Authors, but it goes much further. He gives you that which he only had the power to give, the secret Springs and Motives which influenced his conduct in the various political and military transactions of his life, the arts by which he governed, as well as the power by which he conquered. He acknowledges his weaknesses, honestly owns his errors, describes the difficulties in which he was occasionally involved by those errors, and the policy by which he surmounted and overcame those difficulties. In a word, it is a complete Index to his head and his heart; and though, take it all in all, it redounds to the honour of both the one and the other, yet it was a work by no means calculated for the perusal of his enemies, or or even his ſubjects during his life; ſince it would have enabled thoſe who choſe it, to combat him with his own weapons, or, in other words, to have turned his arts and his policy againſt himſelf. Hence it is reaſonable to ſuppoſe, that the Work in queſtion was entirely unknown during his life; and its ſubſequent temporary obſcurity may, I think, be plauſibly accounted for, by the probability of one copy only exiſting at the time of his death, by the uncertainty into whoſe hands that copy fell, and by the diviſions which followed in his family after the death of *Shaahroch*.

" *Abu Taulib ul Huſſeini*, in the Dedication of his Tranſlation to *Sultaun ul Audil*, ſays, that in the Library of *Jafir*, *Haukim* of *Yemmun*, he met with a manuſcript in the Turki, or Mogul language, which, on inſpection, proved to be the Hiſtory of TIMOUR, written by himſelf; containing an account of his Life and Actions from the ſeventh to the ſeventy-fourth year of his age, &c. &c. He then proceeds to give the Tranſlation of the ſaid Hiſtory, in which are included the Inſtitutes.

" IT may appear remarkable that the Tranſlator ſhould ſay ſo little, or in fact nothing, to prove the authenticity of the valuable work, which he was about to tranſlate. It has an extraordinary appearance, I allow; but, I think, the following inferences only can be drawn from it: either that he thought the work itſelf contained ſufficient proofs of its own authenticity, or that at the period when he tranſlated it, it was ſo well known, as not to admit of doubt, or diſpute. For my part, I think his inattention to this point is a very ſtrong, if not the ſtrongeſt poſſible proof, that the Hiſtory and Inſtitutes of TIMOUR are genuine.

" AN European Critic may ſay, that this ſame *Abu Taulib* might have wrote the work himſelf in the Perſian language, and have impoſed it upon the world as a Tranſlation from the Royal

Royal Mogul author. This I take to be impoſſible. Authors in the Eaſt neither ſold their works to bookſellers, nor publiſhed by ſubſcription, nor depended for ſupport on the applauſe, the generoſity, or the credulity of the public: they were patronized by Princes, who rewarded their labours in proportion to the value of their works. And therefore, if *Abu Taulib* had been capable of writing ſuch a work, he never would have been guilty of ſo dangerous and fooliſh an artifice, which could tend only to diminiſh both his fame and his profit. The applauſe and the reward due to the Tranſlator of an excellent work, muſt, whatever his merit, be inferior to thoſe which are due to the author of ſuch a work; if therefore he had been maſter of abilities to write the Life and Inſtitutes of TIMOUR, as there written, he would have ſpoke in the third perſon inſtead of the firſt (no other alteration being neceſſary,) and have ſtood forth as the author of the firſt and beſt Hiſtory of the Life of TIMOUR, that ever was wrote; for which he muſt have obtained both applauſe and profit tenfold. The ſame mode of reaſoning will hold good to prove that the *Turki* copy could not be wrote by any *Mogul* author, but him to whom it is aſcribed, TIMOUR HIMSELF.

" THE noble ſimplicity of Diction, the plain and unadorned Egotiſm that runs through the whole of the Inſtitutes and Hiſtory of TIMOUR, are peculiarities which mark their originality and their antiquity alſo. The Orientals, for ſome centuries paſt, have adopted a very different mode of writing; the beſt of their hiſtorical works are filled with poetical and hyperbolical Flowers and Flouriſhes, which are ſo numerous, and occur ſo frequently, that many a *folio* volume, weeded and pruned of theſe ſuperfluities, would be reduced to a very moderate *octavo*.

" THE only work bearing the leaſt reſemblance to the Life and Inſtitutes of TIMOUR, which has fallen under my obſervation, is the Hiſtory (or Commentaries) of *Sultaun Babour*, written

written by himself. Babour was descended from TIMOUR in the fifth degree; he was the son of Omer, the son of Abu Saeed, the son of Mahummud, the son of Meraun Shaah, the son of TIMOUR. About eighty years elapsed between the death of TIMOUR and the birth of Babour. Babour in the twelfth year of his age, and the 899th year of the *Hejra*, sat upon the throne of his father, in the kingdom of *Furgauneh*. The earlier part of his life very much resembled that of his great predecessor, TIMOUR: and his abilities in the Field and in the Cabinet, his fortitude in distress, his activity and courage when surrounded with difficulties and danger, and the glory and success with which his Enterprizes were finally crowned, make the resemblance between these two Princes still more striking. Like TIMOUR, Babour wrote an accurate History of his own Life and Actions in the *Turki* language; which though by no means equal to the admirable composition of his renowned ancestor, is a work of infinite merit. Yet this history, great as the Royal Author was, remained in obscurity till the middle of the reign of his grandson *Acbur*, when it was translated into the Persian language by one of his Omrahs, *Khaun a Khaunaun*. It is more difficult to account for the temporary obscurity of this valuable work, than for that of TIMOUR'S; for at the death of Babour it must have fallen into the hands of his son *Humaioon*, and on his death, into those of *Acbur*. Yet till the middle of his reign it remained unknown and untranslated: and if *Acbur* had, in the early part of his life, been driven from his throne, if Divisions had taken place in his family, and his posterity had been scattered abroad, this valuable Manuscript might have fallen into private hands, and have remained unknown for a century longer; possibly, have been totally lost. No Critic, either Oriental or European, pretends to dispute the authenticity of Babour's History; and, as far as I have been able to discover, the Learned of the East consider the Institutes and History of TIMOUR as equally genuine.

"I WAS

" I WAS acquainted with ſeveral great and learned Men in India, both Natives and Perſians: on peruſing the works of TIMOUR, I was led to make the ſame enquiry which you have made, Whether they were, or were not authentic? The anſwers I received were always in the affirmative, and attended with ſome tokens and expreſſions of ſurprize, that I ſhould, or could, doubt their being genuine. SHAAH AULUM, the preſent Mogul, has a beautiful copy of the Hiſtory and Inſtitutes of TIMOUR; which he holds in ſuch eſteem, and of which he is ſo exceedingly careful, that though he granted me the uſe of any other book in his poſſeſſion, this he poſitively excepted by name, as a work ſo rare and valuable, that he could not truſt it to the care of any perſon whatever.

" UPON the whole, if the learned of the Eaſt, for ſeveral generations, have been induced to give implicit credit to the Inſtitutes and Hiſtory of TIMOUR, which is certainly the caſe, I do not ſee how Europeans can, with any degree of propriety, doubt their authenticity. The Oriental Critics have the very beſt materials on which to form their opinions; our ſmall ſtock of knowledge in the language, and ſtill ſmaller ſtock of Aſiatic Hiſtorians, render us very incompetent judges of the point in queſtion. There are a great number of Oriental Manuſcripts in the libraries of the Learned; but I am convinced, that there are ſtill many, very many, which never have found, and poſſibly never will find, their way into Europe; and therefore, though no *hiſtorical* evidence can be produced to prove the authenticity of the Works of TIMOUR, yet no one can pretend to ſay, that ſuch *hiſtorical* Proofs do not exiſt. The learned of the Eaſt muſt be the beſt judges whether they do, or do not merit their belief and veneration; and they have thought proper to beſtow upon them both the one and the other. It is much to be regretted, that the Life of TIMOUR, written by himſelf, is not to be found in Europe: if that, and the Inſti-

tutes

tutes could be tranſlated and publiſhed together, ſuch is the accuracy of the narrative, ſuch the importance of the matter, and ſuch the lights that they would mutually reflect on each other, that it would, I conceive, be impoſſible for any one to read them, without acquieſcing in their Authenticity from the *internal* Evidence alone.

Yours, moſt aſſuredly,

WILLIAM DAVY."

Account of the Portrait of TIMOUR.

The Note and Letter here following are printed from a Book of Eaftern *Portraits given by Mr.* POPE *to the Univerfity. They are fufficiently explicit in themfelves and require no Illuftration.*

" THIS Book (containing one hundred and feventy eight
" Portraits of the Indian Rajahs continued to TAMER-
" LANE and the great Mogols his fucceffors as far as to Au-
" rengzebe) was procured at Surat by Mr. JOHN CLELAND,
" and given to the Bodley-Library, as a token of refpect by

ALEX. POPE."

1737.

To Mr. EVERARD, Fellow of Braze-Nofe College, Oxford.

LONDON, the 8th. *July*, 1760.

" WITH great pleafure it is, SIR, that I comply with your intimation to me of a defire to know fome particulars of that Collection of the Miniature Portraits of the fovereigns of Indoftan prefented by Mr. POPE to the Bodleian library at Oxford, infcribed with his name and mine.

" WHILE I was in India fometime before the year feventeen hundred and forty, one of the Mogul's generals was with an army incamped before the town of Surat, of which Tegbeg Khaun was then governor for the Mogul. On thofe occafions the general never enters the town himſelf, but deputes certain oſſicers to the governor, under pretext of taking cognizance of his conduct, but in fact to receive a bribe, in form of a preſent, not to make too ſtrict a ſcrutiny.

" TEGBEG KHAUN, who was far from being on good terms with the court, being obliged to proportion his preſent to the need he ſtood in of abſolution for the paſt, and protection for the future, ſent the general ſome lacks of rupees, not leſs than to the amount of three or four hundred thouſand pounds. But that ſuch a tranſaction may not appear too barefacedly what it always is, a corrupt bargain, the general uſually makes the governor ſome preſent, which is to paſs for a return. On this occaſion then the Mogul general ſent Tegbeg Khaun a ſabre ſet with rubies, emeralds and diamonds, worth perhaps at moſt three or four thouſand pounds, together with this Book containing a ſet of Miniature Portraits of the ſucceſſive ſovereigns of Indoſtan for ſeveral ages back. They are in colours, on vellum-leaves, and are copies from a ſeries of originals in the Mogul's palace.

" THAT they are not fancy-pictures, there is great reaſon to believe (independent of the preſumption in their favour from the circumſtance of their being a preſent on ſo capital an occaſion from one great officer of ſtate to another, it being well known, that ſuch a ſet of pictures actually exiſts in the royal palace, it hardly ſeems improbable that a copy was taken from them. And here it is obſervable, that the Mogul-moors have nothing of that averſion to images or pictures, which is even a point of religion to the Mahomedans in general. But theſe Moguls retain ſo much of their Tartarian origin as to tolerate all religions, and even to incorporate theirs of the *Thien*, ſuch as the court of China alſo profeſſes, with the predominant religion of whatever country they conquer; for the greater eaſe of preſerving their conqueſts by this political conformity.

THE

" THE portrait of Tamerlan (Timur-lang) in this collection, and perhaps the only one extant in Europe on which any dependence for genuineneſs may be reaſonably had, ſeems to favour the belief of its authenticity, in that you may very clearly remark in it the diſtinctive Tartar lineaments, a broad flattiſh face, with ſmall eyes. Theſe in his ſon and ſucceſſor, are ſomewhat leſs conſpicuous, and, as the line of deſcent proceeds, they melt by degrees wholly into the ſoftneſs of the Indian features.

" IT may alſo be obſerved, that the Moors, or Mahomedan ſovereigns of Indoſtan, are in this collection diſtinguiſhed from the Gentoo ones, by the faſhion of the ſkirts of their robes, which in the Gentoos, hang on each ſide, cut at bottom into an angular form, as all the Rajahs wear them to this day for an enſign of royalty.

" HOWEVER, this book, ſuch as it is, was by the governor Tegbeg Khaun made a preſent of to Mr. Frazer, the ſame who, at my inſtance and requeſt, tranſlated from a Perſian manuſcript the account of Shah Nadir's (the famous Thamas Kooly Khaun's) expedition into India; and who brought home a curious collection of oriental manuſcripts, moſt of which once belonged to the royal library of Iſpahan, and had eſcaped the rage and barbariſm of the Aphgoons, or Ophguan invaders, under Emir Veiſs and his ſucceſſors.

" MR. FRAZER having parted with this Set of Portraits to me, I ſent it to Mr. POPE, with whom I was then in correſpondence; and who wrote me, That judging it too great a curioſity for his private ſtudy, he had done it the honour of preſenting it to the Bodleian Library.

"I NEED not, I presume, insist on how agreeable such a disposal must be to one so penetrated as I have ever been with sentiments of veneration for an university, which in quality both of a spring-head of learning and of a noble conservatory of literature, is so justly considered as a national ornament and honour. But I now receive from that circumstance a fresh pleasure in its furnishing me an occasion of assuring yourself of the truth with which I most respectfully am,

SIR,

Your most obedient

humble Servant,

JOHN CLELAND."

The following ſyſtematized *View of the Matters contained in the Work of* TIMOUR *was ſent me by my learned and reſpected Friend Mr.* HENDERSON *of* Pembroke College, *to whom my Thanks are due for this Communication, and whoſe own Words will beſt ſerve to introduce it.*

SUCH a collection as the following has been acceptable in the editions of various authors. I need not mention the *Penu Tullianum*, or the ſimilar work from SENECA. Hereby the moſt important parts are got together, more ready for uſe: and the book is brought, as it were, to a focus. In ſome authors this is more uſeful than in others, in none quite vane. If we may have nothing to learn from TIMOUR, it will at leaſt pleaſe the curious to ſee in one view ſeveral good things which his mind was acquainted with: we ſhall be pleaſed to know that he knew them.

To avoid ſuperfluity of bulk I have made but three heads, *Political, Military*, and *Theologic* — adding a few remarkable Events.

In *political* management TIMOUR ſeems to have relied chiefly on amuſing perſons, bribing them, keeping them in ſuſpenſe, and dividing them. He was acutely ſagacious, rightly provident and firmly reſolute. He was generally willing by any undeſerved

ſerved or exceſſive kindneſs to make and keep friends: he ſeemed not to know, but readily pardoned enmity and treachery. And ſuch was his delicacy of ſentiment, ſuch the art of his addreſs that he cleared every ſuſpicion of the guilty and fearful; he covered the bluſhes and ſoothed the confuſion of the conſciouſly unworthy. One ſo qualified, with ſo diſcerning an eye, ſo ſenſible yet ſtrong a heart, ſo open yet powerful a hand, ſo free yet ſo forcible an addreſs, what wonder that he was great?

In *military* occaſions his great excellence ſeems to have been hiding or magnifying his ſtrength, ſurpriſe, varying his attacques, and obſtinacy in keeping his ground. His *politics* availed him much in *governing* his army, and he often uſed prayers, his *oracle* of the KORAN, and other *religious* means to *encourage* them.

PARTICULARS in either of theſe parts are not here noticed; but the more generally applicable Sentences.

IN *theologic* matters I have been more ſcant, not meaning a detail of Mahummudan principles. There are only a few notes, tending to ſhew that religion every where has it's force, and is ſerviceable to a general and prince.

I COULD have added *parallel* ſentences from ſacred and other writers in moſt places. But I thought it needleſs to thoſe who knew them, and uſeleſs to the reſt. I only note TIMOUR's Maxims.

POLITICAL

POLITICAL MAXIMS.

TIMOUR's ends "Reduction of kingdoms, obtainment of empire, defeating armies, circumventing enemies, making friends of foes, going out and coming in among friends and enemies."[a] P. 3.

"In conducting the concerns of government take by the hand four assistants, Deliberation, Counsel, Vigilance, and Circumspection." 5.

"Requisites for conducting the concerns of empire are one portion, patience and forbearance; and one portion, pretended negligence and feigning not to know that which thou knowest." ibid.

"The experiened have said, By policy kingdoms may be conquered and numerous hosts may be defeated, which by the swords of united armies cannot be overthrown." 7.

"By experience it is known to me that Counsel and Deliberation, and skilful Measures, are only to be found with the wise and sagacious." 9.

"Though the conclusion of every worldly event is covered by the curtain of fate; yet, according to the holy word of Mahummud, in every enterprise which I undertook, I acted from Counsel and Deliberation." ibid.

"When my counsellors and my advisers were assembled together, I demanded their opinions on the good and on the evil, and on the advantages and on the disadvantages, of undertaking or relinquishing, the enterprise before us. And when I had heard their opinions thereon, I myself examined both sides of their opinions.[b] *N.B.* Every plan in which I discovered a twofold hazard I rejected, and chose that in which the peril was single." 11.

"After examining the avenue of retreat, enter on the execution." ib.

"Those are worthy to be counsellors who stedfastly adhere to that which they say and do." 13.

"Turn the ear to the counsel of the tongue, but treasure the counsel of the heart in the soul."[c] ibid.

When officers are sent to lay waste a province, and it is necessary to the province to gain time, the officers are to be amused with bribes and promises. 19.

They are contracted hearts and eyes to which presents seem great. 21.

If officers be known to have

[a] Of these ends the two last only are essentially good. The others are as their final cause. [b] Hereby, 1. He improved his own wisdom. 2. He had the advantage of every good hint — (And seldom does the wisest not need one.) 3. He pleased the courtiers by giving them the honor and importance of advising their sovereign. But by determining for himself, 1. He kept his counsellors from being too powerful. 2. From being envied. And, 3. Was more likely to have nothing offered him unreasonable or unplausible. [c] First be able to distinguish them.

taken

taken bribes, their prince must cause them to *refund the Bribes*, and displace them.[a] ibid.

People broken by oppression, tho' readily agreeing with an opposition may break their engagements. Mauwur u Nuhur[b]. 33.

An army is the sinews of empire. ibid.

A prince delivered from oppression will sometimes turn against his deliverer, suspecting that else he may seize the government.[c] 47.

When a person aspiring to the throne is known among the people, they will look with observation at him. Therefore he must please them. He must shew royal generosity and liberality.[d] p. 65.

When Timour saw his people divided, and some not heartily with him, he sent for these privately, promising each according to his particular desires. But to each he appointed a *Kotul*, i. e. a person who should succeed, in case of death, desertion, dismission, or the like. By this act he engaged their hearts, he made them watchful to seem worthy their rank, he had a spy over them ready to tell when they deserved dishonour, and he retained two persons by one place. 75.

Since GOD is one, and hath no partner, therefore the vice-gerent over the land of the Lord must be one only. *N.B.* This was said against making confederate princes partakers of their commander's fortune. 89.

Suspected princes are to be divided, that they may be weak. But one must be their reconciler to profit by their united strength. 91. Ki Khissero and Aljauitoo Burdi. 93.

A friend in all places cometh to use. 103.

One obstinately resolved on resistance, who is dangerous, may be won by seeming neglect, or indirect commendations, which he may hear. 111.

An ambassador of use to give intelligence. 127.

Unless it be quite necessary a prince should not displace officers of his own promotion.[e] 133.

Timour having a design against Moosi, complaint was made, and redress sought against Moosi from Timour, by the brother of a governor whom Moosi had slain, and who had been Timour's friend. Timour put the complainant into custody, seeming therein very unjust and giving great offence. Then he said that Moosi and he were on

[a] Perhaps this is not so good. For in this case, people might urge bribes persuasively enough on purpose to ruin an officer. Nor do bribers deserve to recover money so mischievously spent. — Would it not be better to put such bribes in the public stock?

[b] This may admonish at the present time.

[c] As for example. There is a *possibility* of it between the (supposed opprest) Americans, and the (supposed deliverers) the French.

[d] At least he must be better than he whom he rivals.

[e] In some cases this may be necessary. As, 1. When they are known to be less qualified than they seemed at first. 2. When they act very wrong. 3. When they are too important. (But here is need of caution.) 4. When they are found treacherous. 5. When their removal is required by a more powerful. (But this being a physical or political necessity, not an ethical, justice, and the public good, are to be regarded as much as possible.) 6. At the remonstrance of the people, where they have a part of the government.

good

good terms. Which Moosi hearing became secure, and obeyed Timour's summons. By this stratagem Timour took him, and afterwards punisht him. 137.

"I at all times thought that there was nought more worthy the *valor*[a] of princes than conquering of kingdoms and empires, and waging holy wars with infidels."[b] 141.

When seditions are not checked in time, they may grow to open rebellion. ibid.

Seditious people are to be divided by dispersing them.[c] 143.

Such discipline is to be kept that men and officers may maintain without presumption their proper station. 161.

A prince is never to be easy or secure. 163.

It is good to pardon, to be liberal, to be affable, merciful; but chiefly to regard the low and redress the injured. 165.

The valiant are to be distinguisht by a general. And a prince must favor the learned and religious. ib.

Those who labor to hurt others, are not to be admitted to intimacy. 167.

History and politics should be studied by a prince; that he may know what has happened to royalties and realms, and wherefore, and how it happened.[d] ibid.

A prince should learn the conditions of his subjects in all ranks particularly. 169.

For that purpose intelligencers should be dispersed, who should be condignly punisht for falsehood. ib.

The oppressions of inferior governors to be righted and adequately punisht. ibid.

Evil persons are to have scope till they make their selves manifest and odious. 171.

Not only good and great men are to be rewarded, but enemies and traitors on submission are to be pardoned and used as friends, till their suspicions are overcome and their hearts won. Especially if they are brave, wise and eminent. ibid.

One of various fortune learns neither to confide in friends too much, nor fear his foes. 173.

The man who is faithful to an enemy is honest, and *may* be faithful to the other side. ibid. And vice versa. 175.

A prince should make his laws according to the religion of his country. 177.

Teachers of the divine law should be appointed. 179.

The prince is judge of ecclesiastic matters. ibid. 181, et seq.

In weighty matters the divines are to be consulted about religion. 189.

A prince should attend to the minute parts of religion, and make a reformation when they are neglected.

[a] But a prince must be just and good as well as valiant. [b] This is not inserted as a maxim of true, but of Timour's, policy. Have all European princes been more wisely politic? [c] They may be separated without dispersion. And that will be as good. For instance, 1. communication may be cut off by lines of army and fortification; 2. some may be brought over and garrisoned, protected and privileged; 3. seditious people are the easiest to divide by suspicious hints. [d] Timour learnt hence the evil of tyranny and cruelty.

glected.[a] ibid. et ſeq.

It is important to have the approbation of thoſe who are eminent. And they grant concurrence to one who honours them, and courts it. 193, 195.

If a prince would be ſtrong and ſecure, he muſt attach to him the religious. 197.

When thoſe who have injured can be made friends, their injuries are not to be revenged, but forgot. If they ſtill will be evil, they are to be left for a time. Elſe they are to be overcome with good. 199, 201.

Princes ſhould avail their ſelves of the intercourſe with divines, lawyers, ſagacious perſons, holy men whoſe prayer is effectual, warriors, prudent and ſecret men, learned men in ſciences and arts, hiſtorians, aſcetics and ſolitaries, artificers and tradeſmen, and travellers. 209 et ſeq.

Soldiers and ſubjects equal, but one muſt not hurt the other. 209.

Wages of ſoldiers to be advanced, not detained, eſpecially in critical Times. ibid.

Inferior governors well choſen and ordered do much ſervice. 211.

Plenty and population are main ends in a government. ibid.

Merchants may be uſeful not for their wares only, but intelligence from various parts. 217.

It is good to reinſtate perſons who are conquered in their former rank in one's own ſervice. 217.

When merchants from enemies become ſubjects a ſufficient capital ſhould be allowed them. 219. The ſame of the peaſant.

A prince's words and actions ought to be his own, and his ſubjects and ſoldiers ſhould know they are not cauſed by the influence of any other.[b] 221.

A prince ſhould hear advice from every one. But ſo attend to none as to make him equal or ſuperior to his ſelf in ruling. ibid.

A king ſhould be juſt. But eſpecially he ſhould have juſt and good miniſters. Becauſe they can counteract his evil. But if they do evil, it will ruin him.[c] 223.

He muſt act reſolvedly and firmly: giving his orders in perſon, that none may dare or be able to oppoſe. ibid.

A reſolution, enterpriſe or command muſt not be altered. Even tho the conſequence is expected to be bad.[d] ibid.

[a] It makes him, 1. leſs ſuſpected; 2. more revered; and 3. gains him the influence of the religious. *N.B.* The reformation meant is only bringing again into uſe thoſe eſtabliſhed things which by omiſſion were obſolete. — The attention is to maintain and ſpread religion.

[b] This Maxim muſt be qualified. It is a good one in an abſolute government, as Timour's; where the perſon, not the law, rules. But in mixt governments, where the law is underſtood to be above the king, it is more ſecure for the prince to let his ſubjects know that miniſters direct the government, and to give them up when demanded by the people. Unleſs in ſome ſpecial caſes.

[c] This alſo belongs to an abſolute government. See the note foregoing.

[d] This reſolution often brings affairs to an unhoped for iſſue: and ſo gives ſoldiers an opinion of the commander's being infallible and irreſiſtible. Which upon the whole may do more good than evading an evil by change of council. And it is better that a ſuperior do not ſucceed in a buſineſs, than that he ſo ſubmit to the ſubjects as to be expected or conſtrained to ſubmit again.

Too great a ſhare of government ſhould be truſted to none. Neither diſcretionary power. But government is to be divided into as many poſts as may be. Then every one's own buſineſs and watching over others will keep the ſupremacy ſafe. 225.

Rulers ſhould have and maintain a dignity of authority: a majeſty, which can overawe from preſuming at all againſt them. 227.

The power of every officer, even the moſt inferior, to be abſolute over all below.[a] 231.

The learned and divines to have ſubſiſtence from the prince. 235.

A province ſhould be inſpected on the third year. And if populous, plentiful and ſatisfied, the governor ſhould be continued. Elſe removed; and receive nothing for three years. 241.

Tax-gathering may be enforced by menaces: but not corporal puniſhment. ibid.

" The governor whoſe authority is inferior to the power of the ſcourge is unworthy to govern. ib.

Ameers to be tried by their Peers. 245.

Miniſters not to be condemned but on fair trial and clear proof. Becauſe many ſeek their ruin, either envying them, or plotting againſt their ſovereign. ibid.

Peculation in miniſters of revenue to be made good from their own fortunes. 249.

They whom a miniſter patronizes will deceive and betray him: whom he neglects oppoſe him. ibid.

Extortion and rapine in all caſes to be puniſht and righted by reſtitution. 251.

The eccleſiaſtic judge to decide of cauſes and crimes cognizable by eccleſiaſtic law. The civil judge to order the reſt. 253.

A miniſter ſhould be firm and generous, intelligent and ſagacious, be able to live in harmony with the ſubjects, be patient under difficulties, and cultivate peace. ibid.

Such a miniſter ſhould be diſtinguiſht by honor, a poſt of authority, the confidence of his maſter, and diſcretional power. ibid.

The miniſter equal to his office is juſt and moderate (concerning government, land and property) never *appears* a hypocrite, ſpeaks well of the ſoldiers and ſubjects, neither ſays nor hears ill of others, behaves ſo prudently as to turn a man's mind from bad intentions, and does good for evil. 255.

Office muſt not be conferred on the *wicked*, the *envious*, the *revengeful*, or the *ſeditious*. ibid.

If a miniſter be too compliant the worldly-minded will bear him down. 259.

N.B. That miniſter is wiſe who regulateth royalty by a juſt knowledge of mankind. ibid.

The dignity[b] of empire is ſupported by extenſive territories, by a rich treaſury and numerous armies. ibid.

[a] This belongs to an univerſity, or other abſolute government. And is beſt for ſuch. This ſhews how nearly approche ſuch government, ariſtocraſy and democracy. The mere ſubject has *many* lords. [b] The dignity, but not the true welfare. As little army as ſafely may: and well filled, not large territory, are beſt.

A good minister in affairs of the empire, seeth not his enemy.[a] 261.

N.B. That is a valuable minister who keeps in eye the population and cultivation of the country, the prosperity of the subjects, the strength of the army, and the fulness of the treasury. ibid.

He is a skilful minister who can, in fit time, divide or unite the subjects and armies; who can remove the difficulties of his sovereign, and can bring the confused matters of administration to order. 265.

An inferior officer should not do the work of a superior; nor vice versâ. 273.

The several officers of different departments should state to the prince in council the truth of the affairs under their jurisdiction: to be recorded, by official secretaries for the council and a secret one for the prince, in private confidence. 303. et seq.

Regular accompts to be taken of receipts and expenses in each department. 307.

A minister should (at least) do that for the king which he expects from his own steward and Major domo. 313.

A good servant does his duty, because he loves his master. ibid.

A good minister takes not affront nor meditates revenge for the slights or chidings of his prince: but takes his sovereign's faults on his self. 315.

The servant whose eye is on the gleanings of his master will overlook his duty. 315.

He who forgetteth his duty should be trusted no more. ibid.

"The servant who in the hour of trial searcheth after excuses, who on the day of enterprise demandeth his dismission, who keepeth his eye on the means of retreat,[c] and who transferreth till to-morrow the business of to-day, let the names of such servants be held in contempt, and let them be delivered over to the Almighty."[d] ibid.

If a good servant be any how put to shame, let it be repaired. 317.

When one who had forsaken his master, returns of his own accord, let him be received with honor.[e] ibid.

That servant, who was good and faithful to his former master, is to be received with honor, and promoted if he come to another: and the contrary. ibid.

When a servant in policy *pretends* friendship to his master's foe, he should be considered as a wise friend. But if it be earnest, let him be given to the enemy. 321.

When Timour conquered the kingdom of Tooraun, he behaved alike to his friends and enemies;

[a] That is, 1. is intimidated by no opposition to his well-doing; 2. has no consideration of his own private enmities. His power is never the tool of his own revenge.
[b] *N.B.* Under an oriental master. [c] i. e. His *own* safe and advantageous retreat; not that of the adventure. [d] i. e. Be no more concerned with them. [e] How does this consist with the last maxim but two following? Sometimes one is good, sometimes the other. Discretion to be used. As in answering and not answering a fool according to his folly.

even

even to those who had injured him, and had deceived him. So that his foes blushed at his generosity. 323.

The like to those also who envied him. 325.

If a tyrant govern another kingdom it ought to be assaulted, that it may be delivered.[a] 331.

Also if religion be dishonored there. 333.

N.B. Where schism and faction abound the nation is near ruin. And it should be invaded.[b] 335.

Timour informed his self of the dispositions of a people; and indulged their prejudices in his appointments of rulers. 337.

Business is not to be postponed: — lenity and severity have their seasons — the sword is not to be used where negotiation will serve. ib.

"Dominion may be continued to the *infidel*; but to the *tyrant* it shall not be continued."[c] 341.

In conquered kingdoms, Timour reverenced the divines and learned, and provided for them. The rich and the powerful he held as brethren; the poor as his children. He exalted the nobles. He honored the soldiers and soothed the subjects. To the good he did good, expelling the vicious. He kept the base in proper bounds. He suspended all between hope and fear. He opened the portals of equity, and closed the avenues to oppression. 345.

He gave the government again to the subdued prince, holding him obedient by generosity.[d] To the refractory he gave "a *vigorous*, *sagacious* and *upright* Governor." 347.

Thieves were put to death, seditious banisht, and vagrants and buffoons kept out. ibid.

A magistrate watched the soldiers and subjects in every city, and was accountable for all stolen. ibid.

Guards were appointed on the rodes and answerable for losses. ib.

Soldiers were not permitted to enter forcibly a subject's house or seize his property. 349.

Provision was made for mendicants, that begging might be abolisht. ibid.

N.B. *Particulars* of police are recounted after this page, which will not be noted here: only the more general and important.

Beggars persisting to beg were sold into another land. 361.

"I ordained that the revenues and taxes should be collected in such a manner as not to ruin the subject or depopulate the country.[e] For that causeth a diminution of the imperial treasures, and the dispersion of the troops; and the dispersion of the troops, an extinction of the imperial power." 361.

Charters of safety granted to conquered subjects. 363.

The subject paid one third of the *current price* of his commodities into the royal treasury.[f] ibid.

[a] This may have limitations. *N.B.* WILL. III.

[b] When the policy or religion of a country is wrong, Timour would have it righted by a victorious foreign power.

[c] When *men* are injured they are more impatient (and short-sighted) than GOD.

[d] That is not always safe. The subject king has too much power and opportunity (if still reigning) to hurt the conqueror. It is easy to observe that Timour was, like other men, sometimes in extremes. He was too open or too artful.

[e] A necessary consequent on the former.

[f] So taxes were always proportionably tolerable. But the exigencies of the state are so different, that is impracticable; except by varying the tax

Soldiers were paid according to that price also. ibid. in note.

Whoever cultivated waste land, or made an aquæduct or canal was free from tax the first year, in the second what he offered was received, in the third he was regularly taxed. 367.

If a rich injured a poor man, recompense was levied on the wrong-doer. 369.

Waste lands unowned were annext to the crown. If poor, insufficient people owned them, they were enabled to cultivate. ibid.[a]

Bridges repaired and built: Inns supplied. ibid.

In every city a mosque, a school, a monastery,[b] an alms-house, an hospital (with a physician who had salary) a government-house and a court of justice. 371.

An officer (with approbation of ecclesiastic and civil judges) took care of the effects of those who absconded, the insane, those who died intestate, or suffered as malefactors. ibid.

Property given to the lawful heir. If none, expended in public piety. 373.

from one commodity to another; so as that the most saleable bears the burthen. That cannot be where all are taxed in the lump. This is said on supposition that the state may want more than the usual revenue, sometimes. But one third is higher than any rate of taxation with us. [a] *N.B.* Our Commons. [b] Better a college, or the like.

MILITARY PASSAGES.

"ONE experienced and able soldier can direct the efforts of thousands of thousands." p. 7.

If a prince send an army against a foe there is a twofold danger, i. e. that his army may be defeated or revolt. But if he go with them, there is only one peril, i. e. of defeat.[a] 11.

Counsils tending to divide the soldiers are not to be hearkened to. And the dictates of fear are not to be regarded. 15.

One in war, having few men, should abide in the desert. 41.

If the men will not stay in the desert the commander must dispose of them, within call, and go to levy more. ibid.

"And the spirit of glory assaulted me, and said, "Since thou hast advanced forth with pretensions to empire, even this is becoming the dignity and the rank of a king that thou resolve on war. And that thou be either triumphant or be slain in battle." 63.

[a] Timour always preferred the single to the double peril.

"

"And I saw the duration of my power in this, that I should divide among my soldiers the treasures which I had gathered." 65.

"I saw it was good that I should be quick and break their power before they could gather their army." 69.

"I found that my forces were not united with me. And to make them unanimous I saw it was good that I should shew kindness to some, and that with some I should dissemble, and that I should tempt some by riches, and sooth some by promises and persuasions, and engagements." 71.

"I overpowered them at the second charge. And as the night was come I pitched my tents on the ground where I was. And I counselled with myself that I would not let the plain of battle cool.[a] And I considered that if I was guilty of delay something might come to pass which might cause me to stand in need of assistance. And tho Ameer Hoossein was encamped behind me, I did not cause myself to stand in need of his support.[b] But by skilful measures I defeated the forces of Ouleaus Khaujeh, and the men of Jitteh." 77.

"And I saw that they were going troop after troop. And my Ameers and my soldiers called for orders to pursue them. And I said to myself 'I must delay to pursue them until their intentions be known.' And after they had travelled four fursungs they halted. And I discovered their design. Behold their intention was this, that they might bring me down from the mountain apart and assault me." 79.

"And on this account the honor of my station urged me that I should take the castle of Kurshee. And certain of my Ameers counselled that I should go and seize it by force. But I deliberated thus, 'If I attempt to reduce it by a siege, perhaps my forces may be repulsed.' And in a siege several dangers occurred to my mind, and I rejected that measure. And I saw it was good that I should turn my face toward Khoraufaun[c] until the hearts of the keepers of the castle should be at rest: and that then I should return and march with speed and assault the castle by surprise, and reduce it. And I marched and went toward Khoraufaun. When I crossed the Waters of Amuveah, a Kauruvvaun arrived from Khoraufaun, and they were journeying toward Kurshee. And the leader of that Kauruvvaun brought gifts to me. And I asked him of the state of the Ameers of Khoraufaun. And I told him that I was travelling to the kingdom of Khoraufaun. And I dismissed him. And I sent a spy with the people of the Kauruvvaun. And I tarried on the border of the waters of Amuveah until the spy

[a] According to the different circumstances the event of such conduct may be different. [b] Sometimes it may be well to do at almost any rate without help, rather than make one, who might help, of too great consequence. But sometimes this slight may be returned by the slighted person's becoming as important a foe as he would have been a friend. [c] In a different direction. As if he were going else where than to Kurshee.

brought

brought word that the people of the Kauruvvaun had given intelligence to Ameer Moosi saying, 'We saw Ameer Timour on the border of the waters of Amuveah, and he was going toward Khorausaun.' And when Ameer Moosi and the forces of Ameer Hoossein heard this news, they were glad of heart. And they pitched their tents, and spread abroad the carpet of riot and dissipation. And when I received intelligence thereof I selected 243 brave and resolute, and tried, and experienced warriors from among my forces. And I re-crossed the waters of Amuveah. And I marched with great speed. And I alighted at the distance of a fursung from the castle of Kurshee. And I commanded that they should make ready ladders, and bind them together with ropes. And at this time Ameer Jaukoo kneeled before me and said, 'Many of our warriors have remained behind: until they shall arrive, delay is necessary.' And at this time it came into my mind that I should go *alone* and examine the castle. And I took forty warriors with me, and turned my face toward the castle of Kurshee. And when the blackness of the castle appeared, I commanded my warriors to halt. And I took with me Mubbushur and Abdullah, who had been born in my house. And when I came to the border of the ditch I saw that the ditch was full of water. And I looked round about, and I beheld a water-pipe. And water ran through that pipe to the castle, and they had laid it across the ditch. And I delivered my horse to Mubbushur. And I crossed the ditch on that pipe, and I came to the foot of the wall. And I went on to the portal, and struck on the door with my hand, and I discovered that the guards of the portal were asleep.[a] And they had filled up the portal, behind the door, with clay and earth. And I looked round the walls of the castle, and saw the place where the steps of the ladders could be fixed. And I returned, and I mounted my horse, and went back to my warriors. And the troops, who had remained behind, came with the ladders. And they were all armed. And they took up the ladders, and I turned my face toward the castle. And they crossed the ditch on the pipe. And having fixed their ladders they entered on the walls of the castle. And when 40 resolute men had entered the castle, I also placed my foot on the ladder and went in unto them. And they sounded their trumpets.[b] And I obtained possession of the castle. 95.

"And at that time news came unto me, that the Ouzbuks[c] con-

[a] Is not this excellent adventure disgraced by some rashness in this part of it? Timour might have been knocked on the head from the wall. The guards might have rushed out and seized him. This solitary part seems hardly necessary to the rest. At least another might have done it. [b] A common artifice, especially in surprise: that few men make a terrible noise. [c] An unruly, mischievous, oppressive tribe in Mauwur u Nuhur — the government of which had been taken from Timour, and given to Ouleaus Khaujeh. But Timour fought against them for the injured. See p. 25, 27, 29, 35, 61, 65, 77, 79, 81, 83.

tinued

tinued in the caſtles. And I ſaw it was not good that I ſhould ſend my armies againſt them. And I wrote a ſummons, as if from Ouleaus Khaujeh. And I gave it to an Ouzbuk, and I ſent forces with him. And I commanded them to ſhew themſelves, and to raiſe a great duſt. And when the Ouzbuks received the ſummons of Ouleaus Khaujeh,[a] calling them to him,[b] and ſaw the duſt raiſed by my people, they quitted the caſtles, night after night,[c] and fled. And the land of Mauwur u Nuhur was delivered from thoſe oppreſſors, who had ſought to ſlay me. And that kingdom ſubmitted to my government."[d] 105.

"Although I had determined to put them to death, yet as they were warriors, I ſaw it was good that I ſhould diſpel their fears, and employ them in war."[e] 109.

"And I ſaw my ſucceſs in this, that I ſhould throw the people of Khorauſaun into the ſleep of negligence. And I turned toward Summurkund. And when, from the news of my return toward Summurkund, Mullik Gheaus u deen had ſat down quiet, I reſolved thus, 'Now the hearts of the people of Khorauſaun are no longer affraid of me, I muſt fall upon them.' And I turned back. And I marched with ſpeed. And coming to Hurraut I took Mullik Gheaus u deen in the ſleep of ſecurity." 111.

"I ſaw my advantage in this, that I ſhould ſpeak fair to his ambaſſador, and diſmiſs him, and ſhut up the road to the Duſht,[f] and appoint an army to ſet out after the ambaſſador: And that on the day after that on which the ambaſſador ſhould enter the preſence of Auroos Khaun without ſuſpicion, whilſt Auroos Khaun ſhould be unprepared, my forces ſhould aſſault him. And even while the ambaſſador related his ſtory my victorious armies, like an unforeſeen calamity, poured on the head of Auroos Khaun. And Auroos Khaun had not the power to oppoſe them. And the Duſht of Kipchauk was ſubdued." 115.

No more army to be taken on an expedition than can be maintained. (Elſe they will mutiny or decay.)[g] 121.

"And my people were a hungered. And the army of Touktummiſh Khaun were full. And my chiefs and my Ameers ſet not their hearts upon battle, until my ſons and my grandſons came and kneeled down, and devoted their lives unto me. And at this time the ſtandard-bearer of Touktummiſh plotted ſecretly with me.[h] And I found it was good that I ſhould

[a] As they believed. [b] Perhaps to ſtrengthen his army for ſome ſudden expedition. [c] To keep it as ſecret as might be, that the caſtles were unmanned. [d] What became of the Ouzbuks who left the caſtles? Did not they go to Timour's army, taking it for Ouleaus Khaujeh's? Were not they then taken priſoners? Timour ſays nothing of them. [e] But they muſt be watched. [f] Why? To retard the ambaſſador? If he made it quite impaſſable, there muſt have been ſome other (probably longer or worſe) road which the ambaſſador took. [g] This admits ſome variety, when the army can be ſuſtained at coſt of the enemy — as in foraging or plundering the country. [h] See p. 175. for Timour's private opinion, and, in general, public acknowledgment of ſuch behaviour.

ſhould aſſault the foe. And that when the two armies were engaged, the ſtandard-bearer of Touktummiſh Khaun ſhould invert his ſtandard.[a] And when the flames of war and of ſlaughter aſcended high, I commanded that the tents ſhould be pitched, and that they ſhould prepare victuals.[b] And at this time the ſtandard of Touktummiſh Khaun was inverted. And Touktummiſh, diſmaid and confounded, gave the tribe of Jouji to the wind of deſolation; and turned his back on the field of ſlaughter, and fled." 123.

When Timour's Ameers objected to attacking Hindoſtaun, he anſwered them ſaying, "I will ſeek the ſign of war in the Koraun." And they all conſented thereto. And this ſacred verſe came forth, "O Prophet! fight with the infidels and the unbelievers."[c] 131.

"I deliberated with myſelf concerning the Ameers, whether I ſhould throw them down from their commands. But ſince I myſelf had exalted them, I ſought not to pull them down. And I treated them with kindneſs, although they had angered me." 133.

"And the whole of my army was 92 thouſand horſe-men: according to the number of the names of Mahummud, the prophet of God. And I took this number as a fortunate and a happy omen." 135.

"It came into my mind, that if I ſhould reſolve on ſubduing the caſtle of Dehli, perhaps the war might be long and tedious. And I counſelled with myſelf, that I would make myſelf appear weak in their ſight: that the enemy might gain courage, and fight with me on the plane.[d] And I dug a ditch round my army, and I ſtrengthened myſelf within that ditch. And I ſent a force to meet them. And I commanded the ſoldiers that they ſhould ſhew their ſelves weak and fearful. And when the enemies found their ſelves powerful, they exulted. And they came into the plane. And they oppoſed my victorious armies face to face. And Sooltaun Muhmood, the ruler of Dehli, came into battle. And he was defeated, and he fled

a The ſtandard ſeems equally important in moſt armies. b David ſpeaks of a table ſpread in ſight of enemies. Timour did this to ſhew his defiance of the foe, and certainty of victory. This, if he gained the conqueſt, would give him confidence among the ſoldiers. But how if the already falſe ſtandard-bearer had been falſe to Timour? How if his ſeeming plotting with him had been really againſt him? This is one of the many riſques which heroes have been remarked for running. Had they failed they would have been called raſh. Having proſpered they are ſtiled glorious. It may be ſometimes *neceſſary* to dare at hazard. But events alter not the characters of actions. Nor is that the beſt glory which is acquired by chance. c Timour was reſolved in his ſelf. He wiſhed an omen that ſhould ſuit his reſolution. He was prepared to conſtrue a doubtful one in it's favor. Do Chriſtians always conſult their bible more impartially? Even in matters of doctrine, where paſſion and intereſt are generally leſs concerned? —This uſe of the Koraun is of the ſame kind with auguries and other omen-ſeekings. It is an addreſs to popular prejudices. It is applying a ſtrong motive.—How deſirable that princes in Chriſtendom would, at leaſt, as implicitly obey the more peaceable dictates of their goſpel, as the hero Timour did the warlike verſe of his fighting Prophet! d They were in the caſtle.

toward

toward the mountains. And ſpoils, and wealth, above meaſure, fell to my ſoldiers." 139.

"And I let looſe the brave men."[a] 143.

"I gave encouragement to my ſoldiers. And with money, and with jewels, I made them glad of heart. And I permitted them to come into the banquet. And in the field they hazarded their lives. And I withheld not from them my gold nor ſilver. And I educated, and trained them to arms. And to alleviate their ſufferings, I myſelf ſhared in their labors, and in their hardſhips." 161.

"I hazarded my perſon in the hour of danger."[b] 163.

"I kept my ſoldiers ſuſpended between hope and fear." 199.

"The chiefs and the commanders of my forces I admitted to my councils. And I raiſed them to exalted dignities. And I aſſociated, and converſed familiarly with them." 207.

"I loved thoſe intrepid warriors who had given repeted proofs of their courage and abilities.[c] And I propoſed queſtions to them concerning the art of war, and the various modes of advancing in the field of battle, and of retreat in ſituations of peril, and the methods of charging and breaking the lines of the enemy, and of ſkirmiſhing, and all the other operations of war. And I placed confidence in them. And I conſulted their opinions in proportion to their ſkill and experience." 207.

"The brave from among my ſoldiers I diſtinguiſht by gifts and honors." 209.

"I kept my troops in a ſtate of readineſs. And I advanced to them their wages, even before it was due." ibid.

"My ſoldiers of every rank I confined in ſuch ſort to their ſeveral ſtations, that they could not ſtep beyond the limits preſcribed to them." ibid.

"Relative to the various tribes who ſought ſhelter under my government, Thoſe who were ſoldiers I ordered to be incorporated with my troops, and entertained according to their rank &c." 217.

"And the genuine deſcendant of a ſoldier reſolute and brave, of whatever tribe, I ordered to be enrolled in the number of my forces."[d] 219.

N.B. Particular regulations for the army are here omitted. They are detailed, p. 229 &c.

"I commanded that if any one of my ſoldiers, exceding the limits preſcribed him, ſhould injure, he ſhould be delivered into the hands of the injured perſon, that he might retaliate." 251.

"By experience it is known to me, that he only is equal to ſtations of power, who is well acquainted with the military art, and with the various modes of breaking and defeating armies: who in

[a] "Let ſlip the dogs of war." [b] A part of character eſſential to a war-chief.
[c] Both theſe were neceſſary to make a ſoldier important with Timour. And a general, who makes *fit* perſons important, will gain as much conſequence as he gives.—The like is true in all governments as well as the military. [d] Fortes creantur fortibus.

 the

the hour of battle giveth not his heart from his hand, nor permitteth apprehension to take possession of his soul: who can direct the efforts of his troops; and if their ranks be thrown into confusion can by his abilities restore them to order: who can rule armies with majesty and authority, and who hath the vigor to chastise those who rise in opposition to his commands." 269.

A superior officer should not be sent on a service which an inferior can do. 273.

"Every one of the Ameers who from a spirit of enterprise demanded employment, his request should be granted [a]. ibid.

"An atchievement from attention to personal safety in the moment of peril should not be regarded." 275.

"The right of the warrior should not be injured. The soldier grown in years should not be deprived of his station or wages. The actions of the soldier should not be supprest. For those men who sell their *permanent happiness for perishable honor* are worthy of reward." [b] 277.

Every soldier to have the (extra) price of his services paid him.—Hostile soldiers, captive, not to be killed, have it offered to serve in the conqueror's army, or liberty. [c] —If a hostile soldier, brave and faithful to his own commander, from choice or necessity come under another authority, his good qualities and actions to be rated as if originally in the latter service. 279.

"I ordained, that whoever of my Ameers subdued and wrested a kingdom from the hands of the enemy, that for the space of 3 years the vice-gerency of that kingdom should be conferred on him." [d] 291.

The soldier who turns his face from the foe, must appear no more.—He who on the day of enterprise demandeth his dismission, be in contempt &c. 315.

"If one fight valiantly and defeat his foe, let not the insinuations of the envious be heard to his prejudice. Permit not his glory to be concealed. But let it be exhibited in ten-fold splendor." [e] 321.

[a] If he failed, his own self-willed temerity was the cause. If he prospered, the fruit was the prince's. [b] What a sale! What a sentiment! [c] That should be on promise to cease hostility. [d] But care must be taken against his oppression and peculation. [e] For many good military directions, see p. 375. et seq.

REMARKABLE EVENTS.

TIMOUR with 243 warriors ſubdued a caſtle fortified by 1200. P. 7.

He was once brought low. He had but 7 on horſes, and 3 on foot. He carried his wife (whom he calls "honored"[a]) behind on his horſe. He wandered in the deſert, and one night alighted at a well. Three of his people ran away with 3 horſes. So he had 7 men and 4 horſes left. Yet he was ſtrong of heart and did not lament. Then Aali Beg came upon him, carried him off and impriſoned him in a place full of vermin, with a guard over him. There he lay 62 days. Then he wreſted a ſword from his guards, attackt them and they fled. Upon which he preſented his ſelf before Aali Beg. Who being confounded made excuſes, gave him his liberty, reſtored his arms and horſes, adding as a preſent a lean horſe, and a worn out camel: but kept back part of his property. 35.

"And I implored All-mighty God that He would deliver me from that wandering life. And I had not yet reſted from my devotions when a number of people appeared afar off. And I mounted my horſe and I came in behind them. And I aſked of them, ſaying, "Warriors who are Ye?" And they anſwered unto me, "We are the ſervants of Ameer Timour, and we wander ſeeking him, and lo! we find him not." And I ſaid unto them, "I alſo am one of the ſervants of Ameer: how ſay ye if I be your guide and bring you unto Him?" And one of them put his horſe to ſpeed and went and carried news to the leaders, ſaying, "We have found a guide who can lead us to Ameer Timour." And the leaders gave orders that I ſhould appear before them. And they were three troops. And when their eyes fell on me they were overwhelmed with joy. And they alighted from their horſes, and they came and they kneeled, and they kiſſed my ſtirrup. And I alſo came down from my horſe, and took each of them in my arms. And they wept. And I wept. And we mounted our horſes, and came to my dwelling. And I collected my people together and made a feaſt. And on the next day Share Behraum, who had ſeparated from me, in the narrowneſs of his heart, arrived alſo. And he made excuſes. And I took him into my arms. And I accepted his excuſes. And I treated him with ſuch kindneſs that he came forth from his confuſion." 53.

"Ameer Sheikh Mahummud, the ſon of Biaun Suldoze, was always drinking wine and ſtrong ſpirits. And in the end the wine deſtroid him, and he departed from the world. And I took poſſeſſion of his lands." 89.

"When Ameer Hooſſein ſent

[a] Remarkable in the Eaſt.

unto me a Koraun by which he had taken an oath that nought was in his heart but friendſhip and brotherly affection towards me, and ſent a meſſage unto me, ſaying, "If there be ought in my heart contrary to that which I ſay, and if I break my oath and do evil unto thee, may this book of GOD ſeize upon me."[a] Seeing that I thought him a true believer, I put confidence in his words. And he ſent a perſon unto me, and a meſſage, ſaying, "If it may be ſo that we may ſee each other in the paſs of Chukchuk and renew our antient faith, truly it will be better." And this was his deſign: that by perfidy and treachery he might ſeize on me. And altho' I knew that much faith was not to be placed on his word or on his oath, yet out of reſpect to the holy Koraun I reſolved that I would go to meet him. But I determined that I would firſt ſend a number of my reſolute warriors and ſecrete them round about the paſs of Chukchuk, and that I my ſelf would go with another body of my people, and ſee Ameer Hooſſein And I ſent advice to my friends, who were the followers of Ameer Hooſſein, that they ſhould inform me of his deſigns. And Share Behraum, who was of my friends,[b] informed me of the deſigns of Ameer Hooſſein. And Ameer Hooſſein ſlew him:[c] and ſet out with a thouſand horſemen to come upon me. And at that time I had pitcht my tents at the entrance of the paſs, and this news came unto me. And I ordered my forces. And behold the Van guard of Ameer Hooſſein appeared in ſight. And my Kurrauvulaun brought word, ſaying, "It is the army of Ameer Hooſſein. And Ameer Hooſſein cometh not with them. For he hath heard that Ameer[d] is come alone, and he hath ſent an army to ſeize Thee." And behold I was prepared, and two hundred horſe-men were all that were with me.[e] And I waited until the forces of Ameer Hooſſein had entered the paſs. And I ſent a meſſenger to the people whom I had ſent before me, and I commanded them to ſeize the way of retreat. And I my ſelf oppoſed them face to face. And I encloſed my enemies in that paſs, and took many of them priſoners. And Ameer Hooſſein was confounded and made excuſes. And I had faith in him no more. And I was no more deceived by his words." 101.

"When in an engagement with Touktummiſh Khaun my forces were thrown into confuſion by the

[a] Was this imprecation implied in the oath, and only repeted in another form according to the Eaſtern manner? Or is it ſomewhat more? The oath only aſſuring that the profeſſion was as true as that by which it was ſworn. And the (ſuppoſed or real) book of GOD, among it's believers, is eſteemed the pureſt and moſt certain truth. Therefore to ſwear falſely by it is the greateſt crime. It is to ſay that a wicked lye is as true as the divine word. If this be accompted to incur the curſes of the book, the oath implies an imprecation. [b] He had revolted from Timour and was reconciled. p. 55. Yea twice. 87. [c] A reconciled foe, even a faithleſs friend (as in this Inſtance) *reconciled*, may prove a friend faithful unto death. Who then would revenge? [d] Timour. [e] About his perſon. Not including thoſe ſent before, and ſecreted round the paſs.

ſuperior

superior numbers of the enemy, Meer Zeau u deen, noted for the efficacy of his prayers, bared his head and stretched forth his arms in supplication; his prayer was not yet concluded when the effects of his mediation became apparent." 207.

"When one of my wives was afflicted with a deadly distemper, 12 holy Siuds celebrated for their piety assembled together. And each of them devoted a year of his own existence to her preservation. And she was restored to health: and enjoid the full measure of their donation."[a] 207.

"Several of those in whom I confided, from envy and malice communicated fictitious tales to me, both in public and private, to the prejudice of Ameer Ubbaus; who was one of my most powerful and most faithful chiefs. And they kindled the fire of my resentment by their false reports. And in the moment of anger I ordered him, unheard and unexamined, to be put to death. And in the end I discovered the perfidy of his accusers. And I was ashamed and confounded at my own conduct."[b] 247.

"Mullick Shaah Siljokee disgraced his Vizzeer Nizzaum ul Moolluk, who was adorned with every great and shining quality; and appointed an ignoble and worthless man in his place. By the ill conduct, viciousness and villainy of that minister the foundation of the power of Mullick Shaah was overturned." 255.

"Munguli Booghau advanced with an army against me. And before the engagement I sent proposals to him, and endeavored to draw him over to my side.[c] But he forgot not his duty to Tughulluk Timour Khaun. And he formed his troops in order of battle. And he charged my forces with undaunted resolution. And he was defeated. And when he afterwards voluntarily came unto me, I raised him to an exalted station. And such were the favors which I conferred upon him, that if any resentment remained in his heart, it was obliterated. And he signalized his self in my service, and conferred obligations on me. And when I encountered Kurrau Eusoof, in the moment that my troops were discouraged and thrown into confusion he placed on his spear the head of a hostile commander. And he named it the head of Kurrau Eusoof, and called to my forces, that Kurrau Eusoof was slain. And he gave courage to my soldiers. And he rusht on the centre of Kurrau Eusoof's line, and drove him from the fields." 281.

"When the Khaukaun advanced against Hurmuz, the son of Nousharevaun, with an army of 3 hundred thousand sanguinary Toorks, that prince sent forth Behraum

[a] i. e. Lived 12 years longer. Could not he get a farther prolongation of her life? or was he tired of her? [b] What must be the feelings of an honest, humane mind, in such a case! From the horrible misery of such conduct how happily are those princes secured whose authority and it's acts the laws define! What then is he who would be absolute? knows he his own weakness? knows he the craft of others? or cares he not for mischief? [c] Timour knew it would be for his advantage to seduce Munguli Booghau. Had he yielded to the temptation, Timour would have despised, detested, perhaps punisht him.

Joubeen, who had been the minister, and the counsellor, and the general[a] of his father, with 320000 Persians to oppose him. And he engaged that prince. And for 3 days and for 3 nights the slaughter continued with great fury. At length he defeated the Khaukaun, and dispatcht intelligence of his victory to Hurmuz. And he also sent unto him the spoils which he had taken. And the envious and the slanderous, who influenced the councils of Hurmuz, forged accusations against him, saying, "Behraum hath secreted the treasures of the enemy. And he hath seized to his self the sword and the crown, and the buskins of the Khaukaun, ornamented with jewels of price." And Hurmuz forgot the services of Behraum. And he credited the accusations. And he pronounced him a traitor. And, in token of his anger and contempt, he sent a chain to him, and a collar, and the veil of a woman.[b] And Behraum Joubeen placed the collar on his neck, and on his feet he fastened the chain. And he clothed his self in the female attire. And he called the Ameers and the chiefs of his soldiers together. And thus habited he gave public audience to his people. And when they beheld Behraum they uttered revilings against their prince. And they turned their hearts from their duty to Hurmuz. And under the banners of Behraum Joubeen they proceded to the palace of the king. And they deprived him of his regal authority."[c] 285.

[a] In warring countries it may be often convenient to unite these characters. [b] How poor females are despised in the East! Yet no where more loved. So do esteem and love differ. [c] Contrast with this Chughtai Khaun's story. p. 249.

THEOLOGIC AND RELIGIOUS SENTENCES OF TIMOUR.

VICTORY procedeth not from the greatness of armies, nor defeat from inferiority of numbers. For conquest is obtained by the divine favor [and skilful measures.] P. 7. et seq.

"If the canopy of heaven were a bow, and if the earth were the cord[a] thereof, and if calamities were the arrows, if mankind were the mark for those arrows, and if Allmighty GOD (the tremendous and

[a] It appears hence that the convexity of the terraqueous globe was not thought of by the Caliph. He considered the flat, horizontal surface of the earth as like the cord.

the

the glorious) were the unerring archer —— to whom could the ſons of Adam flee for protection ? The ſons of Adam muſt flee unto the Lord."[a] 17.

Timour in all his actions ſought an omen from the Koraun —— his Bible.[b] 19, 75, 89 &c.

"And I gave praiſe unto GOD, and I ſaid unto my ſelf, GOD doeth great things for me." 49. *N.B.* So he ſays on all ſuch occaſions.

"And on that night, which was a holy night, I kept watch. And when the morning broke I was emploid in prayer. And after repeting the prayers preſcribed by the law I lifted up my hands in ſupplication. And in the midſt of my ſupplication I wept. &c." 51. *N.B.* He was then diſtreſt. Mark the good effect of this in "Remarkable Events." ibid.

"And the hour of prayer was arrived. And we prayed together."[c] 55.

"I opened the holy book for an omen. And this ſacred verſe came forth as a ſign. "How oft do the weak vanquiſh the powerful, by the permiſſion of All-mighty GOD." 75.

"The forces of Ouleaus Khaujeh ſpent that night in watching. And I in that night, on the top of that hill, was emploid in humiliations and ſupplications to the throne of All mighty GOD. And between ſleeping and waking I heard a voice as of ſome one ſpeaking to me, ſaying, "Timour, victory and conqueſt, and triumph, are thine." And when the morning broke I praid with my people."[d] 79.

"And at this time Baubau Aali Shaah came before me, and ſaid, "Timour, GOD All-mighty hath declared, that if there were two GODS in the Heavens and in the earth, the order of the univerſe would end in horror and confuſion." And I took warning by his words." 89.

"By the favor of All-mighty GOD I obtained poſſeſſion of the caſtle."[e] 99.

Timour having received an inſidious invitation, wherein he ſuſpected treachery and danger, yet becauſe it was accompanied with a Koraun, on which amity had been ſworn, out of reſpect to the Koraun he reſolved to go."[f] 101.

"And I reſted on the favor of the All-mighty."[g] 127.

"I will turn to All-mighty GOD, that whatever be the will of GOD, that I may do." 131.

"Having pitcht my tents to-

[a] This is applied to ſhew, one muſt repair to a hoſtile ſuperior, too ſtrong to be reſiſted, in ſubmiſſion. [b] This has been (with our Bible) an immemorial practice among Chriſtians.) (And a ſimilar among many people.) Auſtin notes ſome that took *Sortes* from the goſpels. (Ep. 119.) The ſame with the pſalms or goſpels, or any thing elſe, is condemned in Charles the Great's Capitular. (Cap. 4.) Cedrenus relates that Heraclus ordered his army to live purely three days, then opening the goſpels he conſtrued the place preſented as an order to winter in Albany. Peter Bleſenſis conſtrued a viſion of his from a paſſage opened on in the pſalter. (Ep. 30.) & plura, &c. Beſide the *Sortes Virgilianæ*, and the like. [c] Vid. Remarkable Events. ibid. [d] Immediately follows a ſignal victory. [e] This was after a moſt painful and perilous adventure. Yet he attributes the ſucceſs to GOD alone. [f] And eſcaped, having defeated thoſe who attackt him. [g] And proſpered.

ward Hindoſtaun I repeted the prayer of victory." 133.

"Praiſe is due to the GOD of the univerſe, that He hath brought under my authority many of the kingdoms of the world." 147.

"May GOD be merciful to that ſervant[a] who knoweth his own limits: and who placeth not the foot of temerity beyond his proper bounds." ibid.

"And among the rules which I eſtabliſht for the ſupport of my empire, the firſt was, That I promoted the worſhip of Almighty GOD: and at all times, and in all places, ſupported the true faith."[b] 159.

"It is known to me by experience that every empire, which is not eſtabliſht in morality and religion, ſhall paſs away." 175.

"I appointed a man of holineſs and illuſtrious dignity to watch over the conduct of the faithful, that he might regulate the manners of the times,[c] and appoint ſuperiors in holy offices: and eſtabliſh in every city and in every town a doctor learned in the ſacred law:[d] and ordain ſalaries for ſuperior eccleſiaſtics and for holy men, and for men of knowledge."[e] 177.

"I commanded that they ſhould build places of worſhip in every city." 179.

"He put an end to thoſe diviſions. And by ſo doing gave ſtrength to our holy law."[f] 183.

"Encreaſe thou thy good actions that thy benevolent Creator may encreaſe his mercies to thee." 197.

"The different offices in an earthly empire are ſymbols of thoſe in the empire of the Creator. In which are laborers, agents &c. And they are all buſied in their proper departments. And they ſeek not to overleap the bounds allotted them. And they wait in perpetual obedience to the will of the Lord." 201.

"We cannot be profuſe[g] in our offerings to Almighty GOD." 203.

"I granted admiſſion to Theologians, and to holy men. And they reſorted at all times to my palace. And they adorned my imperial aſſembly by their preſence." 205.

"I revered devout and pious men. And I implored their prayers

[a] This was addreſt to Bajazet. Would all princes conſider and conduct their ſelves as the *ſervants* of GOD! [b] Thus far is right. But whatſoever is more cometh of evil. Support the true faith. Promote it. It cannot be enforced. To attempt that is the effort of a zeal not according to knowledge, ſet on fire of hell. The faith of force is not that which worketh by love. Therefore not that which fulfils the law. Much the ſame may be ſaid of puniſhing hereſy. The civil power ſhould puniſh civil crimes. What hurts the ſtate is a civil crime. Nothing elſe comes under the magiſtrate's vindictive power. [c] That was great authority. Timour (not to derogate from the purity of his intention) found his accompt in favoring the religious. They are important. And he gained their favor. 179 &c. [d] The appointer was an arch-biſhop, as it were. Here we ſee ſome regal power in the church. Indeed if a prince muſt ſupport religion, he muſt have ſome eccleſiaſtic authority. [e] "The prieſt ſhall preſerve knowledge." — Beſide all this power, this man had the appointment of judges and ſupervisors of the markets. [f] Is this unworthy the attention of Chriſtians? Would not our ſtrength be ſtrengthened by union? Yet can we hope it? Scarcely while any among us, like thoſe divided ones, "fulminate curſes and denounce execrations" one at another. Much leſs, while, like them, any "procede to hoſtilities."
[g] Taking that word in a bad ſenſe.

in the hour of retirement. And I ſupplicated their bleſſings on my actions. And in war, and in peace, and in my councils, and in my deliberations, I reaped the greateſt advantages from their mediation." [a] 207.

"I united my ſelf with holy and pious men: with thoſe to whom the All-mighty had given wiſdom. And I aſſociated with them. And I heard from them the word of GOD. And I acquired knowledge of the bleſſings of a future ſtate. And I ſaw them perform miracles and wonderful things. And I reaped delight from their converſation." 215.

[*Annotation* on the NOTE, P. 215.

Timour is often tautologic and indiſtinct. But I am willing to allow that the firſt, third, and tenth Orders were really different. (I mean that whether different or not in their ſelves, eſſentially, they were ſome how diſtinguiſht then and there.) Yet I aſſent not to the diſtinction in this Note. None of theſe claſſes is ſaid by Timour to live in ſecluſion. [b] And perhaps both the third and tenth might live ſo. The Eaſtern hermits are not more alike than the Weſtern. Timour's variety appears to me thus. The firſt were regular, authoritative divines. The third were good men: whoſe merits and interceſſions have generally been believed to avail. The tenth were ſuch as moreover had extraordinary communications with heaven: receiving thence miraculous revelations, gifts and powers. Theſe are really diſtinct in their ſelves.]

"Relative to the various tribes who ſought ſheltre under my government, I commanded that thoſe who were Theologians ſhould be received with reverence: and that all their deſires ſhould be fulfilled: and that they ſhould be ſupported in affluence." 217.

"Thy good actions, and the bleſſings which the people of the All-mighty receive from thy hands, are equal to all the merits of pilgrimage and ſanctity." [c] 263.

"In every nation He that feareth GOD, and worketh Righteouſneſs, is accepted with Him."

[a] The notion that good perſons are ſo acceptable to GOD, that for their ſakes he confers favors on the leſs deſerving, is not peculiar to the Chriſtian or Moſaic œconomy. ——The blood of JESUS is ſaid to ſpeak better than that of Abel. Not that the latter, as ſome conſtrue it, cried for vengeance. But the former was a better mediator. Abel was conſidered as a mediator, and petitions offered to GOD in his name. His blood was eſpecially ſacred.

[b] Solitude no more proves ſanctity than ſanity. Many a ſpiritual as well as carnal peſt-houſe ſtands alone. — This is borrowed from Fuller's "holy ſtate."

[c] Let this be ſet againſt ſuperſtition.

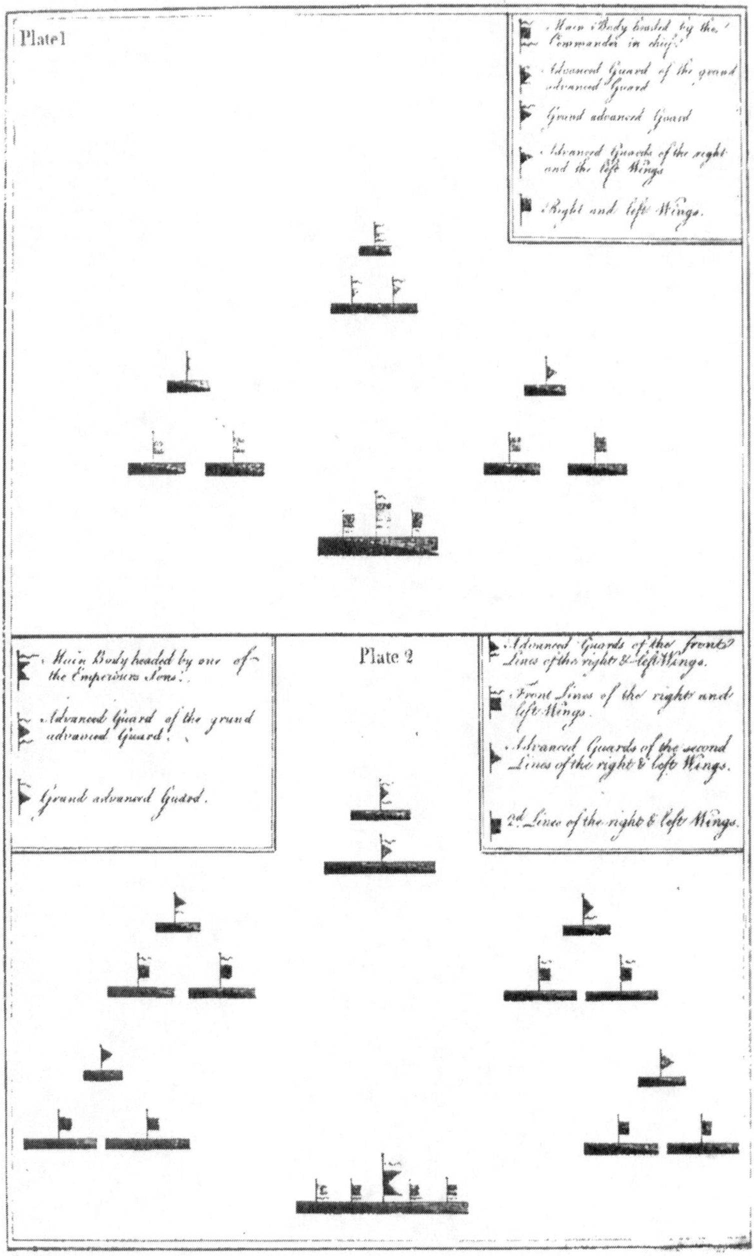
Plate 1
Main Body headed by the Commander in chief.
Advanced Guard of the grand advanced Guard
Grand advanced Guard
Advanced Guards of the right and the left Wings
Right and left Wings.
Plate 2
Main Body headed by one of the Emperours Sons.
Advanced Guard of the grand advanced Guard.
Grand advanced Guard.
Advanced Guards of the front Lines of the right & left Wings.
Front Lines of the right and left Wings.
Advanced Guards of the second Lines of the right & left Wings.
2d Lines of the right & left Wings.

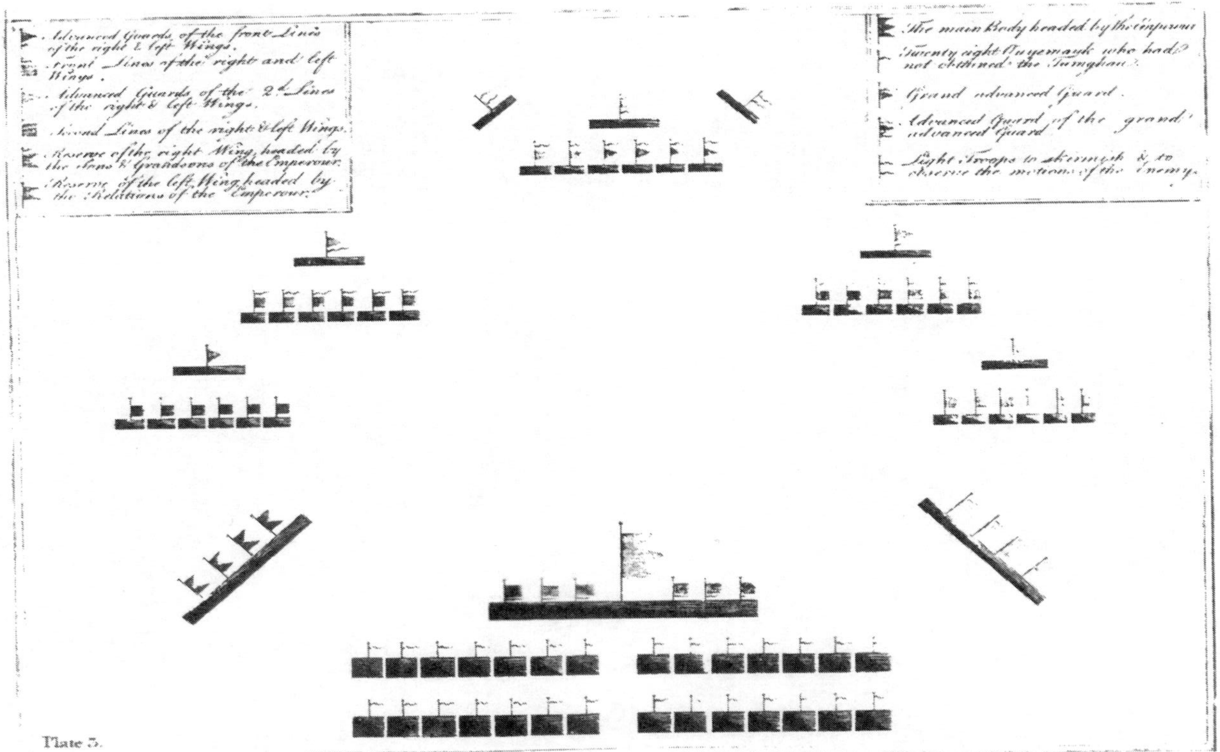
Advanced Guards of the front Lines of the right & left Wings.
Front Lines of the right and left Wings.
Advanced Guards of the 2d. Lines of the right & left Wings.
Second Lines of the right & left Wings.
Reserve of the right Wing, headed by the Sons & Grandsons of the Emperour.
Reserve of the left Wing headed by the Relations of the Emperour.
The main Body headed by the Emperour
Twenty eight Ouyemayk who had not obtained the Tamghau.
Grand advanced Guard.
Advanced Guard of the grand advanced Guard.
Light Troops to skirmish & to observe the motions of the Enemy.

Plate 5.

تزوكات تيمور

مقالت اول

في تدبيرات وكنكاشها

THE INSTITUTES OF TIMOUR.

BOOK THE FIRST.

DESIGNS AND ENTERPRISES.

مقالت اول

في تدبيرات وكنكاشها

تزوك

وكنكاش * امور ملككيري وجهانداري ولشكرشكني ودشمن را بدام آوردن ودوست ساختن مخالفان ودر آمدن وبر آمدن بميان دوستان ودشمنان چنين كردم

* In order to account for the abruptness of this Exordium, it is necessary to inform the Reader, that this part of the Work in the Original followed the INSTITUTES, and by the Royal author was undoubtedly considered as a part of them, under the Denomination of DESIGNS and ENTERPRISES; which he appears to have given as Models of Conduct to others in similar situations. But as it is presumed that little more than the Name of TIMOUR is known to the generality of Europeans, and as this part of the Work contains an abridged account of his most

Book the First.

DESIGNS and ENTERPRISES.

* THUS I formed meaſures and deſigns for the reduction of kingdoms, and for the obtainment of empire, and for defeating armies, and for circumventing enemies, and for making friends of foes, and for going out, and for coming in, amongſt friends and enemies.

moſt important Schemes and Enterpriſes, which conſequently lead to a knowledge of the genius, abilities, and extraordinary actions of the man; it has been deemed a proper introduction to that part of the Work, which may with propriety be ſtiled his INSTITUTES. Another reaſon for prefixing this part of the Work to the other, is, that from the ſimplicity of the Narrative, it will (in the beginning) be better adapted to the uſe of thoſe who are inclined to ſtudy the Perſian Language.

که پیـر من بمن نوشت که ابـو
المنصور تیمور در امـور سلطنت چـهار امررا بدست
بکیرد یعني کنکاش ومشورت وحزم واحتیاط

که هر سلطنتي که از کنکاش ومشورت
خالي باشد چـون شخصي است جاهل که انچه
کند وکوید همه غلط باشد وکفتار وکردارش سر
بسر پشیماني وندامت بار آورد پس بهتر است که در
تمشیت امور سلطنت خودرا بمشاورت وتدبـیـر عمل
نماي تا آخر نادم وپشیمان نکردي

وبدان که در امور سلطنت یک حصه
صبـر وتحمل است ویک حصه تغافل وتجاهل بعد
از تعارف واز کار کردن بعزیمت وصبر واستقامت
وحـزم واحتیاط وشجاعت جمیع امـور میسر میشود
والسـلام

وکویا این مکتوب هادي بود که مرا
راه نمود وظـاهـر ساخت که در امـور سلطنت نه

† Koottub ul Aktaub Sheikh Zine u deen Aboo Bukkur: a devout and learned man descended from the Mahummudan Lawgiver, who foretold to TIMOUR the power and greatness to which he would arrive. It appears that this prince considered him in the light of a ghostly father, consulted him

حصه

For my PEER † wrote unto me, ſaying, "Let Abu'l Munsour Timour, in conducting the "important concerns of government, take by the hand "four aſſiſtants; to wit, Deliberation, and Counſel, and "Vigilance, and Circumſpection.

"For every government which ſhall be "void of deliberation and counſel, is like unto a fooliſh "man, who erreth in all which he ſayeth and doeth; "and whoſe actions and words bring forth no fruit but "ſhame and repentance. It is therefore good that in "conducting the affairs of thy government, thou act "with deliberation and with counſel; that thou mayeſt "not in the end be aſhamed and confounded.

"And know, that the requiſites for con- "ducting the concerns of empire are one portion pa- "tience and forbearance, and one portion pretended neg- "ligence and feigning to know not that which thou "knoweſt—and that by acting with reſolution, and with "uprightneſs, and with patience, and with vigilance, and "with caution, and with bravery, every undertaking "will become eaſy and ſucceſsful. Farewell."

And behold this letter was a guide which pointed out to me the way; and ſhewed unto me, that

him on all occaſions, and paid the moſt implicit attention to his counſels. *Peer* in the Perſian language ſignifies *old* or *aged*; hence a *Father*: which is the appellation by which Timour diſtinguiſhes him throughout this work.

حصه مشاورت وتدبیر وکنکاش است ویک حصه
شمشیر

که گفته اند به تدبیري ملکها توان
کشاد ونوجها توان شکست که بشمشیرهاي لشکرها
میسر نشود

وبتجربه من رسید که یک مرد کاردیده
شجاع مردانه صاحب عزم وتدبیر وحزم بهتر از هزار
مرد بي تدبیر وحزم است چه یک مرد کاردیده هزار
هزار مردرا کار فرماید

وبتجربه من رسید که غالب شدن بر
مخالفان نه از بسیاري لشکر است ومغلوب شدن
نه از کمي سپاه بلکه غالب شدن بتایید وتدبیر
است

چنانچه من با دو صد وچهل وسه کس
از روي کنکاش وتدبیر بر سر قلعه قرشي که امیر
موسي وملک بهادر با دوازده هزار سوار در قلعه
وحوالي قلعه نشسته بودند آمدم وبتایید تنکري
تعالي وتدبیر درست قلعه قرشي را مسخر کردانیدم
وبا

of the requisites for conducting the affairs of dominion nine tenths are Deliberation, and Counsel, and provident Measures; and that the Sword is one portion only. Book I.

For the experienced have said, "By Po-"licy kingdoms may be conquered, and numerous hosts "may be defeated, which by the Swords of united ar-"mies cannot be overthrown."

And by experience it is known unto me, that one tried soldier, of magnanimity, and of bravery, and of resolution, and of skill, and of circumspection is more valuable than a thousand men who want discretion and knowledge. For one experienced and able soldier can direct the efforts of thousands of thousands.

And by experience it is known unto me, that victory over the foe proceedeth not from the greatness of armies, nor defeat from inferiority of numbers: for conquest is obtained by the Divine Favour, and by skilful and judicious measures.

Thus, aided by deliberation and foresight, with two hundred and forty three warriors only, I came down on the castle of Kurshee. † And in the castle and the neighbourhood thereof, Ameer Moosi and Mullik Bahaudur had sat down with twelve thousand horsemen; and by the aid of Almighty God and by skilful measures I subdued the castle of Kurshee.

† A city of Mauwur u Nuhur, or Transoxiana, Long. 99. Lat. 39.

And

وبا دوازده هزار سوار امير موسي وملك
بهادر آمده مرا در قلعه ترشي محاصره نمودند ومن
اعتماد بر تاييد ايزدي كردم واز روي تدبير واحتياط
از قلعه بر آمدم ومرتبه بمرتبه جنـگ كردم وباين
دو صد وچهل وسه كس دوازده هزار سواررا شكست
دادم وچند فرسنگ راه تعاقب ايشان نمودم

وبتجربـه من رسيد كه راي وتدبـير
وكنكاش با مردي دانا دل هوشيار مي آيد اكرچه
تهشيت كارها در پرده تقدير مستور است ليكن بر
سنت سنيه محمدي صلي الله عليه وسلم هر كاري
كه كردم بمشاورت كردم

وچون ارباب راي وكنكاش جمع مي
آمدند از خير وشر ونفع وضرر كردن وناكردن كارها
كه در پـيش بود پرسش مينمودم وچـون سخنان
ايشان را مي شنيدم هر دو طرف آنرا ملاحظه مي كردم
ونـفـع وضرر آنرا بخـاطر مي آوردم ومخاطرات آن
كـار

AND Ameer Moosi and Mullik Bahaudur, with their twelve thousand horsemen, came and surrounded me in the castle of Khurshee. And I rested on the favour of the Almighty, and I sallied forth with skill and with circumspection from the castle, and I assaulted them repeatedly. And with those two hundred and forty and three people I defeated twelve thousand horsemen, and pursued them for many Fursungs.*

AND by experience it is known unto me, that counsel, and deliberation, and skilful measures are only to be found with the wise and the sagacious. Therefore, notwithstanding the conclusion of every worldly event, is covered by the curtain of Fate, yet, according to the holy word of Mahummud (on whom be the Blessing of the Almighty) in every enterprise which I undertook, I acted from counsel and deliberation.

AND when my counsellors and my advisers were assembled together, I demanded their opinions on the good and on the evil, and on the advantages and on the disadvantages of undertaking, or relinquishing, the enterprise before us. And when I had heard their opinions thereon, I myself examined both sides of their opinions. And I duly weighed the advantages and the disadvantages;

* Fursung is a league of about six thousand yards.

كاررا بنظر اعتبار ميديدم وهر كاري كه در آن دو خطر ميديدم طرح ميكردم وكاري كه يك خطر داشت اختيار مي نمودم

چنانچه من به تغلغتيهور خان صلاح دادم در وقتي كه امراي وي در دشت جته علم مخالفت برافراختند از من كنكاش خواست وبوي كفتم كه اكر فوج بدفع ورفع ايشان بفرستي دو خطر متصور است واكر خود متوجه شوي يك خطر ووي به كنكاش من عمل كرد ومتوجه دشت شد وچنان شد كه بوي كفته بودم

ودر جميع كارها مشاورت بكار بردم ودر انصرام آن كار تدبير درست ميكردم وراه بر آمدن آن كاررا ملاحظه نموده شروع در آن كار ميكردم واز روي تدبير وعزم درست وحزم واحتياط وپيش بيني ودور انديشي باتمام ميرسانيدم

وبتجربه

advantages; and I considered the perils thereof with the eye of attention. And every plan, in which I discovered a two-fold hazard, I rejected; and I chose that in which the peril was single. Book I.

Thus I advised Tughulluk Timour Khaun, when his Ameers exalted the standard of rebellion in the Dusht of Jitteh. Behold he demanded counsel from me; and thus I said unto him—"If thou send an army "to disperse and expel them, a two-fold danger may be "apprehended therefrom: * but if thou thyself advance "against them, one peril only." And he acted according to my counsel, and turned towards the Dusht of Jitteh: and that which I had fore-told unto him, came to pass.

And I entered on every measure with counsel and advice; and in the execution of that measure I acted on a plan which was uniform and good. And after examining the avenue of retreat, I entered on the execution thereof. And by skill, and by resolution, and by caution, and by circumspection, and by fore-sight, and by penetration I brought that enterprise to a fortunate conclusion.

* i.e. If he sent Forces, and went not himself, they might be defeated; or they might be prevailed upon to join the rebels: but the latter, if he went himself, was not to be apprehended.

وبتجربه من رسید که صاحب کنکاش
جهعی توانند بود که از روی اتفاق بر کفتار وکردار
خود عازم باشند واز آن کار بهیچ وجه
نکذرند واکر کویند نکنیم پیرامون آن کار
نکردند

وبتجربه من رسید که کنکاش دو
قسم است زبانی وته دلی انچه زبانی می شنیدم
کوش میکردم وانچه ته دلی می شنیدم در کوش
دل جای میدادم

ودر هنکام لشکرکشیها از صلح وجنک
پرسش مینهودم ودلهای امرای خود را می جستم
که جنک جویند یا صلح واکر از صلح سخن میکردند
منافع صلح را با ضرر جنک مقابله می نهودم واکر
از جنک حرف میزدند نفع وفایده آنرا با ضرر صلح
ملاحظه میکردم هرکدام غالب در نفع بود همان را
اختیار مینهودم

وهر

And by experience it is known unto me, that thoſe are worthy to be counſellors, who ſteadfaſtly adhere to that which they ſay, and to that which they do; and who on no account relinquiſh the meaſures on which they have reſolved; and who, if they ſay, "We "will not do this," keep far from the action which they have condemned.

And by experience it is known unto me, that there are two kinds of counſel—that which proceedeth from the tongue, and that which proceedeth from the receſs of the heart. I turned my ear to that which proceeded from the tongue; but to the counſel of the heart, which I heard, I gave a place in the treaſury of my ſoul.

And in times of hoſtility I ſought counſel relative to peace and to war; and I ſtudied the hearts of my chiefs, whether they were deſirous of war or of peace. And if they adviſed peace, I compared the advantages of peace with the perils of war. And if they propoſed war, I oppoſed the profits and advantages thereof to the inconveniences and dangers that might follow from peace: and which ever appeared moſt profitable, that I preferred and approved.

And

وهر كنكاشي كـه سپاه را دو دل مى
ساخـت از استماع آن احتراز ميكردم وهـر صاحـب
كنكـاش كه مضطربانه كنكاش ميكفت آنرا كوش
ميكردم ومردي كه عاقلانـه ومردانه سخـن ميكرد
آنـرا مـي شنـيـدم

وكنـكاش از همه كس مي پرسيدم
ليكن خـيـر وشـر هـر سخن را ملاحظه مي نمودم
وطرف صلاح وصواب آنرا اختيار ميكردم

چنانچه در وقتي كه تغلقتيـمور خان
نبيره چنكيز خان بعزم تسخير ماوراالنهر از آب خجند
كذشت ويرليغ طلب بنام من واميـر حاجي برلاس
وامير بايزيد جلاير صادر ساخت وايشان از من كنكاش
خواستند كه با اهل والـوس خـود بجانب خراسان
بـرويم يـا رفته تغلقتيمور خان را به بينم من بايشان
كنكاش كفتم كـه در ديـدن تغلقتيمور خـان
دو نفع است ويك ضرر ودر رفتن خـراسـان دو ضرر

* i. e. Such as occasioned a disunion of sentiments among them, or rendered them doubtful or apprehensive.

† i. e. To Timour &c. commanding them to submit and come in to him.

‡ *Ameer* signifies a *Prince*, or *Leader*; and is a title given to all the nobility

AND I hearkened not to those counsels which divided the hearts of my soldiers.* And every counsellor who gave his opinion under the dominion of fear, I turned my ear unto him: but to the man who spoke with judgment and with firmness, I listened with attention.

AND I asked counsel from all: but I considered the good and the evil of every opinion; and from each I selected those things which were just and expedient.

THUS when Tughulluk Timour Khaun, of the line of Chungaze, crossed the waters of Khujjund with a determination to reduce the kingdom of Mauwur u Nuhur, and issued mandates of summons in my name,† and in the names of Ameer Haujee Burlaus ‡, and Ameer Bauezzeed Jullauir; those chiefs asked counsel of me, saying, "Shall we flee into Khorausaun, with our families and with our hords, or shall we go and see Tughulluk Timour Khaun?" I counselled them, saying, "There are two advantages and one peril in seeing Tughulluk Timour; and in fleeing to Khorausaun

bility of the first rank in the Mogul empire; also to the commanders of bodies of troops. Ameer Haujee Burlaus was the uncle of Timour. He and Ameer Bauezzeed Jullauir were both chiefs of tribes in the kingdom of Mauwur u Nuhur.

"there

است وبیک نفع ایشان کنکاش مرا قبول نکردند
ومتوجه خراسان شدند ومن در رفتن خراسان ودیدن
تغلقتیمور خان دو دله شدم

ودرین امر از پیر خود کنکاش خواستم
ایشان درجواب من نوشتند که از خلیفه چهارم
کرم الله وجهه سوال کردند که هرگاه اسمانها
کمانها کردند وزمینها زه آن کمانها شوند وحوادث
تیرها شوند وآدمیان هدف آن تیرها کردند
وتیرانداز خداي باشد جل جلاله آدمیان بکجا
بگریزند خلیفه در جواب فرمود که آدمیان را است
که در خدا گریزند پس تراست که درینوقت در
تغلقتیمور خان گریزي وتیر وکمانرا از دست وي
بگیري واز رسیدن این جواب توي دل گشتم
ورفته تغلقتیمور خانرا دیدم

* i. e. By obeying the ſummons of Tughulluk Timour it was poſſible that they might preſerve their country from depredation, and enſure the ſafety of their families and effects, at the riſque perhaps of their own lives. Whereas by diſobeying the ſummons, and retiring into Khorauſaun, they would

لیکن

"there are two perils, and but one advantage."* And Book I. they approved not of my counsel, and they turned towards Khorausaun: and I also was divided within myself, whether I should retire into Khorausaun, or whether I should see Tughulluk Timour.

And on this occasion I asked counsel of my Peer; who in his answer wrote unto me, saying, "It was once demanded of the fourth Khulleefeh † (on "whom be the mercy of the creator), If the canopy of "heaven were a bow; and if the earth were the cord "thereof; and if calamities were the arrows; if man-"kind were the mark for those arrows; and if Almighty "God (the tremendous and the glorious) were the uner-"ring Archer; to whom could the sons of Adam flee "for protection?" The Khulleefeh answered, saying, "The sons of Adam must flee unto the Lord? Thus, it "is thy duty at this time to flee unto Tughulluk Timour; "and to take from his hand the bow and the arrows of "wrath." And when I received this Answer, I became strong of heart, and I went, and I saw Tughulluk Timour Khaun.

would be banished from their country, and deprived of their Principalities; with no other advantage, but that of having secured for a time their own personal safety.

† The Caliph Aali.

لیکن در هر امري از امور که کنکاش
بر آن قرار مي یافت بقران فال مي کشادم وبحکم
قران عمل مي نمودم

وچون در دیدن تغلغتیمور خان
بمصحف فال کشودم سوره یوسف علیه السلام بر
آمد وبحکم قران مجید عمل کردم

کنکاش اول که در دیدن تغلغتیمور
خان از مشرق دلم سر بر زد این بود

که چون بمسامع من رسید که
تغلغتیمور خان بیکچک وحاجي بیک ارکنت والغ
تغتیمور کریت را با دیکر امراي جته سه فوج ساخته
بتاخت وغارت مملکت ماورالنهر تعین نموده بودند و
افواج امراي سه کانه در منزل خزار نزول نموده اند
چون کنکاش دیدم که اول رفته امرا را بمال
فریفته تطمیع نمایم که از تاخت وقتل وغارت ولایت
ماورالنهر عنان بکشند تا آنکه من رفته تغلغتیمور
خان را بـه بـینـم

وچون

BUT in every action of the actions of my life, on which I had deliberated, I drew an omen from the sacred KORAUN, and I acted according to the direction thereof. Book I.

AND when I sought a presage in the KORAUN concerning the seeing of Tughulluk Timour, the Chapter of Eusoof* (peace be with him) came forth: and I followed the direction of the sacred book.

THE FIRST MEASURE which my heart dictated unto me concerning the seeing of Tughulluk Timour, was this. DESIGN I.

HAVING heard that Tughulluk Timour Khaun had appointed Begchuk, and Haujee Beg of the Tribe of Arkunut, and Allugh Tuktimour of the Tribe of Kurreet, and other Ameers of Jitteh, with three armies, to ravage and lay waste the kingdom of Mauwur u Nuhur; and that those three armies under those Ameers were arrived at Khuzzaur, behold, I deemed it necessary that I should first go unto them, and deceive them by presents, and excite their avarice by temptations, that they might withdraw their hands from desolating and ravaging the kingdom of Mauwur u Nuhur, and from slaughtering the inhabitants thereof; until I should go and see Tughulluk Timour Khaun. A. D. 1369. A. TIM. 25.

* i.e. Joseph. Alluding to the protection which that patriarch afforded to his family, when in Egypt. See Sale's *Al* Koran. Chap. 12.

وچون امراي مذكوررا ديدم سطوت
من در ايشان اثر كرد واز راه تعظيم وتكريم پيش
آمدند وچون دلهاي ايشان مانند چشمهاي تنك
بود وساوري كه بديشان دادم در نظر ايشان بسيار
نمود ودست از تاخت وتاراج ماورالنهر باز داشتند
ومن رفته تغلقتيمور خان را ديدم ووي ديدن مرا
شگون گرفت واز من كنكاش خواست وانچه از
من شنيد همه را پسنديده داشت

ودرين حال بمسامع تغلقتيمور خان
رسيد كه امراي افواج سه كانه مبلغهاي وساوري
از اهالى ماورالنهر كرفته اند ودر ساعت آن مبلغ را
بر ايشان اطلاق كرد و تحصيلدار تعيين نمود
وايشان را از رفتن ماورالنهر منع كرد وايشانرا معزول
ساخت وحاجى محمود شاه يسوري را بجاي ايشان
نصب كرد
وچون اين خبر بمسامع امرا رسيد
علم مخالفت بر افراخته مراجعت نمودند
ودر اين حال به اغلان خواجه كه ديوانبيكى
واميـر

And when I came unto those Ameers, my power * made an impression upon them, and they received me with honour and respect. And behold their hearts, like unto their eyes, were blind and contracted, and the presents which I gave unto them, seemed great in their sight: and they withdrew their hands from ravaging and destroying the kingdom of Mauwur u Nuhur. And I went, and saw Tughulluk Timour Khaun; and he took my coming for a happy omen: and he asked counsel of me, and all that which he heard me say, he approved.

And at this time news came to the ears of Tughulluk Timour Khaun that the Ameers of the three armies had taken monies and gifts from the inhabitants of Mauwur u Nuhur: and he instantly commanded those sums to be delivered up, and he appointed collectors thereof. And he forbad them to enter into Mauwur u Nuhur; and he turned them out from their commands; and he appointed Haujee Muhmood Shaah Yessoori to supply their place.

And when intelligence of these things reached the ears of the chiefs, they elevated the ensign of enmity, and they retired towards their homes. And at this time they were met on their way by Aghlaun

* Having taken all his own tribe, and all the principal people of Mauwur u Nuhur along with him. Vide Fragm. Hist. p. 327 et 328. MS Hunter.

Khaujeh

وامیـر کنکاج خان بود برخوردند واورا هم از خود کرده بجانب جته روان شدند

وهمدریـن وقت خبر رسید که امرای تغلقتیمور خـان در دشت قیچاق عـلـم مخالفت بر افراشته اند خان مضطرب شد واز من کنکاش خواسته روی بطرف دشت جته باز نهاد

وماوراالنهر را بمن کـذاشـت ودرین باب یرلیغ وعهد نوشت وتومان امیر قـراچـار نویـان را از ماوراالنهر بمن باز کذاشت ومن بر ولایت ماوراالنهر تا کنار آب جیحون فرمان فرما کشتم واین کنکاش در ابتدای دولت وسلطنت من بود وبتجربـه مـن رسید که یک تدبیر درست کار صد هـزار سـوار میـکـنـد

* The president of his council.

† This circumstance is erroneously related in Aali Yezzudi; who says that the Toumaun of Kurrauchaur Nooyaun only was conferred upon him, and that not by Tughulluk Timour Khaun himself, but by the *Leaders of his advanced guard*. Vide Petis de la Croix's Histoire de Timour Bek. Tom. 1. p. 30.

‡ A Toumaun is a military fief capable of sending forth ten thousand fighting men: it also signifies that number of men collected together.

Nooyaun, in the Mogul language signifies *a prince*, or *the descendant of a prince*. Kurrauchaur Nooyaun was the fifth ancestor of Timour, and

Khaujeh, who was the Deewaunbeghee,* and the chief counsellor of the Khaun, and they drew him also over to their side: and they proceeded on their way to Jitteh. Book I.

And at this time also news arrived that the Ameers of Tughulluk Timour had exalted the standard of rebellion in the Dusht of Kipchauk: and the Khaun was disturbed in heart, and he asked counsel of me; and he turned back his face to the Dusht of Jitteh.

And he gave unto me the government of Mauwur u Nuhur,† and in this matter he wrote a commission and an agreement; and he restored unto me the Toumaun‡ of Ameer Kurrauchaur Nooyaun in that kingdom: and I became the ruler of all the kingdom of Mauwur u Nuhur, even to the waters of Jihoon.§ And this action came to pass in the beginning of my fortune and power. And I found by experience that one skilful plan can perform the service of a hundred thousand warriors.

and the Vizzeer of Chughtaï Khaun, one of the sons of Chungaze Khaun. (Ghenghis Can.)

§ Thus it appears that Tughulluk Timour Khaun, who had advanced no farther than Khojjund on the river Sihoon, and was unable to prosecute the reduction of Mauwur u Nuhur on account of the dissensions which Timour had sown betwixt him and the chiefs of his army, and also on account of the rebellion of his Ameers in the Dusht of Kipchauk, took advantage of the submission of Timour to obtain a nominal dominion over Mauwur u Nuhur, by conferring upon him the title of Viceroy in that kingdom.

THE

کنکاش دویم که در عنوان سلطنت

خود کردم این بود

که چون تغلقتیمور خان مرتبه دیکر بر

مملکت ماورالنهر لشکر کشید ونقض عهد کرد

وحکومت ماورالنهر را از من کرفت وبالیاس خواجه

پسر خود سپورد ومرا سپه سالار ومشیر وي ساخت

وعهد نامه قاجولي بهادر وقبل خانرا ظاهر ساخت

من هم بنابر قول وعهد بزرکان سپه سالاري را

قبول کردم

* Kubbul Khaun and Kaujooli Bahaudur were twin brothers, and the ſons of Toumuneh Khaun. Kubbul Khaun was the great grandfather of Chungaze Khaun [Ghenghis Can], and Kaujooli Bahaudur was the eighth anceſtor of Timour, and the great grandfather of Kurrauchaur Nooyaun, mentioned before.

Thus it appears, that Chungaze Khaun and Timour both ſprang from the ſame ſtock, i.e. from Toumuneh Khaun; who was the fourth anceſtor of Chungaze Khaun, and the ninth anceſtor of Timour. Toumuneh Khaun was ſucceeded by his ſon Kubbul Khaun, and Kubbul Khaun was ſucceeded by Burtun Khaun in the ſovereignty of the Moguls.

And it appears that an agreement had taken place between Kubbul Khaun and Kaujooli Bahaudur (at the deſire perhaps of their father Toumuneh Khaun) that the former (who was the elder brother) and his poſterity ſhould ſucceed to the dignity of Khaun, and that the latter (who was the younger brother) and his poſterity ſhould always fill the poſt of chief miniſter and leader of the forces; and that the deſcendants of both ſhould, by this agreement between their fathers, be bound to live in conſtant friendſhip and amity with each other. And this is the agreement ſhewn by Tughulluk Timour Khaun, who was deſcended in a right line from Chungaze and Kubbul Khaun,

THE SECOND DESIGN which I formed in the beginning of my fortune and power, was this. Book I.

DESIGN II.

A.D. 1370. A. TIM. 26.

WHEN Tughulluk Timour Khaun drew an army on the kingdom of Mauwur u Nuhur a ſecond time, and broke his engagements, and took from me the government of Mauwur u Nuhur, and delivered it over to Ouleaus Khaujeh his ſon, and offered me the poſt of counſellor and general to that prince, and ſhewed unto me the agreement between Kaujooli Bahaudur, and Kubbul Khaun; * I alſo, on account of the engagements and agreements of my anceſtors, conſented to lead his armies.

Khaun, to Timour, deſcended in a right line from Kaujooli Bahaudur: who, on peruſing the above-mentioned agreement, conſidered himſelf bound to accept the appointment offered him by Tughulluk Timour. Thus Timour, in *Fragm. of Hiſt.* p. 128. l. 3. MS. HUNTER, ſays,

در شهور سنه هفصد وششت ودو كه تغلقتيمور خان
مرتبه دويم به ماورالنهر لشكر كشيد نامه در بـاب
طلب بمن فرستاد ومن هم استقبال كرده ويرا ديدم
ووي نقـص عهد كرده ماورالنهر به پسر خود الياس
خـواجـه داد ومرا سپهسالار ساخت وچون مرا تيره
يافـت عهد نامه قاجولي بهادر جد من وقبل خان را
ظاهر ساخت چون من آن عهد نامه را كه بر صفحه
فـولاد نقش كرده بودند كه خاني بر اولاد قبل
خان متعلق باشد وسپه سالاري به اولاد قاجولي بهادر
ومخالفت

وچون ظلم وتعدی اوزبکیه در ماورالنهر
بسیار شد چنانچه هفتاد سید وسیدزاده را اسیر
ساخته بودند والیاس خواجه از سلطنت بهره نداشت
ودر منع ظلم وتعدي ایشان عاجز بود من از روي
سطوت بر اوزبکان غلبه کردم ومظلومان را از دست
ظالمان خلاص ساختم واین معني سبب عناد امراي
الیاس خواجه واوزبکان شد

وبه تغلقتیمور خان نوشتند که تیمور
علم مخالفت بر افراخته است وخان این افترا را
راست دانسته یرلیغ بکشتن من صادر کرد وآن
یرلیغ بدست من افتاد

ومخالفت یکدیگر نکنند مطالع کردم بنابر وفاي
عهد مخالفت نه نمودم وسپهسالاري را قبول کردم

i. e. "In the beginning of the year of the Hejra 762 [A. D. 1360] when "Tughulluk Timour Khaun drew an army a ſecond time into Mauwur u "Nuhur, he ſent unto me a mandate, ordering me before him; and I "went to meet him, and I ſaw him. And he broke his engagements, and "delivered over Mauwur u Nuhur to his ſon Ouleaus Khaujeh, and ap-"pointed me the leader of his forces. And when he ſaw that I was diſſa-"tisfied with his proceedings, he ſhewed unto me the agreement between "my anceſtor Kaujooli Bahaudur and Kubbul Khaun. And when I read "that agreement (which they had engraved on a tablet of ſteel) ſetting "forth,

وکشته

AND when the cruelties and the oppressions of the Ouzbuks became great in the kingdom of Mauwur u Nuhur, (for behold they had carried into slavery seventy Siuds, and sons of Siuds) and the power of Ouleaus Khaujeh availed him nought, and he was no longer able to restrain their cruelties and oppressions; in the spirit of authority I rushed upon the Ouzbuks, and I delivered the oppressed from the hand of the oppressors. And this circumstance was the cause of disobedience in the Ameers of Ouleaus Khaujeh, and in the soldiers under them.

AND they wrote unto Tughulluk Timour Khaun, saying, "Timour hath exalted the standard of "rebellion." And the Khaun thought that the accusation was true: and he issued an order to put me to death: and that order fell into my hands.

"forth, that the dignity of Khaun should appertain to the posterity of "Kubbul Khaun, and that the post of minister and general should belong "to the posterity of Kaujooli Bahaudur, and that they should live in amity "with each other: I also to fulfil the engagement of my ancestors, refrained from enmity, and consented to lead his armies."

This note is formed from authorities found in Abulghazi Khan's genealogical history of the Tartars, in D'Herbelot, and in the Fragment of the history of Timour, p. 153. l. 9.——And the passages illustrated here and in the notes on page 23. will to the oriental scholar serve to refute the falsehoods of the Arabian author Ibn Arabshaab, and to prove the superior accuracy and authenticity of the life of Timour written by himself *over that composed by* Alli Yezzudi; *who has hitherto been considered by the learned of Europe as the most perfect and faithful narrator of the actions of Timour.*

 AND

وکشته شدن خود را معاینه کردم ودر
علاج آن چنین تدبیر کردم که جوانان بهادر
الوس برلاس را بر سر خود جمع آورم وایشان را بخود
متفق سازم واول کسي که دست متابعت بمن داد
ایکو تیمور بود ودویم امیر جاکو برلاس ودیکر
بهادران از جان ودل اختیار متابعت من نمودند

چون اهالي ماورالنهر از داعیه من آکاه
شدند که اراده کرده ام که بر اوزبکان خروج
نمایم چون دلهاي ایشان از طایفه ظالم اوزبکان
منحرف شده بود اکابر واصاغر اهالي ماورالنهر
بمن متفق شدند وعلما ومشایخ فتوي بدفع ورفع
طایفه اوزبکیه نوشتند وبعضي امرا الوسات وقشونات
نیز برین معني اتفاق نمودند
وصورت فتوي وعهدي که کرده
بودند وبر کاغدي ثبت نمودند اینست

* *Alous*, of which *Alousaut* is the plural, signifies *a tribe*, or *hord*. A true explanation of the Tartar word *Kushoon* has not been met with. Mr. Petis de la Croix calls it a *body of a hundred soldiers*: but this interpretation is undoubtedly erroneous. The words *Kubbeeleh, Taueefeh, Ouemauk, Alous* and *Kushoon*, (some of which are Arabic) all appear to signify *a tribe* or *hord*; but there must be some distinction between them unknown to Europeans.

که

AND I reflected upon my danger: and to remedy the evil, this was the design which I formed—that I should gather round me the valiant youth of the tribe of Burlaus, and attach them unto me. And the first man who gave unto me the hand of obedience, was Eekou Timour; and the second was Ameer Jaukoo Burlaus: and after him other warriors, from their hearts and from their souls, consented to receive my commands. Book I.

WHEN the inhabitants of Mauwur u Nuhur obtained knowledge of my purpose, that I had resolved to rise in opposition to the tribe of Ouzbuk; as their hearts were turned aside from that oppressive people, both the rich and the poor of the people of Mauwur u Nuhur united themselves unto me. And the religious, and the holy men issued forth a decree, authorizing the expulsion and the extirpation of the Ouzbuks. And in this undertaking certain of the Ameers of Alousaut and and of Kushoonaut joined also. *

AND the decree and the engagement to which they had agreed, and which they caused to be written, is this. "According to the conduct and the ex-

Europeans. The *Kushoonaut* (which is the plural of *Kushoon*) may here mean *bodies of military men drawn from tribes or hords*, as the word *Toumaun* sometimes signifies. The number of the *Toumaun* is known to be ten thousand; that of the *Kushoon* may perhaps be somewhat less: but it can hardly signify so insignificant a number as a hundred men. Several particulars in this work tend to confirm this opinion.

"example

که مطابق سیرت وصورت خلفاي راشدین رضوان الله تعالـي علیهم واجمعین اهل اسلام سپاه ورعیت وعلما ومشایخ وبرا کرام دیده ملقب بر سلطنت قطب السلطنه امیر تیمورا ایده الله نموده اند که بمال وجان در رفع ودفع وقلع وقمع طایفه اوزبکیه که دست ظلم وتعدي به عرض وناموس ومال واسباب مسلمانان دراز کرده اند کوشش نمایند

وما در عـهـد وبیعت خـود درسـت پیمان باشیم واکر خلاف پیمان وعـهـد نمایـم از حول وقوت آلهي برآمده داخل حول وقوت شیطان بـاشـیـم

وچون فـتـوي را بمن نمودار ساختند خـواسـتـم کـه علم قتال وجدال بر افرازم وبر سر اوزبـکـان لشکر بکشم وداد مظلومـون از ظالمان بـکـیـرم لیکن بعضي مردم اراذل این راز را فاش کـردنـد

ودیکر باره خود بخود کنکاش کردم که اکر در سمرقند بمقابله ومقاتله اوزبکان اشتغال نمایم

"ample of the orthodox Khulleefehs, † (on whom be Book I.
"the favour of Almighty God) the followers of Islaum,
"the doctors, and the holy men, and the soldiers, and the
"subjects, seeing Him noble and worthy thereof, HAVE
"NOMINATED AMEER TIMOUR (the Polar star of dominion, on whom be the favour of God) to the empire: and with their wealth, and with their lives they
"will exert themselves in expelling and in driving out,
"and in extirpating and in destroying the tribe of Ouzbuk,
"who have stretched forth the hand of cruelty and rapine over the families and over the wealth, and over
"the property and over the effects of the faithful."

"AND we will be firm in our engagements;
"and if we deviate from our agreement and from our
"compact, may we be deprived of the grace and of
"the protection of Almighty God; and be delivered
"over to the power and the dominion of the devil!""

AND when they shewed unto me the decree, I was eager to exalt the standard of war and of slaughter, and to draw down an army on the people of Jitteh, and to revenge the oppressed on the heads of the oppressors: but certain of the worthless revealed my intentions.

AGAIN, I deliberated with myself, that if I made war upon them in the city of Summurkund, it might come to pass that the people of Mauwur u Nu-

† The Caliphs Abaubukkur, Omur, Osmaun and Aali.

hur

نـمـایـم مبارا اهل ماورالنهر کوتاهي کنند پس چنین کنکاش دیدم که از سمرقند برآمده در کوه مقام کنم تا هر کس کـه بمن متفق باشد نزد من آید انکـاه جمیعت کرده بقتال وجدال اوزبکان مـبـادرت نـمـایـم

چـون از سمـرقـنـد بـر آمـدم زیـاده از ششت سوار دیکر کسي با من بر نیآمد ودانستم که در کنکاش خود غلط نکرده ام

وچون یکهفته در آن کوه توقف نمودم وکسي بمن در نیآمد خود بخود کنکاش کردم که بجانب بدخشان رفته شاهان بدخشان را بخود متفق سازم

وسوار شـدم وبخدمت امیر کلال رفتم ایـشـان مرا ارشاد نمودند که بجانب خوارزم عنان عزیمت معطوف دارم ومن مال یکساله سمرقند را نذر ایشان کردم که اکر بر اوزبکان ظفر یابم با ایشان بکذرانم وایشان فاتحه فتح خوانده مرا رخصت دادند

وچون از خدمت ایشان بر آمدم همکي شـشت سوار با من بود وچون خبر نهضت من در خوارزم

hur might ſhrink back from their engagements: therefore I reſolved to come forth from Summurkund, and to fix my habitation in the hills, that every one who was united with me might come in unto me; and that having gathered together an army, I might advance and make war upon the Ouzbuks. Book I.

And when I came forth from Summurkund, ſixty warriors only came forth with me; and I ſaw that I had not erred in my deliberations.

And when I had remained ſeven days in thoſe hills, and no one had come in unto me, I determined with myſelf that I would proceed to Buddukhſhaun, and draw unto my ſtandard the princes thereof.

And I ſet out, and I went into the preſence of Ameer Goolaul.* And he directed me that I ſhould turn the reins of my intention towards Khauruzm. And I promiſed unto him the revenue of Summurkund for one year—that I would lay it before him, if I proved victorious over the Ouzbuks. And he repeated over me the prayer of victory, and permitted me to depart.

And when I came forth from the preſence of Ameer Goolaul, ſixty horſemen were all that were with me. And when the news of my arrival in Khauruzm reached the ears of Ouleaus Khaujeh, he wrote

* A religious man, celebrated for his piety.

خوارزم بالیاس خواجه رسید به تکل بهادر حاکم خیوق نوشت که بر سر من آمده مرا ضایع سازد وتکل بهادر با هزار سوار بر سر من آمد ومن با شصت سوار خود وبا امیر حسین که در راه آمده بمن ملحق شده بود رو برو شدم وبجنک در آمدم وتا بحدي جنک وکوشش نمودم که از هزار کس وي پنجاه کس ماند واز شصت سوار من ده کس ماند تا آنکه در معنی فتح از جانب من شد

وچون خبر فتح من بمسامع الیاس خواجه وامرا جته رسید باهم کفتند که تیمور عجب مردي وصاحب اقبال وتاییدات است واین فتح را بر خود شکون * کرفتم وچشم اوزبکان از من تیره شد

کنکاش سیوم که در اصلاح سلطنت خود کردم این بود

که در آن وقت که احوال دولت من مختل شد واساس سلطنت من از هم کسیخته شد چنانچه زیاده از ده کس همراه من نبود که هفت کس سوار بودند وسه پیاده وجز آنها کسي دیکر با من نماند وهمشیره امیر حسین که حرم محترم من

* An asterisk placed after a word (in the Persian text) signifies that it is of Mogul origin.

unto Tukkul Bahaudur the governor of Khiook, that he ſhould fall upon me and deſtroy me. And Tukkul Bahaudur came upon me with a thouſand horſemen: and I oppoſed him with my ſixty warriors, and with Ameer Hooſſein who had come and joined me in the way; and I entered into battle. And I fought with ſuch obſtinacy and reſolution, that of the one thouſand horſemen of Tukkul Bahaudur fifty remained, and of my ſixty warriors ten remained; and the victory in effect was mine. Book I.

AND when the news of my ſucceſs reached the ears of Ouleaus Khaujeh and the Ameers of Jitteh, they ſaid among themſelves, "Timour is a wonderful man: fortune and the Divine favour are with him." And I called this victory a favour from heaven conferred upon me: and the eyes of the tribe of Jitteh were darkened by my ſucceſs.

THE THIRD DESIGN which I formed for the reſtoration of my power, was this. DESIGN III.

AT the time when the ſtate of my fortune was reduced low, and when the foundation of my power was broken aſunder, ſo that my aſſociates were ten only (and ſeven of them were on horſes, and three of them were foot-men) and none other remained with me; in thoſe days the ſiſter of Ameer Hooſſein, who was my honoured wife, I placed behind me on my horſe, and I

من بود ویرا با خود بر اسپ خود سوار ساخته بودم
ودر صحراي خوارزم سر کردان می کشتم تا آنکه شبي
بسر چاهي فرود آمدم وهمان شب آن سه نفر خراسانی
بیوفا سه اسپ را کرفته وسوار شده کریختند ودر میان
هفت کس چهار اسپ ماند واحوال من بسیار مختل
شد لیکن قوي دل بودم وافشاي خطا نکردم

واز سر آن چاه روان شدم ودر این وقت
علـی بیک چون غرباني بر سر من آمد ومرا برده
در خانه پر از کیک محبوس ساخت ونکاهبانان بر
من تعیین نمود وششت ودو روز مرا در قید نکاهداشت
وخود بخود کنکاش کردم وبتایید آلهي
موید شده بقوت بازوي جلادت شمشیري از
نکاهبانان کشیده بر ایشان حمله آوردم ونکاهبانان
روي بکریز نهادند ومن پیش علي بیک رفته ایستادم
ووی از عمل نا شایسته خود که مرا مقید ساخته
بود شرمنده ومنفعل شد وعذر خواست
واسپان ویراق مرا حاضر آورد ویک اسپ
لاغر ویک اشتر نا توان آورده بمن پیشکش نمود
وارمغان که برادرش محمد بیک بمن فرستاده بود
در آن طمع نمود وپاره نکاهداشت ومرا رخصت نمود
وبجانب

wandered to and fro in the desart of Khauruzm, until on a certain night I alighted at a well. And even in that night the three faithless Khorausauni * seized on three horses, and mounted them and fled: and four horses only remained for seven people, and my distresses were very great: but I was strong of heart, and I lamented not over my misfortunes. Book I.

AND I departed from the well; and at this time Aali Beg Choun Ghoorbauni came upon me, and he carried me away, and confined me in a habitation filled with vermin, and placed a guard over me, and kept me imprisoned for sixty and two days.

AND I deliberated with myself, and aided by the assistance of Almighty God, with the strength of the arm of vigour I wrested a sword from my guards and I rushed upon them: and the guards turned their faces to flight, and I went and stood before Aali Beg. And he was ashamed and confounded at his evil conduct, that he had thrown me into prison; and he made excuses.

AND he ordered my horses and my arms to be brought forth; and he gave me a horse that was lean, and a camel that was past service as a present. But he thirsted after the gifts which his brother Mahummud Beg had sent unto me, and he kept back a part thereof; and he suffered me to depart.

* Natives of Khorausaun.

AND

وبجانب بيابان خوارزم روان شدم
ودوازده سوار بر سر من جمع آمدند وبعد از دو روز بموضعي رسيدم ودر خانه نزول نمودم وجمعي از تركمانان كه در آن موضع مي بودند اغري * كفته بر من حمله آوردند ومن همشيره امير حسين را در خانه مضبوط ساختم وبذات خود بر آن جماعه حمله كردم ودر اين وقت شخصي حاجي محمد نام كه در ميان تركمانان بود مرا بشناخت وفرياد بر آورد كه امير تيمور است ومردم را از جنك منع كرده زانوزد ومن ويرا تسلي كردم ومنديل خود را بر سر وي نهادم ووي آمده با برادران خود ملازم من شد

كنكاش چهارم كه در اوايل سلطنت خود كردم اين بود

كه چون شست سوار نزد من جمع آمدند بخود كنكاش كردم كه اكر در موضعي كه رسيده بودم اقامت نمايم مبادا اهل آن موضع دست

* The word thus tranſlated is in the original *Aghuri*, and evidently of Mogul origin. The Mogul language is, in this work and in moſt other oriental authors, called *Toori Zubaun* and *Zubaun a Toorki*, or the language of the Toorks. But notwithſtanding the language, known in Europe by the name of Turkiſh, muſt have been derived from the ſame origin, this and ſeveral other Mogul words retained by the Perſian tranſlator in

تطاول

Book I.

AND I set out toward the desart of Khauruzm, and twelve horsemen united themselves unto me. And after two days I came to an inhabited place, and I alighted at one of the dwellings thereof. And certain of the Toorkummauns, who were in that place, gave a loud shout,* and rushed upon me. And I secured the sister of Ameer Hoossein in the house, and I assaulted those people in my own person. And at this time a man among the Toorkummauns, whose name was Haujee Mahummud, knew me again; and he exclaimed aloud, "It is Ameer "Timour." And he ordered the people to desist, and he kneeled before me. And I received him kindly, and I placed my turban on his head; and he came with his brethren, and was my servant.

THE FOURTH DESIGN which I formed in the early days of my power, was this. DESIGN IV.

WHEN sixty horsemen were gathered round me, I reflected with myself, that if I continued in the place where I then sojourned, perhaps the inhabitants thereof might extend the hand of treachery over me, and send news of my condition to the tribe of Jitteh.

in this work, are not to be found in any Lexicon, and are consequently unknown. Where the probable sense is discoverable from the context, as in the present case, an interpretation is given in the translation; and wherever the meaning is beyond the reach of conjecture, the Mogul word is retained in the version; its origin in both cases being marked for the benefit of the Persian scholar. See note on pag. 34.

And

تطاول بر من دراز كنند وخبر مرا در اوزبكان
فرستند وصلاح حال خود در اين ديدم كه از آن موضع
بر آيم ودر صحراي كه از معموره دور باشد نزول نمايم
تا آنكه لشكر كه بازوي سلطنت است نزد من جمع آيد

واز آن موضع بجانب خراسان متوجه شدم
ودر راه مبارك شاه سنجري حاكم ماخان با يكصد
سوار نزد من آمد واسپان خوب پيشكش كرد وجمعي
از سادات واهالي نيز بمن ملحق كشتند وقريب دو
صد نفر سوار وپياده در آن صحرا با من همراه كشت

ودرينوقت مبارك شاه وسيد حسن وسيد
ضياء الدين بمن عرض كردند كه توقف نمودن درين
صحرا باعث پريشاني است بطرفي بايد رفت وولايتي
جهت بودن مسخر بايد ساخت ومن خود بخود
كنكاش كردم وبا ايشان كفتم كه بخاطرم اين كنكاش
رسيده كه متوجه طرف سمرقند شويم وشهايانرا در موضع
مضافات بخارا متفرق سازم وخود بحوالي سمرقند رفته
وبهيان اهل والوسات در آمده ايشانرا بخود متفق سازم
ولشكري جمع ساخته وشهايانرا طلب داشته با لشكر جته
والياس خواجه درافتم ومملكت ماورالنهر را مسخر سازم
ايشان

And I ſaw that my ſafety conſiſted in this — that I ſhould come forth from that place, and that I ſhould ſojourn in the deſart, far from the habitations of men; until an army, which is the ſinews of Empire, ſhould be gathered around me. Book I.

AND I journeyed from that place toward Khorauſaun; and Mubauruk Shaah Sunjuri, the governor of Maukhaun, came to me on the way with an hundred ſoldiers, and preſented ſome choſen horſes to me: and certain of the deſcendants of the prophet and of the inhabitants alſo came in unto me; and near two hundred men, horſe-men and foot-men, joined me in the deſart.

AND at this time Mubauruk Shaah, and Siud Hooſun, and Siud Zeau u deen ſaid unto me, "Our tarrying in this deſart is the cauſe of our diſtreſs; "we muſt go from hence, and we muſt ſeize on ſome "Province for an habitation." And I deliberated with myſelf, and I ſaid unto them, "This meaſure occurreth "to my mind — that we advance towards Summurkund, "and that I diſperſe you in the ſecure places of Bokh-"aura; and that I myſelf go into the parts adjacent to "Summurkund, and enter among the people and the "tribes, and unite them with me: and having collected "an army, and called you unto me, that I encounter "Ouleaus Khaujeh and the forces of Jitteh, and ſubdue "the kingdom of Mauwur u Nuhur."

 THEY

ایشان همکي این کنکاش وتدبیر مرا
پسندیدند ودرین عزیمت فاتح خوانده روان شدم
وایسن دو صد کس را در حوالي بخارا متفرق ساختم
والجاي ترکان آغا همشیره امیر حسین را پنهاني در
آن موضع کذاشتم ومتوجه سمرقند شدم

وتهوکه توچین با پانزده سوار آمده در
راه بمن ملحق شد وراز خودرا بوي کفته ویرا نزد
مبارک شاه فرستادم وخود میان الوسات در آمده قریب
دو هزار کس را با خود متفق ساختم که هرکاه در
سمرقند علم سلطنت برافرازم ایشان خودرا برسانند

وشب پنهانی داخل شهر سمرقند شدم
وبخانه تنلغ ترکان اغاي خواهر کلان خود رفته
نزول نمودم وشب وروز در فکر وتدبیر بودم وچهل
وهشت روز پنهاني کذرانیدم تا آنکه بعضي از اهالي
شهر بر آمدن من اطلاع نمودند ونزدیک بود که
سر من فاش شود ناچار با پنجاه سوار که در شهر
با من بودند شب از سمرقند بر آمده بطرف خوارزم
متوجه شدم وجمعي از پیادکان هم با من رفاقت
کردند

THEY all approved of my counſel and my deſign; and having repeated the prayer of ſucceſs on our attempt, I proceeded forward. And I diſperſed thoſe two hundred people in the environs of Bokhaura, and I ſecreted Aljaié Turkaun Aughau, the ſiſter of Ameer Hooſſein, in that place; and I advanced toward Summurkund.

AND Tumookeh Kouchein met me on the way with fifteen horſemen, and joined me. And I communicated my ſecret unto him, and ſent him to Mubauruk Shaah. And entering myſelf among the tribes, I confederated with me near two thouſand of the people: and whenever I exalted the ſtandard of empire in Summurkund, they were to join me.

And I entered the city of Summurkund under the cover of the night; and going to the dwelling of my eldeſt ſiſter Kuttulugh Turkaun Aughau, I ſojourned therein. And I was buried in thought and reflection night and day. And I paſſed forty eight days undiſcovered; until at length certain of the inhabitants gave information of my arrival, and my ſituation was near to be revealed. I was without remedy; and with fifty horſemen, who were with me in the city, I came forth from Summurkund by night, and I proceeded toward Khauruzm: and certain of the foot-ſoldiers alſo came with

کردند ودر اثناي راه چند اسپ از کله ترکمانان بدست آوردم وپیادکان خودرا سوار ساختم

وآمده در موضع اچیغي در کنار آب آمویه در زمین پست وبلند نزول نمودم ودر همین جاي اهل حرم ومبارک شاه وسید حسن وجماعه را که در حوالي بخارا کذاشته بودم آمده بمن ملحق شدند وتیمور خواجه اغلان وبهرام جلایر با افواج خود آمده ملازمت نمودند وقریب هزار سوار نزد من جمع آمدند واز اینجا خود با خود کنکاش کرده روانه باختر زمین وقندهار شدم وآن ملک را مسخر کردانیدم

کنکاش پنجم که در ایام خروج خود کردم این بود

که چون بجانب باختر زمین وقندهار روان شدم بکنار آب هیرمن رسیدم ونزول نمودم ویورتي بجهته خود ساختم وچند روز بتیمارداري سپاه در کنار آن آب توقف نمودم

ودر این وقت سپاه ورعیت ولایت کرمسیر

* It may be proper to obferve, for the credit of Timour, that before he took thofe horfes, he enquired out the owners and fent for them, and gave them a written order for their value. This happened in the principality of Kufh.

رجوع

me. And on the road I took horſes from among the droves of the Toorkummaun;* and I mounted my foot-ſoldiers thereon. Book I.

AND I came and I encamped at Atcheghi in the hilly grounds on the banks of the waters of Amuveah: in this place my family, and Mubauruk Shaah, and Siud Hooſſun, and all thoſe whom I had left in the environs of Bokhaura, came and joined themſelves unto me. And Timour Khaujeh Aghlaun and Behraum Jullauir, with their forces, came and ſerved me; and near a thouſand horſemen were gathered round me. And I deliberated with myſelf, and I ſet out from thence towards Baukhtur Zemeen and Kundahaur, and I ſubdued thoſe countries.

THE FIFTH DESIGN which I formed in the days of enterpriſe, was this. DESIGN V.

WHEN I departed towards Kundahaur and Baukhtur Zemeen, I came to the border of the river of Hiremun, and I ſojourned there, and I made for myſelf an habitation; and I tarried ſome days on the border of that river to refreſh my people.

AND at this time the ſoldiers and the inhabitants of Kurrumſeer came in unto me; and near a thouſand

Kuſh. Vide Timour's full account of this tranſaction in the Fragment of his Hiſtory. pag. 355. l. 5. MS. HUNTER.

رجوع آوردند و تریب بهزار سوار از ترک وتاچک نیز بر
من جمع شد وولایت کرمسیر مسخر من کشت

ودر این وقت کنکاش کردم که بر
ولایت سیستان ترکتاز آورم وچون خبر بوالی سیستان
رسید ارمغان وساوري* فرستاد وطلب مدد کرد که
جمعي از دشمنان بر من ظلم کرده وملک مرا با هفت
قلعه متصرف شده اند اکر دست دشمنان از ملک
من کوتاه شود شش ماهیه علوفه سپاه را برسانم

وکنکاش درین دیدم که عنان عزیمت
بجانب سیستان معطوف دارم واز هفت قلعه که
دشمنان وي متصرف شده بودند پنج قلعه را جبرا
وقهرا کرفتم در دل والي سیستان هراس راه یافت
ودشمنان خودرا با خود دوست کرد وبا خود کنکاش
کردند که اکر امیر تیمور درین ملک اقامت کند ملک
سیستان از دست ما بدر خواهد رفت وسپاه ورعیت
تمامي مملکت سیستان حشر کردند وبر سر من آمدند

وچون دیدم که والي سیستان بعهد
خود وفا ننمود ناچار شدم وسر راه بر ایشان کرفته
قتال وجدال نمودم وتیري آمد وبر بازوي من خورد
ونیز یک تیر دیکر بر پاي من رسید آخر بر ایشان
ظفر یافتم

وچون

thousand horsemen also, Toork and Taucheek, were gathered round me; and the country of Kurrumseer submitted to my authority. Book I.

AND at this time I resolved that I would invade the province of Seistaun. And when the ruler of Seistaun received accounts thereof, he sent offerings and rich gifts unto me, and he demanded succour, saying, "Certain of my enemies have oppressed me, and they "have seized upon my lands, and upon seven castles.— "If the hands of my enemies be withdrawn from my "dominions, I will advance six months wages to the soldiers."

AND I saw it was good that I should turn the reins of my intentions toward Seistaun. And of the seven castles which were in the hands of his enemies, I subdued five castles by force and by assault. — And fear found admission into the heart of the ruler of Seistaun, and he made his enemies his friends; and they said among themselves, "If Ameer Timour tarry in this country, the province of Seistaun will pass out from our hands." And they gathered together the soldiers and the people of all the country of Seistaun, and they came upon me.

AND when I saw that the ruler of Seistaun fulfilled not his engagement, I was without remedy; and I advanced toward them, and gave them battle. And an arrow came and pierced my arm, and another arrow also came upon my foot, but in the end I obtained the victory over them.

AND

وچون آب وهواي آن ملک را بمزاج خود
موافق ندیدم برخاسته به گرمسیر آمدم ودر آن ولایت
دو ماه اقامت نمودم تا آنکه زخمهاي من به شد

کنکاش ششم که در وقت خروج خود
کردم این بود
که چون گرمسیر مسخر من گردید
وزخمهاي من به شد کنکاش درین دیدم که رفته
در کوهستان سرحد بلخ اقامت نمایم وجمعیت کرده
بتسخیر ملک ماورالنهر متوجه شوم وچون برین کنکاش
عزیمت بستم سوار شدم وهمگی چهل سوار با من بودند
اما همه اصیل واصیل زاده وامیر زاده بودند وتنگري
تعالي را شکر گفتم که در چنین پریشاني همچنین
مردم بي زر وبي توشه آمده همراهي واطاعت مرا قبول
کرده اند وبا خود گفتم الله تعالی را بمن کار بسیار
است که این نوع مردم همسر مرا بمن مطیع ساخته

وبجانب کوهستان بلخ نهضت نمودم ودر
اثناي راه صدیق برلاس از اولاد یلدرین تراچار نویان
که بطلب من سر گردان مي گشت با پانزده سوار آمده
بمن ملحق شد ومن آمدن ویرا شگون* گرفتم
ودرین

Book I.

AND when I ſaw that the air and the water of that country ſuited not with me, I departed from thence, and I came back to Kurrumſeer; and I ſojourned in that land for two months, until my wounds were healed.

DESIGN VI.

THE SIXTH DESIGN which I formed in the days of enterpriſe, was this.

WHEN Kurrumſeer had ſubmitted to my authority, and my wounds were healed, I ſaw it was good that I ſhould go and ſojourn in the mountains on the borders of Bullukh; and having collected an army, that I ſhould proceed to ſubdue the kingdom of Mauwur u Nuhur. And when I reſolved on this meaſure, I departed from thence: and forty horſemen were all that were with me. But they were all reſolute men, and the ſons of reſolute men, and the ſons of Ameers. And I gave praiſe unto God, for that in ſuch diſtreſs ſuch men ſhould come, without purſe and without ſcrip, and follow me, and be obedient unto me. And I ſaid unto myſelf, God Almighty doeth great things for me; ſeeing he hath made ſuch men, even my equals, my ſervants.

AND I went on towards the mountains of Bullukh, and Suddeuk Burlaus (of the race of Yeldureen Kurrauchaur Nouyaun) who was wandering in ſearch of me, met me in the way with fifteen horſemen, and joined me; and I took his coming for a happy omen.

ودرين ايام بكوشت شكار اوقات مي كذرانيديم وپيش مي رفتيم ودر اثناء راه ديدم كه فوجي بر پشته ايستاده وساعت بساعت زياده مي شدند واستاده قراولان فرستادم تا خبر آورند وقراولان بآن جماعت رسيده خبر آوردند كه قرانچي بهادر نوكر قديم امير است كه با صد سوار از لشكر جته جدا شده وبطلب امير سر كردان مي كردد من سجده شكر تنكري تعالي بجا آوردم وامر باحضار قرانچي كردم ووي آمده زانوزد ودر پاي مرا بوسه داد ومن ويرا تسلي نمودم ومنديل خودرا بر سر وي نهادم ومتوجه دره ارصنى شدم

وبدره ارصنى رسيده نزول نمودم وروز ديكر سوار شدم ودر آن دره در آمدم ودر ميان دره بلندي بود بغايت خوش هوا ومن رفته برآن بلندي جاي كرفتم ولشكريان هريك در حوالي آن پشته فرود آمدند

ومن آن شب كه جمع بود زنده داشتم وچون صبح بدميد بنماز مشغول شدم وبعد از اداي نماز دست برداشته بدعا مشغول شدم ودر اثناي

AND in thoſe days we paſſed our time in hunting, and we proceeded forward. And on the way I beheld a body of men ſtanding on a hill; and their numbers increaſed from time to time: and I halted, and ſent people to obtain intelligence. And they went in among thoſe men, and brought back intelligence, ſaying, "It is "Kurraunchee Bahaudur, the old ſervant of Ameer,* who "with an hundred horſemen hath ſeparated from the ar-"mies of Jitteh, and is wandering in ſearch of thee." I bowed in gratitude to Almighty God, and I ſent orders for Kurraunchee to approach. And he came, and he kneeled before me; and he kiſſed my feet. And I received him with affection, and I placed my own turban on his head. And I went on to the valley of Arſuff.

AND I came to the valley of Arſuff, and I pitched my tents. And on the next day I mounted my horſe, and entered into the valley. And in the midſt of that valley there was a hill; and the air thereof was very delightful. And I went and dwelt upon that hill; and my people, each of them, pitched their tents in the neighbourhood thereof.

AND on that night, which was a holy night,† I kept watch; and when the morning broke, I was employed in prayer. And after repeating the prayers

* i. e. Timour.

† Friday, the Mahummudan ſabbath.

 preſcribed

اثنــاي دعـا مرا رقتي دست داد واز تنكري تعالي
درخواست كردم كه مرا از اين سركرداني نجات دهد

وهنوز از دعا فارغ نكشته بودم كه فوجي
از دور نهودارشد كه از برابر بلندي ميكذرد ومن سوار
شده از عقب آن فوج در آمدم تا احوال ايشانرا معلوم
نهايم كه ايشان چه مردم اند وايشان همكي هفتاد سوار
بودنــد از ايشان پرسيدم كه بهادران شما چه كسانيد
وايشان كفتند ما نوكران امير تيموريم كه بطلب امير
ميكرديم واينك ويرا نهي يابيم ومن بديشان كفتم كه
مــن هم يكي از نوكران امير ام چونست كه شمارا
راهبري كرده بامير برسانم ويكي از ايشان اسپ خودرا
تاخته ورفته خبر بسرداران برد كه راهبري يافته ايم
كه مارا به امير تيمور رساند وايشان عنان اسپان خودرا
كشيدند وحكم باحضار من نهودند وايشان سه فوج
بودند وسردار فوج اول تغلق خواجه برلاس بود وسردار
فوج دويم امير سيف الدين بود وسردار فوج سيوم توبك
بهادر بود وچون نظر ايشان بر من افتاد بيخود شده از
اسپان خود پياده شدند وآمده زانو زدند وركاب مرا
بوسيدند من هم از اسپ فرود آمدم وهركدام را در
بغل

prefcribed by the law, I lifted up my hands in fupplication. And in the midft of my fupplication I wept: and I implored Almighty God, that he would deliver me from that wandering life. Book I.

AND I had not yet refted from my devotions, when a number of people appeared afar off: and they were paffing along in a line with the hill. And I mounted my horfe, and I came in behind them: that I might know their condition, and what men they were. And they were in all feventy horfemen; and I afked of them, faying, "Warriors, who are ye?" And they anfwered unto me, "We are the fervants of Ameer Timour, "and we wander in fearch of him; and lo! we find him "not." And I faid unto them, I alfo am one of the fervants of Ameer: how fay ye, if I be your guide, and conduct you unto him? And one of them put his horfe to fpeed, and went and carried news to the leaders, faying, "We have found a guide, who can lead us to "Ameer Timour." And the leaders drew back the reins of their horfes, and gave orders that I fhould appear before them. And they were three troops. And the leader of the firft troop was Tughulluk Khaujeh Burlaus, and the leader of the fecond troop was Ameer Sife u deen, and the leader of the third troop was Toubuk Bahaudur. And when their eyes fell upon me, they were overwhelmed with joy; and they alighted from their horfes, and they came and they kneeled, and they kiffed my ftirrup. And

I alfo

بغل کرفتم ومندیل خودرا بر سر تغلق خواجه نهادم وکمربند خودرا که بسیار پر کار وزر بافت بود بر کمر امیر سیف الدین بستم وجامهء خودرا بر توبک بهادر پوشانیدم وایشان رقت کردند ومرا هم رقت شد ووقت نماز دررسید وبجمعیت نمازرا ادا کردیم وسوار شده وآمده بیورت نزول نمودیم ومجلس ساخته طوي دادم

وروز دیکر شیر بهرام هم که از روي خوردي از من جدا شده بود واراده زمین هندوستان در دل داشت رسید ومرا ملازمت نمود وعذر خواست ومن ویرا در کنار کرفتم وعذرش را پذیرفتم وآن قدر مهرباني کردم که از خجالت بر آمد

کنکاش هفتم که در ایام خروج خود کردم این بود

که چون سان لشکر خود دیدم که همکي سه صد وسیزده سوار بودند بخود کنکاش کردم که یکي از قلاع را بدست آورده جاي بودن قرار دهم وچنین کنکاش کردم که اول قلعه الاجورا که از جانب الیاس خواجه منکلی بوغا سلدوز در آن قلعه مي بود مسخر سازم وجاي نکاه

I alſo came down from my horſe, and took each of them in my arms. And I put my turban on the head of Tughulluk Khaujeh; and my girdle, which was very rich in jewels and wrought with gold, I bound on the loins of Ameer Sife u deen, and I cloathed Toubuk Bahaudur in my coat. And they wept, and I wept alſo. And the hour of prayer was arrived, and we prayed together. And we mounted our horſes, and came and alighted at my dwelling: and I collected my people together and made a feaſt. Book I.

AND on the next day Share Behraum, who had ſeparated from me in the narrowneſs of his heart, and had reſolved to go into the land of Hind, arrived alſo. And he came into my preſence, and he made excuſes. And I took him into my arms, and I accepted his excuſes; and I treated him with ſuch kindneſs, that he came forth from his confuſion.

THE SEVENTH DESIGN which I formed in the days of enterpriſe, was this. DESIGN VII.

WHEN I ſaw the number of my forces, that they were in all three hundred and thirteen horſemen; I determined with myſelf that I would ſeize on one of the caſtles, and make to myſelf a reſidence. And thus I reſolved, that I would firſt reduce the caſtle of Aulaujou; (and Munguli Booghau Suldoze, on the part of Ouleaus Khaujeh, was in that caſtle,) and that I would make

نگاه داشتن بار وپرتل خود گردانم وباین عزیمت
روانه قلعه الاجو شدم

وشیر بهرام با وي از قدیم اشناي
داشت والتماس کرد که من رفته منکلي بوغا را
ایل گردانم

وچون شیر بهرام بحولی قلعه رفت
مرا پیغام داد که منکلی بوغا اظهار میکند چون
این قلعه را الیاس خواجه بمن سپرده از مردي ومروت
دور است که من بامیر تیمور ایل شده قلعه را
بسپارم ودر دادن قلعه اهمال نمود

لیکن این قدر شد که از خبر توجه
من واهمه در دل وي جاي کرد وقلعه را گذاشته
رو بگریز نهاد وسه صد مرد از قوم دولان جاون که
در قلعه با وي بودند واز قدیم در سلک ملازمان من
انسلاک داشتند آمده بمن ملحق گشتند

وبموضع دره صوف رسیدم ودرین وقت
املس پسر تومن بهادر که بحوالی بلخ بجهته تاخت
آمده بود خبر رسیدن مرا شنید وبا دو صد سوار آمده
ملازمت نمود ومن ویرا تسلي داده مستمال ساختم
واز

make it a place wherein to keep my baggage and my effects. And with this intention I ſet out toward the caſtle of Aulaujou.

AND Share Behraum had long acquaintance with the governor of that caſtle: and he ſpoke unto me, ſaying, "I will go and I will bring Munguli Booghau "over to our ſide."

AND when Share Behraum went near to the caſtle, he ſent word unto me, ſaying, Munguli Booghau ſayeth, "Since Ouleaus Khaujeh gave this caſtle "in charge unto me, it is far from manhood and from "fidelity that I ſhould come over to Ameer Timour, and "give up the caſtle:" and he refuſed to deliver it up.

BUT thus much came to paſs, that on receiving information of my approach, terror took poſſeſſion of his heart, and he left the caſtle, and he turned his face to flight. And three hundred men of the tribe of Doulaun Jauwun, who were with him in the caſtle, and who from old times were included in the train of my ſervants, came and united themſelves unto me.

AND I arrived at the defile of Souf, and in thoſe days Umlis, the ſon of Toumun Bahaudur, who had come down into the neighbourhood of Bullukh to plunder, received news of my coming; and he came with two hundred horſemen and joined me: and I received him kindly, and I encouraged him.

واز همین جا تموکه بهادررا با سه سوار فرستادم که از آب ترمذ کذشته خبر لشکر جته بیآورد واز اراده وکنکاش ایشان خودرا اکاه سازد

تموکه بعد چهار روز آمده خبر رسانید که لشکر جته بولایت ترمذ رسیده وبقتل وغارت مشغول اند چون این خبر بمن رسید عنان عزیمت بجانب دره کز معطوف داشتم وکنکاش درین دیدم که رفته در دره کز اقامت نمایم وقابو یافته بر سر لشکر جته ترکتاز آورم

وچون بدره کز در آمدم ودر میدان ایلچي بوغا کنار آب جیحون نزول نمودم خبر من بالیاس خواجه رسید که بدره کز رسیده ام وافواج خود را بر سر من تعیین نمود

ودرین وقت خبر رسید که امیر سلیمان برلاس وامیر موسي وامیر جاکو برلاس وامیر جلال الدین وامیر هندوکه برلاس که در لشکر جته بودند از امراي جته رو کردان شده وبا لشکر خود جدا کردیده بترمذ کهنه رسیده اند وتولان بوغا را که نزد من

AND even from this place I ſent Tummookeh Bahaudur with three horſemen, that having paſſed over the waters of Turmuz, he ſhould bring intelligence of the army of Jitteh, and inform himſelf of their counſels and deſigns.

AND Tummookeh returned after four days, and brought intelligence, ſaying, "The army of Jitteh "is arrived in the land of Turmuz, and they are em-"ployed in rapine and in ſlaughter." When I received this intelligence, I turned the reins of my intention towards the ſtreights of Guz. And I ſaw it was good that I ſhould go into the ſtreights of Guz, and ſojourn there: and ſeizing an opportunity, that I ſhould go down on the army of Jitteh.

AND when I came into the ſtreights of Guz, I pitched my tents in the plain of Ilchee Booghau, on the border of the waters of Jihoon. And Ouleaus Khaujeh received news of me, that I was arrived in the ſtreights of Guz; and he ſent his forces upon me.

AND in thoſe days intelligence came, that Ameer Soolamaun Burlaus and Ameer Jullaul u deen and Ameer Hindookeh (who were in the army of Jitteh) having turned their faces from the leaders of that tribe, and ſeparated from them with their forces, were arrived at old Turmuz: and Toulaun Booghau, whom they had

 ſent

من فرستاده بودند رسيده ملازمت نمود وخبر رسيدن ايشان را بعرض رسانيد که با هزار سوار بملازمت ميرسند

وآمدن ايشان را بر خود شکون * گرفتم وبر من کنکاش گفتند که شب بر لشکر جته شبخون بايد برد چون سوار شدم خبر رسيد که لشکر جته رسيده مى آيد من افواج خودرا تزوک کرده در مقابل ايشان ايستاده شدم وآب در ميان لشکر ايشان ولشکر من حايل بود

وکنکاش دربين ديدم که مخالفان را بحرف وحکايت نکاهدارم وآتش سوزش ايشانرا به آب تدبير فرو نشانم وايشان را بخود رام سازم

وبسردار لشکر جته که امير ابو سعيد بود سخن کردم وانچه بوي کفتم قبول کرد ليکن امراي ديکر مخالفت وي کرده بر جنک قرار دادند وآتش غيرت من هم شعله کشيد وافواج خودرا ترک کردم

کنکاش هشتم که در شکست دادن لشکر جته کردم اين بود

که با خود کفتم اکر با لشکر جته جنک کنم چون ايشان بسيارند مبادا چشم زخمي بلشکر

ſent unto me, arrived and ſaw me, and informed me of their approach, that they were coming to ſerve me with a thouſand horſemen. Book I.

AND I took their coming for a good omen: and they counſelled me, ſaying, "Thou muſt fall upon "the army of Jitteh by ſurpriſe in the night." And when I mounted my horſe, news was brought that the army of Jitteh was arrived and coming down upon me. And I put my forces in order, and I ſtood over againſt them; and the water was between their army and my army.

AND I ſaw it was good, that I ſhould amuſe the enemy with words and with perſuaſions, and extinguiſh the fire of their animoſity with the water of policy, and bring them over unto me.

AND I ſpoke to the leader of the army of Jitteh (who was Ameer Aboo Saeed), and that which I ſaid unto him, he took well. But the other leaders oppoſed him and reſolved on war. And the fire of my ſpirit alſo flaſhed forth, and I formed my forces in order of battle.

DESIGN VIII.

THE EIGHTH DESIGN which I formed (in defeating the army of Jitteh) was this.

I SAID unto myſelf, "If I fight with the "army of Jitteh, ſeeing they are very many, perhaps evil "may come unto my people." And at this time the ſpirit of

بلشکر من برسد درین حال غیرت کریبان کیر من شد وکفت که چون بدعوي سلطنت خروج کردهء لایق شان ومرتبه سلطنت همین است که بر جنک عازم کردي یا مظفر ومنصور شوي یا کشته کردي

چون برین عزیمت عازم شدم دیدم که غنیم سه فوج شده راه جنک مي طلبند ومن لشکر خودرا هفت فوج ساختم وکنکاش کردم که دفع بدفع افواج هفتکانه خودرا بر ایشان کشاده دهم وچون نایرهء قتال وجدال بلند شد امر نمودم که افواج هراول بخانه کمان در آمده تیر باران نمایند

وافواج شغاول وچپاول را * امر کردم بچپقولش * در آیند وخود با افواج جرانغار وبرانغار* بحرکت در آمدم ودر حمله اول ودوم فوج امیر ابو سعید که امیر الامراي لشکر جته بود برداشتم

درین حال حیدر اندخودي ومنکلی بوغا بمبارزت پیش آمدند من خود بایشان رو برو شدم ودر حمله اول ایشانرا نیز متفرق ساختم وتمامي لشکر جته از هم فرو ریخته متفرق وپراکنده شدند

کنکاش

of glory assaulted me and said, Since thou hast advanced forth with pretensions to empire, even this is becoming the dignity and the rank of a king, that thou resolve on war; and that thou be either victorious and triumphant, or be slain in battle. Book I.

AND when I had resolved on this measure, I saw that the enemy were divided into three bodies; and that they were eager to engage. And I divided my forces into seven squadrons; and I determined that I would send down my seven squadrons upon them, one after the other. And when the flames of war and of slaughter ascended high, I commanded the advanced guards to take to their bows, and to rain arrows upon the enemy.

AND I commanded the squadrons of the front lines of the left and the right wings to go into battle. And I myself advanced with the troops of the second lines of the left and the right wings. And in the first and the second charge I drove back the squadrons of Ameer Aboo Saeed, who was the chief leader of the army of Jitteh.

AND it came to pass at this time, that Hydur Andookhodee and Munguli Booghau advanced to the fight. And I myself opposed them face to face; and in the first charge I defeated them also. And all the forces of Jitteh dissolved away, and were scattered and dispersed abroad.

کنکاش نهم که در قوام سلطنت
خود کردم این بود
که چون بر امراي لشکر جته ظفر یافتم وخبر خروج
من بدعوي سلطنت در توران زمین منتشر شد
عزیمت بستم که بداد ودهش فرمان فرما کردم
کنکاش استقامت سلطنت خودرا درین یافتم که خزانه
که فراهم آورده بودم از نقد وجنس بر سپاه قسمت
نمایم واول قلعه قهلقه را مسخر کردانم

چون لشکر خود را تغار داده تزوک
کردم وبکنار آب جیحون رسیدم واز کذر ترمذ
عبور کردم وقراولان بطرف قهلقه فرستادم ودر کنار
آب جیحون چند روز مقام نمودم ومنتظر خبر قراولان
مي بودم

چون خبر من بالیاس خواجه رسید
الچون بهادر برادر بیکچک را با انواج کران بر سر
من تعیین کرد وقراولان غافل شده بخواب رفته
بودند واز ایشان کذشته وشب بشب آمده بر سر من
شبخون آورد

وزمیني

THE NINTH DESIGN which I formed in establishing my regal power, was this. Book I.

WHEN I had obtained the victory over the leaders of the army of Jitteh, and the news of my advancing forth, and aspiring to the throne, was made public throughout the land of Tooraun; I resolved that I would become a king by generosity and by liberality. And I saw the duration of my power in this, that I should divide among my soldiers the treasures which I had gathered together, both the money and the effects: and that I should first subdue the castle of Kehulkeh.

AND when I had given subsistence to my army, I put them in order, and I arrived on the border of the waters of Jihoon. And I crossed at the passage of Turmuz; and I sent out my Kurrauvul * towards the castle of Kehulkeh; and I halted some days on the border of the waters of Jihoon, expecting intelligence from my Kurrauvul.

AND when Ouleaus Khaujeh heard where I was, he sent Alchoun Bahaudur, the brother of Begchuck, with a mighty army upon me. And my Kurrauvulaun were negligent, and went to sleep: and the enemy passed by them, and advanced night after night, and came upon me by surprise.

* Scouts, light troops.

وزمیني که در آن نزول نموده بودم جزیره
بود واز سه طرف آب داشت چند خیمه که بیرون
جزیره بودند بتاراج لشکر جته رفتند ومردم بیرون
آمده داخل جزیره شدند

ومن استعداد جنک کرده آمده در کنار
جزیره ایستادم چون چشم غنیم ترسیده بود وبجنک
مبادرت ننمودند

ومن تا ده روز در آن جزیره اقامت
نمودم وبعد از آن از جزیره بر آمده در کنار آب
آلجوتها* زده تا مدت یکماه در برابر لشکر جته نشستم
تا آنکه غنیم هراس یافته مراجعت کرد ومن از آب
کذشته در منزل ایشان فرود آمدم وفوجي را بتعاقب
ایشان فرستادم

کنکاش دهم که در استقامت سلطنت
خود کردم این بود
که چون لشکر جته را شکست دادم
صلاح کار خود درین دیدم که رفته ولایت بدخشان را
مسخر سازم وامور سلطنت خودرا رواج دهم واز کنار
آب کوچ کرده در موضع خلم نزول نمودم

وامیر حسین نبیره امیر ترغن که
همشیره

AND the land in which I had pitched my tents was a peninſula: and it had water on three ſides. Some tents, which were without the peninſula, were plundered by the forces of Jitteh: and the people that were without, came and entered into the peninſula.

AND I formed my troops in order, and went and ſtood on the neck of the peninſula: but the enemy were fearful, and they did not advance to the attack.

AND I tarried ten days in that peninſula; and I afterwards came forth from thence, and pitched my tents † on the border of the river. And I ſat down oppoſite to the army of Jitteh for the ſpace of one month; even till they were ſeized with fear, and returned back. And I croſſed the river, and came down in their camp, and ſent forces to purſue them.

THE TENTH DESIGN which I formed for the advancement of my power, was this.

WHEN I had broken the forces of Jitteh, I ſaw it was good that I ſhould go and ſubdue the country of Buddukhſhaun, and extend my dominions. And I marched from the border of the river, and encamped at the place called Khullum.

AND Ameer Hooſſein, the grandſon of Ameer Kurghun, whoſe ſiſter was in my houſe, came;

† Literally, temporary huts or cantonements.

همشیره وي در خانه من بود آمده باهم ملاقات نمودیم وطویهاي دادیم وکنکاش درین یافتم که روانه بدخشان شوم چون بقندز رسیدم در آن موضع اقامت نمودم تا آنکه سرداران ایل یورلداي جمع آمده بمن پیوستند وبهریک خلعتي داده تسلي نمودم

چون خبر اراستکي فوج من بشاهان بدخشان رسید مستعد جنک شدند کنکاش درین دیدم که پیش دستي کرده تا ایشان لشکرهاي خودرا جمع سازند ایشانرا درهم شکنم وایلغار کرده خودرا بطالخان رسانیدم

چون خبر رسیدن من بطالخان بمسامع شاهان رسید از راه مصالحه در آمده ملازمت کردند من از کنکاش خود راضي شدم ودیدم که غلط نکرده بودم وسلطنت من در ولایت بدخشان رواج یافت واکثري از سپاه بدخشان آمده ملازمت اختیار کردند

کنکاش یازدهم که در رواج سلطنت خود کردم این بود

که چون شاهان بدخشان با طاعت من در آمدند متوجه ختلان شدم چون بمملکت ختلان در آمدم بولاد بوغا وشیر بهرام از بد سلوکي امیر حسین جدا شده بالوس خود رفتند

ومن

and we ſaw each other, and we made a feaſt. And I found it was right, that I ſhould go on towards Buddukhſhaun. And when I came to Kunduz, I halted in that place until the chiefs of the people of Yeurldaiee came together and joined me. And I gave to each of them a robe of honour, and I encouraged them. Book I.

AND when the news of the order and the ſtrength of my forces arrived to the princes of Buddukhſhaun, they prepared for war. And I ſaw it was good that I ſhould be quick, and break their power, before they could gather their army together. And I marched with expedition, and I came to Taulkhaun.

AND when the news of my arrival at Taulkhaun reached the ears of the princes, they came in at the avenue of peace and ſaw me. I was ſatisfied with my own deliberations, and ſaw that I had not done wrong. And my power was eſtabliſhed in the country of Buddukhſhaun; and many of the ſoldiers of Buddukhſhaun came unto me and choſe my ſervice.

THE ELEVENTH DESIGN which I formed for extending my power, was this. DESIGN XI.

WHEN the princes of Buddukhſhaun came and ſubmitted to my authority, I turned towards Khuttulaun. And when I came into the kingdom of Khuttulaun, Boulaud Booghau and Share Behraum, on account of the ill conduct of Ameer Hooſſein, ſeparated and returned to their tribes.

ومن رفته در جلكاي دشت كولك

اقامت نمودم وجاسوسان تعين كردم كه رفته از لشكر

جته والياس خواجه خبر آورند

وجاسوسان بعد از ده روز خبر آوردند

كه امراي جته اول ايشان كوج تيمور پسر بيكچك

است ودوم ايشان تيمور نويكان است وساريق بهادر

وشنكوم وتغلق خواجه برادر حاجي بيك با بيست هزار

سوار از موضع خلاتي تا پل سنكين نزول نموده اند

وايلچي نزد من فرستادند كه احوال مرا

ولشكر مرا بخاطر آورند من لشكر خودرا دو باره بنظر

ايلچي در آوردم وايلچي را رخصت دادم

وكنكاش خودرا درين يافتم كه متعاقب

ايلچي روان شوم ليكن لشكر خودرا بخود متفق نديدم

ودر متفق ساختن لشكر خود كنكاش چنين ديدم

كه به بعضى مروت نمايم وبه بعضى مدارا كنم

وكروهي را بمال فريفته سازم وجمعى را بسخن وقول

وعهد تسلي دهم

درين حال خبر رسيد كه تغلق

سلدوز وكي خسرو كه از نوكران من

بودند

AND I went and ſojourned in the paſture-lands of the Duſht of Koulauk. And I appointed ſpies, that they ſhould go and bring news of the armies of Jitteh and of Ouleaus Khaujeh.

AND after ten days the ſpies brought back intelligence, ſaying; "The Ameers of Jitteh (and the firſt of them is Kooch Timour, the ſon of Begchuck; and the ſecond of them is Timour Noubukaun; and the others are Saureek Bahaudur, and Shungoom, and Tughulluk Khaujeh, the brother of Khaujee Beg) with twenty thouſand horſemen, have pitched their tents from the town of Khillautee even to the bridge of Sungheen."

AND they ſent an ambaſſador unto me, that they might know my ſituation and the ſtrength of my army. And I drew out my army twice in the ſight of the ambaſſador, and diſmiſſed him.

AND I ſaw my advantage in this, that I ſhould ſet out after the ambaſſador: but I found that my forces were not united with me. And to make them unanimous, I ſaw it was good that I ſhould ſhew kindneſs to ſome, and that with ſome I ſhould diſſemble; and that I ſhould tempt ſome by riches, and ſoothe ſome by perſuaſions, and promiſes, and engagements.

AND at this time news arrived, that Tughulluk Suldoze, and Ki Khiſſero (who were of my ſervants)

بودند شش هزار سوار جته سر کرده بر سر من مي
آورند چون اين خبر بمسامع لشکر من رسيد تفرقه
خاطر ايشان پيشتر شد وانديشناک کشتند ليکن
امير جاکو وايکو تيمور وامير سليمان وامير جلال
الدين را بخود يافتم

کنکاش دوازدهم که در باب اتفاق
لشکر خود کردم اين بود

که امير جاکو وايکو تيمور وامير سليمان
وامير جلال الدين را بخلوت طلب داشته خواستم
ايشانرا بخود متفق کردانم چون بايشان خلوت
کردم سخن بديشان اين بود که ايشانرا شريک
دولت خود ساختم تا بر عزيمت خود راسخ شدند

وطايفه که در مقام بي اتفاق بودند
يک يک را بخلوت طلب داشته جداکانه صحبت
داشته آنهاي که حريص وطماع بودند بمال ومنال
فريفته ساختم وکروهي را که نظر بر جاه ومنصب
ومملکت داشتند انچه از ملک وولايت مسخر من
شده بود بديشان نامزد کردم وهمه را در ميانه اميد

* This expreffion occurs in feveral places, and is very obfcure. Perhaps it means, that if he fucceeded in his views on the kingdom of Mauwur

ويبم

vants) had taken the command of ſix thouſand horſemen of Jitteh, and were bringing them down upon me. And when this news reached the ears of my people, the terror of their hearts was increaſed, and they were ſore afraid. But I found that Ameer Jaukoo, and Eekoo Timour, and Ameer Soolamaun, and Ameer Jullaul u deen were with me. Book I.

Design XII.

THE TWELFTH DESIGN which I formed (in uniting the hearts of my people) was this.

I CALLED unto me in private Ameer Jaukoo and Eekoo Timour, and Ameer Soolamaun, and Ameer Jullaul u deen; and I ſought to confederate them with me. And when I retired with them in private, my words with them were theſe —"That I had made them "the partners of my fortune." * And they united firmly in my deſigns.

AND of thoſe who were diſſatisfied, I called each of them unto me in private, and ſpoke to them ſeparately. And thoſe who were covetous and avaricious, I tempted by wealth and by riches; and thoſe who fixed their eyes on dignities, and commands, and governments, among them I ſhared out the countries and the provinces which I had ſubdued: and I kept them all ſuſpended

wur u Nuhur, certain principalities ſhould be given to them, and rendered independent of the crown.

وبيم نكاهداشتم واز براي هريكي كوتلي* تعين كردم وسـايـر سپاه را به لقمه وخرقه اميدوار كردانيدم وبشرين زباني وكشاده روي ايشانرا فريفته خـود سـاختم وخدمات ايشانرا يكى بده باز نموده خـوشـدل كردانيدم تا آنكه موافق ومنافق همكى بمن متفق كشتند وعـهـد بستند كه با من در موافقت وجانسپاري بتقصير راضي نشوند

چـون خاطرم از لشكر جمع شد مستعد جنك الياس خواجه شدم ودر دفع ايشان وروش جنك چنين كنكاش كردم كه پيش دستي بكار برم وتا ايشانرا خبر شود بر ايشان تركتاز آورم

دريـن باب بقران مجيد فال كشادم اين اية كريمه بفال آمد كم من نية قليلة غلبت نية كثيرة باذن الله

وچـون ايـن بشارت يافتم لشكر خودرا تـزوك كرده وهفت فوج مرتب ساخته روان شدم بر وقت صبح بـر سـر تغلق سلدوز و كى خسرو كه

* *Kotul* is a Mogul word, and ſignifies one appointed to ſucceed to the government on the death or diſmiſſion of the governor. By this artful policy he not only ſecured his authority over the provinces which he divided among

between hope and fear, and I appointed a Kotul * to each. Book I.

AND I raiſed the hopes of all my ſoldiers by gifts and by preſents: and I drew them over unto me by kind words, and by an open countenance. And the ſervices which they had done, I extolled ten-fold, and made them joyful: even until thoſe who were with me, and thoſe who were againſt me, all joined with me firmly. And they took an oath, that in ſupporting me, and in devoting their lives unto me, they would not be wanting.

AND when my heart was at reſt concerning my army, I prepared for the war of Ouleaus Khaujeh. And in defeating him, and in planning the order of battle, thus I determined — that I would uſe ſpeed, and that I would go down upon them before they were aware.

AND concerning this I opened the holy book for an omen; and this ſacred verſe came forth as a ſign, "How oft do the weak vanquiſh the powerful by "the permiſſion of Almighty God!"

AND when I had obtained this token, I formed my ſoldiers in order, and I divided them into ſeven ſquadrons, and I ſet out. And I came in the morning upon Tughulluk Suldoze and Ki Khiſſero, (who,

among his Ameers, by placing a ſpy (for ſuch was the Kotul) over the conduct of each of them, but made every province anſwer the purpoſe of ſatisfying *two* inſtead of *one* of his Ameers.

 being

هراول شده می آمدند رسیدم ودر حمله دوم ایشانرا مقهور ساختم وتا کنار پل سنکین که منزل الیاس خواجه بود هزیمت دادم

چون شب در آمد بسر زمینی که رسیده بودم نزول نمودم با خود کنکاش کردم که میدان جنک افسرده نکردانم وکرم کرم بسر لشکر الیاس خواجه که قریب به سی هزار اند ترکتاز آورم

وکنکاش کردم که اکر توقف نمایم مبادا امري روي دهد که در علاج آن محتاج کومک کردم با آنکه امیر حسین در عقب منزل داشت لیکن من خودرا بمدد وي محتاج نکردانیدم وبه کنکاش درست لشکر الیاس خواجه را شکست دادم

کنکاش سیزدهم که در شکست دادن لشکر جته والیاس خواجه نمودم این بود

که اول لشکر الیاس خواجه را بجمعي از افواج قاهره مقید ومعطل نکاهدارم بدین جهته امیر موید ارلات واوج قرا بهادر وامیر موسي را با دو هزار سوار بر سر پل رو بروي الیاس خواجه نکاهداشتم . ومن

being the Hurrauvul, * were advancing) and I overpowered them at the second charge, and I drove them back to the head of the bridge of Sungheen, which was the station of Ouleaus Khaujeh. Book I.

AND as the night was come, I pitched my tents on the ground where I was, and I counselled with myself, that I would not let the plain of battle cool; but that I would charge quick and hot on the army of Ouleaus Khaujeh: and they were near thirty thousand.

AND I considered, that if I was guilty of delay, something might come to pass, which might cause me to stand in need of assistance. And although Ameer Hoossein was encamped behind me, I did not cause myself to stand in need of his support; but by skilful measures I defeated the forces of Ouleaus Khaujeh, and the men of Jitteh.

THE THIRTEENTH DESIGN which I formed, (in defeating the army of Jitteh and Ouleaus Khaujeh) was this. DESIGN XIII.

FIRST, I saw it was good, that by a body of my victorious army, I should confine and make useless the people of Jitteh: and for this purpose I stationed Ameer Muviud Arlaut, and Ouj Kurrau Bahaudur, and Ameer Moosi, with two thousand horsemen, at the head of the bridge of Sungheen, opposite to Ouleaus Khaujeh.

* Advanced guard.

AND

ومن خود با پنج هزار سوار از آب كذشته
بر كوهي كه مشرف بر لشكر الياس خواجه بود برآمدم
وفرمودم كه شب آتش بسياري برافروزند

وچون آتشها بنظر لشكر جته در آمد وفوج
كلاني در سر پل سنكين ديدند مضطرب شدند وآن
شب را لشكر الياس خواجه بحاضر باش بكذرانيدند

ومن در آن شب ببالاي كوه بعجز ونياز
بدركاه تنكري تعالي مشغول بودم وصلوات بر محمد
صلي الله عليه وآله واصحابه وسلم ميفرستادم

ودر ميان خواب وبيداري اوازي بمسامع
من رسيد كه شخصي ميكويد كه تيمور فتح وفيروزي
وظفر تراست چون صبح صادق طلوع كرد نماز
بجماعت ادا كردم

ودرينوقت ديدم كه الياس خواجه با امراء
خود سوار شده فوج فوج روان شدند وامرا وسپاه من
در تعاقب نمودن حكم خواستند ومن بخود كنكاش
كردم كه در تعاقب نمودن ايشان تاخير بايد كرد
تا مقصد ايشان معلوم شود

چون چهار فرسنك راه رفتند فرود آمدند
من

AND I myself passed over the river with five thousand horsemen, and came forth on a hill, which was higher than the army of Ouleaus Khaujeh. And I commanded that in the night they should make many fires.

AND when the people of Jitteh beheld the fires, and when they saw a strong army at the head of the bridge of Sungheen, they were afraid: and the forces of Ouleaus Khaujeh passed that night in watching.

AND I in that night, on the top of that hill, was employed in humiliations and supplications to the throne of Almighty God; and I sent forth prayers on Mahummud (may the blessing of God be upon him, and upon his descendants, and upon his companions).

AND between sleeping and waking I heard a voice, as of some one speaking to me, saying, "TIMOUR, "victory and conquest and triumph are thine." And when the morning broke, I prayed with my people.

AND I saw at this time that Ouleaus Khaujeh and his Ameers were mounted on their horses, and going troop after troop: and my Ameers and my soldiers called for orders to pursue them. And I said unto myself, I must delay to pursue them until their intentions be known.

AND after they had travelled four fursungs, they halted: and I discovered their design. Behold, their intention

من کنکاش ایشانرا در یافتم که مطلب ایشان اینست
که مرا از کوه جدا بمیدان در آورند وجنک اندازند

وامرای هرلول را که شکست داده بودم
ایشان بالیاس خواجه پناه برده بودند ووی ایشان را
سرزنش کرده بود

درین وقت دیدند که من از کنکاش
ایشان واقف شده ام واز کوه بیرون نمي آیم بالضرورة
برکشته بر سر من تاخت آوردند

ومن کنکاش چنین یافتم که در دامن
کوه افواج خودرا تزوک سازم وبجنک در آیم چون
لشکر جته آمده بدامن کوه در آمدند ومعطل شدند
بهادرانرا امر نمودم که مخالفان را بشپهء تیر کرفتند
وبسیاري از مخالفان را زخمدار ساختند وچون شب
شد ودیدند که کاري نتوانستند ساخت در دامن کوه
فرود آمدند که کوه را محاصره نمایند من در آن
شب چنین کنکاش یافتم که لشکر خودرا چهار فوج
ساخته بذات خود بر ایشان شبخون آورم چون این
کنکاش دل نشین امراي من شد قریب بصبح سوار
شدم واز چهار طرف بر مخالفان شبخون آوردم

وتبا

intention was this — that they might bring me down from the mountain apart, and assault me. Book I.

And the chiefs of the advanced guard, whom I had defeated, had fled unto Ouleaus Khaujeh for shelter; and he had reproved them.

And they saw at this time, that I had discovered their intentions; and that I came not down from the hill: and from necessity they turned back, and came upon me.

And I found it was good, that I should draw up my forces on the declivity of the hill, and enter into battle. And when the army of Jitteh advanced, and came up on the slope of the hill, and were unable to act, I gave orders to my warriors, that they should annoy the enemy with flights of arrows. And they wounded numbers of the foe. And as the night was come, the forces of Jitteh saw that they could effect nothing: and they encamped on the skirts of the hill, that they might surround it. And in that night I resolved thus — that forming my army into four squadrons, I myself would assault them by surprise. And when this resolution was impressed on the hearts of my Ameers, I mounted my horse, and I assaulted the enemy in four different places unawares, toward the morning.

وتا لشکر جته خودرا جمع سازند بهادران
من ایشان را متفرق ساختند ودر چپقولش* که شد مردم
جنکي از طرفین کشته شدند ولشکر جته الفرار کفتند
وکریزان شدند ومن خودرا بالیاس خواجه رسانیده یول
بولشن* کفتم وچون آواز من بمسامع الیاس خواجه
رسید وي از روي غضب لشکر خودرا نهیب داد
ولشکریان وي بر کشتند

وتا طلوع آفتاب میانه لشکر من ولشکر
وي جنک چپقولش* بود وترکشها خالي شد وغنیم
جنک در کریز میکردند تا آنکه در چهار فرسنکي که
یورت ایشان بود شکسته حال رفته نزول نمودند ومن
هم از تعاقب ایشان عنان باز کشیدم ودر همان سر
زمین فرود آمدم

چون لشکر جته خودرا مغلوب ومقهور
دیدند دیکر بجنک مبادرت ننمودند ومن سپاه خودرا
بر دور اردوي الیاس خواجه متفرق ساختم ومحاربات
ومجادلات مینمودم تا آنکه الیاس خواجه از روي اضطرار
از آب خجند کذشت ومن هم تعاقب ایشان را
کذاشته مظفر ومنصور بماوراالنهر مراجعت نمودم

ودر استقلال سلطنت خود کنکاشها کردم
وآن

And before the forces of Jitteh could gather themſelves together, my ſoldiers diſperſed them; and in the ſkirmiſh many warriors of both ſides were ſlain. And the forces of Jitteh cried out, "Let us flee;" and they fled. And I came up to Ouleaus Khaujeh and ſaid, Yole Boliſhun. † And when he heard my voice, he rallied his forces in wrath; and they returned.

And there was ſkirmiſhing between my army and his army until the riſing of the ſun. And the quivers were emptied, and the enemy fought flying. And they fled even to the diſtance of four furſungs, where their tents were pitched; and they halted there in a broken condition. And I alſo drew in the reins from purſuing them, and came down ‡ in the place where I was.

When the forces of Jitteh ſaw that they were broken and defeated, they ventured not to renew the fight. And I ſpread my ſoldiers round the camp of Ouleaus Khaujeh, and I fought with them continually: even until Ouleaus Khaujeh, from extreme neceſſity, croſſed the waters of Khujjund. And I alſo left off purſuing them, and I returned victorious and triumphant to Mauwur u Nuhur.

And I deliberated concerning the eſtabliſhment of my power; and my deliberations were theſe —

† A Mogul expreſſion of ſalutation, the preciſe meaning of which is not known. ‡ i. e. encamped on the ſpot where he had arrived.

وآن کنکاشها این بود که امرای که هریک خودرا
امیرعظیم الشان میدانستند وهریک خودرا از دیکری
بزرکتر میکرفتند مطیع ومنقاد خود کردانم اول
امیرحسین نبیره امیر ترغن که در ماورالنهر علم
سلطنت برافراخته بود ویرا شریک دولت خود خواندم
وبوي مدارا کردم ووي اکرچه ظاهر بمن اظهار دوستي
میکرد اما همیشه در مقام نفاق وحسد با من مي بود
ومیخواست که خود بر تخت سلطنت
ماورالنهر متمکن شود وچون بروي اعتماد نداشتم ویرا
بمزار خواجه شمس الدین برده بر دوستي خود قسم
دادم وبمن عهد وقول کرد که خلاف دوستي نکند
وسه مرتبه دیکر قسم بمصحف مجید در
باب دوستی من خورد وچون آخر نقض عهد کرد
نقض عهد ویرا بمن کرفتار ساخت

وشیخ محمد پسر امیر بیان سلدوز خودرا
امیر کلاني میدانست وویرا استمالت دادم وبا هفت
تشون ایل ومطیع خود کردانیدم وملازم خود ساختم
وبهریک از امراي تشونات مذکور ولایتي ارزاني داشتم

وشیر

that I ſhould render the Ameers obedient and ſubmiſſive unto me. For each of them thought himſelf a chief of exalted dignity; and each of them deemed himſelf greater than the reſt. And firſt, I named Ameer Hooſſein (the grandſon of Ameer Kurghun) who had exalted the ſtandard of power in Mauwur u Nuhur, the partner of my fortune; and I treated him with attention. And although he outwardly ſhewed friendſhip toward me, yet did he always envy and oppoſe me. Book I.

AND he wanted that he himſelf ſhould be eſtabliſhed on the royal throne of Mauwur u Nuhur. And I had no faith in him, and I carried him to the ſepulchre of Khaujeh ſhums u deen, and made him ſwear friendſhip unto me. And he promiſed and ſwore that he would not ſwerve from his engagement.

AND concerning his friendſhip with me, he took an oath three times on the holy book. And when at laſt he broke his oaths, his breach of faith delivered him into my hands.

AND Sheikh Mahummud, the ſon of Ameer Biaun Suldoze, thought himſelf a mighty chief. And I gained his affections by ſoothings; and I brought him with ſeven Kuſhoons to ſubmit unto me, and I made him my ſervant. And to each of the Ameers of thoſe Kuſhoons I gave the command of a province.

AND

وشیر بهرام که جدا شده بالوس خود
رفته بود ودر مقام تمرد مي بود ویرا استمالت داده
طلب نمودم ووي بالوس خود آمده اطاعت مرا قبول
کرد وملازم خود ساخته ولایتي بوي ارزاني داشتم

وچون میانهء من وامیر حسین خویشي
بود من هرچند مروت ومدارا کردم دوست من نشد
تا آنکه ولایت بلخ وحصار شادمان را از من گرفت
ومن هم بخاطر همشیرهء وي که در خانهء من بود
مضایقه نکردم وچندان بوي مدارا کردم که امراي
که با من در مقام مخالفت بودند مطیع من کشتند
لیکن امیر حسین همیشه در مقام شکست من ومکر
وفریب با من مي بود تا آنکه کنکاش کار وي چنین
کردم که بضرب شمشیر ویرا مطیع نمایم

وچون بر ولایت توران مستولي کشتم
وولایت ماورالنهر از خس وخاشاک وجود اوزبکان پاک
ساختم بعضي از امراي اولوسات سر باطاعت من فرو
نیاوردند وهریک با قبایل خود نازش میکردند وبعضي
از امراي من سفارش ایشان میکردند که چون همه
شریک دولت اند ایشانرا نیز شریک دولت باید دانست
لیکن سخنان ایشان در غیرت سلطنت اثر نمي کرد
بخود

And Share Behraum, who had ſeparated from me and returned to his tribe, and remained in a ſtate of diſobedience; to him I gave encouragement, and called him unto me. And he came with his tribe, and ſubmitted to my authority. And I made him my ſervant, and I conferred a province upon him.

And there was relationſhip between me and Ameer Hooſſein: and although I treated him with affection and with kindneſs, he was not my friend; and he even took from me the country of Bullukh and the caſtle of Shaudumaun. And I alſo, for the ſake of his ſiſter who was in my houſe, regarded it not. And I ſhewed ſuch kindneſs unto him, that the Ameers who were in a ſtate of enmity with me, ſubmitted to my authority. But Ameer Hooſſein ſtill acted towards me with treachery and fraud, and ſought to overthrow me: even until I reſolved that I would force him to ſubmiſſion by the edge of the ſword.

And when I became the lord of the land of Tooraun, and had made clean the kingdom of Mauwur u Nuhur from the abominations † of the Ouzbuks; certain of the Ameers of Auloofaut ſubmitted not to my government. And they, with their tribes, diſſembled with me. And certain of my Ameers ſpoke in their behalf, ſaying, "Since we are all partners of the ſame fortune, they muſt be conſidered as the partners of thy fortune alſo." But their words made no impreſſion upon me.

And

† Literally, the weeds and the briars.

بخــود کنکاش کردم که چون خدا
یک است ولا شریک له است پس کدخداي ملک
وي تعالي وتقدس هم باید که یکی باشد
درین وقت بابا علي شاه نزد من آمده
کفت تیمور تنکري تعالي فرموده که اکر در زمین
وآسمان دو خدا باشد کار عالم بفساد انجامد ومن
بسخن وي هدایت یافتم

وبـقـران مجید فال کشادم این آیة
کریمه بفال آمد که انا جعلناک خلیفه في الارض
واین فال را شکون* کرفتم ودر مطیع ساختن امراي
کـه خـودرا شـریـک دولـت وسلطنت میدانستند
کنکاشـهـا کـردم

واول بمنزل ویورت امیر حاجی بـرلاس
رفته ویرا بخود متفق ساختم
وامـیـر شیخ محـمـد پسر بیان سلدوز
چـون همیـشـه بشراب وخمر مشغول بود آخر شراب
ویرا کلو کیر ساخت وعالم را وداع نمود ولایت اورا
بتصرف در آوردم

وامیر

AND I deliberated with myself, saying, Book I. Since God is one and hath no partner, therefore the vicegerent over the land of the Lord (the Almighty and the Holy) must be one only.

AND at this time Baubau Aali Shaah † came before me and said, "TIMOUR, God Almighty "hath declared, that if there were two Gods in the "heavens and in the earth, the order of the universe "would end in horror and confusion." And I took warning by his words.

AND I opened the holy book for an omen, and this sacred verse came forth as a sign, "TRULY WE "HAVE APPOINTED THEE VICEGERENT UPON "EARTH." And I took this omen as a favour from heaven; and I formed measures for reducing to submission those Ameers who thought themselves the partners of my fortune and dominion.

AND I first went to the station, and to the dwelling, of Ameer Haujee Burlaus, and I united him with me.

AND Ameer Sheikh Mahummud, the son of Biaun Suldoze, was always drinking wine and strong spirits; and in the end the wine destroyed him, and he departed from the world, and I took possession of his lands.

† One of those Dervishes who professed ideotism. The East is full of this kind of Santons, who are held in great veneration by the Mahummudans.

وامير بايزيد جلاير كه ولايت خجند را
متصرف بود بوي نصيحت كردم اما دروي اثر نكرد تا
آنكه مردم الوس وي بروي خروج كرده وكرفتار ساخته
نزد من آوردند ومن ويرا بنواختم وشرمنده ساختم†

وايلچي بوغا سلدوز در بلخ علم سلطنت
برافراخته بود وامير حسين كه طلب تختكاه جد
خودرا اميرقزغن مينمود بوي در انداختم

ومحمد خواجه ايردي كه از اويماق
نايمن بود ولايت شيرغانات را متصرف شده علم
مخالفت من برافراخته بود وديكر ولايت بوي دادم
ووي را نوكر خود ساختم

وشهان بدخشان كه ولايت بدخشانات را
متصرف شده رايت مخالفت من برافراخته بودند با
هريك از ايشان سازكاري كردم تا بيكديكر در
افتادند وبمن رجوع آوردند

وكي خسرو والجايتو بردي ولايت
ختلان وارهنك را متصرف شده بودند وبه كي
خسرو مدد فرستادم تا رفته ولايت الجايتو بردي را
متصرف شد والجايتو بمن پناه آورد

† i.e. By the extraordinary favours, which he conferred upon him, he made him ashamed of his former conduct.

Book I.

AND to Ameer Bauezeed Jullauir, who was ruler over the province of Khojjund, I gave advice: but it made not an impreſſion upon him, until the people of his tribe roſe up againſt him, and ſeized him, and brought him unto me. And I exalted him and cauſed him to bluſh. †

AND to Ameer Ilchee Booghau Suldoze, who had exalted the ſtandard of power in the city of Bullukh, I oppoſed Ameer Hooſſein; who laid claim to the imperial city ‡ of his grandfather, Ameer Kurghun.

AND Mahummud Khaujeh Erudee (who was of the hord of Tauemun) having ſeized on the country of Shereghaunaut, had exalted the ſtandard of enmity againſt me: and I gave him another province, and made him my ſervant.

AND the princes of Buddukhſhaun, who ruled over the countries of Buddukhſhaun, had elevated the enſigns of hoſtility againſt me. And I dealt artfully with each of them, || until they diſputed among themſelves, and returned back unto me.

AND Ki Khiſſero, and Aljauitoo Burdi had ſeized on the countries of Khuttulaun, and Arhung. And I ſent aſſiſtance to Ki Khiſſero, until he went and took poſſeſſion of the lands of Aljauitoo Burdi: and Aljauitoo Burdi came to me for ſhelter.

‡ i.e. The city of Bullukh.

|| i.e. Sowed animoſities among them, and by that means obliged them to ſubmit.

وامیر خضر یسوری ولایت تاشکنت را
باتفاق احشام یسوري متصرف شده بود والجایتو بردي
وکي خسرو را بیکدیکر آشتی دادم وجماعه را همراه
ایشان کردم تا رفته احشام یسوري را تاخت وتالان
کردند وامیر خضر عاجز شده پناه بمن آورد

چون ولایت ماورالنهر را از هرج ومرج پاک
ساختم افواج قاهره من قوت تمام یافت والوس برلاس
نامدار شد وتشونات وتومانات چغتاي از همت
من بلند آوازه کردید

وبر جمیع ایل وتشونات وتومنات
واحشام فرما کشتم لیکن بعضي قلعهاء
ماورالنهر در تصرف امیر حسین بود حکم من در
آنجا جاري نبود

وامیر حسین چون عظمت وشوکت مرا
مشاهده نمود عرق حسدش بحرکت در آمد وعلم
مخالفت برافراخت ونقض عهد نمود من بجانب وي
بسیار رفتم واو هیچ بطرف من نیامد وبلطایف
الحیل قلعه ترشي را از من کرفت وامیر موسی را
با هفت هزار سوار بقلعه قرشي تعیین
کرد

Book I.

AND Ameer Khizzur Yessooree, assisted by the tribe of Yessoor, had taken possession of the province of Taushkund. And I reconciled Aljauitoo Burdi and Ki Khissero to each other, and sent forces with them; until they went, and over-run, and pillaged the tribe of Yessoor. And the power of Ameer Khizzur was reduced low, and he fled to me for protection.

AND when I had cleared the kingdom of Mauwur u Nuhur from discord and anarchy, my armies acquired great strength; and the tribe of Burlaus obtained renown; and the Kushoonaut and the Toumaunaut of Chughtauee became celebrated on account of my exploits.

AND I became the ruler of all the tribes, and of the Kushoonaut, and of the Toumaunaut, and of the people. But certain castles of Mauwur u Nuhur were in the possession of Ameer Hoossein; and in them my authority was not established.

AND when Ameer Hoossein beheld my might and my power, his envy was excited against me. And he exalted the standard of hostility, and he broke his oaths. And I advanced a great way toward him, and he came not at all toward me. † And he took from me the castle of Kurshee by fraud. And he appointed Ameer Moosi, with seven thousand horsemen, to guard the castle

† i. e. Endeavoured to bring about a reconciliation, to which Ameer Hoossein continued adverse.

of

کرد وپنج هزار سوار دیکر هم فرستاد ودر مقام
استیصال من در آمد

وازین جهته غیرت سلطنت من طغیان
کرد که قلعه ترشی را از وي بکیرم بعضي امراي
من کنکاش دادند که رفته بجنک قلعه را مسخر
کردانم من کنکاش کرفتن قلعه ترشي را
چنین کردم که اکر خواهم که بجنک مسخر
کردانم مبادا چشم زخمي بلشکر من برسد ودر جنک
چند خطر بخاطر من خطور کرد جنک را طرح کردم
وکنکاش درین دیدم که بجانب خراسان
متوجه شوم تا خاطر قلعه داران جمع شود وآنکاه
برکشته ایلغار کنم وشبخون بقلعه برده مسخر کردانم
وکوچ نموده متوجه خراسان شدم
چون از آب امویه عبور نمودم کاروانی
از جانب خراسان آمده بود ومتوجه ترشی میرفت
وقافله سالار آن کاروان ارمغاني بمن آورد من از احوال
امراي خراسان از وي پرسش کردم ورفتن خودرا
بولایت خراسان بوی اظهار نمودم وایشانرا رخصت دادم
وجاسوسي همراه کاروانیان کردم
وخود در کنار آب مقام نمودم تا آنکه
جاسوس

of Kurshee: and he afterwards sent five thousand horsemen more. And he took measures for my destruction.

AND on this account the honour of my station urged me on, that I should take from him the castle of Kurshee. And certain of my Ameers counselled me, that I should go and seize it by force. But concerning the reduction of the castle of Kurshee I deliberated thus — If I attempt to reduce it by a siege, perhaps my forces may be repulsed. And in a siege several dangers occurred to my mind; and I rejected that measure.

AND I saw it was good that I should turn my face toward Khorausaun, until the hearts of the keepers of the castle should be at rest; and that then I should return and march with speed, and assault the castle by surprise, and reduce it. And I marched, and went toward Khorausaun.

WHEN I crossed the waters of Amuveah, a Kauruvvaun arrived from Khorausaun; and they were journeying toward Kurshee. And the leader of that Kauruvvaun brought gifts unto me, and I asked of him the state of the Ameers of Khorausaun. And I told him that I was travelling to the kingdom of Khorausaun; and I dismissed him.

AND I sent a spy with the people of the Kauruvvaun, and I tarried on the border of the waters of Amuveah

جاسوس خبر آورد که کاروانیان خبر بامیر موسی
رسانیدند که امیر تیمور را در کنار آب امویه دیدیم
که بطرف خراسان میرفت

چون این خبر بامیر موسي ولشکر امیر
حسین رسید خوشدل شدند ورحل اقامت انداخته
بساط عیش وعشرت بکسترانیدند

چون این خبر بمسامع من رسید از
لشکر خود دو صد وچهل وسه جوان بهادر مردانه کار
کرده آزموده را جدا ساختم واز آب کذشته ایلغار
کردم ودر موضع شیرکنت رسیدم ویک شب ویک روز
مقام کردم واز آنجا ایلغار کرده در یك فرسنکي قلعه
قرشي نزول نمودم

وفرمودم که چند نردبان بریسمانها باهم
بسته طیار سازند درین وقت امیر جاکو زانو زده بعرض
رسانید که جماعه از بهادران در عقب مانده اند
تا رسیدن ایشان توقف ضرور است درین وقت بخاطرم
رسید که تا رسیدن بهادران خود تنها رفته قلعه را
ملاحظه نمایم

وچهل سوار بهادر را همراه کرفته رو
بطرف قلعه قرشی آوردم چون سیاهی حصار بنظر
در

Amuveah until the ſpy brought word, that the people of the Kauruvvaun had given intelligence to Ameer Mooſi, ſaying; "We ſaw Ameer Timour on the border of the "waters of Amuveah; and he was going toward Kho-"rauſaun." Book I.

AND when Ameer Mooſi and the forces of Ameer Hooſſein heard this news, they were glad of heart; and they pitched their tents, and ſpread abroad the carpet of riot and diſſipation.

AND when I received intelligence thereof, I ſelected two hundred and forty three brave, and reſolute, and tried, and experienced warriors from among my forces; and I re-croſſed the waters of Amuveah. And I marched quick, and I arrived at Sharekund. And I halted for one night and for one day. And I marched from thence with great ſpeed; and I alighted at the diſtance of a furſung from the caſtle of Kurſhee.

AND I commanded that they ſhould make ready ladders, and bind them together with ropes. And at this time Ameer Yaukoo kneeled before me, and ſaid, "Many of our warriors have remained behind: until they "ſhall arrive, delay is neceſſary." And at this time it came into my mind that I would go alone and examine the caſtle.

AND I took forty warriors with me, and I turned my face toward the caſtle of Kurſhee. And when the blackneſs of the caſtle appeared in ſight, I commanded

در آمد بهادران را امر نهودم که توقف نهایند ومبشر وعبد الله که خانه زاد بچکان من بودند همراه کرفته وچون بکنار خندق رسیدم دیدم که خندق پر از آب است ونظر بر اطراف کردم وترناوي که آب از آن بقلعه میرفت وبر روي خندق انداخته بودند بنظرم در آمد

واسپ را به مبشر سپرده واز بالا ترناو از خندق کذشته بخاک ریز قلعه رسیدم وخودرا بدروازه رسانیدم ودستي بر در زدم ویافتم که دروازهبانان در خوابند

ودروازه را بپشت در بخاک وکل انپاشته اند واطراف دیوار قلعه را ملاحظه نهودم وجايء که زینه ونردبان توان کذاشت دیدم ومراجعت نهودم وسوار شده خودرا به بهادران رسانیدم

وفوجي که در عقب مانده بود با نردبانها رسیدند وهمکي مسلح شده ونردبانها را برداشتند ورو بقلعه آوردم واز خندق بر روي ترناو کذشتند وزینه ها کذاشته بدیوار قلعه بر آمدند چون چهل مرد مردانه داخل قلعه شدند من هم قدم بر نردبان کذاشته بقلعه در آمدم وکرنا وبرغو* کشیدند وبتوفیق تنکري تعالی قلعه را مسخر کردانیدم

چون این خبر بهسامع امیر حسین رسید در مقام مکر وفریب در آمد ومیخواست که در لباس اشنايء ودوستي مرا در قید خودرا آورد

کنکاش

my warriors to halt. And I took with me Mubbuſhur and Abdullah, who had been born in my houſe. And when I came to the border of the ditch, I ſaw that the ditch was full of water. And I looked round about, and I beheld a waterpipe; † and water ran through that pipe to the caſtle, and they had laid it acroſs the ditch. Book I.

AND I delivered my horſe to Mubbuſhur, and I croſſed the ditch on that pipe, and I came to the foot of the wall. And I went on to the portal, and ſtruck on the door with my hand; and I diſcovered that the guards of the portal were aſleep.

AND they had filled up the portal behind the door with clay and with earth. And I looked round the walls of the caſtle, and ſaw the place where the ſteps of the ladders could be fixed. And I returned, and I mounted my horſe, and went back to my warriors.

AND the troops who had remained behind came with the ladders, and they were all armed; and they took up the ladders, and I turned my face toward the caſtle. And they croſſed the ditch on the pipe; and having fixed their ladders, they entered on the walls of the caſtle. And when forty reſolute men had entered the caſtle, I alſo placed my foot on the ladder, and went in unto them. And they ſounded their trumpets; and by the favour of Almighty God I obtained poſſeſſion of the caſtle.

AND when this news reached the ears of Ameer Hooſſein, he entered into the road of deceit and diſſimulation; and, under the cloak of friendſhip and intimacy, he ſought to bring me into his power.

A trunk of a tree hollowed into a pipe

THUS

کنکاش خلاص خود از مکر وخدعهٔ امیر
حسین که میخواست مرا دستگیر سازد چنین کردم
که چون امیر حسین مصحفی که بآن
قسم خورده بود که مرا بجز دوستی ومراعات خویشی
چیزی دیگر بخاطر نیست نزد من فرستاد وگفته
فرستاد که اگر خلاف انچه میگویم امری دیگر بخاطرم
باشد واگر نقض عهد نموده ترا بدی بکنم این
مصحف خدا مرا بگیرد وچون ویرا مسلمان میدانستم
بر قول وی اعتماد کردم تا آنکه کس نزد من فرستاد
وپیغام داد که اگر چنان شود که در تنگ چکچک
با یکدیگر ملاقات نماییم وتجدید عهد سابق کنیم
حقا که بهتر خواهد بود

ومقصدش این بود که بمکر وفریب مرا
دستگیر نماید ومن میدانستم که بر عهد وقول وی
چندان اعتمادی نیست اما بنابر تعظیم مصحف قرار
دادم که بملاقات وی نهضت نمایم وکنکاش کردم
که اول جمعی از بهادران مردانه را فرستاده در حوالی
وحواشی دره چکچک پنهان سازم وخود با جمعی
رفته با امیر حسین ملاقات نمایم

وبدوستان خود که در خدمت امیر حسین
بودند

THUS I acted for my deliverance from the treachery and perfidy of Ameer Hooſſein, who ſought to make me his priſoner.

WHEN Ameer Hooſſein ſent unto me a KORAUN, by which he had taken an oath that nought was in his heart but friendſhip and brotherly affection towards me; and ſent a meſſage unto me, ſaying, "If there "be ought in my heart contrary to that which I ſay; "and if I break my oath, and do evil unto thee, may "this book of God ſeize upon me;"—ſeeing that I thought him a true believer, I put confidence in his words: even until he ſent a perſon unto me, and a meſſage, ſaying, "If it may be ſo that we may ſee each "other in the paſs of Chukchuk, and renew our antient "faith, truly it will be better."

AND this was his deſign, that by perfidy and treachery he might ſeize upon me. And although I knew that much faith was not to be placed on his word, or on his oath; yet, out of reſpect to the holy KORAUN, I reſolved that I would go to meet him. But I determined that I would firſt ſend a number of my reſolute warriors, and ſecrete them round about the paſs of Chukchuk, and that I myſelf would go with another body of my people and ſee Ameer Hooſſein.

AND I ſent advice to my friends, who were the followers of Ameer Hooſſein, that they ſhould inform

بودند پیغام دادم که از اراده امیر حسین مرا آکاه
کردانند وشیر بهرام که از دوستان من بود مرا بر اراده
امیر حسین آکاه ساخت وامیر حسین اورا بقتل آورد
وبا هزار سوار بر سر من روان شد

در آن وقت من در سر دره فرود آمده
بودم که این خبر بمن رسید وتزوک فوج خود کردم
ودرین حال طلایهء لشکر امیر حسین نمودار شد
وقراولان خبر آوردند که فوج امیر حسین است
واینک امیر حسین خود نمي آید چون شنیده که
امیر تنها آمده است فوج بکرفتن شما تعین نموده

ومن مستعد شدم وهمکي با من دو صد
سوار بودند وصبر کردم تا آنکه فوج امیر حسین بدره
در آمد وبمردمي که پیش از خود فرستاده بودم امر
کردم که راه برکشتن ایشانرا بکیرند ومن خود
بایشان رو برو شدم ومخالفانرا در آن دره در میان
کرفتم واکثر را دستکیر کردم ومردم خود را جمع
ساخته وتزوک نموده روانه ترشي شدم وبتجربه من
رسید که دوست در همه جا بکار مي آید

وبامیر حسین مضمون این بیت بترکي
نوشتم

صبا

inform me of his designs. And Share Behraum, who was of my friends, informed me of the designs of Ameer Hoossein. And Ameer Hoossein slew him; and set out with a thousand horsemen to come upon me. Book I.

AND at that time I had pitched my tents at the entrance of the pass, and this news came unto me. And I ordered my forces: and, behold, the vanguard of Ameer Hoossein appeared in sight. And my Kurrauvulaun brought word, saying, "It is the army of Ameer "Hoossein; and, lo! Ameer Hossein himself cometh "not with them: for he hath heard that Ameer † is come "alone, and he hath sent an army to seize thee."

AND, behold, I was prepared; and two hundred horsemen were all that were with me. And I waited until the forces of Ameer Hoossein had entered the pass: and I sent a messenger to the people whom I had sent before me, and I commanded them to seize the way of their retreat. And I myself opposed them face to face. And I enclosed my enemies in that pass, and I took many prisoners. And I gathered my people together, and I ordered them, and set out towards Kurshee. And by experience it was known unto me, that a friend in all places cometh to use. ‡

AND I wrote to Ameer Hoossein the sense of this verse, in the Toorki || language;

† i. e. Timour.

‡ Alluding to the intelligence which he had received from Share Behraum.

|| i. e. the Mogul.

Say,

صبا بکوي بآن يار دام مکر نهنده
که مکر باز نکردد مکر بمکر کننده

چون پیغام من بامیر حسین رسید خجل ومنفعل شد وعذر خواست ومن دیکر بروي اعتماد نکردم وبسخنان وي فریفته نشدم

کنکاش در پاک ساختن توران زمین از بقیه السیف طایفه اوزبک چنین کردم

که چون لشکر جته والیاس خواجه را از ماورالنهر بر آوردم واز آب خجند کذرانیدم بعضي افواج اوزبکان در قلعهاي ماورالنهر مستحکم بودند وچون خواستم که افواج بر ایشان تعین کنم وبخاطرم خطور کرد که مبادا کار بدور ودراز بکشد

در آن وقت خبر بمن رسید که اوزبکان در قلعها قایم شده اند وصلاح در آن ندیدم که افواج خودرا بر ایشان تعین نمایم ویرلیغي از جانب الیاس خواجه نوشتم وبه اوزبکي دادم ونوجی همراه وي کردم وامر نمودم که خودرا نمودار سازند وکرد وغبار برانکیزند

وچون برلیغ طلب الیاس خواجه بایشان رسید

"Say, O Zephyr, to that friend, the layer of the snares
"of treachery,
"Doth not the treachery return back to the doer of
"treachery?"

And when Ameer Hoossein received my message, he was ashamed and confounded; and he made excuses. And I had faith in him no more, and I was no more deceived by his words.

In making clean the land of Tooraun from those of the tribe of Ouzbuk who had escaped the sword, thus I acted.

When I drove forth from Mauwur u Nuhur the armies of Jitteh, and of Ouleaus Khaujeh, and forced them to cross the waters of Khujjund, certain of the troops of Ouzbuk were enclosed in the castles of Mauwur u Nuhur; and when I sought to send forces upon them, it came into my mind that perhaps the war might be tedious and of long duration.

And at that time news came unto me, that the Ouzbuks continued in the castles; and I saw it was not good that I should send my armies against them. And I wrote a summons, as if from Ouleaus Khaujeh, and I gave it to an Ouzbuk, and I sent forces along with him. And I commanded them to shew themselves, and to raise a great dust.

And when the Ouzbuks received the summons of Ouleaus Khaujeh, calling them unto him,

رسید وگرد وغبار افواج را دیدند شب بشب قلعها را
خالي ساخته بدر رفتند وساحت ماوراالنهر از وجود
آن ظالمان که قصد کشتن من کرده بودند پاک
شد وآن مملکت مسخر من کشت

ومن صلهٔ رحم نکاهداشته ولایت بلخ
وحصار شادمانرا بامیر حسین ارزاني داشتم ووي قدر
احسان ومروت مرا ندانست وقصد استیصال من کرد
ومن کنکاش در استیصال امیر حسین چنین کردم
که چون وي اثار فتح ونصرت مرا دید
عرق حسدش بحرکت درآمد وازارها بمن وهمشیره اش
که در خانه من بود رسانید وقصد کرد که ماوراالنهر از
من بکیرد وبکشتن من کمر بست وبارها بمصاف
من برآمد وهر مرتبه شکست یافت

چون بی اعتدالي وبي انصافي وي
بحد افراط رسید ونزدیک شد که بر من غالب آید
ومرا مستاصل کرداند در آن وقت امراي وي از بد
سلوکي که بایشان میکرد از وي برکشتند وبرادر امیر
کي خسرو حاکم ختلان را هوچي بقتل آورد وامیر
کی خسرو در ختلان باغي شد
چون امراي وي در مقام نفاق بودند ووي
ایشانرا

and ſaw the duſt raiſed by my people; they quitted the castles, night after night, and fled. And the land of Mauwur u Nuhur was delivered from thoſe oppreſſors who had ſought to ſlay me: and that kingdom ſubmitted to my government. Book I.

AND I regarded the ties of kindred, and gave to Ameer Hooſſein the country of Bullukh and the caſtle of Shaudumaun. And he perceived not the degree of my kindneſs and regard; and he ſought to deſtroy me. And in reducing Ameer Hooſſein thus I determined.

WHEN he ſaw the ſigns of my victories and conqueſts, his envy was excited; and he moleſted me, and he moleſted his ſiſter who was in my houſe; and he ſought to take Mauwur u Nuhur from me. And he girded up his loins to ſlay me. And he came forth many times to fight with me: and he was defeated every time.

WHEN his iniquity and injuſtice had reached the limits of exceſs, and it was near that he ſhould become conqueror over me, and expel me; in thoſe days his Ameers, becauſe of the evils which he had done unto them, turned back from him. And he ſlew Humoochee, the brother of Ameer Ki Khiſſero, the ruler of Khuttulaun. And Ameer Ki Khiſſero rebelled in Khuttulaun.

AND his Ameers were in a ſtate of enmity; and he thought that they were his friends. And he

ایشانرا از اهل وناق میدانست وبقصد دفع ورفع من از خطه بلخ پیشخانه بیرون کشید واین خبر بمن آوردند وتابوي خودرا درین دیدم که تا امیر حسین بحرکت در آید خودرا بر سر وي برسانم

وبا جماعه که حاضر بودند متوجه بلخ شدم ودر راه افواج قاهره از اطراف وجوانب آمده جمع شدند وبحوالي خطه بلخ رسیده نزول نمودم وامیر حسین بمدافعه ومقاتله بر آمد وصرفه نبرد وبقلعه در آمده متحصن شد وآمد بر سرش انچه آمد

در باب ایل ساختن آنها که با من بدیها کرده ازمن متوهم بودند ونظر بر بدیهاي خود نموده در خاطر داشتند که من آنها را خواهم کشت چنین کنکاش کردم

که چون امیر حسین بدست من کرفتار شد نوکران وامراي وي بر من کمان کردند که ایشانرا خواهم کشت اکرچه من در مقام کشتن ایشان بودم اما چون سپاهي بودند کنکاش درین دیدم که ایشانرا مستمال ساخته بکارهاي سپاهکري تعین نمایم

† He was obliged to deliver up the castle to Timour, from whom he received a promise of personal safety; but was slain nevertheless some days after by certain of that prince's officers whom he had formerly injured. Vid. *Histoire de Timur-Bec*, Tom. I. p. 191.

وامیر

brought forth his tents from the land of Bullukh, with a resolution to drive me out and destroy me. And they brought unto me this news, and I saw my advantage in this, that even before Ameer Hoossein could put himself in motion, I should go down upon him.

AND I turned toward Bullukh, with the people that were with me: and my victorious forces came from all parts, and from all sides, and were gathered together. And having arrived on the borders of the land of Bullukh, I pitched my tents. And Ameer Hoossein came forth to fight with, and expel, me; and it availed him not. And he entered into the castle, and was enclosed therein. And that befel him which did befall him. †

CONCERNING those who had done evil unto me, and who, reflecting on their evil doings, thought in their hearts that I should slay them, thus I acted.

WHEN Ameer Hoossein fell into my hands, and his Servants and his Ameers were suspicious of me, that I would slay them; although I had determined to put them to death, yet, as they were warriors, I saw it was good that I should dispel their fears, and employ them in war. ‡

‡ The principal Ameers of Bullukh having revolted from Timour, and submitted to their former prince Sooltaun Ahmud Iullauir.

AND

وامير الامراء وي كه در بدخشانات حاكم
بود وبارها بمن رو برو شده وشمشيرها زده بود وچون
شنيد كه امير حسين بقتل رسيد از سياست من
ترسيد وخودرا جمع ساخت واكر من لشكر بكرفتن
وي تعين ميكردم لايق نمي بود

ودر كار وي تغافل كردم وكنكاش
درين ديدم كه در مجالس ومحافل ذكر خير وتعريف
شجاعت ومردانكي وي كردم تا آنكه دوستان وي
بوي نوشتند كه امير با تو در مقام مرحمت وعنايت
است ووي بمن عرضه داشت كرده تكيه بر عنايت
ومروت من نمود وپناه بمن آورد

كنكاشي كه در تسخير دار الملك خراسان
كردم اين بود كه چون ولايت بلخ وحصار شادمان
وبدخشانات مسخر من شد وامير حسين مقتول
كرديد خبر آن بملك غياث الدين حاكم خراسان
رسيد وبر خود بلرزيد ودر مقام جمعيت سپاه ولشكر
در آمد وميخواست كه خودرا استحكام دهد

كنكاش خودرا درين ديدم كه اهل
خراسان را در خواب غفلت اندازم وازين جهته عنان
عزيمت

AND the Ameer ul Omurau of Ameer Hooſſein was the governor of Buddukhſhaun; and he had met me face to face many times, and had fought againſt me. And when he heard that Ameer Hooſſein was ſlain, he feared my juſtice, and he collected himſelf together. And if I had appointed an army to ſeize him, it would not have been proper.

AND I feigned negligence toward him; and I ſaw it was good that I ſhould ſpeak well of his conduct, and praiſe his courage and his magnanimity in the aſſemblies, and among the people: until his friends wrote unto him, ſaying, "Ameer Timour is inclined to ſhew "favour and mercy unto thee." And he ſupplicated me ſubmiſſively, and he reſted on my clemency and favour; and he came to me for protection.

THE DESIGN which I formed for ſubduing the capital city of Khorauſaun, was this. When the kingdom of Bullukh, and the caſtle of Shaudumaun, and the countries of Buddukhſhaun were ſubdued; and when Ameer Hooſſein was ſlain; the news thereof came to Mullik Gheaus u deen the ruler of Khorauſaun, and he trembled for himſelf. And he began to gather together his ſoldiers and his army; and he ſought to ſecure himſelf.

AND I ſaw my ſucceſs in this, that I ſhould throw the people of Khorauſaun into the ſleep of negligence: and for this reaſon I turned back the reins

of

عزیمت بطرف سمرقند معطوف داشتم وبعد از آن نامه پیر من بمن رسید که ملک غیاث الدین بظلم وجور مشغول است

وچون از خبر مراجعت من بطرف سمرقند ملک غیاث الدین بخاطر جمع نشسته بود کنکاش کردم که الحال خاطر خراسانیان از طرف من جمع کشت باید که بر ایشان ترکتاز آورم

واز حوالي بلخ برکشته با لشکري که در بلخ کذاشته بودم ایلغار کردم وخودرا بهرات رسانیده ملک غیاث الدین را در خواب غفلت کرفتم ووي ناچار از شهر هرات بر آمد وخزاین ودفاین ومملکت خودرا بمن پیشکش کرد وملک خراسان مسخر من کردید وامراي خراسان همکي اطاعت من کردند

وکنکاش دیکر که در تسخیر ممالک سیستان وقندهار وافغانستان کردم اینست که چون مملکت خراسان بتسخیر در آمد امراي من کنکاش کفتند که افواج به تسخیر این سه ملک تعین باید کرد من کفتم که اکر با افواج کار میسر نشود ناچار مرا عنان عزیمت بدآن صوب معطوف باید

of my intention toward Summurkund. And after that a letter from my PEER came unto me, ſaying; "Mullik "Gheaus u deen is employed in tyranny and oppreſſion." Book I.

AND when, from the news of my return toward Summurkund, Mullik Gheaus u deen had ſat down quiet and ſecure, I reſolved thus —— "Now the hearts "of the people of Khorauſaun are no longer afraid of me, "I muſt fall upon them."

AND I turned back from the neighbourhood of Bullukh; and with the army which I had left in Bullukh, I marched with ſpeed: and, coming to Hurraut, I took Mullik Gheaus u deen in the ſleep of ſecurity. And he was helpleſs, and he came forth from the city of Hurraut, and he preſented unto me his treaſures, and his wealth, and his kingdom. And the kingdom of Khorauſaun was ſubdued; and the Ameers of Khorauſaun, every one of them, ſubmitted unto me.

THE DESIGNS which I formed for conquering the countries of Seiſtaun, and Kundahaur, and the land of the Afghauns, were theſe. When the kingdom of Khorauſaun was reduced to obedience, my Ameers counſelled me, ſaying, "Thou muſt ſend armies "to ſubdue theſe three countries." I anſwered them, ſaying, If the matter be not brought to paſs by the armies, without remedy, I myſelf muſt turn the reins of

بـايد داشت واينک مرا کار بسياري در پيش است
کنکاش دربن ديدم که يرليغهاي استمالت
به حکام آن ديار بنويسم با اين مضمون که اکر بمن
در آييد بر آييد واکر در افتيد بر افتيد وانچه بينيد
وتدبير موافق تقدير بود وبمجرد رسيدن يرليغها ايشان
سر اطاعت بر جادهء فرمان برداري نهادند

کنکاشي که در استيصال اروس خان
وتسخير دشت قپچـاق کردم اين بود که چون
تقتمش بداخان از اروس خان شکست يافته پناه بمن
آورد بخـود کنکاش کردم که بهمراهي تقتمش
بداخان فوج بفرستم يا خود بروم

دربـنـوقـت ايلچـي اروس خان رسيد
کنکاش را چنين يافتم که ايلچي ويرا تسلي نمايم
ورخصت دهم وراه دشـت را بربندم ومتعاقب ايلچي
لشکري تعين کنم که در روزي که ايلچي
بخـاطـر جـمـع بمجلس اروس خان در آيد ووي
غـافـل شـود روز ديکر افـواج مـن بر سر وي
ترکتاز آورد

چون

my intention that way: and, behold, I have very much business before me. Book I.

AND I saw it was good, that I should write mandates of encouragement to the rulers of those countries, to this purport — "If ye come in unto me, "come; and if ye refuse, refuse: and do that which ye "see best." And, behold, the measure was good: and as soon as my mandates arrived, they placed the forehead of submission on the path of obedience.

THE DESIGN which I formed for vanquishing Auroos Khaun, and for subduing the Dusht of Kipchauk, was this. When Touktummish Buddau Khaun was defeated by Auroos Khaun, and fled to me for shelter, I counselled with myself whether I should send an army with Touktummish Khaun, or whether I should go myself.

AND at this time the ambassador of Auroos Khaun arrived. And I saw my advantage in this — that I should speak fair to his ambassador, and dismiss him, and shut up the road to the Dusht, and appoint an army to set out after the ambassador;—and that on the day after that on which the ambassador should enter the presence of Auroos Khaun, without suspicion; whilst Auroos Khaun should be unprepared, my forces should assault him.

چون چنین کردم تدبیر موافق تقدیر آمد که چون ایلچي اروس خان رسید وحکایت میکرد که افواج قاهره من چون بلاي ناکهاني بر سر اروس خان ریختند واروس خان تاب مقاومت نیآورد وترار بر فرار داد ومملکت دشت قپچاق مسخر من شد

کنکاش که در تسخیر ممالک کیلان وجرجان ومازندران واذربایجان وشروان وفارس وعراق کردم این بود که در ایامي که عرایض اهل عراق از تعدي آل مظفر وملوک طوایف بمن رسید اراده یساق عراق کردم

ودرین حال بخاطرم رسید که ملوک آن ممالک اکر بیک اتفاق در مقابل من در آیند جنک را آماده باید بود وامراي من همچنین کنکاش کفتند که باستعداد جنک باید رفت ومن با خود چنین کنکاش دیدم که یک یک از ایشان را بخود رام کردانم وهرکس رام نشود ویرا بسزا رسانم

اول کسي که بمن پناه آورد امیر علي حاکم مازندران بود که بمن پیشکش فرستاد

AND when I did ſo, the meaſure proved ſucceſsful. For when the ambaſſador arrived, even whilſt he related his ſtory, my victorious armies, like unto an unforeſeen calamity, poured on the head of Auroos Khaun. And Auroos Khaun had not the power to oppoſe them; and he reſolved on flight. And the Duſht of Kipchauk was ſubdued. †

THE DESIGNS which I formed for ſubduing the countries of Kilaun, and Jurjaun, and Mauzinduraun, and Azzurbauejaun, and Shurwaun, and Fauris, and Erauk, were theſe. In thoſe days, when the petitions of the people of Erauk, on account of the oppreſſions of the race of Muzzuffur, and of the rulers of the nations, came unto me, I reſolved to go down upon Erauk.

AND at this time it came into my mind, that if the rulers of thoſe countries ſhould join together to oppoſe me, I muſt be well prepared for war: and my Ameers gave this counſel, ſaying, "We muſt go prepa-"red for war." And I reſolved with myſelf, that I would make them obedient unto me, one by one; and that I would chaſtiſe thoſe who refuſed to ſubmit.

AND the firſt perſon, who ſought my protection, was Ameer Aali the ruler of Mauzinduraun,

† Upon the death of Auroos Khaun, which happened ſoon after his defeat, Touktummiſh Khaun was eſtabliſhed on the throne of the Duſht of Kipchauk, by the aſſiſtance of Timour.

who

فرستاد ودر مکتوبی که نوشته بود قید کرده بود که
ما جمعي که از آل علي ايم قناعت باين سر زمين كرده
ايم ان تاخذوا قدرتكم اقوي وان تعفوا اقرب للتقوي
يعني اگر بگيريد قدرت شما قويتر است واگر عفو
كنيد نزديک به پرهيزكاري است

من رجـوع حاكم مازندران را شكون*
گرفتم ومتوجه مملكت گيلان وجرجان شدم وچون
حـكـام آنجا بمن رجوع نياوردند وافواج قاهره بر سر
ايشان تعين نمودم وخود بعراق لشكر كشيدم
واصفهان را مسخر ساختم وبر اهل اصفهان
اعتماد كرده قـلـعـه را بدست ايشان سپردم وايشان
باغي شده داروغه را كه بر ايشان تعين كرده بودم
بـا سـه هزار كس از سپاه بقتل آوردند من هم
حكم بقتل عام اهالي اصفهان كردم

كنكـاشي كه در تسخير دار الملك
فارس وتنبه عراق كردم اينست
كه چون شـيـراز را به آل مـظـفـر
گـذاشـتـم ودر اصـفـهـان سـه هـزار كـس
تعين

who ſent gifts unto me; and in the letter which he wrote unto me, he inſerted this — "We, who are of the "poſterity of Aali, have reſted ſatisfied with this land. "ان تاخذوا قدرتكم اقوي وان تعفوا اقرب " "للتقوي † That is to ſay; *If thou wilt take it from* "*us, thy power is greater than ours; but if thou wilt* "*ſpare us, it will come nearer to clemency.*" Book I.

I CONSIDERED the ſubmiſſion of the ruler of Mauzinduraun as a happy omen; and I turned toward the countries of Kilaun and Jurjaun. And when the princes of thoſe countries ſubmitted not unto me, I appointed troops to go down upon them; and I myſelf drew my army into Erauk.

AND I conquered the city of Isfahaun. And I truſted in the people of Isfahaun; and I delivered the caſtle into their hands. And they rebelled; and the Daurogheh, whom I had placed over them, they ſlew, with three thouſand of the ſoldiers. And I alſo commanded that a general ſlaughter ſhould be made of the people of Isfahaun.

THE DESIGN which I formed for the reduction of the chief city of Fauris, and the reſt of Erauk, is this.

WHEN I left Sharauze in the hands of the deſcendants of Muzzuffur, and ſtationed three thouſand

† Arabic.

تعین نمودم وبجهته دفع ورفع تقتمش خان بجانب دشت قپچاق لشکر کشیدم اهل اصفهان داروغه را بقتل رسانیده بودند واهالي شیراز نیز قدم اطاعت بیرون گذاشته بودند

لهذا تجدید یساق مملکت عراق نمودم وهشتاد هزار سوار موجود ساختم وکنکاش کردم اگر بیک مرتبه با این لشکر کران بعراق در آیم گنجایش نخواهد بود وانواج را مقرر ساختم که نوج نوج بمملکت عراق ترکتاز آورند

چون چنین کنکاش کردم لشکر خودرا سه فوج ساختم وپیش از خود تعین نمودم ولشکرهاي متفرقه که در عراق جمع آمده بودند همه پراکنده شدند وبر شیراز لشکر کشیدم وشاه منصور بمن رو برو شد وبسزاي خود رسید

کنکاشي که در شکست دادن تقتمش خان کردم این بود

که در دشت قپچاق لشکریان من بواسطه آنکه پنج ماه در تعاقب تقتمش خان معطل شدند قحطي وتنکي در لشکر من بسیار شد چنانچه

men in Isfahaun, and drew my armies towards the Dusht of Kipchauk, to reduce and drive out Touktummish Khaun, † the people of Isfahaun put my Daurogheh to death: and the inhabitants of Sharauze also turned aside from their obedience.

AND on these accounts I went down upon the kingdom of Erauk a second time, and I collected together eighty thousand horsemen. And I reflected, that if I entered into Erauk at one time with this mighty army, that they could not be supported. And I commanded my armies, that they should invade the kingdom of Erauk, one after the other.

AND when I had resolved thus, I divided my forces into three armies, and sent them down before me. And the divided troops who had come together in the kingdom of Erauk, were all dispersed abroad. And I drew an army on Sharauze: and Shaah Munsoor opposed me face to face. And he met with his reward. ‡

THE DESIGN which I formed in defeating Touktummish Khaun was this.

WHEN my armies were weakened by a pursuit of five months after Touktummish Khaun in the Dusht of Kipchauk, famine and scarcity were very great in my army, even so that for many days my people lived

† Who, forgetting the repeated services and assistances which he had received from Timour, had during his absence in Persia &c. made incursions into Mauwur u Nuhur.

‡ i. e. was slain in the action.

چنـانچه چند روز بآش یلماق* وکوشت شکار وتخم مرغان صحرايء اوقات میکذرانیدند تا آنکه تقتمش خان احوال لشکر مرا شنیده فرصت یافت وبا لشکري پیشتر از مور وملخ آمده بمن رو برو شد

ولشکریان من بسیار کرسنه بودند ولشکر تقتمش خان آسوده وسرداران وامراي من دل نهاده جنک نمي شدند تا آنکه فرزندان ونبایر آمده زانو زدند واختیار جانسپاري نمودند

ودریـن وقت علمدار تقتمش خان بمن سازش کرد وکنکـاش چنین یافتم که جنک بیندازم ودر هنکـام مقابله هر دو صف علمدار وي علم ویرا نکونسار سازد

† To render the importance of this DESIGN intelligible, it may be proper to obſerve, that in aſiatic encounters the diſappearance or retreat of the grand ſtandard of the prince has ever been, and ſtill is, attended with the loſs of the battle. This ſtandard is conſpicuous for its ſize, and accompanies that body of troops immediately headed by the prince himſelf. The eyes of the whole army are fixed upon it. While it continues diſplayed and advancing, the troops are ſatisfied that their prince is with them; but the moment it diſappears, or retreats, they conclude that he is either ſlain or flying from the field: and the diſperſion of his forces immediately follows.

Aali Yezzudi appears to be totally ignorant of the good underſtanding which had taken place between Timour and the ſtandard-bearer of Touktummiſh Khaun. Unacquainted with this circumſtance, he is at a loſs to account for certain of the emperor's actions prior to the battle. In relating the movements of the army a ſhort time before the action, he ſays, "Tocat-

"mich

چون

on the flesh of the beasts of the forests, and on the eggs of the birds of the desert. And Touktummish Khaun heard of the state of my people, and found his advantage; and, with an army more numerous than the ants and the locusts, came upon me, and opposed me face to face. Book I.

AND my people were an hungered, and the army of Touktummish Khaun were full. And my chiefs and my Ameers set not their hearts upon battle, until my sons and my grandsons came, and kneeled down, and devoted their lives unto me.

AND at this time the standard-bearer of Touktummish plotted secretly with me. And I found it was good that I should assault the foe; and that, when the two armies were engaged, the standard-bearer of Touktummish Khaun should invert his standard. †

" mich s'étoit imaginé que lorsque Timur arriveroit au fleuve de Tic, il le " traverseroit par les passages ordinaires, c'est pourquoi il s'étoit mis en em- " buscade pour le surprendre dans ce passage: mais l'Empereur *s'étoit pré- " cautionné* contre les desseins de Tocatmich; il avoit passé le fleuve à la " nage par un autre endroit, et il étoit arrivé près de lui sans peril. *Quoi- " qu'il en soit*, ce Prince *ayant compris* la maniere d'agir de Tocatmich Can, " il s'arrêta dans ce lieu là, jusqu'à ce que toutes les Troupes s'y fussent " rendues, &c." Vid. *Hist. Timur-Bec*, Tom. II. p. 98.

This is another proof of the superiority of the history of Timour, written by himself, over that written by Aali Yezzudi; who, though a tolerably accurate narrator of the exploits of Timour, appears to be, in most cases, an absolute stranger to the secret springs and motives which influenced his conduct.

 AND

چون خبر زانو زدن فرزندان بمسامع امرا ونونيان رسيده همکي قوي دل کشته دل نهاد جنک شدند

وامير زاده ابا بکر با هشت هزار سوار هراول ساختم وچون آتش قتال وجدال بلند شد امر کردم که خيمهارا بر پا سازند وبطبخ طعام مشغول شوند

ودرين وقت علم تقتمش خان سر نکون شد وتقتمش خان شکسته رکاب وکسسته عنان الوس جوجي را بباد غارت داده پشت بمعرکه کرد وفرار نمود

کنکاشي که در تسخير دار الاسلام بغداد وعراق عرب کردم اين بود

که بعد از آنکه عراق عجم وفارس را مسخر ساختم درين وقت مکتوب قطب الاقطاب پير من بمن رسيد که قهرمان عراق عرب وعجم عراق را بتو ارزاني داشته

در تسخير بغداد چنين کنکاش کردم که اول ايلچي نزد سلطان احمد جلاير فرستادم تا

† i. e. At the time that the advanced guard was engaged, Timour, assured of success from his intrigue with the standard-bearer of Touktummish,

احوال

AND when it reached the ears of the Ameers and the Leaders, that my children had kneeled before me, and had offered to devote their lives unto me, they became ſtrong of heart, and they reſolved on battle. Book I.

AND I appointed the prince Abau Bukkur, with eight thouſand horſemen, the advanced guard. And when the flames of war and of ſlaughter aſcended high, I commanded that the tents ſhould be pitched, and that they ſhould prepare victuals. †

AND at this time the ſtandard of Touktummiſh Khaun was inverted: and Touktummiſh, diſmayed and confounded, gave the tribe of Jouji to the wind of deſolation; and turned his back on the field of ſlaughter, and fled.

THE DESIGN which I formed for the reduction of Bughdaud (the city of Iſlaum) and Erauk a Arrub, was this.

AFTER I had ſubdued Erauk a Ajjum and Fauris, in thoſe days a letter from Koottub ul Aktaub, my PEER, came unto me, ſaying, "The lord of Erauk "a Ajjum and Arrub hath given Erauk unto thee."

AND thus I acted in the reduction of Bughdaud. I firſt ſent an ambaſſador to Sooltaun Ahmud Jullauir, that he might inform himſelf of the prowefs

miſh, ordered in contempt the cavalry of his main body to diſmount and prepare their victuals Vid. *Hiſt. Timur-Bec*, Tom. II. p. 114.

and

احوال شجاعت ومعاش سلطان احمد والي بغداد ولشکر ویرا معلوم نماید

وایلچي به بغداد رفته بمن عرضه داشت نمود که سلطان احمد پارچه گوشتي است ودو چشم دارد

من تکیه بر تایید ایزدي نموده ایلغار کردم وخودرا باستعجال به بغداد رسانیدم وسلطان احمد جلایر ترار بر فرار داده وبطرف کربلا گریخت ودار الاسلام بغداد مسخر من گشت

کنکاشي که در استیصال تغتمش خان کردم این بود

که چون الوس جوجي خان را بغارت داده وهزیمت یافته بود در وقت فرصت لشکرهاي گران از راه دربند وشیروان بر ولایت ازربجان فرستاد وآغاز فتنه وفساد کرد ومن چون عراقین را مسخر ساخته بودم در استیصال وي چنین کنکاش کردم که با لشکرهاي فراوان از راه دربند بدشت قپچاق در آیم

وعرض لشکر خودرا ملاحظه نمودم لشکرهاي من تا چهار فرسنک راه یسال بسته ایستاده بودند شکر آلهي بجاي آوردم

واز

and the conduct of Sooltaun Ahmud the ruler of Bughdaud, and of the ſtrength of his forces. Book I.

And the ambaſſador went to Bughdaud, and wrote word unto me, ſaying, "Behold, Sultaun Ahmud is a piece of animated fleſh: and lo, he hath two eyes." †

And I reſted on the favour of the Almighty; and I marched with ſpeed, and I came to Bughdaud ſuddenly. And Sooltaun Ahmud Jullauir reſolved on flight, and he fled toward Kurbullau: and Bughdaud, (the houſe of Iſlaum) was conquered.

The design which I formed for extirpating Touktummiſh Khaun was this.

After he had given up the tribe of Jouji to the wind of deſolation, and had been put to flight; he, in the hour of advantage, ſent down a mighty army on the kingdom of Azzurbauejan by the way of Durbund and Sharevaun, and began to raiſe commotions therein. And when I had conquered the two Erauks, thus I reſolved to deſtroy him — that I would go into the Duſht of Kipchauk with a mighty army by the way of Durbund.

And I reviewed my armies, and, behold, they ſtood on four furſungs of ground ‡ in battle array: and I gave thanks to God.

† A mode of ſpeech uſed by the ambaſſador to expreſs his contempt of the abilities of Sooltaun Ahmud.

‡ About 13 Engliſh miles.

And

واز آب تیمور عبور نموده بایل والوس

دشت برلیغها نوشتم که هرکس بمن در آید بر آید

وهر کس در افتد بر افتد

ودر سنه ۷۹۷ بدشت تپچاق در آمدم

وتا اقصاي زمین شمال رفتم وایل والوس جوجي را

که راه مخالفت من مي پیمودند خراب ومستاصل

ساختم وولایت والوسات وقلعهاي اقلیم پنجم وششم را

مسخر ساختم ومظفر ومنصور معاودت نمودم

کنکاشي که در تسخیر هندوستان

کردم این بود که اول بسبیل مزاج داني از

فرزندان وامرا کنکاش خواستم

امیر زاده پیر محمد جهانکیر

کفت که چون مملکت هند را بکیریم از زر هند

عالم کیر شویم

وامیر زاده محمد سلطان کفت هند را

میکیریم لیکن هندوستان را حصارها است اول دریاها

دوم جنکلها وبیشها سیوم سپاه سلاح دار وفیلان

آدم شکار

امیر

AND I crossed the waters of Timour †. Book I.
And I wrote mandates to the people, and the tribes of the Dusht of Kipchauk, saying; Whoever cometh in unto me, let him come; and whoever refuseth, let him refuse.

AND in the year seven hundred and ninety seven I entered the Dusht of Kipchauk. And I went to the boundaries of the land of the north; and the people, and the tribes of Jouji, who opposed me, I destroyed. And I subdued the countries and the castles of the fifth and of the sixth region. ‡ And I returned victorious and triumphant. A.D. 1394.

MY DESIGN, for reducing the empire of Hindostaun, was this. First, to discover the thoughts of my Sons and of my Ameers, I demanded counsel of them.

THE prince Peer Mahummud Jehaungheer said; "Behold, when we shall subdue the empire of "Hind, with the gold of Hind, we shall become the "conquerors of the world."

AND the prince Mahummud Sooltaun spoke, saying; "We may subdue Hind: yet Hindo-"staun hath many ramparts. First, the rivers; and se-"condly, the wildernesses and the forests; and thirdly, "the soldiers clad in armour; and fourthly, the ele-"phants, destroyers of men."

† The word *Timour* is probably an error.

‡ He penetrated to Moscow, at that time the capital of Russia, which he pillaged. Vid. *Hist. Timur-Bec*, Tom. II. p. 363. See also note on p. 131.

امیر زاده سلطان حسین کفت که
چون هند را بکیریم بر چهار اقلیم حاکم وفرمان فرما
کردیم
امیر زاده شاه رخ کفت که در قوانین
ترک خوانده ام که پنج پادشاه عظیم الشان اند که
از بزرکی ایشانرا بنام نمیخوانند پادشاه هندرا دارا
میکویند وپادشاه روم را قیصر میخوانند وپادشاه خطا
وچین وماچین را نغفور مینامند وپادشاه ترکستان را
خاقان میکویند وپادشاه ایران وتوران را شهنشاه
میخوانند وحکم شهنشاه همیشه بر ممالک هندوستان
جاري بوده وچون ایران وتوران زمین بتصرف ما
است لازم است که هندوستان را هم مسخر
کردانیم
وامرا کفتند که اکرچه هند را میکیریم
لیکن اکر اقامت نماییم نسل ما ضایع شود واولاد
واحفاد ما از ترکیب بدر آیند وهندي زبان کردند
چون بر عزیمت تسخیر هند کمر همت
بسته بودم نخواستم که ترک عزیمت خود نمایم ودر
جواب ایشان کفتم که به تنکري تعالي متوجه میشوم
واز قران فال جنک مي بینم تا انچه امر تنکري
تعالي

THE prince Sooltaun Hooſſein ſpoke, and ſaid; "When we ſhall have conquered Hindoſtaun, we "ſhall become the lords and the rulers of four re- "gions." †

THE prince Shaahrokh ſaid; "I have read "in the Toorki annals, that there are five mighty "kings, whom, becauſe of their greatneſs, they mention "not by their names. For, behold, they call the king "of Hind, Daurau; and the king of Room they call "Keeſur; and the king of Khuttun, and Cheen, and "Maucheen, they ſtile Fughfoor; and they call the king "of Toorkiſtaun, Khaukaun; and they call the lord of "Eraun, and of Tooraun, King of kings. And, lo! "the power of the King of kings hath, in all times, been "over the empire of Hindoſtaun: and ſince the land of "Eraun, and the land of Tooraun are in our hands, it "behoveth us to conquer Hindoſtaun alſo."

THE Ameers ſpoke, and ſaid; "Although "we may ſubdue Hind, yet if we tarry in that land, our "poſterity will be loſt; and our children, and our grand "children, will degenerate from the vigour of their fore- "fathers, and become ſpeakers of the language of Hind."

AND I had reſolved on the conqueſt of Hindoſtaun, and I was loth to deſiſt from my reſolution: and I anſwered them, ſaying; "I will turn to Almighty "God, and I will ſeek the ſign of war in the KORAUN,

† i.e. Four ſevenths of the known world. For the Arabians and Perſians, following the antient Greek writers, diſtribute what they imagine the habitable parts of the earth, into ſeven regions or climates.

تعالي باشد بدآن عمل نمايم وايشان همه قبول کردند

چون از مصحف مجيد فال کشادم اين

آية کريمه بر آمد يا ايها النبي جاهد الکفار والمنافقين†

وچون علما مضمون آية را بامرا خاطر نشان کردند

سرها در زير انداخته خاموش شدند ومرا دل از

خاموشي ايشان افسرده شد

بخون کنکاش کردم که امراي که به

تسخير هندوستان راضي نميشوند ايشانرا از مرتبه امارت

بيندازم وافواج وقشونات ايشانرا بکوتل* ارزاني دارم

ليکن چون تربيت کرده من بودند نخواستم که

ايشانرا خراب سازم وبديشان ملايمت کردم اکرچه

ايشان خون در دل من انداختند ليکن چون آخر

متفق شدند چيزي در خاطر نياوردم

ومرتبه ديکر کنکاش کردم وپيشخانه اقبال

بجانب هندوستان بر آورده فاتحه فتح خواندم

وکنکاش تعين نمودن لشکرها بر دار

الملک هندوستان چنين کردم که امير زاده پير محمد

جهانکيررا با سي هزار سوار لشکر جرانغار* که در کابل

بود امر نمودم که از راه کوه سليماني رفته واز آب سند

کذشته بر ولايت ملتان ترکتاز آورد ومسخر کرداند

وسلطان

† Arabic.

"that whatever be the will of God, that I may do." Book I.
And they all consented thereto.

AND when I sought an omen in the holy book, this sacred verse came forth — "O PROPHET "FIGHT WITH THE INFIDELS AND THE UNBE-"LIEVERS." And when the doctors of the law explained the meaning of the verse to the Ameers, they hung down their heads, and they were silent. And my heart was grieved by their silence.

AND I deliberated with myself concerning the Ameers who opposed the reduction of Hindostaun, whether I should throw them down from their commands, and give their troops, and their Kushoons to their Kotuls: but since I myself had exalted them, I sought not to pull them down. And I treated them with kindness: and although they had angered me, yet, as they were unanimous at last, I regarded it not.

AND I called a council a second time; and having pitched my tents toward Hindostaun, I repeated the prayer of victory.

THUS I resolved to send down armies on the chief city of Hindostaun. I commanded the prince Peer Mahummud Jehaungheer, who was at Kaubul with thirty thousand horsemen of the left wing of the army, that, going by the way of the mountain of Soolamaun, and crossing the Sind, he should go down upon Mooltaun and subdue it.

AND

وسلطان محمد خان وامير زاده رستم را
وديكر امرا را با سي هزار سوار برانغار* امر نمودم كه از
آب سند كذشته از راه دامن كوه كشمير بر ولايت
لاهور تركتاز آورند ومن خود با سي ودو هزار سوار
قول* شدم

وچون مجموع لشكر من نود ودو هزار
سوار بودند موافق ومطابق عدد اسم محمد رسول الله
صلي الله عليه وآله وسلم اين عدد را بفال نيكو
ومبارك كرفتم

وسوار شدم ودر موضع اندرآب سرحد
بدخشان فرود آمدم وتنبيه كفار كوه كتور نموده متوجه
غزاي دار الحرب هندوستان شدم

وكنكاش پاك ساختن راه هندوستان از
اوغانيان چنين كردم

كه چون بعرض من رسيد كه بعضي از
اوغانيان متعرض راه هندوستان شده رهزني مينمايند
خصوصا موسي اوغان كه كلانتر تبيله كركس است
وبر لشكر شاه اوغان كه از چاكران ودولتخواهان

† According to D'Herbelot (*Bibl. Orientale*, p. 603.) the Mahummudans have given 99 names or attributes to their prophet, the same number by which they distinguish the Creator. By this account the names of the prophet

Book I.

And I ordered Sooltaun Mahummud Khaun, and the prince Rooſtum, and other Ameers with thirty thouſand horſemen of the right wing, that, croſſing the waters of Sind, they ſhould go down on the country of Lahore, by the way of the ſkirts of the mountains of Kuſhmeer. And I myſelf with thirty and two thouſand horſemen, was the main body.

And behold the whole of my army was ninety and two thouſand horſemen, correſponding and according to the number of the names of Mahummud, the prophet of God, † (be the bleſſing of the Almighty on him and on his poſterity) and I took this number as a fortunate and an happy omen.

And I ſet out, and I came and pitched my tents at Anduraub on the border of Budukhſhaun: and having puniſhed the infidels of the mountains of Kuttoor, I went on to the holy war of Hindoſtaun.

The design which I formed for clearing the road to Hindoſtaun, from the Oughauns, ‡ was this.

It was reported unto me that certain of the Oughauns infeſted the road to Hindoſtaun, and robbed and plundered therein: and eſpecially Mooſi the Oughaun, who was the head of the tribe of Gurkus. And he came down on Luſhkur Shaah the Oughaun, who was

phet appear to be only ninety two in number, which ſeems moſt probable.

‡ Or Afghauns. The word is written ſometimes *Oughaun* and ſometimes *Afghaun* in the MS.

one

من بود وويرا امير زاده پير محمد به محافظت قلعه ايراب كذاشته بود تركتاز آورد ووبرا بقتل رسانيد وهرچه داشتند ونداشتند بغارت داده وهمدرين وقت ملك محمد برادر لشكر شاه آمده داد فرياد كرده حقيقت كشته شدن برادر خوردرا از تعدي موسي بعرض رسانيد

ومن بحبس وي فرمان دادم وكفتم كه موسي دولتخواهي من است وامراي من سخن بر ظلم من كردند

اما چون خبر حبس ملك محمد وحرف من بكوش موسي رسيد قوي دل كشت وچون يرليغ طلب كه نوشته بودم بوي رسيد بي دهشت آمد وقلعه را پيشكش كرد

چون من بتماشاي آن قلعه رفتم يكي از سپاهيان وي تيري بقصد من انداخت وموسي بسزا وجزاي خود رسيد وراه هندوستان مفتوح شد

كنكاشي كه در شكست دادن سلطان محمود حاكم دهلي وملو خان كردم اين بود

† When Moosi submitted, Timour found it prudent to continue him for a time in his government, and supplied him with people and necessaries to put the castle of Ireaub in a proper state of defence. The emperor, on his

كه

one of my servants and well-wishers (and the prince Peer Mahummud had left him to defend the castle of Ireaub) and he slew him, and plundered all that he had. And at this time Mullik Mahummud, the brother of Lushkur Shaah, came and demanded justice; and he set forth unto me the murder of his brother by the cruelty of Moosi.

AND I gave orders that Mullik Mahummud should be thrown into prison; and I said that Moosi was my well-wisher; and my Ameers spoke of my injustice.

BUT when the news of the confinement of Mullik Mahummud, and of that which I had said, reached the ears of Moosi, he became strong of heart. And when the mandate which I had written unto him arrived, he came without fear and he delivered up the castle.

AND when I went to view the castle, one of his soldiers shot an arrow with an intention to slay me: and Moosi met with his reward. † And the road to Hindostaun was open.

THE DESIGN which I formed for vanquishing Sooltaun Muhmood the ruler of Dehli, and Mulloo Khaun, was this.

his arrival in that neighbourhood, went to view the castle; when one of the people of Moosi let fly an arrow at him. As he had all along determined to chastise Moosi, he immediately caused him to be seized and put to death. Vid. *Hist. Timur-Bec*, Tom. III. p. 39.

که سلطان محمود وملو خان با پنجاه
هزار سوار وپیاده ویک صد وبیست زنجیر فیل قلعه
دهلي را استحکام داده بقصد جنک من در آمد

وبخاطرم خطور کرد که اکر بکرفتن قلعه
دهلي مقید شوم مبادا کار بدور ودراز بکشد

با خود کنکاش کردم که خودرا زبون
نمودار کردانم تا آنکه غنیم دلیر شود بجنک صف
مبادرت نماید

واز این جهت در دور لشکر خندق کندم
ومیان خندق خودرا استوار ساختم وفوجي را باستقبال
ایشان فرستادم وامر کردم که خودرا زبون وترسان
نمودار ساخته غنیم را دلیر سازند

وچون غنیم خودرا غالب یافت خیره
شده در میدان آمده با افواج قاهره رو برو شدند
وسلطان محمود حاکم دهلي بجنک مبادرت نمود
وشکست یافت وبطرف کوهستان بکریخت وغنایم واموال
بي قیاس از نقود واجناس نصیب سپاهیان من شد

ودر میان یک سال دار الملک هند را مسخر
ساختم ودر اواخر سنه مذکور بدار السلطنت سمرقند
معاودت نمودم

کنکاشي

Book I.

SOOLTAUN Muhmood and Mulloo Khaun, with fifty thouſand men, horſemen and footmen, and one hundred and twenty elephants, made ſtrong the caſtle of Dehli, and prepared to oppoſe me.

AND it came into my mind, that if I ſhould reſolve on ſubduing the caſtle of Dehli, perhaps the war might be long and tedious.

AND I counſelled with myſelf, that I would make myſelf appear weak in their ſight; that the enemy might gain courage, and come, and fight with me on the plain.

AND on this account I dug a ditch round my army, and I ſtrengthened myſelf within that ditch: and I ſent a force to meet them. And I commanded the ſoldiers that they ſhould ſhow themſelves weak and fearful, that they might give courage to the enemy.

AND when the enemy found themſelves powerful, they exulted: and they came into the plain, and they oppoſed my victorious armies face to face. And Sooltaun Muhmood, the ruler of Dehli, came into battle, and he was defeated, and he fled toward the mountains. And ſpoils and wealth above meaſure, in money and in effects, fell to the lot of my ſoldiers.

AND in the ſpace of one year I conquered the chief city of Hind: and at the end of the ſame year I returned toward the imperial city of Summurkund.

کنکاشي که در تسخیر ممالك کرجستان
کردم این بود
که چون از هندوستان مظفر ومنصور
معاودت نمودم هنوز از رنج سفر هند نیآسوده بودم
که عرایض حکام عراقین رسید که کفار کرجستان قدم
از جادهء حد خود بیرون کذاشته اند
وهمیشه در فکر مي بودم که پادشاهانرا
بهتر از غزا وجهاد با کفار وملك کیري وجهان
ستاني چیزي دیکر نیست
ودرین وقت که خبر طغیان کرجستانیان
بي ایمان رسید کنکاش کردم که اکر دفع ورفع ایشان
اهمال نمایم مبادا مفسدان آن دیار بطغیان در آیند
ودر دفع ایشان سرعت بکار بردم
وسپاهیان را که از یساق هند آمده
بودند مختار ساختم که هرکس خواهد بجاي خویش
باشد وهرکس خواهد همراهي نماید
وبلشکرهاي خراسان وقندهار وسیستان
وکرمان وطبرستان وکیلان ومازندران وفارس یرلیغها
صادر کردم که تهیه یساق نمایند ودر حوالي اصفهان
آیند وبلشکر ظفر اثر ملحق شوند
وکنکاش

THE DESIGN which I formed for ſubduing the countries of Goorjiſtaun, was this.

WHEN I returned victorious and triumphant from Hindoſtaun, I had not yet reſted from the fatigues of the war of Hind, when the petitions of the governors of the two Erauks arrived, ſaying; "The infidels of Goorjiſtaun have advanced beyond their boundaries."

AND, behold, I at all times thought that there was nought more worthy the valour of princes than the conquering of kingdoms and empires, and the waging holy wars with infidels and unbelievers.

AND, in thoſe days, when the news of the irruption of the infidel inhabitants of Goorjiſtaun arrived, I reflected, that if I delayed to chaſtiſe them, perhaps the ſeditious of that country might riſe into open rebellion: and in chaſtiſing them I uſed expedition.

AND I gave liberty to the ſoldiers, who had returned from the war of Hind, that every one of them who choſe to ſtay at home, might ſtay; and that every one who choſe to go with me, might go.

AND I ſent forth orders to the armies of Khorauſaun and Kundahaur, and Seiſtaun and Kurmaun, and Tubburiſtaun, and Kilaun, and Mauzinduraun, and Fauris; that they ſhould make ready for war, and come down into the neighbourhood of Isfahaun, and be united to my victorious forces. †

† i. e. To the army which he commanded in perſon.

AND

وکنکاش کردم که کردن کشان هر
ملک را متفرق سازم چنانچه بعضي کردن کشان
خراسان وفارس را بتوران زمین فرستادم وساحت آن
ممالک را از مخالفت ایشان پاک ساختم وبه تسخیر
قلاع ولایت کرجستان عنان عزیمت مصروف نهودم

وبه کنکاشي که پسندیده سپاهیان بود
عمل مینمودم وخود فولادي بر سر نهادم وزره داودي
در بر کردم وشمشیر مصري حمایل نهودم وبر سربر
مبارزت نشستم

ودلیران توران وبهادران خراسان ومردان
مازندران وکیلان را نهیب دادم وقلعه سیواس وقلاع
کرجستان را مسخر ساختم وجماعه که در قلعه ها
بودند همکي را مستاصل کردانیدم وغنایم آن قلعه ها
را بر عساکر منصوره قسمت نهودم ومفسدان واوباش
اذربایجان را تنبیه کردم

وبعد از آن متوجه بتسخیر قلاع ملطیه
وآن حوالي شدم وچون خاطرم از تسخیر ونسق قلاع

† Viz. To set forward in great martial pomp, as afterwards described.

‡ Timour, in his first incursion into Georgia, reduced Tiflis the capital, and took prisoner Ipocrates the christian king of that country, who afterwards

جمع

AND I resolved that I would disperse and scatter abroad the rebellious and seditious of every country. Thus I sent into the land of Tooraun certain of the seditious of Khorausaun and of Fauris, and delivered those countries from their machinations. And I turned the reins of my intention to the reduction of the castles of Goorjistaun. Book I.

AND I determined on that measure which was agreeable to my soldiers. † And I placed a helmet of steel on my head, and I cloathed myself in the armour of Dauood, ‡ and I hung a scymetar of Missur by my side, and I sat on the throne of war.

AND I let loose the brave men of Tooraun, and the valiant men of Khorausaun, and the mighty men of Mauzinduraun, and of Kilaun; and I subdued the castle of Seewaus, and the castles of Goorjistaun; and I destroyed all the people who were in those castles: and the spoils of those castles I divided among my victorious forces. And I chastised the seditious and the plunderers of Azzurbauejaun.

AND after this I went to reduce the castles of Mulluteah and the neighbourhood thereof. And when I had subdued the castles, and had taken possession of them,

wards turned Mahummudan, and became a great favourite with Timour; to whom he gave a suit of Armour, which he pretended Dauood (i.e. David) the king of Israel had forged with his own hands in a smith's shop. Vid. *Hist. Timur-Bec*, Tom. I. p. 400.

This is the armour which Timour put on, on the present occasion.

I resolved

جمع شد بر تسخير حلب وحمسا همت بستم وباندك توجهي آن مملكت را مفتوح ساختم وكمر عزيمت بر تسخير ممالك مصر وشام بستم

وكنكاشي كه در مفتوح ساختن مصر وشام كردم اين بود

كه چون خبر شوكت وقدرت من بمسامع قيصر رسيد كه قلاع سيواس وملطيه وتوابع آنرا مسخر كردم ولشكرهاي ويرا كه در قلاع بودند همكي متفرق وپراكنده كردانيدم عرق غيرت وي بحركت در آمد وباغواي قرا يوسف تركمان كه ازصدمه لشكر من كريخته بود وپناه بقيصر برده بود بجنك قرار داد

ونكبت وزوال قيصر نزديك رسيده بود وقرا يوسف ويرا ترغيب نمود كه بر من لشكر كشد وقيصر باغواي قرا يوسف با لشكر كران بحركت در آمد وافواج مصر وشام را هم بمدد خواسته بود

ومن كنكاش كردم كه اكر من هم لشكر خودرا سه فوج سازم بهتر است اما فتح وهزيمت در پرده تقدير محجوب اند واز امرا كنكاش خواستم وسپاهيانه كنكاش كفتند كه بجنك مبادرت بايد نمود

وچون

I resolved to conquer Hullub and Humsau: † and I subdued that country with little labour. And I girded up the loins of my resolution to subdue the countries of Missur and of Shaum. ‡ Book I.

THE DESIGN which I formed for the reduction of Missur and of Shaum, was this.

WHEN the news of my power and my strength reached the ears of Keesur, || that I had conquered the castles of Seewaus and Mulluteah, and the dependencies thereof, and that I had dispersed and defeated all his soldiers, who were in those castles, he was very wroth. And at the instigation of Kurrau Eusoof, the Toorkumaun (who had fled from the shock of my army, and had sought shelter with Keesur) he resolved on war.

AND, behold, the ruin and overthrow of Keesur was at hand; and Kurrau Eusoof urged him that he should draw an army upon me. And Keesur, at the instigation of Kurrau Eusoof, came down with a mighty army; and he called the forces of Missur and of Shaum to his aid.

AND I reflected, that if I also divided my people into three armies, it would be better. But, behold, victory and defeat are hidden by the curtain of fate: and I demanded counsel of my Ameers. And they gave soldier-like counsel, saying, "Thou must go down to battle "with speed."

† Aleppo and Emessa. ‡ Egypt and Syria.

|| Cæsar: the title given by the Asiatic nations to the Turkish emperors.

وچون بخود فکر کردم چنین کنکاش
یافتم که آتش قیصر را بگرمي وسردي اطفا نمایم
ومکتوبي بقیصر نوشتم وخلاصه مضمونش آنکه
شکر است خداوند زمین وآسمان را که
اکثري از ممالک هفت اقلیم را در زیر فرمان من در
آورده وسلاطین وحکام عالم حلقه اطاعت مرا در گوش
جان کشیده اند خداي رحمت کند بر آن بنده که
حد خودرا بشناسد وپا جسارت از حد خویش فراتر ننهد
وبر عالمیان ظاهر است که نسب ونسبت
تو بکجا منتهي میشود پس مناسب حال تو آنست
که قدم جسارت پیش نکذاري وخودرا در ورطه رنج وبلا
نیندازي وباغواء جمعي از دولت راندکان که بواسطه
اغراض خود پناه بتو برده اند وفتنه خوابیده را بیدار
ساخته اند در فتنه وآشوب را بر روي دولت خود وا
نکني لیکن که ترا یوسف را نزد من فرستي والا آنچه
در پرده تقدیر است بعد از مقابله صفین بر تو ظاهر
خواهد شد

وچون این نامه را مصحوب ایلچیان
کاردان نزد قیصر فرستادم کنکاش خود را
درمین

AND when I reflected by myself, thus I found it was good, that I should extinguish the fire of Keesur by policy. And I wrote a letter to Keesur; and the substance of it was this.

"PRAISE is due to the God of the universe, that he hath brought under my authority many of the kingdoms of the seven regions of the world; and that the princes and rulers of the earth have submitted unto me. May God be merciful to that servant who knoweth his own limits, and who placeth not the foot of temerity beyond his proper bounds.

"WHERE thy race and lineage endeth, is known to all men. † It is therefore worthy of thy condition, that thou advance not forward the foot of presumption, and that thou throw not thyself into the abyss of affliction and calamity; and that thou open not the door of discord and desolation on thy empire at the instigation of the evil-minded, who have fled unto thee for their own ends, and have awakened the sleeping destruction; but that thou send bound unto me Kurrau Eusoof, the Toorkumaun: otherwise, that which is concealed by the curtain of fate, after our armies meet, will be known unto thee."

WHEN I had sent the letter to Keesur by the hands of experienced ambassadors, I found my advan-

† Alluding to the descent of Bajazet, which was supposed to have been from a Toorkumaun sailor.

درين يافتم كه بجانب دار ملک شام نهضت نمايم واز راه حمص وحلب روان شدم وچون بحلب رسيدم شنيدم كه ملک فرج پسر ملک برقوق از شنيدن خبر رسيدن من از مصر متوجه دمشق شد

ومن ايلغار كردم كه افواج مصر وشام را نگذارم كه بيكديكر ملحق شوند وملک فرج پيش دستي كرده خودرا بدمشق رسانيد ومن در عقب وي رسيده دمشق را مسخر ساختم

كنكاشي كه در تسخير بلاد روم وشكست دادن قيصر كردم اين بود

كه چون بلاد شام را مسخر كردانيدم وملک فرج پادشاه مصر وشام از جنگ من بگريخت وايلچي من از روم با جواب نا صواب ايلدرم بايزيد مراجعت نمود وعرض كرد كه چون خبر شكست عساكر مصر وشام بقيصر رسيد متفكر واشفته كرديد وتهيه يساق نمود

من تسخير دمشق وبلاد الشام نموده از راه موصل به بغداد نهضت نمودم وكنكاش كردم كه بجانب اذربايجان متوجه شوم تا قيصر اگر بر عزيمت خود مصمم باشد ظاهر شود

وچون

tage in this, that I ſhould go toward the chief city of Shaum. And I ſet out by the way of Hums and Hullub. And when I came to Hullub, I heard that Mullik Furruj, the ſon of Mullik Burkook, on hearing the news of my coming from Miſſur, had gone to Dummiſhk. †

AND I marched with ſpeed, that I might not permit the forces of Miſſur and the armies of Shaum to join themſelves together: but Mullik Furruj was quicker than I, and got to Dummiſhk. And I arrived after him at Dummiſhk, and reduced that city.

THE DESIGN which I formed for ſubduing the cities of Room, and for defeating the armies of Keeſur, was this.

WHEN I had conquered the cities of Shaum, and Mullik Furruj (the king of Miſſur and Shaum) had fled from my battle; my ambaſſador returned from Room, and brought the defiance of Yeldurrum Bauezzeed, ‡ and ſet forth — that when the news of the defeat of the armies of Miſſur and of Shaum came to Keeſur, that he was amazed and confounded, and prepared for war.

HAVING conquered Dummiſhk and the cities of Shaum, I went towards Bughdaud by the way of Mooſul. And I reſolved that I would turn toward Azzurbauejaun, that if Keeſur ſhould perſiſt in his intentions, it might be known.

† Damaſcus. ‡ Bajazet.

وچون بجانب تبریز روانه شدم بعضي از
امیر زادکانرا با افواج کران بر سر بغداد فرستادم
وسلطان احمد جالبر فرخ نامي را از نوکران خود
باسباب قلعه داري وجمیعت بسیار بمحافظه شهر
وقلعه بغداد کذاشته بود.

وامیر زادکان به بغداد رسیدند وشهر را
محاصره کردند وکار بجنک انجامید وحقیقت را
بمن عرضه داشت کردند

ومن کنکاش درین یافتم که خود رفته
شهر وقلعه بغداد را مستخلص کردانم واز راه تبریز
مراجعت نمودم وایلغار کردم وخودرا به بغداد رسانیدم
وبتدبیر واحتیاط سپاهکري ولوازم قلعه کیري پرداختم
وبعد از آنکه مدت محاصره بدو ماه وچند روز
کشید قلعه وشهر مسخر ومفتوح کردید

وفرخ قلعهدار در آب دجله غرق شد ومن
بشهر در آمدم وامر نمودم که جمیع مفسدان واوباش
شهر را بقتل رسانند وقلعه وعمارت شهر را انداخته
بخاک برابر سازند

واز بغداد بطرف اذربایجان عنان عزیمت
معطوف داشتم وچندکاه در آن مملکت طرح اقامت
انداختم

وچون

AND when I ſet out toward Tubburaze, I ſent down certain of the princes, with a mighty army upon Bughdaud. And Sooltaun Ahmud Jullauir had left one of his ſervants, whoſe name was Furrukh, with numerous forces, and the neceſſaries and the implements of defence, to guard the city and the caſtle of Bughdaud.

AND the princes arrived at Bughdaud, and they ſurrounded the city; and the people in the city oppoſed them: and they informed me thereof.

AND I found it was good that I myſelf ſhould go and reduce the city and the caſtle of Bughdaud. And I turned back by the way of Tubburaze, and I marched with ſpeed, and came to Bughdaud. And I beſieged Bughdaud; and when the ſiege had continued for two months and ſome days, the caſtle and the city of Bughdaud were conquered and ſubdued.

AND Furrukh, the governor, was drowned in the waters of the Tigris. And I entered into Bughdaud, and I commanded that they ſhould ſlay the ſeditious inhabitants of that city; and that they ſhould throw down the caſtle and the buildings thereof, and make them level with the earth.

AND from Bughdaud I turned the reins of my intention toward Azzurbauejaun; and I ſojourned in that kingdom for ſome time.

AND

وچون بمسامع من رسید که قیصر افواج
بر بلاد حلب وحمص ودیار بکر تعین نموده وقرا یوسف
ترکمان که از من گریخته بود وپناه بقیصر برده
براهزني وآزار قافله که بحرمین شریفین آمد وشد مي
نمایند مشغول است ودرین وقت جماعه آمدند واز
تعدي وستم وي دادخواه شدند وبر من لازم شد
که سزاي قرا یوسف را در کنارش نهم وقیصر را از
خواب غفلت بیدار سازم

درین باب کنکاش چنین یافتم که از
هر شهري وقبیله لشکر طلب دارم وحشر کرده بر سر
قیصر روان شوم وچون لشکرها جمع آمده بودند در
ماه رجب سنه هشتصد وچهار هجري از اذربایجان
بعزم رزم قیصر روانه شدم

وپیشتر از خود افواج تعین نمودم که
بر مملکت روم ترکتاز آورند وفوج دیکر تعین کردم
که منازل وآب وعلف را ملاحظه کنند واز راه انکوریه
متوجه شدم وقیصر با چهار صد هزار کس از سوار
وپیاده بمقابله ومدافعهء من شتافت وجنک انداختم
وفتح کردم وقیصر را لشکریان من دست کیر کرده
بحضور آوردند وبعد یورش هفت ساله مظفر ومنصور
بسمرقند مراجعت نمودم

AND when it reached my ears that Keesur had sent down armies on Hullub and on Hums, and on Deaur-a-bukkur; and that Kurrau Eusoof, the Toorkumaun (who had fled from before me and sought protection with Keesur) was employed in assaulting and molesting the Kauruvvaun which went to the sacred cities; (and at this time people came and demanded protection from his cruelty and oppression) it became my duty that I should chastise Kurrau Eusoof, and awaken Keesur from the sleep of forgetfulness.

AND in this matter I found it was good, that I should call out the forces of every city and of every tribe, and collect them together and go down upon Keesur. And when my forces were collected together, in the month of Rujjub, in the year of the Hijreh 804, I set out from Azzurbauejaun to wage war with Keesur.

AND I sent an army before me to ravage the kingdom of Room; and I sent another army to examine the stages, and the water, and the forage; and I went by the way of Angooreah. And Keesur with four hundred thousand men, horse-men and foot-men, advanced with speed to oppose and to expel me. And I assaulted him and obtained the victory; and my soldiers seized upon Keesur, and brought him into my presence. And after a war of seven years, I returned victorious and triumphant to Summurkund.

تزوكات تيمور

مقالت دوم

BOOK THE SECOND.

THE INSTITUTES OF TIMOUR.

تزوکات تیمور

مقالت دوم

فرزندان

ملک گیر کامکار ونبابر ذوي القدر جهاندارررا معلوم باد که چون از درگاه تنکري تعالي امید دارم که بسیاري از فرزندان واولاد واحفاد من بر مسند سلطنت ومملکت داري خواهند نشست بنابرین بر امور سلطنت خود تزوکات بر بسته دستور العمل آنرا انشا نمودم که هریک از فرزندان واولاد واحفاد من بدآن موجب عملنموده دولت وسلطنت مرا که برنجها ومحنتها وقزاقیها وجنکها بتاییدات رباني ومیامن نیروي ملت محمدي صلي الله علیه وسلم ودوستي آل عظام واصحاب کرام آنحضرت بچنک اورده ام نکاهباني نمایند

واین

BOOK THE SECOND.

THE INSTITUTES OF TIMOUR.

BE it known to my fortunate sons, the conquerors of kingdoms; to my mighty descendants, the lords of the earth; that since I have hope in Almighty God that many of my children, descendants, and posterity, shall sit upon the throne of power and regal authority; upon this account, having established laws and regulations for the well-governing of my dominions, I have collected together those regulations and laws as a model for others: to the end, that every one of my children, descendants, and posterity, acting agreeably thereto, my power and empire, which I acquired through hardships, and difficulties, and perils, and bloodshed, (by the divine Favour, and by the influence of the holy religion of Mahummud, (God's peace be upon him) and with the assistance of the powerful descendants and illustrious followers of that prophet) may be by them preserved.

AND

واين تزوكات را در امور سلطنت خويش دستور العمل سازند تا دولت وسلطنتي كه از من بايشان برسد از خلل وزوال ايمن باشد

اكنون سبيل فرزندان كامياب نامدار ونباير ممالك ستان ذوي الاقتدار آنكه همچنانچه من به دوازده امر كه شعار خود ساختم وبمرتبه سلطنت رسيدم وبدين دوازده امر مملكت كيري وملك داري كردم واورنك سلطنت خودرا زيب وزينت دادم ايشان نيز بهمين تزوك عملنمايند ودولت سلطنت مرا وخودرا نكاهباني كنند

واز جمله تزوكاتي كه بر دولت وسلطنت خود بر بستم اول اين بود كه دين خدا وشريعت محمد مصطفي را در دنيا رواج دادم وهميشه وهمه جاء تقويت دين اسلام نمودم

دويم آنكه با جماعه دوازده طبقه وطايفه ملك كيري وجهانداري كردم واركان دولت سلطنت خودرا بديشان استوار نمودم ومجلس خودرا از ايشان

† The maxims here mentioned are not the twelve following rules, but those given at length in the 18th, 19th, and 20th pages of the MS.

آراسته

AND let them make these regulations the rule of their conduct in the affairs of their empire, that the fortune, and the power, which shall descend from me to them, may be safe from discord and dissolution.

NOW therefore be it known to my sons, the fortunate and the illustrious, to my descendants, the mighty subduers of kingdoms; that, in like manner as I by twelve maxims, † which I established as the rules of my conduct, attained to regal dignity; and with the assistance of these maxims conquered and governed kingdoms, and decorated and adorned the throne of my empire; let them also act according to these regulations, and preserve the splendor of mine and their dominions.

AND among the rules which I established for the support of my glory and empire, the FIRST was this—That I promoted the worship of Almighty God, and propagated the religion of the sacred Mahummud throughout the world; and at all times, and in all places, supported the true faith.

SECONDLY, with the people of the twelve classes and tribes I conquered and governed kingdoms; and with them I strengthened the pillars of my fortune, and from them I formed my assembly. ‡

‡ The twelve classes of men, here alluded to, are fully described in a subsequent part of the institutes.

آراستـه ساختـم

سیوم آنکه بمشاورت وکنکاش وتدبیرات وحـزم واحتیاط فوجهارا شکستم وملکهارا مسخر خود ساختم وامـور سلطنت خـودرا بمدارا ومروت وتحمل وتغافل از پیش بردم وبدوستان وبدشمنان مدارا نمودم

چهارم به توره وبه تزوک کارخانه سلطنت خودرا بند وبست نمودم وبه تـوره وبـه تزوک خودرا بمرتبه قایم نگاهداشتم که امرا ووزرا وسپاه ورعیت از مـرتبه خود تجاوز نتوانستند نمود وهریک حافظ مرتبه خود مي بـودنـد

پنجـم امـرا وسپاه خودرا باولي* دادم وایشان را بـزر وزیـور خـوشدل ساختم ودر بزمها اورن دادم ودر رزمها جـانفشاني کردند ودرم ودینار را از ایشان دریغ نداشتم وبجهت آساني کارهاي ایشان محنت ومشقت ایشـان را خود بر میداشتم وتربیت ایشان مینمودم تا آنکه ببازوي مـردي ومردانکي

† The word which I have rendered *policy*, cannot be tranflated into the Englifh language with any degree of force or energy. It fignifies *political* inattention

واتفاق

THIRDLY, by consultation, and deliberation, and provident measures; by caution, and by vigilance I vanquished armies, and I reduced kingdoms to my authority. And I carried on the business of my empire by complying with times and occasions, and by generosity, and by patience, and by policy; † and I acted with courteousness towards my friends and towards my enemies.

FOURTHLY, by order and by discipline I regulated the concerns of my government; and by discipline and by order I so firmly established my authority, that the Ameers, and the Vizzeers, and the soldiers, and the subjects, could not aspire beyond their respective degrees; and every one of them was the keeper of his own station.

FIFTHLY, I gave encouragement to my Ameers and to my soldiers, and with money and with jewels I made them glad of heart; and I permitted them to come into the banquet; and in the field of blood they hazarded their lives. And I withheld not from them my gold nor my silver. And I educated and trained them to arms; and to alleviate their sufferings, I myself shared in their labours, and in their hardships; until, with the arm of fortitude and resolution, and with the unanimity of my

inattention or negligence, or *pretending* not to see or discover such things as it would be improper, or impolitical, to take notice of.

واتـفـاق امـرا وسپهسـالاران وبهادران بضرب شمشیر تختگاه بیست وهـفـت پادشاه را مسخر ساختم ودر ممالـک ایران وتـوران وروم ومغرب وشام ومصر وعراق عرب وعجم ومازندران وگیلانات وشروانات وازربایجان وفـارس وخراسان ودشت جته ودشت قپچاق وخوارزم وخـتن وکابلستان وباختر زمین وهندوستان پادشاه شدم وفرمان فرما گشتم

وچـون جامـهء سلطنت در پوشیدم از عـافـیـت وغنودن بر بستر راحت چشم پوشیدم واز دوازده سالگي تنرها زدم ومحنتها کشیدم وتدبیرها کـردم وفوجها شکستم واز امرا وسپاه نفاقـهـا دیدم وسخنان تلخ شنیدم وبتحمل وتغافل گذرانیدم وبذات خـود شمشیرها زدم تا آنکه بر ولایات وممالـک مسلط شـدم ونـامـور گـشـتـم

ششم به عدالـت وانصاف خلق خدارا از خود راضي داشتم وبر گناه کار وبي گناه رحم کردم

chiefs, and my generals, and my warriors, by the edge of the ſword I obtained poſſeſſion of the thrones of ſeven and twenty kings; and became the king and the ruler of the kingdoms of Eraun and of Tooraun; and of Room, and of Mughrib, and of Shaum; and of Miſſur, and of Erauk-a-Arrub, and of Ajjum; and of Mauzinduraun, and of Kylaunaut; and of Shurvaunaut, and of Azzurbauejaun; and of Fauris, and of Khorauſaun; and of the Duſht of Jitteh, and the Duſht of Kipchauk; and of Khauruzm, and of Khuttun, and of Kauboolıſtaun; and of Hindoſtaun, and of Baukhtur Zemeen. Book II.

AND when I cloathed myſelf in the robe of empire, I ſhut my eyes to ſafety, and to the repoſe which is found on the bed of eaſe. And from the twelfth year of my age I travelled over countries, and combated difficulties, and formed enterpriſes, and vanquiſhed armies; and experienced mutinies amongſt my officers and my ſoldiers, and was familiarized to the language of diſobedience; (and I oppoſed them with policy and with fortitude) and I hazarded my perſon in the hour of danger; until in the end I vanquiſhed kingdoms and empires, and eſtabliſhed the glory of my name.

SIXTHLY, by juſtice and equity I gained the affections of the people of God; and I extended my clemency to the guilty as well as to the innocent; and I

کردم وحکم بر حق کردم وباحسان در دلهاي خلق مقام نهودم وبسياست وانصاف سپاه ورعيت مرا در ميانه اميد وبيم نکاهداشتم وبر رعايا وزيردستان ترحم کردم وبسپاه انعام دادم

وداد مظلوم از ظالم کرفتم وبعد از اثبات ظلم مالي وبدني موافق شرع در ميانه ايشان محاکمه نهودم وبکناه ديکري ديکري را نکرفتم

وکساني که بمن بديها کرده بر من شهشيرها کشيده بودند ودر کار من شکستها رسانيده بودند چون بمن التجا آوردند اعزاز ايشان نهوده بر مرتبه ايشان افزودم وبر کردارهاي بد ايشان قلم نسيان کشيدم وبنوعي بايشان سلوک نهودم که اکر خدشه در خاطر ايشان بود بالکليه محو شد

هفتم سادات وعلما ومشايخ وعقلا ومحدثين اخباررا برکزيده داشتم وتعظيم واحترام ايشان نهودم وارباب شجاعت را دوست داشتم چه

تنکري

paſſed that ſentence which truth required: and by benevolence I gained a place in the hearts of men; and by rewards and puniſhments I kept both my troops and my ſubjects divided between hope and fear. And I compaſſionated the lower ranks of my people, and thoſe who were diſtreſſed. And I gave gifts to the ſoldiers.

AND I delivered the oppreſſed from the hand of the oppreſſor; and after proof of the oppreſſion, whether on the property or the perſon, the deciſion which I paſſed between them was agreeable to the ſacred law. And I did not cauſe any one perſon to ſuffer for the guilt of another. †

THOSE who had done me injuries, who had attacked my perſon in battle, and had counteracted my ſchemes and enterpriſes, when they threw themſelves on my mercy, I received them with kindneſs; I conferred on them additional honours, and I drew the pen of oblivion over their evil actions. And I treated them in ſuch ſort, that if ſuſpicion remained in their hearts, it was plucked out entirely.

SEVENTHLY, I ſelected out, and treated with eſteem and veneration, the poſterity of the Prophet, and the Theologians, and the Teachers of the true Faith, and the Philoſophers, and the Hiſtorians. And I loved

† In this obſervation he alludes to a too frequent cuſtom of the Eaſt, of involving the whole family and connections of an attainted perſon in the ſame puniſhment with the guilty ſubject.

men

تنکري تعالي شجاع را دوست ميدارد وبا علما صحبت داشتم وبر دلهاي اصحاب قلوب رفتم واز ايشان دريوزه همت نمودم واز انفاس متبرکه ايشان التماس فاتحه کردم ودرويشان وفقرا را دوست داشتم وايشان را آزرده ومحروم نساختم واشرار وبدکويانرا در مجلس خود راه ندادم وبسخن ايشان عمل نکردم وبدکويء ايشان را در حق هيچکس نشنيدم

هشتم بعزيمت عمل کردم وبر هر کاري که عازم مي شدم همان کار پيش نهاد همت خود ميساختم وتا باتمام نميرسانيدم دست از آن کار باز نميداشتم وبر کفتار خود عامل مي بودم وبر هيچکس سخت نکرفتم وهيچ کاري را به تندي نکردم تا تنکري تعالي بر من سخت نکيرد وکار من بر من تنک نسازد

وقوانين وسيرت سلاطين کذشته را از آدم تا خاتم واز خاتم تا اين دم از دانايان پرسش نمودم وسلوک ومعاش وافعال واقوال يکان يکان را بخاطر آوردم واز اخلاق حسنه وصفات پسنديده ايشان نسخه برداشتم وسبب زوال دولتهاي ايشان پرسش نمودم

men of courage and valour; for God Almighty loveth the brave. And I associated with good and learned men; and I gained their affections, and I entreated their support, and I sought success from their holy Prayers. And I loved the Dervishes, and the poor; and I oppressed them not, neither did I exclude them from my favour. And I permitted not the evil and the malevolent to enter into my council; and I acted not by their advice: and I listened not to their insinuations to the prejudice of others.

EIGHTHLY, I acted with resolution; and on whatever undertaking I resolved, I made that undertaking the only object of my attention: and I withdrew not my hand from that enterprise, until I had brought it to a conclusion. And I acted according to that which I said. And I dealt not with severity towards any one, and I was not oppressive in any of my actions; that God Almighty might not deal severely towards me, nor render my own actions oppressive unto me.

AND I enquired of learned men into the laws and regulations of antient princes, from the days of Adam to those of the prophet, and from the days of the Prophet down to this time. And I weighed their institutions, and their actions, and their opinions, one by one. And from their approved manners, and their good qualities, I selected models. And I enquired into the causes of the subversion of their power, and I shunned those

actions

نمودم وانچه موجب زوال وانتقال دولت بود از آن
اجتناب کردم واز ظلم وفسق که انقطاع نسل میکند
وقحط ووبا مي آرد احتراز لازم دانستم

نهم از احوال رعیت آگاه شدم وکلانان
ایشان را بمنزله برادر وخوردان ایشان را بجاي فرزند
دانستم وبر مزاج وطبایع هر ملک وهر شهر خودرا
وافق ساختم وبه اهالي واکابر واشراف اشناي
کردم وموافق مزاج وطبیعت وخواهش ایشان بر
ایشان حاکم تعین نمودم

واز احوال اهالي هر دیار آگاه مي بودم
واخبار نویسان راست قلم با دیانت در هر مملکت
تعین کردم که کیفیت اطوار واوضاع واعمال
وافعال سپاه ورعیت را ومواقعي که در میان ایشان
بوقوع آید بمن نویسند واگر خلاف انچه نوشته
بودند بر من ظاهر مي شد اخبار نویسان را
سیاست مي نمودم وانچه از ظلم وجور حاکم وسپاه
ورعیت مي شنیدم تدارک آنرا بانصاف وعدالت
مي کردم

دهم

actions which tend to the destruction and overthrow of regal authority. And from cruelty and from oppression, which are the destroyers of posterity, and the bringers of famine and of plagues, I found it was good to abstain.

NINTHLY, the situation of my people was known unto me. And those who were great among them, I considered as my brethren; and I regarded the poor as my children. And I made myself acquainted with the tempers and the dispositions of the people of every country and of every city. And I contracted intimacies with the citizens, and the chiefs, and the nobles; and I appointed over them governors adapted to their manners, and their dispositions, and their wishes.

AND I knew the circumstances of the inhabitants of every province. And in every kingdom I appointed writers of intelligence, men of truth and integrity, that they might send me information of the conduct, and the behaviour, and the actions, and the manners, of the troops and of the inhabitants, and of every occurrence that might come to pass amongst them. And if I discovered ought contrary to their information, I inflicted punishment on the intelligencer; and every circumstance of cruelty and oppression in the governors, and in the troops, and in the inhabitants, which reached my ear, I chastised agreeably to justice and equity.

دهم هر طايفه وهر قبيله از ترک وتاچک
وعرب وعجم که بدولتخانه من در آمدند بزرگان
ايشان را گرامي داشتم وساير ايشانرا فراخور احوال
نوازش نمودم وبه نيکان ايشان نيکي کردم وبدان
ايشانرا به بدي ايشان سپردم

وهر کس بمن دوستي کرد قدر دوستي
ويرا فراموش نکردم وبوي مروت واحسان نمودم وهرکس
خدمت من کرد حق خدمت ويرا ادا کردم وهر
کس بمن دشمني کرد وپشيمان شده بمن التجا
آورد وزانوزد دشمني ويرا فراموش کردم وبدوستي
ومروت خريدار وي شدم

چنانچه شير بهرام امير الوس بمن همراه
بود ودر وقت کار مرا گذاشت وبغنيم ملحق شد
وبر من شمشير کشيد وآخر نمک من ويرا گرفت
وباز بمن التجا آورد وزانوزد چون مردي بود اصيل
ومردانه وکارکرده از کردارها بد وي چشم پوشيدم
وويرا بنواختم وبر مرتبه وي افزودم وويرا بمردانکي
وي بخشيدم

يازدهم

TENTHLY, whatever tribe, and whatever hord, whether Toork or Taucheek, or Arrub or Ajjum, came in unto me, I received their chiefs with diſtinction and reſpect, and their followers I honoured according to their degrees and their ſtations. And to the good among them I did good, and the evil I delivered over to their evil actions.

AND whoever attached himſelf unto me, I forgot not the merit of his attachment, and I acted towards him with kindneſs and generoſity: and whoever had rendered me ſervices, I repaid the value of thoſe ſervices unto him. And whoever had been my enemy, and was aſhamed thereof, and flying to me for protection, humbled himſelf before me, I forgot his enmity; and I purchaſed him with liberality and kindneſs.

IN ſuch manner Share Behraum, the chief of a tribe, was along with me. And he left me in the hour of action, and he united with the enemy, and he drew forth his ſword againſt me. And at length my ſalt, which he had eaten, ſeized upon him; and he again fled to me for refuge, and humbled himſelf before me. As he was a man of illuſtrious deſcent, and of bravery, and of experience, I covered my eyes from his evil actions; and I magnified him, and I exalted him to a ſuperior rank; and I pardoned his diſloyalty in conſideration of his valour.

یازدهم فرزندان وخویشان وآشنایان وهمسایکان وکساني که با من آشنایي داشتند ایشانرا در وقت دولت ونعمت بنواختم وحق ایشان را ادا کردم وبا فرزندان وخویشان قطع صلهء رحم ننمودم وبکشتن وبستن ایشان امر نکردم

وهر کسرا بهر طرزي شناخته بودم فراخور شناخت خود بوي سلوک نمودم چون کرم وسرد روزکار بسیار دیدم وتجربها برداشتم با دوست ودشمن سازکاربها کردم

دوازدهم سپاه دوست ودشمن را عزیز داشتم که متاع باقي خودرا بمال فاني میفروشند ودر معارک ومهالک خودرا مي اندازند وجان فشاني مینمایند

ومردي که از جانب دشمن با من خصمي کرد وشمشیر کشید ونسبت با ولي نعمت خود راسخ الاعتقاد بود ویرا بسیار دوست داشتم وچون نزد من آمد قدر ویرا دانسته معتمد خود ساختم وبوفا وحقیقت ویرا شناختم

† Timour appears to allude to those persons whom he knew in the days of his obscurity.

Book II.

ELEVENTHLY, my children, and my relations, and my aſſociates, and my neighbours, and ſuch as had been connected with me, † all theſe I diſtinguiſhed in the days of my fortune and proſperity, and I paid unto them their due. And with reſpect to my family, I rent not aſunder the bands of conſanguinity and mercy; and I iſſued not commands to ſlay them, or to bind them with chains. ‡

AND I dealt with every man, whatever the judgment I had formed of him, according to my own opinion of his worth. As I had ſeen much of proſperity and adverſity, and had acquired knowledge and experience, I conducted myſelf with caution, and with policy, towards my friends and towards my enemies.

TWELFTHLY, ſoldiers, whether aſſociates or adverſaries, I held in eſteem; thoſe who ſell their permanent happineſs to periſhable honour, and throw themſelves into the field of ſlaughter and battle, and hazard their lives in the hour of danger.

AND the man, who drew his ſword on the ſide of my enemy, and committed hoſtilities againſt me, and preſerved his fidelity to his maſter, him I greatly honoured; and when ſuch a man came unto me, knowing his worth, I claſſed him with my faithful aſſociates; and I reſpected and valued his fidelity and his attachment.

‡ This obſervation is ſtrictly conſiſtent with his conduct: for though ſeveral of his relations, and ſome of his children, at different times rebelled againſt him, he ever ſubſtituted *pardon* in the place of *puniſhment*.

AND

وآن سپاهي که حق نمک ووفا داري را
فراموش کرد ووقت کار از صاحب خود رو کردان
شد ونزد من آمد ويرا دشمنترين مردم دانستم
ودر جنک توقتمش خان امراي وي
بمن پيغامها کردند وعرايض نوشتند وحق نمک
توقتمش خان را که صاحب ايشان ودشمن من بود
فراموش کردند بر ايشان نفرين کردم که حق ولي
نعمت خودرا فراموش کرده حقيقت ووفارا بر کوشه
نهاده اند ونزد من آمدند با خود کفتم که با مربي
خود چه وفا کردند که با من خواهند کرد

وچون بتجربه من رسيد که هر دولتي
که به ديني وآييني قايم نباشد وبتوره وتزوک استوار
نبود شکوه وسطوت وبند وبست از آن سلطنت برخيزد
وآن سلطنت مثل مردي برهنه باشد که هرکس ويرا
به بيند چشم بپوشد وچون خانه باشد که سقف
ودر ودربند نداشته باشد وکس ناکس در آن داخل
توانند شد
بدين جهت بناي سلطنت خودرا به
دين وآيين اسلام وبه توره وتزوک استحکام دادم
وواقعات وامورى که مرا در سلطنت پيش مي
آمد

AND the ſoldier, who forgot his duty and his honour, and in the hour of action turned his face from his maſter, and came in unto me, I conſidered as the moſt deteſtable of men. Book II.

AND in the war with Touktummiſh Khaun, his Ameers forgot their duty to Touktummiſh, who was their maſter and my foe, and ſent propoſals and wrote letters unto me. And I uttered execrations upon them; becauſe unmindful of that which they owed to their lord, they had thrown aſide their honour and their duty, and come in unto me. I ſaid unto myſelf, What fidelity have they obſerved to their liege lord? What fidelity will they ſhew unto me?

AND, behold, it was known unto me by experience, that every empire, which is not eſtabliſhed in morality and religion, nor ſtrengthened by regulations and laws, from that empire all order, grandeur and power ſhall paſs away. And that empire may be likened unto a naked man, who, when expoſed to view, commandeth the eye of modeſty to be covered: and it is like unto a houſe, which hath neither roof, nor gates, nor defences; into which, whoever willeth, may enter unmoleſted.

THEREFORE, I eſtabliſhed the foundation of my empire on the morality and the religion of Iſlaum; and by regulations, and laws I gave it ſtability. And by laws and by regulations, I executed every buſineſs and every

آمد بتوره وتزوک آن کاررا انجام میدادم

واول تزوک که از مشرق دلم سرزد
رواج دین وتقویت شریعت محمدي بود صلي الله
علیه وسلم ودر ممالک واقطار وامصار عالم دین اسلام
وشریعت خیر الانام را رواج دادم وسلطنت خودرا
بشریعت آراسته ساختم

تزوک رواج دین مبین چنین کردم که
یکي از سادات ذي قدررا بصدارت اهل اسلام مقرر
کردم که ضبط اوقات نماید ومتولیان تعین کند
وبهر شهري وبلدي اقضي القضات ومفتي ومحتسب
معین سازد وسیورغال ووظایف از براي سادات وعلما
ومشایخ وارباب استحقاق گرداند

وقاضي از براي عسکر وقاضي
از براي رعیت نصب نمودم وبهر مملکتي

† The man appointed to fill the station mentioned in the original, is called *Sedr*. He is a person of great authority in the empire, who has the absolute

شیخ

every tranſaction that came before me in the courſe of my government. Book II.

AND the firſt regulation which my heart dictated unto me, was the promulgation of the true faith, and the ſupport of the ſacred tenets of Mahummud (God's peace be upon him). And I encouraged the progreſs of the holy laws and the religion of Iſlaum through all the cities, and the provinces, and the kingdoms of the earth; and I adorned my empire by the ſacred laws.

THUS I regulated the promulgation of the true faith. I appointed a man of holineſs,† and of illuſtrious dignity, to watch over the conduct of the faithful, that he might regulate the manners of the times, and appoint ſuperiors in holy offices; and eſtabliſh in every city and in every town a judge of penetration, and a doctor learned in the ſacred law, and a ſupervisor of the markets, of the weights and of the meaſures: and that he might ordain penſions and ſalaries for the deſcendants of the prophet, and for ſuperior eccleſiaſtics, and for holy men, and for men of knowledge.

AND I eſtabliſhed a judge for the army and a judge for the ſubjects: and I ſent into every province

abſolute management of church lands, and what revenues are appropriated towards the maintaining of public ſchools, ſalaries to learned men, and other pious uſes.

 and

شیخ الاسلامي فرستادم که اهل اسلام از معاصي باز
دارد وامر معروف نماید

وامر کردم که در هر شهري مساجد
وخانقاهها تعمیر نمایند وبر سر راهها رباطات بنا کنند
وبر نهرها پل بر بندند

وعلما ومدرسان بهر شهري تعین کردم
که اهل اسلام را مسایل دیني وعقاید شرعي تعلیم
دهند وعلم دین از تفسیر وحدیث وفقه بمسلمانان
درس کویند

وامر نمودم که صدر وقاضي مهمات
شرعي ممالک محروسه را بعرض من میرسانیده
باشند وامیر عدل تعین نمودم که مرافعات عرفي
سپاه ورعیت را بعرض رساند

چون تزوک دین نمودم ودر بلاد اسلام
شریعت را رواج دادم وچون اوازه رواج دین واسلام
بمسامع صغار وکبار اهل اسلام رسید علماي اسلام
فتوي نوشتند —— که چون الله تعالي در هر
صد سال مروجي ومجددي از براي رواج
وتجدید

and kingdom an inſtructor in the law, to deter the faithful from thoſe things which are forbidden, and to lead them in the truth. Book II.

AND I commanded that they ſhould build places of worſhip and monaſteries in every city; and that they ſhould erect ſtructures for the reception of travellers on the high roads, and that they ſhould make bridges acroſs the rivers.

AND I appointed eccleſiaſtics and religious teachers in every city, to inſtruct the followers of Iſlaum in the abſtruſe and fundamental principles of our holy law; and to preach to them the doctrines of religion, with the holy traditions, and the ſacred commentaries upon them.

AND I ordered that the ſuddur † and the judge, from time to time, ſhould lay before me all the eccleſiaſtical affairs of my empire; and I appointed a judge in equity, that he might tranſmit unto me all civil matters of litigation, that came to paſs amongſt my troops and my ſubjects.

WHEN I had regulated all religious concerns, and had promoted the progreſs of the ſacred tenets throughout the cities of Iſlaum; and when the rumour of the promulgation of the true faith had reached the ears of all ranks of the faithful; the doctors of our holy faith publiſhed a decree — That as Almighty God in each century had ſent a promoter and propagator of the faith,

† Or *Sedr*: ſee note on p. 177.

وتجديد دين محمدي صلي الله عليه وسلم بر
مي انكيزند ودرين صد هشتم تجديد دين را
امير صاحب قران نموده پس مجدد دين محمدي
ايشان باشند

ومير سيد شريف كه از فحول علماي
زمان بود درين باب مكتوبي بمن نوشت —— كه
اتفاق علماي خلف وسلف برين رفته كه در سر
هر صد سال از حضرت رسالت پناه الله تعالي از براي
رواج دين محمدي صلي الله عليه وسلم مجددي
مي انگيزد وچون درين سر صد هشتم امير
صاحب قران دين متين را رواج داده اند ودر اقطار
وامصار عالم دين واسلام رواج يافته بتحقيق رسيد كه
مروج دين امير صاحب قران است وصورت مكتوب
اينست

كه اللهم انصره من نصر دين محمد
واخذل من خذل دين محمد
چون از زمان هجرت حضرت رسالت
پناه الي يومنا هذا هشت صد سال گذشته ودر سر
هر

for the promulgation and restoration of the religion of Mahummud (God's peace be upon him); and as in the eighth century AMEER SAUHIBA KURRAUN† hath restored the purity of the holy laws, he therefore must be THE RESTORER OF THE RELIGION OF MAHUMMUD. Book II.

AND Meer Siud Shurreef, the most respectable of the doctors of the age, wrote unto me on this subject, saying, 'The holy men of all ages have agreed, 'that in every century from the days of the prophet, 'Almighty God hath sent forth a propagator of the faith, 'for the purpose of promulgating the religion of Mahummud (God's peace be upon him): and since in the 'beginning of this the eighth century, Ameer Sauhiba 'Kurraun, hath propagated the laws of the holy prophet, and the true religion hath been diffused throughout the different cities and kingdoms of the earth; 'it is apparent that Ameer Sauhiba Kurraun is the true 'promoter and supporter of the faith.' And the Letter is this.

"O God assist thou the promoter of the religion of thy prophet, and abandon thou the deserter of the faith of Mahummud.

"SINCE from the time of the Hijrut of the great and holy apostle down to the present period 800 years have elapsed, and since the pure and omnipotent

† *Sauhiba Kurraun* is a royal title first assumed by Timour. It literally signifies *Lord of the Conjunction*; it being said, that there was a fortunate conjunction of planets at his birth.

Creator

هر صد سال الله تعالي وتقدس از براي رواج دين
رسول وحبيب خود مروجي ومجددي بر انكيخته
كه تجديد دين وملت آنحضرت نمايد الحمد لله
كه در سر صد هشتم الله تعالي امير صاحب قران را
مجدد ومروج دين اسلام بر انكيخته كه دين
محمدي را در بلاد وممالك رواج داده اند

واز انچه علماي سلف از احوال مجددان
دين تتبع نموده در تصانيف خود نوشته اند اين اثير
از آنست
كه در سر مايهء اول از هجرت مجدد
دين عمر عبد اللعزيز است كه چون دين اسلام
بواسطه طعن ولعن كه خوارج بر منابر بر حضرت علي
مي كفتند ضعيف شده بود بر طرف ساخت
وبغض وعداوتي كه ميان اهل اسلام
بوقوع آمده بود چنانچه كروهي خلفاء راشدين را
لعن وطعن مخصوص ميداشتند وجمعي ديكر بر
امير المومنين علي وحسين وعباس لعن ميكردند وبا
يكدكر در مقام تعصب ونقاضت مي بودند رفع
نمود وتجديد دين كرد

ودر

Creator hath in each century inſpired and ſent forth a promoter and reſtorer of religion, for the advancement of the faith of his meſſenger and friend, and the re-eſtabliſhment of his ſacred doctrines; praiſe be to the moſt high! that in the beginning of this the eighth century Ameer Sauhiba Kurraun, who hath encouraged and eſtabliſhed the holy religion of Mahummud in various nations and regions of the earth, is by the Almighty evidently appointed the reſtorer and promoter of the faith of Iſlaum. Book II.

"FROM all that former Theologians have diſcovered and inſerted in their works concerning the promoters of our holy faith, the following are ſelections.

"IN the FIRST CENTURY from the Hijrut Omur Abdul Azeez ſtood forth the ſupporter of the faith. For when the holy religion of Iſlaum was weakened by the revilings of the ſchiſmatics, who dared to execrate from their pulpits the moſt excellent Aali, he aboliſhed that profane practice.

"AND whereas diviſions and hatred had ſprung up amongſt the followers of Iſlaum, ſo that one faction fulminated curſes on the three orthodox Khalifs, whilſt their opponents denounced execrations on Aali (the commander of the faithful) on Hooſſein and on Ubbaus; and at length proceeded to open diſſentions and hoſtilities; he put an end to thoſe diviſions, and by ſo doing gave ſtrength to our holy law.

AND

ودر سر مايهء دوم مجدد دين مامون
الرشيد است كه هفتاد دو مذاهب باطله را بر طرف
ومنسوخ ساخته مذهب بر حق سنت وجماعت را رواج
داد وعلي ابن موسي جعفر را رضي الله عنهم از
خراسان طلب نمود وويرا ولي عهد گردانيد وباذن
وي در مملكت تصرف مي نمود

ودر سر مايهء سيوم مروج دين محمدي
صلي الله عليه وسلم مقتدر بالله عباسي است كه
چون قوم قرامطه كه ريس ايشان ابو طاهر بود بر مكه
معظمه مستولي شد وسي هزار محرم را در روز عرفه
قتل نموده بدرجه شهادت رسانيد وحجر الاسود را
از اركان خانه كعبه بركند وبلاد اسلام خراب كرده
قتل وغارت مينمود وبدين جهت دين اسلام ضعيف
شد مقتدر بالله بر آن قوم لشكر كشيد وايشانرا
برانداخت ودين اسلام وشريعت را رواج داد

ودر سر مايهء چهارم از مروجان دين محمدي
صلي الله عليه وسلم عضد الدوله ديلمي است كه
چون

"AND the ſupporter of the faith in the SECOND CENTURY was Maumoon ul Ruſheed. For he abrogated and annulled ſeventy two pernicious and unorthodox tenets, and eſtabliſhed the true rites and ceremonies on the faith of the Sunna, and on the ſacred traditions. And he called Aali, the ſon of Mooſi Jaufir (on whom be the bleſſing of God) from Khorauſaun; and appointed him ſucceſſor to the Immaumut, and with his conſent took poſſeſſion of the government. Book II.

"AND in the THIRD CENTURY Mocktaudir Billau Ubbauſi was the promoter of the faith. For when the ſect of the Kuraumuteh, headed by Abou Tauhir, ſeized the holy city of Mecca, and martyred 30,000 pilgrims on mount Auruffaut; when that impious chief cauſed the Black Stone to be torn from the corner of the ſacred Caaba, deſolated the cities of Iſlaum, and plundered and ſlaughtered the inhabitants (by which a mighty blow was given to our holy religion) Mocktaudir Billau drew forth his armies againſt that abandoned ſect, and extirpated them from the face of the earth: and thus ſupported and defended the laws and the faith of Iſlaum.

"AND in the FOURTH CENTURY Azzud u Dowla Delumi was the ſupporter of the religion of Mahummud, on whom be God's peace and bleſſing. For when, on

چون بواسطه نسق وفجور مطيع لامر الله عباسي وظلم توابع ولواحق وي دين اسلام ضعيف شده بود ودر بلاد اسلام انواع فسق ومنهيات شيوع يافته بود عضد الدوله ويرا از خلافت عزل نمود وپسر وي طالع بالله ولي عهد ساخت

وعضد الدوله خود متصدي رواج دين شد ورفع ودفع بدعت ونا مشروعات وظلم وجور نموده شريعت محمدي را رواج داد

ودر سر مايهء پنجم مروج دين وشريعت سلطان سنجر ابن سلطان ملكشاه است كه شيخ احمد جامي وحكيم سناي معاصر وي بوده واو بديشان مريد بود دربن ايام ملاحده وجهال دين اسلام را ضعيف ساخته بودند وي بقتل وقمع ملاحده مبادرت نمود وبمرتبه در اطاعت ومتابعت دين محمدي صلي الله عليه وسلم مبالغه مينمود كه خلاف شريعت از وي امري سر نميزد

ودر سر مايهء ششم مجدد دين غازان خان بن ارغون خان بن هلاكو خانست كه چون دين اسلام بواسطه استيلاي كفره تركستان ضعيف شد

account of the wickedneſs and corruption of Muttei la-umurilla Ubbauſi, and the oppreſſions and perſecutions exerciſed by his ſervants and dependants, our holy religion was neglected, and corruption and impiety became notorious in the cities of Iſlaum; Azzud u Dowla depoſed him from the Khillaufut, placed his ſon Taulaa Billau on the vacant throne, and by his exertions re-eſtabliſhed the true faith. Book II.

AND Azzud u Dowla aboliſhed innovations and things unlawful, ſtopped the current of injuſtice and oppreſſion, and thus ſupported the holy laws of Mahummud.

AND Sooltaun Sunjur, the ſon of Sooltaun Mullik Shaah, and the contemporary and diſciple of Sheikh Ahmud Jaumi and Hukkeem Sunaï, was the promoter of the faith and the laws in the FIFTH CENTURY. For he extirpated the heretics who in thoſe days had weakened the faith of Iſlaum; and paid ſuch pious obedience to the holy doctrines of Mahummud (God's peace be upon him) that in the period of his life he was not guilty of one action prohibited by the ſacred laws.

IN the SIXTH CENTURY the ſupporter of the faith was Ghauzaun Khaun the ſon of Arghoon Khaun, the ſon of Hullaukoo Khaun. For when the holy religion was almoſt annihilated by the conqueſts of the infidels of Toorkiſtaun, Ghauzaun Khaun with one hundred

شـد الله تـعـالي غـازان خانـرا با صد هزار ترک
بر انگيخت که همکي بيک مرتبه در صحراي لار
بدست شيخ ابراهـيـم حموي ايمان آورده مسلمان
شدند وزبان بکلمه لا اله الا الله ومحمد رسول الله
کويا ساختند

واثار کفر وبدعت بر انداختند وشريعت را
در بلاد وامصار رواج دادند

ودر سر مايهء هفتم الجايتو سلطان بن
ارغون خان است که ملقب بسلطان محمد خدابنده
شد که در سنه مذکـور بعد از برادرش غازان خان
بـر تخت سلطنت نشست وچـون بمسامع وي رسيد
که دين محمدي بمرتبه ضعيف شده که در نماز
بعد از تشهد صلوات بر محمد وبر آل محمد نميفرستند
خود برخاسته بمسجد جامع سلطانيه حاضر آمد وحکم
باحضار علماي اسلام نمود

از فـضايـل در بـاب صلوات فـرستادن
بر پيغمبر وآل پيغمبر سوال نمود علما باتفاق کفتند
که بحکم خداي تعالي صلوات بر محمد وبـر آل
محمد بايد فرستاد

ودرين

dred thousand Toorks (such was the will of the Almighty) were at one time converted to the Mahummudan faith by Sheikh Ibraheem Hummuee in the plain of Laur; and joined in the sacred exclamation, "There is no God but "God, and Mahummud is the Apostle of God." Book II.

"AND Ghauzaun Khaun rooted out idolatry and heresy; and established the holy laws amongst the surrounding nations.

"THE supporter of the faith in the SEVENTH CENTURY was Aljauetoo Sooltaun, the son of Arghoon Khaun, who was also named Sultaun Mahummud Khodau Bundeh. For when he succeeded his brother Ghauzaun Khaun at the above period, and was informed that the duties of our holy religion were neglected to such a degree, that the people, after the profession of their faith, did not include the posterity of Mahummud in their blessings and benedictions on that holy prophet; he himself arose and went forth to the imperial Musjid, and commanded the Theologians to be assembled before him.

"AND he demanded of the doctors of the law the cause of this omission; and ordered them to deliver their sentiments concerning the propriety or impropriety of including the sacred posterity of the prophet in their prayers. They replied with one accord, that by the express command of Almighty God the prayers of the faithful were due not only to the holy messenger, but to his descendants also.

SEVERAL

ودرين وقت جمعي از علما كفتند كه امام شافعي نمازرا بدون صلوات بر محمد وآل محمد فاسد شمرده وجمعي كفتند كه امام اعظم فرمود كه نمازي كه بصلوات بر محمد وآل محمد مقرون نباشد مكروه است

آنكاه از علما سوال كرد كه چرا بر هريك از آل وي در صلوات ذكر نميكنند ودر صلوات بر خاتم انبيا ذكر ميكنند چون علما در جواب فرو ماندند سلطان كفت

مرا در جواب اين سوال دو دليل بخاطر ميرسند اول آنكه چون دشمنان ويرا ابتر خوانند ايزد تعالي ابتري را بر ايشان انداخت كه نسل ايشان منقطع شده واكر باشد هم ايشانرا كسي نشناسد ونام نبرد وذريت آل پيغمبر آن قدربهم رسيدند كه تعداد ايشان را جز خداي تعالي ديكري نداند ودر صلوات بمتابعت پيغمبر صلي الله عليه وسلم بر ايشان درود ميفرستند

ديكر آنكه اديان جميع انبيا ورسل وعهد ايشان در معرض نسخ وتبدل بود وامضاي احكام

"SEVERAL of the doctors said, that Immaum Shaufeï had declared, that the sacred service unattended by the usual benedictions on Mahummud and his posterity, were impious. Others acknowledged, that Immaum a Aazum had pronounced the prayers, in which the usual petitions in behalf of Mahummud and his posterity were omitted, to be void and of no effect.

"HE then demanded of them, why, when they mentioned the prophet in their prayers, they included not his immediate descendants. The doctors of the law were unable to reply, and the Sooltaun proceeded.

"IN proof of the necessity of including the successors and posterity of the prophet in our prayers two arguments occur to me. First, that as the wicked excluded the descendants and successors of our holy lawgiver from the benefit of their benedictions, so Almighty God hath excluded them from the benefit of his protection, and hath cut off their posterity from the face of the earth: for if any of their descendants remain, none know them, none regard them: whereas the posterity of the prophet are increased to such a degree, that no one except the Almighty knoweth their numbers, and those in respect and obedience to the holy apostle (on whom be the blessing of God) still offer up their prayers for his immediate descendants.

"SECONDLY, the religious rites and institutions of all former prophets and messengers have been either altered or annulled; for the rules prescribed by the religions

احکام دین ایشان علي الدوام لازم نبود بخلاف دین محمدي صلي الله عليه وسلم که تا قيامت تغير وتبديل در آن راه نخواهد يافت

پس بر متابعان آنحضرت لازم باشد که در صلوات بمتابعت نام مبارک آنحضرت را ذکر ميکنند اولادرا نيز ذکر کنند تا بر امت معلوم شود که حاميان دين محمدي ومفسران وحي الهي وحافظان شريعت احمدي ايشانند ووراث علوم انبيا ومرسلين اند وعلوم دين وفرايض اسلام از ايشان فرا گيرند ومتابعت وحرمت ايشانرا از لوازم شمارند

چون سلطان اين کلمات را بر زبان راند خلايقي که در مسجد جمع آمده بودند بيک مرتبه زبان بصلوات پيغمبر وآل پيغمبر کشارند

آنگاه سلطان گفت که چون اول آل محمد علي وآخر ايشان محمد مهدي موعود است پس مارا است که در ملک محمد بدون اذن اولادش تصرف ننمايم واگر نمايم غاصب باشم

چون

religions which they eſtabliſhed were not adapted to all times and to all ſituations. On the contrary, the religion of Mahummud (the peace of God be upon him) will continue, without change or abolition, to the end of time. Book II.

" IT is the duty therefore of the followers of our holy prophet, who in their prayers reſpectfully mention his name, to include his deſcendants alſo: that it may be known to the people that they are the ſupporters of the religion of Mahummud, the expounders of the divine revelations, the guardians of the holy law, and the heirs of the prophets and apoſtles: that the knowledge of the true religon and the divine ordinances of Iſlaum may be perpetuated by them, and that obedience and reſpect to the deſcendants of the prophet may be conſidered as an indiſputable and important duty.

" WHEN the Sooltaun had concluded, the people who were collected together in the Musjid, inſtantly and with one voice, offered up their benedictions in favour of the prophet and his ſacred deſcendants.

" THE Sooltaun proceeded thus. " Since Aali has been acknowledged to be the firſt, and Mahummud Mehdi the laſt, of the ſucceſſors and immediate deſcendants of the prophet, it cannot be lawful for me to aſſume authority over the dominions of the holy Mahummud without the aſſent of his and their poſterity; ſince by ſo doing I ſhould be an uſurper."

چون کلمات سلطان بمسامع خاص
وعام رسید همه علما اذعان نمودند بعد اذعان علما
سلطان امر نمود که چون حقیقت برین منوال است
باید که خطبه تمام اهل بیت بخوانند وسکه بنام
ایشان بر زنند

وانچه علما درین وقت فتوي نوشته اذعان
نموده اند این است که الجایتو سلطان مروج دین
وشریعت اند

در سر مایهٔ هشتم امیر صاحب قران است
که در امصار واقطار عالم شریعت را رواج داده وسادات
وعلمارا اعزاز واحترام نموده وباذن ذریت آل رسول الله
در ملک او تصرف کرده اند

چون مکتوب میر سید شریف بمن
رسید تنکري تعالي را شکر کفتم وبمحمد وآل
محمد التجا بردم که مرا توفیق تجدید دین
وشریعت حاصل آید

ومکتوب را

"WHEN this declaration of the Sooltaun reached the ears of the people, those of the posterity of the prophet immediately granted their consent. Having thus obtained their approbation of his authority, the Sooltaun ordained that agreeably to this regulation, the Khutbeh should be pronounced from the pulpits in the names of each of the successors of the prophet, and that their names also should be impressed on the coins of the empire. Book II.

"THE ecclesiastical decree which the theologians promulgated on this occasion, and to which they subscribed their assent, is as follows, "Aljauetoo Sooltaun "is the supporter of the faith, and the restorer of the "laws."

"IN this the eighth century AMEER SAUHIBA KURRAUN IS THE SUPPORTER OF OUR SACRED RELIGION; since he hath revived and encouraged obedience to the holy laws in the different cities and nations of the earth, hath protected and reverenced the posterity of the prophet of God, and with their assent and approbation hath assumed dominion over the empire of Mahummud."

WHEN the letter of Meer Siud Shureef came unto me, I offered up thanks to Almighty God, and I invoked the holy Mahummud and the descendants of Mahummud, that I might obtain their guidance and support in promoting our holy faith and in establishing the laws.

ومکتوب را بجنس نزد پیر خود فرستادم
ایشان بر حاشیه همان مکتوب نوشتند که مروج
الدین والشریعت تیمور صاحب قران ایده الله تعالي
معلوم نماید که این موهبتي است عظمي وتاییدي
است کبري که آن قطب السلطنت را الله تعالي
توفیق تجدید دین ورواج شریعت ارزاني داشته
بیغزا تا بیغزایند.

چون مکتوب موشح بخط پیر من بمن
رسید تعظیم واحترام سادات وعلماي اسلام بجا آوردم
ودر رواج شریعت پیشتر از پیشتر سعي کردم وامر
کردم که صورت این مکتوب را در دفتر وقایع من
ثبت نمایند

چون تزوک دین وشریعت کردم شروع
در تزک کارخانه سلطنت خود نمودم وبه توره وتزوک
مراتب سلطنت خود نکاهداشتم تزک نکاهداشت
مراتب سلطنت خودرا برین نهج کردم
اول قواعد سلطنت خودرا بدین اسلام
وشریعت خیر الانام ومحبت آل واصحاب واجب الاحترام
آنحضرت

AND the Letter itſelf I ſent unto my PEER, who wrote thus on the border of that Letter. " Be it " known to Ameer Sauhiba Kurraun, the promoter of " the faith, the eſtabliſher of the laws (with whom be " the protection of Almighty God) that this is a bleſſing " extraordinary, and a mercy inconceivable, which the " omnipotent creator hath vouchſafed to thee, the axis of " empire, in appointing thee the re-eſtabliſher of the " faith, and the ſupporter of the ſacred laws. Encreaſe " thou the number of thy good actions, that thy benevo- " lent creator may encreaſe his mercies unto thee!"

WHEN the epiſtle, bearing the ſubſcription of my PEER, was returned unto me, I reverenced and reſpected the poſterity of the prophet, and the teachers of the doctrine of Iſlaum; and in enforcing the ſacred laws I exerted myſelf more than before. And I commanded that the ſubſtance of the letter ſhould be inſerted in the regiſter of my tranſactions.

WHEN I re-eſtabliſhed the faith and the holy laws, I then began to form my civil regulations; and by law and by order I ſtrengthened my government. And the regulations for giving ſtability to my government, I formed in this manner.

FIRST, I kept firm the foundation of my power by the true religion, and by the laws of the prophet, and by the love of the deſcendants and venerable compa-

آنحضرت استوار داشتم وحفظ مرتبه سلطنت خود بتوره وتروک چنان کردم که احدي را ياراي نبود که در سلطنت من دخل تواند کرد

دوم سپاه ورعيت را در مرتبه اميد وبيم نکاهداشتم ودوست ودشمن را در مرتبه مروت ومدارا داشته کردار وکفتار ايشانــرا به تحمل وتغافل در کذرانيدم

وهرکس از دوست ودشمن که التجا بمن آوردند دوستان را در مرتبــه نکاهداشتم که بر دوستي خود افزودند وبا دشمنان بمرتبهء سلوک نمودم که دشمني را بدوستي مبدل ساختند

وهرکسرا بر من حقي بود حق ويــرا ضايــع نساختم وهرکسرا بروي شناختم ويــرا از نظر نينــداختــم

وهرکس از اوان طلوع دولت وسلطنت من بمن التجاآ ورده بودند از نيکو کار وبد کردار خــواه بمن نيکي کرده بودند خواه بدي چون بر تخــت سلطنت نشستم ايشانرا شرمنده احسان خــود ساختــم وبديهاي که بمن کرده بودند نا کرده انکاشتم وقلم عفو بر جريده اعمال ايشان کشيدم

سيوم

companions of that holy legislator; and by regulations and by order I so secured my regal authority, that no one had the power to interpose in my government. Book II.

SECONDLY, I kept my soldiers and my subjects suspended between hope and fear; and conducting myself towards my friends and my enemies with gentleness and with humanity, I either over-looked or patiently bore with their words and their actions.

WHOEVER, whether friends or enemies, fled unto me for protection; if they were friends, I treated them in such sort as tended to increase their friendship; and if they were enemies, I so conducted myself towards them that their enmity was speedily converted into affection.

WHOEVER had a demand upon me, I attempted not to diminish the value thereof: and those whom I personally knew, I threw not forth from my presence.

AND whoever, from the first shining forth of my fortune and power, had sought my protection, whether worthy or unworthy, whether their conduct towards me had been good or evil, when I ascended the throne of empire, I caused them to blush by my bounty and kindness; and I considered as undone the evil which they had done unto me, and I drew the pen of oblivion over the register of their actions.

THIRDLY,

سیوم در مقام انتقام هیچکس نشدم وانتقام نکشیدم وبد کنندکان خودرا به پروردکار سپردم

ارباب شجاعت ومردان کارکردهء ازموده نکاهداشتم ومردم اصیل وسادات وعلمای وفضلا را بخود راه دادم واشرار وبد نفسان ولیمان را از مجلس خود راندم

چهارم بکشاده رویء ورحم وشفقت خلق خدارا بخود رام کردم وبعدالت کرویدم واز ظلم وجور دوری کزیدم

درین وقت پیر من بمن نوشت که ابو المنصور تیمور ایده الله تعالی را معلوم باد که کارخانه سلطنت نمونهء از کارخانه آلهی است که در آن عمله وفعله ونایبان وحجاب اند وهریک در مرتبه خود بکار خود مشغول اند واز مرتبه خود تجاوز نمیکنند ومنتظر امر آلهی می باشند

پس ترا احتیاط باید که وزرا ولشکریان وعمالان وکارکنان وسپهسالاران هریک در حد مرتبه

THIRDLY, I never gave way to the thirst of revenge, nor did I ever satiate my resentment on any one. Those who had injured me, I delivered over to the justice of the Almighty.

I retained in my service warriors of approved valour, and soldiers of tried experience. And I admitted to my society men of exalted lineage, and the posterity of the prophet, and theologians, and doctors learned in the law. And the seditious, and the wicked, and the inglorious I drove far from my presence.

FOURTHLY, I drew to me the obedience of the people of God by complacency, and by mercy, and by indulgence. And I ever adhered to equity and justice; and I retired far from cruelty and oppression.

AT this time my PEER wrote unto me, saying, " Be it known to Abu'l Munsour Timour (on whom " be the blessing of Almighty God) that the different " offices in an earthly empire are symbols of those in the " empire of thy creator; in which there are labourers, " and agents, and deputies, and chamberlains; and they " are all busied and occupied in their own proper depart-" ments, and they seek not to over-leap the bounds allotted " them; and they wait in perpetual obedience to the " will of the Lord.

" THEREFORE, thou must be watchful, " that thy vizzeers, and thy soldiers, and thy labourers, " and thy servants, and thy officers, being each of them

مرتبه خود بوده منتظر حکم تو باشند وهر طایفه وهر قوم را در مرتبهء ایشان بدار تا مرتبه سلطنت تو بنظام وانتظام در آید

واگر حفظ مراتب هرچیز وهرکس نکني بسي خلل وفساد در امور سلطنت راه یابد پس تراست که پایه قدر ومنزله هرچیز وهرکس نگاهداري

ومرتبه آل محمدرا از جمیع مراتب برتر داري وتعظیم واحترام ایشان بجا آري وافراط را در محبت ایشان اسراف نداني که هرچه از براي خدا باشد در آن اسراف نباشد به دوازده طایفه سلطنت خودرا آراسته وپراسته بدار والسلام

چون این نامه پیر من بمن رسید هرچه فرموده بودند بجا آوردم ومراتب سلطنت خودرا نسق وانتظام دادم ومرتبه سلطنت خودرا به توره وتزوک زیب وزینت بخشیدم وبدوازده طایفه سلطنت خودرا

استوار

" restricted to their proper stations, attend with due sub-" mission thy commands. And restrain thou every " people and every tribe under thy dominion within their " proper limits: that thy empire may be established on " the basis of regularity and good order.

" But if thou regardest not the due ar-" rangement of thy concerns, and attendest not to the " just subordination of thy people, corruption, and vio-" lence, and disorders shall find their way into every de-" partment of thy government. Be it therefore thy care " to watch over and confine thy people, and thy concerns, " within the limits of subordination and good order.

" And thou shall exalt the sacred posterity " of the prophet above all other ranks of thy people; " and thou shalt revere and honour them, and thou shalt " not consider the greatest instances of liberality, which " thy love for them shall call forth, as the effects of pro-" fusion. We cannot be profuse in our offerings to Al-" mighty Cod. Regulate and govern thou thy empire by " the Twelve select Classes; and farewell."

When I received this letter from my Peer, I acted in obedience to all which he had commanded, and I gave order and connexion to the different departments of empire; and I ornamented and beautified my power by regulations and laws: and I made my authority durable by the twelve classes.

استوار ساختم تزوك مرتبه

سلطنت وقواعد سلطنت خودرا بدوازده طايفه مربوط ومضبوط ساختم واين دوازده طايفه را بمنزله دوازده برج فلك ودوازده ماه كارخانه سلطنت خود قرار دادم

اول طايفه سادات وعلما مشايخ وفضلا را بخود راه دادم وهميشه ببارگاه من آمد شد مي نمودند ومجلس مرا بزيب وزينت نگاه مي داشتند ومسايل علوم ديني وحكمي وعقلي مذكور مي ساختند ومسايل حلال وحرام از ايشان استفسار مينمودم

طايفه دويم عقلا واصحاب كنكاش وارباب حزم واحتياط ومردم كهنه سال پيش بين را در مجلس خاص خودرا راه دادم وبايشان صحبت داشتم ونفع يافته تجربها حاصل ميكردم

طايفه سيوم ارباب دعارا گرامي داشتم ودر خلوت از ايشان دريوزه دعوات كرده مدعيان خودرا استدعا مينمودم ودر مجالس ومحافل وبزم ورزم از

REGULATIONS. By the TWELVE CLASSES I rendered ſtrong and permanent the baſis and ſuperſtructure of my government; and I conſidered thoſe Claſſes as the twelve months, and as the twelve ſigns of the zodiac, predominating over the concerns of my empire.

THE FIRST CLASS. I granted admiſſion to the deſcendants of the prophet, and to theologians, and to doctors learned in the laws, and to holy men. And they reſorted at all times to my palace, and they beautified and adorned my imperial aſſembly by their preſence. And they converſed on ſacred knowledge, and on government, and on wiſdom: and to them I propoſed queſtions concerning thoſe things which were lawful, and thoſe which were forbidden.

THE SECOND CLASS. Perſons of wiſdom, and deliberation, and vigilance, and circumſpection, and aged men endowed with knowledge and foreſight, I admitted to my private councils: and I aſſociated with them, and I reaped benefit, and acquired experience from their converſation.

THE THIRD CLASS. I revered devout and pious men; and I implored their prayers in the hour of retirement: and I ſupplicated their bleſſings on my actions. And in war, and in peace, and in my councils, and in

از ایشان برکتي تمام مي یافتم ودر روز جنک از ایشان ظفرها میدیدم

چنانچه در وقتي که لشکر من بواسطه کثرت لشکر توقتمش خان در جنک مضطرب شدند میر ضیا الدین سبزواري که صاحب الدعوت بود سر خودرا برهنه ساخت ودست بدعا بر آورد وهنوز دعاي وي باتمام نرسیده بود که اثر دعاي وي ظاهر کردید

وچنانچه در وقتي که یکي از اهل حرم سراي مرا بیماري صعب عارض شده بود دوازده سید دعاکوي جمع آمده هریک یک سال از عمر خود بوي بخشیدند ووي صحت یافت ودوازده سال زندکاني کرد

چهارم طایفه امرا وسرهنکان وسپهسالاران را در مجلس خود اورن دادم وبمراتب علیا سر بلند داشتم وبا ایشان صحبت داشته سخنان مي پریدم

وارباب شجاعت را که بارها شمشیرها زده بودند دوست داشتم واز رزم ودر آمدن وبر آمدن در معارک ومهالک وشکستن صفها وحرب وضرب وچپقولشها

in my deliberations, I reaped the greatest advantage from their mediation. And by them I obtained victories in the day of battle.

THUS it came to pass, when in an engagement with Touktummish Khaun my forces were thrown into confusion by the superior numbers of the enemy, Meer Zeau u deen (of Subzvaur) who was noted for the efficacy of his prayers, bared his head, and stretched forth his arms in supplication: his prayer was not yet concluded, when the effects of his mediation became apparent.

AND so also it came to pass, at a time when one of the inhabitants of my Hoorrum Surrai † was afflicted with a deadly distemper. Twelve holy Siuds, celebrated for their piety, assembled together; and each of them devoted a year of his own existence to her preservation: and she was restored to health, and enjoyed the full measure of their donation.

THE FOURTH CLASS. The Ameers, and the chiefs, and the commanders of my forces, I admitted to my councils; and I raised them to exalted dignities; and I associated, and conversed familiarly, with them.

AND I loved those intrepid warriors who had given repeated proofs of their courage and abilities. And I proposed questions to them concerning the art of war, and the various modes of advancing in the field of battle, and of retreat in situations of peril, and the me-

† One of his wives.

thods

وچپتولشها از ایشان سوالات مینهودم ودر مرتبه سپاهکري ایشانرا معتهد میداشتم وکنکاش از ایشان میطلبیدم

پنجم طایغه سپاه ورعیت را بیک چشم دیدم واشجعان سپاه را از بهادران ودلاوران به اوتاغه* کهر وترکش خاصه سر بلند ساختم

وکلانتران وکدخدایان هر ملک وممکلت را کرامي داشتم وبایشان جزا دادم ونغع کرفتم

وسپاه را حاضر نکاهداشتم وعلونه ایشان را پیش از طلب میدادم چنانچه در یساق روم هغت ساله علونه از کذشته وآینده به سپاه دادم وسپاه ورعیت را بنوعي ضبط نهودم که از هیچ یک بر دیکري تعدي وعنغي واقع نهي شد

وسابر سپاه را علي مراتب درجاتهم در مراتب خود نکاه میداشتم که از حد خود قدم بیرون نهي کذاشتند ومرتبه ایشان را نه بلند بلند ساختم ونه پست پست واز هر کدام که خدمتي بوتوع مي آمد بجلدو وانعام امتیاز میدادم

وشجاعت

thods of charging and breaking the lines of the enemy, and of ſkirmiſhing, and all the other operations of war: and I placed confidence in them; and I conſulted their opinions in proportion to their ſkill and experience. Book II.

THE FIFTH CLASS. The ſoldier and the ſubject I regarded with the ſame eye. And the brave and the reſolute from amongſt my warriors I diſtinguiſhed by gifts and by honours.

AND I treated with dignity and attention the rulers and the chiefs of every province and kingdom; and I conferred rewards upon them, and I reaped benefit from their ſervices.

AND I kept my troops in a ſtate of readineſs, and I advanced to them their wages even before it was due. Thus in my expedition againſt Room, I gave unto my ſoldiers ſeven years wages; part thereof due, and the remainder in advance. And ſuch was the diſcipline which I eſtabliſhed amongſt my troops and my ſubjects, that the one was never injured or oppreſſed by the other.

AND my ſoldiers of every rank I confined in ſuch ſort to their ſeveral ſtations, that they could not ſte beyond the limits preſcribed to them: and I neither exalted them above, nor depreſſed them below the reſt of my ſubjects. And thoſe of them who ſignalized themſelves by eminent ſervices, I rewarded with honours and donations.

وشجاعت وعقل هر کس از سایر سپاه را که بمیزان عیار مي سنجیدم تربیت کرده بمرتبه امارت میرسانیدم وفراخور کار ایشان بر مراتب ایشان مي افزودم

طایفه ششم از خردمندان معتمد راسخ الاعتقاد که سزاواران بودند که رازهاي امور سلطنت بایشان سپارم ومشوره امور سلطنت بایشان کنم طایفه را صاحب اسرار نهاني خود ساختم وامور مخفي واسرار نهاني خودرا بدیشان سپردم

هفتم طایفه از وزرا وکتاب ومنشیان دیوان سلطنت خودرا آراسته ساختم وایشان را آینه دار ممالک خود ساختم که وقایع ملک ومملکت وسپاه ورعیت را بمن نمودار میساختند

وخزانه ورعیت وسپاه مرا معمور نگاه میداشتند ورخنه ملک را بتدبیر لایق بر میبستند، ومداخل ومخارج کارخانه سلطنه مرا مضبوط نگاه میداشتند ودر توفیر ومعموري ملک ساعي مي بودند.

هشتم

AND those of my officers whose resolution and abilities I had weighed and proved in the balance of trial, I received into my especial favour, and I promoted them to the rank of commanders: and, in proportion to their conduct, I advanced them to superior stations.

THE SIXTH CLASS. From amongst the wise and the prudent, who merited trust and confidence, who were worthy of being consulted on the affairs of government, and to whose care I might submit the secret concerns of my empire, I selected a certain number, whom I constituted the repositories of my secrets. And my weighty and hidden transactions, and my secret thoughts and intentions I delivered over to them.

THE SEVENTH CLASS. By the vizzeers, and the secretaries, and the scribes I gave order and regularity to my public councils. I made them the keepers of the mirrour of my government; in which they shewed unto me the affairs of my dominions and my empire, and the concerns of my armies and my people.

AND they kept rich my treasury; and they secured plenty and prosperity to my soldiers and to my subjects. And by proper and skilful measures they repaired the disorders incident to empire; and they kept in order the revenues and the expences of government; and they exerted themselves in promoting plenty and population throughout my dominions.

هشتم طبقه حکما واطبا ومنجمان
ومهندسان که مصالح کارخانه سلطنت اند بر خود
جمع آوردم
وباتفاق حکما واطبا معالجه بیماران
مي کردم واز طبقه منجمان سعادت ونحوست ایام
کواکب وسیر ایشان ودور افلاک را مشخص مینمودم
وباتفاق مهندسان عمارات عالي بنا نهاده تعمیر کردم
وطرح باغات انداختم

نهم طایفه محدثین وارباب اخبار
وقصص را بخود راه دادم واز قصص انبیا واولیا واخبار
سلاطین روزکار وکیفیت رسیدن ایشان بمرتبه
سلطنت وزوال دولت ایشان ازین طایفه مي
شنیدم
واز قصص واخبار ایشان وکفتار وکردار
هریک تجربها برمیداشتم واخبار وآثار عالم از ایشان
مي شنیدم وبر احوال عالم اطلاع حاصل مي
نمودم

دهم طایفه بمشایخ وصوفیان وعارفان
خدا پیوستم وبایشان صحبتها داشتم وفواید
آخروی

THE EIGHTH CLASS. Men learned in medicine, and thoſe ſkilled in the art of healing, and aſtrologers, and geometricians, who are eſſential to the dignity of empire, I drew around me.

AND, by the aid of phyſicians and chirurgeons, I gave health to the ſick. And, with the aſſiſtance of aſtrologers, I aſcertained the benign or malignant aſpect of the ſtars; their motions, and the revolutions of the heavens. And, with the aid of geometricians and architects, I laid out gardens, and planned and conſtructed magnificent buildings.

THE NINTH CLASS. Hiſtorians, and ſuch as were poſſeſſed of information and intelligence, I admitted to my preſence. And from theſe men I heard the lives of the prophets and the patriarchs; and the hiſtories of ancient princes, and the events by which they arrived at the dignity of empire, and the cauſes of the declenſion of their fortunes.

AND from the narratives and the hiſtories of thoſe princes, and from the manners and the conduct of each of them, I acquired experience and knowledge. And from thoſe men I heard the deſcriptions and the traditions of the various regions of the globe, and acquired knowledge of the ſituations of the kingdoms of the earth.

THE TENTH CLASS. I united myſelf with holy and pious men, with thoſe to whom the Almighty

آخروي اخذ نمودم وسخنان خداي مي شنيدم وكرامات وخوارق عادات از ايشان مشاهده مي نمودم ومرا از صحبت ايشان سرور وحضور تمام حاصل مي آمد

يازدهم طايفه ارباب صناعت را از هر طايفه وهر صنفي بدولتخانه خود آوردم ودر اردوي خود ايشانرا اورن دادم كه در سفر وحضر ما يحتاج سپاه را حاضر داشته باشند

طايفه دوازدهم مترددين ومسافران هر ملك وديار را تسلي دادم كه اخبار ممالك را بمن برسانند

وتجارانرا وقافله سالاران را تعين نمودم كه بهر ملك وهر ديار رفته از ختا وختن وچين

† The first, the third, and this (the tenth) class, appear on a superficial view to be the same people, i.e. men devoted to the duties of religion; but, on a nearer examination, it is evident that they were classes distinct from each other. The first were undoubtedly the heads of the Mahummudan church, the posterity of Aali, the dignified prelates, and the eminent doctors of the law. The third class appears to be a selection (from the first) of such eminent men as had rendered themselves celebrated by their superior piety and religious attention to the laws. And by this (the tenth) class Timour evidently means such religious men, as had retired from the world and

وماچين

mighty had given wisdom; † and I associated with them; and I heard from them the word of God; and I acquired knowledge of the blessings of a future state. And I saw them perform miracles and wonderful things; and I reaped delight and satisfaction from their conversation.

THE ELEVENTH CLASS. I brought into my palace artificers of every sort, and of every denomination; and I admitted them into my camp; that both at home and abroad they might supply, and keep in readiness, the necessaries requisite to my soldiers.

THE TWELFTH CLASS. To travellers, and to voyagers, of every country I gave encouragement; that they might communicate unto me the intelligence and transactions of the surrounding nations.

AND I appointed merchants and chiefs of Kauruvvauns to travel to every kingdom, and to every country; that they might bring unto me all sorts of valuable merchandize and rare curiosities, from Khuttau, and from Khut-

and devoted themselves to solitude, to the study of the Koraun, and the regular performance of the religious duties prescribed by their law-giver. These hermits, or monks, like their brethren of the western church, acquired in all times a large share of popular respect and veneration by their austerities and apparent sanctity. They too performed their miracles and wonderful things; and, if the eastern historians may be credited, with as much dexterity and address as any of those holy men and women on whom the honour of saintship has been conferred by the infallibility of the Roman Pontiffs.

tun,

وماچین وهندوستان وبلاد عرب ومصر وشام وروم
وجزایر فرنک متاع نفیس وتحفهاي لایق بجهت من
بیاورند واحوال واوضاع واطوار متوطنان وسکنه آن
دیار را بعرض من رسانند وسلوک حکام هر مملکتي را
با رعایا بخاطر آورده نهودار سازند تروک طوایفي که
از ترک وتاچیک وعرب وعجم بدرگاه من التجا
آوردند چنین کردم

که اول امر نهودم که هر طایفه وهر
طبقه را که سادات وعلما باشند اعزاز واحترام نهایند
وهر مطلبي که ایشانرا بوده باشد
با نجاح مقرون کردانند ورعایت احوال ایشان بواجبي
نهایند

واکر طایفه سپاه بوده باشد ایشانرا اورن
داده فراخور احوال پرداخت احوال ایشان نهایند

واکر از ارباب معرفت وصناعت باشد
در کارخانجات سلطنت ایشانرا بکار دارند وسایر

† i. e. Whether Tatars or Persians, Arabs or Syrians. Such are the confined meanings of the words *Taucheek* and *Ajjum*; but they frequently convey a more extensive idea: for the Tatars use the word *Taucheek*, and the

الناس

tun, and from Cheen, and from Maucheen, and from Hindostaun, and from the cities of Arabia, and from Missur, and from Shaum, and from Room, and from the islands of the Christians; that they might give me information of the situation, and of the manners, and of the customs of the natives and the inhabitants of those regions; and that they might observe, and communicate unto me, the conduct of the princes of every kingdom, and of every country, towards their subjects. Book II.

RELATIVE to the various tribes, whether Toork or Taucheek, Arrub or Ajjum,† who sought shelter under my government; these were the REGULATIONS which I established.

FIRST, I commanded that those who were of the posterity of the prophet, or theologians learned in the laws, should be received with reverence and respect; and that all their wishes and desires should be fulfilled; and that they should be supported in affluence and honour.

AND those who were soldiers, I ordered to be incorporated with my troops, and entertained according to their rank and their circumstances.

AND those who were skilled in mechanic arts, I directed to be employed in my service. And the

the Arabs the word *Ajjum* or *Ajjumi* to distinguish any person, or people, of a different nation from their own. Thus *Taucheek* and *Ajjum* answer to our word *foreigner*.

الناس را از نقرا ومساكين كه استطاعت داشته باشد فراخور احوال وطبقه مرسوم قرار دهند

وحكم كردم كه هر تاجري كه راس المال را از دست داده باشد بوي آن قدر زر دهند كه باز راس المال خويش سازد وهر مزارعي ورعيتي كه از رعيتي وزراعت بي استطاعت شده باشد مصالح زراعت وعمارت بوي مقرر دارند وهر طايفه وهر صنفي كه شيوه سپاهگري اختيار كند وي را سپاهي سازند

وسپاهي زاده شجاع اصل از هر طايفه كه باشد اورا اورن دهند وفراخور كار تربيت نمايند

وامر نمودم كه هركس از هر طايفه كه بمجلس من در آيد ويرا از خوان نعمت سلطنت من محروم نكردانند

وهركس را بنظر من در آورند ونظر من بروي افتاد تشريفات فراخور احوال بوي ارزاني دارند وهركس از كنه كاران وبي كناه كه بديوان عدالت من در آيد بروي به بخشايند ودر كناه دوم وسيوم فراخور كناه سزا دهند

تزوك

body of the people, the indigent and the poor, who had capacity and abilities, I commanded to be accommodated agreeably to their situations. Book II.

I ordered that the merchant who had lost his property, should have such sums of money given unto him as were sufficient to restore his capital to its original state; and that every husbandman and every peasant, who was not possessed of the implements of husbandry and cultivation, should be supplied therewith; and that those, of whatever class or rank, who chose the occupation of arms, should be received into military service.

AND the genuine descendant of a soldier, resolute and brave, of whatever tribe or hord he might be, I ordered to be enrolled in the number of my forces, and to be promoted in proportion to his conduct and behaviour.

AND I ordained that no person, whatever his rank, who entered my palace, should be excluded from the table of my imperial bounty.

AND whoever was brought into my presence, and attracted my notice, I commanded that honours should be conferred upon him in proportion to his rank; and that every criminal who came for the first time before my tribunal, should be pardoned; but that for the second, and the third, crime he should meet with punishment adequate to his offences.

 THUS

تــزوک استقلال سلطنت خــود چنین کــردم

که دوازده چیز را شعار خود ساختم تا باستقلال تمام بر تخت سلطنت نشستم وبه تجربه من رسیده است که با هر پادشاهي که این دوازده امر نباشد از سلطنه بهره نداشته باشد

اول باید که کردار وکفتارش از خود بـاشــد یعني سپاه ورعیت بدانند که انچه بادشاه میکوید ومیکند خود میکوید ومیکند ودیکري را در آن دخلي نیست

پس بایــد که پادشاه بکفتار وکردار دیکران بنوعي که شریک مرتبه سلطنت کردند عمل نکند اکرچه سخن خوب از همه کس باید شنید اما نــه بمرتبه که از کفتار وکردار در امــور سلطنت شریک وغالب کردند

دویم سلطانرا باید که در همه چیز عدالت بکار برد ووزراي عادل با انصاف در خدمت خود نکاهدارد واکر پادشاه ظلم کــنــد وزیــر عادل

THUS I established rules for the security of my government. Book II.

I regulated my conduct by TWELVE CERTAIN MAXIMS: and by them I seated myself firmly on the throne of empire. And from experience it is known unto me, that every prince who adhereth not to these Twelve Maxims, shall reap little advantage from his dominion and regal station.

FIRST. It is necessary that his words and his actions be his own. That is to say, that his soldiers and his subjects may know that what the king sayeth and doeth, he sayeth and doeth from himself; and that no other person hath influence therein.

THEREFORE it is requisite that a king be not so guided by the conduct and the counsels of others, as to make them his associates in his regal authority. For although he be obliged to hear good advice from all, yet he must not to that degree attend unto them, as to enable them by their measures and their counsels to become his equals, and in the end his superiors, in the concerns of his government.

SECONDLY. It is necessary to a king that he adhere to justice in all his actions, and that he receive into his service ministers who are just and virtuous. For if a king be guilty of oppression, an upright minister may counteract the evil thereof. But if the minister be unjust

عادل تدارک آن نماید اما اکر وزیر ظالم باشد زود
باشد که خانه سلطنت خراب کردد

چنانچه امیر حسین وزیري داشت ظالم
که بحق وناحق جریمها از سپاه ورعیت میکرفت تا در
اندک زمانسي از ظلم آن وزیري بي انصاف خانه
سلطنت امیر حسین خراب شد

سیوم در اوامر ونهي استقلال بکار برد
وبذات خود حکم کند که دیکري را زهره آن
نباشد که در آن حکم دخل کند وتغیر دهد

چهارم بر عزیمت خود راسخ باشد یعني
بر هر کاري که عزیمت بندد فسخ آن نکند وتا
باتمام نرساند دست از آن کار باز ندارد

پنجم جریان حکم است چه حکمي
که بکند باید که آن حکم جاري کردد وکه کسي را
یاراي آن نباشد که رد آن حکم تواند کرد اکرچه
در آن حکم ضررها متصور باشد

چنانچه

unjust and cruel, it shall speedily come to pass, that the edifice of his masters's power and dominion shall be levelled with the earth. Book II.

Thus Ameer Hoossein had a cruel and a wicked minister, who levied oppressive fines on the soldiers and on the subjects; until in a short time by the oppressions of that unjust and cruel minister, the fabric of the dominion of Ameer Hoossein was laid in the dust.

Thirdly. In his injuctions and in his prohibitions he must act with resolution and with firmness. And he himself must issue his royal commands, that no one may have the temerity, or the power, to interpose, to alter, or to corrupt them.

Fourthly. He must be firm and constant in all his determinations. That is to say, on whatever plan or enterprise he shall resolve, he must not alter his resolution, nor withdraw his hand from that enterprise, until he hath brought it to a fortunate conclusion.

The fifth is the spirit of command. For whatever command he giveth, it is necessary that that command should be obeyed; that no one should have the power to act in opposition thereto, even though inconvenience or mischief should be the expected consequence of that command.

So

چنانچه بمسامع من رسید که سلطان
محمود غزنوي حکم کرد که سنکي بر سر میدان
غزنین بینداختند واز آن سنک اسپان مردم رم
میکردند هرچند بعرض رسانیدند که آن سنکرا از
سر راه بر دارند کفت که حکمي کرده ام از حکم
خود بر نمیکردم وخلاف حکم نمیکنم

ششم امور سلطنت خودرا من حیث
الاستقلال بدیکري نسپارد وعنان اختیار خود بدست
دیکري ندهد که دنیا غدار است وعاشق بسیار دارد
وزون باشد که آن صاحب اختیار میل بر سلطنت
نموده متصرف مرتبه سلطنت کردد
چنانچه وزراي سلطان محمود با وي
کردند وویرا از مرتبه سلطنت خلع نموده ومملکت
وسلطنت ویرا متصرف کشتند پس باید که امور
سلطنت متابع کرداند بچند کس معتبر ومعتمد
که تا هر یکي بکار خود مشغول بوده طمع در مرتبه
سلطنت ننمایند

هفتم

So it hath been related unto me, that Sooltaun Muhmood, emperor of Ghizni, ordered on a certain occaſion that a ſtone ſhould be caſt down at the entrance of the plain of Ghiznein: and the horſes of the people ſtarted and ſprang back from that ſtone. And although his ſervants ſolicited his permiſſion that they might remove the ſtone from the entrance of the road, he refuſed his aſſent: he anſwered unto them, 'I have iſſued 'forth the order; and I will not turn back from, or con- 'tradict, my own commands.'

SIXTHLY; (for from hence proceedeth ſecurity and power) he muſt not truſt the concerns of his government to others, nor deliver over the reins of his authority into the hands of a ſervant: for the world is full of treachery, and hath many lovers; and it may ſoon come to paſs that the powerful ſervant ſhall aſpire to regal dignity, and ſeat himſelf on the throne of his maſter.

SUCH was the conduct of the miniſters of Sooltaun Muhmood towards their lord. They expelled him from the imperial throne, and they divided his dominions and his power amongſt themſelves. It is neceſſary therefore that the powers and important affairs of government be divided; and that they be entruſted to the care of divers perſons of approved fidelity, and of known loyalty; ſo that being employed in their own proper departments, no one of them may aſpire to the ſupreme authority.

هفتم در امور سلطنت از هر کس سخن
بشنود انچه پسندیده باشد در خزانه خاطر خود
نکاهدارد ودر وقتش بکار برد

هشتم در امور سلطنت وسپاه ورعیت
بقول ونعل هر کس عمل نکند واز وزرا وامرا که در
حق شخصي سخني کویند بشنود خواه نیک وخواه
بد لیکن در عمل نمودن بآن تامل نماید تا آنکه
حقیقت حال بروي ظاهر کردد

نهم باید که سطوت سلطنتش در دلها
سپاه ورعیت بنوعي جاي کیرد که هیچکس را یاراي
تخلف از امر وحکم وي نباشد واز اطاعت ومتابعتش
عصیان نورزند

دهم انچه کند بذات خود کند وانچه
کوید بر سخن خود راسخ باشد چه پادشاه را جز اعزاز
حکم چیزي دیکر بهره نباشد که خزانه ولشکر ورعیت
وسلاطین همین حکم ایشان باشد

بازدهم

SEVENTHLY. On the affairs of his government he muſt liſten to the opinions of his ſervants: thoſe which are good, he muſt lay up in the treaſury of his heart, and call them forth into action at their proper ſeaſons.

EIGHTHLY. In the concerns of dominion, and in thoſe things which relate to his ſubjects and his ſoldiers, he muſt not act by the aſſiſtance and the advice of others. If his Vizzeers or his Ameers ſpeak unto him concerning any one, whether that which they ſay be good, or whether it be evil, let him hearken to them; but in forming his determination thereon let him be cautious and circumſpect, until the truth be apparent unto him.

NINTHLY. It is neceſſary that the majeſty of his dominion be ſo impreſſed on the hearts of his ſoldiers and his ſubjects, that none ſhall dare to diſobey his orders and commands, or to revolt from their duty and obedience to his royal authority.

TENTHLY. What the king doeth he muſt do from himſelf; and he muſt adhere to that which he ſayeth: for unto a prince there is nothing ſo valuable as a juſt veneration for his royal word. This word is unto him a family of princes, and a rich treaſury; it maketh to him numerous ſubjects and powerful armies.

یازدهم در امور سلطنت واجرای
احکام خودرا بی شریک داند وکسی را شریک
سلطنت نکرداند

دوازدهم از حال اهل مجلس خود
آگاه باشد وهوشیاری بکار برد که اکثر خواهش
عیوب باشند وخبر به بیرون رسانند واز گفتار وکردار
پادشاه خبر به امرا ووزرا بگویند چنانچه این قضیه
بر من بوقوع آمده چون جمعی از اهل مجلس
خاص من جاسوسان امرا ووزرا من بودند

تزوک نگاهداشت سپاه

امر نمودم که چون ده نفر سپاهی
اصیل کارکرده جمع آیند یکی از ایشان که بجوهر
شجاعت ومردی مخصوص باشد بصلاح ورضاء آن
نه نفر دیگر ویرا بر ایشان امیر گردانند ویرا اون
باشی نام نهند

وچون ده اون باشی جمع شوند یکی
از ایشان که بکارگذاری وکاردانی آراسته باشد بر
ایشان امیر گردانند وویرا یوز باشی نام کردانند

وچون

ELEVENTHLY. In the affairs of his government, and in the iſſuing forth his orders and commands, he muſt conſider himſelf as ſingle and alone; nor muſt he aſſociate any one with him in the adminiſtration of his authority. Book II.

TWELFTHLY. He muſt be acquainted with the manners and the diſpoſitions of his favourites and his confidents. And he muſt act with caution and circumſpection: for many are lovers of ſlander and of calumny, who may carry reports abroad, and communicate to the Vizzeers and the Ameers the words and the actions of their prince. Thus, it once happened unto me at a time when ſeveral of thoſe whom I admitted to my private council proved to be the ſpies of my Vizzeers and my Omraus.

REGULATIONS FOR THE FORMING OF MY ARMY.

I ordained, when ten ſelect ſoldiers, men of proof, were collected together, that one of them, who was diſtinguiſhed for valour and for bravery, ſhould, with the advice and the conſent of the remaining nine, be appointed commander over them; and that he ſhould be called Ounbauſhee:

AND when ten Ounbauſhee were aſſembled together, that one of them who was qualified by ſervice and abilities, ſhould be appointed their leader; and that he ſhould be ſtiled Euzbauſhee:

AND

وچـون ده یوز باشي جمع آیند امیر زاده عاقل اصیل بهادر مردانه را بریشان امیر گردانند ووبرا منک باشي وامیر هزاره خطاب دهند

واون باشیان را مختار ساختم که اگر یکي از تابینان ایشان فوت شود یا فرار نماید دیگري را بجـاي وي مقرر سازند وهمچنین یـوز باشي اون باشي را ومنـک باشي یوز باشي را تعین نـمـایند وکیفیت فـوت یا فـرار او ونصب کردن دیگري را بـعـرض رسانند

وهمچنین امر کردم که در چار پلچار* وامور سلطنت حکم منک باشي بر یوز باشي وحکم یوز باشي بر اون باشي وحکم اون باشي بر تابـیـنـان جاري باشد واگر خلاف نمایند بسزا رسانند واگر در چار پلچار* کوتاهي نمایند اخراج نموده عوض نـگـاه دارنـد

تـزوک قـرار علوفـه سپاه

امر کردم که علوفه سپاه از امرا ومنک باشیان

AND that, when ten Euzbaushee were collected together, an officer of exalted lineage, the son of a chief, of approved knowledge, and valour, and intrepidity, should be appointed commander over them; and that he should be called Mingbaushee, and Leader of a thousand.

AND I gave power to the Ounbaushees, that if any soldier under their command should die, or should desert, that they should appoint another soldier in his place. In the like manner I ordained, that the Euzbaushee should appoint the Ounbaushee, and the Mingbaushee the Euzbaushee; and that they should lay before me an account of the person who had died or deserted, and of the appointment of another in his stead.

AND I commanded in the like manner, that, on military service and in every concern that related to government, the authority of the Mingbaushee should be established over the Euzbaushee; and the authority of the Euzbaushee over the Ounbaushee; and the authority of the Ounbaushee over the common soldier; that they should chastise those that were disobedient; and that those who in the day of battle were deficient in performing their duty, should be expelled; and that others should be appointed in their place.

THE ESTABLISHMENT OF THE PAY OF MY FORCES.

I commanded that the subsistence of my troops, of the Omraus, and the Mingbaushees, and the Euzbaushees,

باشيان ويوز باشيان واون باشيان وساير سپاه برين
نهج مقرر كردانند

كه علوفه ساير سپاه بشرط اصالت
وسپاهكري بهاي اسپ وي مقرر باشد وعلوفه
بهادرانيكه از بهاء دو اسپ تا چهار اسپ معين باشد

وعلوفه اون باشي ده برابر علوفه تابينان
وي باشد وعلوفه يوز باشي دو برابر علوفه اون باشي
وعلوفه منك باشي سه برابر علوفه يوز باشي
معين باشد

وحكم كردم كه هريك از سپاه كه
در چار پلچار* كوتاهي نمايد ده يك از علوفه وي
كم نمايند وامر نمودم كه اون باشي به تصديق
يوز باشي علوفه بكيرد ويوز باشي بتصديق منك
باشي ومنك باشي به تصديق امير الامرا علوفه
بكيرد

† This mode of fixing the pay of the ſoldier is ſtill practiced in Hindoſtaun. Every ſoldier finds his own horſe, and receives pay in proportion to his value. Select men are ſtill taken into ſervice with two, and ſome-times

وامر

Euzbaushees, and the Ounbaushees, and the common soldiers should be fixed and determined according to the following order. Book II.

I ordained that the subsistence of each of the private soldiers, if he were a sufficient and able man, should be fixed at the value of his horse; † and that the subsistence of my select and chosen warriors should be estimated at the value of from two to four horses each.

AND I ordered that the subsistence of the Ounbaushees should be ten times as much as the subsistence of the soldiers under them; and that the subsistence of the Euzbaushees should be twice as much as that of the Ounbaushees; and that the subsistence of the Mingbaushees should be three times as much as the subsistence of the Euzbaushees.

AND I ordained that the soldier who neglected his duty, ‡ should be fined in one tenth of his pay. And I commanded that the Ounbaushees should receive their subsistence under the controul of the Euzbaushees; and that the Euzbaushees should receive their subsistence under the controul of the Mingbaushees; and that the Mingbaushees should receive their subsistence unde. the controul of the Ameer ul Omrau. ‖

times three, horses each; which are mounted by their servants, and they receive pay in proportion.

‡ The word thus translated is Mogul, and the sense doubtful.

‖ i.e. The chief of the Ameers or Nobles.

وامر نمودم که علوفــه امیر الامرا ده برابر علوفــه تابینان ایشان بوده باشد وهمچنان امر نمودم که علوفه دیوان بیکي ووزرا ده برابــر امــرا باشد وعلوفه یساولان وجساولان وتلقچیان* از هزار تا ده هزار مقرر باشد٭

وعلوفه مجلسیان از سادات وعلما وفضلا وحکما واطبا ومنجمان وارباب قصص وروایــات فراخور نسبت ایشان سیــورغال* ووظیفه وعلوفه معین دارند وعلوفه پیادکان وخدم وفراشان از صد تا هــزار مقرر نمــاینــد

وامر کردم که امیر الامــرا بتصدیــق دیوان بیکي ووزرا علوفه بکیرد وعرض مراتب علوفــه هــریــک را دیوانبیکي ووزرا بــعــرض من رسانــنــد وتنخــواه دهــنــد

وامر نمودم که یرلیغ علوفه بهریــک از سپاه نوشته بسپارند انچه بوي رسانند در پست همان یرلیغ وصول آن مبلغ بنویسند

† This regulation is not underſtood by the the tranſlator. The words *Yuſſauwullaun*, *Juſſauwullaun*, and *Kulluckcheaun* are Mogul.

AND I commanded that the pay of the Ameer ul Omrau should be ten times as much as the pay of the officer subordinate unto him. And, in like manner, I ordained that the stipends of the Dewaunbeghi and of the Vizzeers should be ten times as much as the subsistence of the Ameers; and that the subsistence of the Yussauwullaun, the Jussauwullaun, and the Kulluckcheaun should be established at from one thousand to ten thousand. †

AND I ordained that pensions, and salaries, and subsistence should be conferred on the posterity of the prophet, and the theologians, and the men of science, and the learned in medicine, and on the astrologers, and the historians, in proportion to their different ranks and stations: and that the subsistence of the foot-soldiers, and the domestics, and the Furraushaun ‡ should be fixed at from a hundred to a thousand.

AND I ordained also that the Ameer ul Omrau should receive his subsistence under the inspection of the Dewaunbeghi and the Vizzeers. And I commanded that the Vizzeers and the Dewaunbeghi should lay before me the statement of the salaries of each of my people, and pay them agreeably thereto.

AND I ordained that a written order for his subsistence should be delivered to each of my soldiers; and that the sums which from time to time were advanced unto him, should be written down on the back of that order.

‡ The *Furraushaun* are the people employed to erect the tents, &c.

تزوک تنخاه ورسانیدن علوفه بسپاه

امر نمودم که یکساله علوفه پیادگان
وقلغچیان ویساولان وجساولان را * بر آورد نموده
مبلغ ایشانرا در دیوانخانه آورده بدیشان
برسانند

وعلوفه سایر سپاه وبهادرانیکه را امر نمودم
که شش ماهه بر آورد نمایند ووجه علوفه ایشانرا از
خزانه تنخاه دهند

وامر نمودم که علوفه اون باشي ویوز
باشي بر مال اماني شهري وملکي نقد برات
نویسند ومنک باشیانرا در میان ولایت یتول* بدهند
وامرا وامیر الامرا را در سرحدها ولایت مقرر نمایند

وامر نمودم که قسمت ولایات بدین
طریق نمایند

که جمع حاصل ولایات ومهالک را
تقسیم نمایند ودر یرلیغها کم وزیاده بنویسند وآن
یرلیغها را در دیوانخانه آورده هریک از امرا ومنک
باشیان

CONCERNING THE APPOINTMENT AND PAY OF MY TROOPS.

I commanded that the accompt of twelve months subsistence for the infantry, and the Kulluckcheaun, and the Yussauwullaun, and the Jussauwullaun should be made out at one time; and that the money which was their due should be brought forth into the hall of audience, and there delivered unto them.

I ordered that the accompts of the subsistence of my cavalry in general should be made out every six months; and that appointments to the amount of their pay should be delivered unto them from the treasury.

AND I ordained that for the subsistence of the Ounbaushees and the Euzbaushees written orders should be given on the Maulaumauni † of the cities and the country; and that the interior districts should be allotted for the payment of the Mingbaushees; and that the stipends of the Ameers and the Ameer ul Omrau should be granted on the revenues of the frontier provinces.

AND I COMMANDED THAT THE DISTRIBUTION OF THE PROVINCES, AND THE DISTRICTS, SHOULD BE MADE IN THIS MANNER:

THAT the amount of the revenues of the various provinces and kingdoms should be divided into lots for more or for less, and that a royal assignment for the payment of each of those lots should be made out; and that those assignments should be brought into the hall

† Imposts, duties.

باشيان يرليغي بردارند واكر از علوفه وي زيـاده باشد ديكري را بخود شريک سازد واكر كم باشد برليغ ديكري را بردارد

وامـر نمودم كه امرا ومنک باشيان در تحصيل مال وجهات از رعيت چيزي زياده از اصل المال وساوري وتنلغه وشيلان* بها طلب ندارند

وهر مملکت را كه يتول* بدهند دو وزير بدآن مملکت تعين نمايند يكي جمع ولايت بنويسد ونسق رعيت نمايد تا خرابي بحـال رعيت راه نيابد وجاكيردار ظلم وتعدي بر رعايا نتواند كرد وانچه از ولايت تحصيل شود در مداخل جمع نمايد ووزيـر ديكر مخارج بنويسد وبر سپاه قسمت نمايد

وبـهـر اميري كه يتول* بدهند تا سه سال بحـال نكاهدارند وبعد از سه سال ملاحـظـه

† *Jaugheer* is a royal grant of certain lands; or more properly an assignment of the crown revenues of a certain district to any one, and revocable at the pleasure of the prince. The holder of this grant is called *Jaugheerdaur*.

نمايند

of audience; and that the Ameers and the Mingbaushees should each of them take one of those assignments; and that if the amount thereof exceeded the sum of his subsistence, some one else should participate with him; and if it were less, that another should be given in exchange, or added unto it. Book II.

AND I commanded that the Ameers and the Mingbaushees, in collecting the revenues from the subjects, should not on any account demand more than the taxes and duties established.

AND to every province on which a royal assignment was granted, I ordained that two supervisors should be appointed to that province: that one of them should inspect the collections and watch over the concerns of the inhabitants, that they might not be impoverished, and that the Jaugheerdaur † might not ill-use or oppress them; and that he should take an account of all the sums which were collected in the province: and that the other supervisor should keep a register of the public expences, and distribute the revenues among the soldiers.

AND every Ameer who was appointed to a Jaugheer, ‡ I ordained that for the space of three years it should remain unto him; and that after three years the state of the province should be inspected. If the inhabi-

‡ In the original *Yettool*; which is Mogul, and has the same meaning with *Jaugheer*.

tants

نمايند اكر ملك اباد ورعايا راضي باشند بحال خود دارند واكر بر خلاف اين باشد آن ولايت را بخالصه ضبط كنند وتا سه سال آن جاكيردار را علوفه ندهند

وامر نمودم كه مال از رعيت بسه بيم وترسانيدن تحصيل نمايند نه بچوب وشلاق چه حكم حاكمي كه از چوب وشلاق كمتر باشد آن حاكم سزاوار حكومت نباشد

مراتب علوفه فرزندان ونبايىر

امر نمودم كه فرزند اولين كه محمد جهانكير است وولي عهد من باشد دوازده هزار سوار را علوفه وولايت بكيرد

وفرزند دويمين كه عمر شيخ است ده هزار سوار را علوفه وولايت بكيرد

وفرزند سيومين كه ميران شاه است نه هزار سوار را علوفه بكيرد وبر ولايت متصرف كردد

وفرزند جهارمين كه شاهرخ است هفت هزار سوار را علوفه وولايت بكيرد

ونبيركان

tants were satisfied, and if the country was flourishing and populous, that he should be continued therein: but if the contrary should appear, that the Jaugheer should return unto the crown; and that for the three following years, subsistence should not be granted to the holder thereof. Book II.

And I ordained that the collection of the taxes from the subject might, when necessary, be enforced by menaces and by threats; but never by whips and by scourges. The governor whose authority is inferior to the power of the scourge, is unworthy to govern.

Concerning the subsistence of my children and descendants.

I commanded that my eldest son, the heir to my throne, who is Mahummud Jehaungheer, should receive the subsistence of twelve thousand horsemen, and the assignment of territories sufficient to defray the same:

And that my second son, who is Omur Sheikh, should receive the subsistence of ten thousand horsemen, and lands correspondent thereunto:

And that my third son, who is Meeraun Shaah, should receive the subsistence of nine thousand horsemen, and the assignment of a province for the payment of the same:

And that my fourth son, who is Shaahrokh, should receive the subsistence of seven thousand horsemen, and the assignment of a Jaugheer equivalent thereto:

ونبیرکان بقدر استعداد از سه هزار تا
هفت هزار سواررا علوفه وولایت بکیرند

دیکر جماعت را که بمن قرابت داشتند
فراخور حالت واستعداد وامارت وایالت از مرتبه امیر
اول تا امیر هفتم بدهند وهریک در مرتبه حد خود
بوده از حد خود تجاوز نه نمایند وچون خلاف ظاهر
شود مخاطب کردند

در باب سیاست فرزندان ونبیرکان
وخویشان وامرایان ووزرا

امر نمودم که اکر از فرزندان یکي
مدعي مرتبه سلطنت شود درکشتن وبستن وي
جرات نکنند واعضاي ایشان را ناقص نسازند لیکن
در قید نکاهدارند تا از دعوي خود باز آیند تا در
ملک خدا فساد نشود

ونبایر وخویشان اکر مخالفت نمایند
ایشانرا درویش سازند

وامرا

And that my grandſons ſhould receive ſubſiſtence and lands for from three to ſeven thouſand horſe, each according to his capacity and abilities.

To all others who were related unto me, I commanded that ſubſiſtence and appointments ſhould be given, from the rank of firſt Ameer to the rank of ſeventh Ameer, according to the abilities, and the dignity, and the rank of each; and that every one of them ſhould reſt content with the ſtation wherein he was placed, and preſume not to exceed the limits preſcribed unto him; and that if any one of them ſhould diſobey this order, he ſhould be called to a ſtrict account.

Concerning the punishments of my children, and my grandchildren, and my relations, and my chiefs, and my ministers.

I ordained, if either of my ſons ſhould aſpire to the imperial throne, that they ſhould not preſume to put him to death, nor load him with chains; neither ſhould they injure him in his limbs, or his organs; but that they ſhould confine him in a priſon, until he returned back from his evil ways: that civil wars and convulſions might not ariſe in the land of the Lord.

And if any one of my grandchildren, or relations, roſe in enmity againſt me, I ordered him to be reduced to the ſtate of a Dervaiſh. †

† i. e. To be deprived of his honours and fortune; to be reduced to a ſtate of beggary.

وامرا کـه حصار ملک اند اکر در وقت
کار نفاق کنند ایشانرا از امارت وایـالت مـعـزول
کردانند واکر از ایشان کاري بظهـور رسد که از
آن کار فسادي در ملک ظـاهـر شـود تابین امرا
نهایند واکر در امور سپاهکري کاهلي نهایند داخل
نویسندکان سازند واکر بعد آن تقصیري وکوتاهي
از ایشان بظهور رسد بار ندهند

در بــاب وزرا که معتمدان ومعتبران
سلسله دولت اند

امر نهودم اکر در امور سلطنت خیانتي
از ایشان ظاهر شود وزوال سلطنت اراده نهوده باشند
درکشتن ایشان تعجیل نه نهایند

وتحقیق کنند که مدعي وتـقـریـر
کنندکان ایشان چه کسان اند اول راستي وراست
کويء مدعیان بر محک امتحان تجربه نهایند چه
حـاسدان ومفتریـان بسیار باشند که از روي حسد
وطمع امر دروغي را بلباس راستي بـیارایند تا کار
خودرا ساخته کردانند

وبسیار از سفلکان لـیـم بـاشند که
دشمنان دولت را تسلي نهایند ودولتخواهان جانسپاررا
بحیله

AND if the Ameers, who are the bulwarks of empire, ſhould diſobey in the hour of action, I ordered that they ſhould be degraded from their commands, and deprived of their powers and their dignities; and that if any of them ſhould be guilty of actions, from whence diſturbances might ariſe in my dominions, that they ſhould be delivered over to the judgement of their peers; and that if they were guilty of neglect in the line of their military duty, they ſhould be claſſed amongſt the ſcribes; and, if in that ſtation they were diſobedient and refractory, that they ſhould be expelled from the imperial ſervice.

CONCERNING THE MINISTERS, WHO ARE THE MOST RESPECTABLE AND CONFIDENTIAL OF THE SERVANTS OF ROYALTY.

I ordained, if they ſhould be guilty of treachery in the concerns of the empire, or form attempts for the ſubverſion of the imperial authority, that their judges ſhould not be precipitate in conſigning them over to death:

AND that they ſhould diſcover and aſcertain who were their accuſers, and firſt try the honeſty and truth of the witneſſes on the touchſtone of examination and proof: for the invidious and the ſlanderers are many; who from envy and ſelf-intereſt will cloath falſehood in the garment of truth, that they may accompliſh their own deſigns.

AND many there are, worthleſs and wicked men, who will ſupport and encourage the enemies of their prince; and who by fraud, and artifice and trea-

بحیله کري ومکاري خراب سازند وبه مکر وغدر در حصار مملکت رخنه اندازند

چنانچــه امیر حسین به یکي از وزراي من در ساخت وویـرا تطمیع کرد که امیـر ایکو تیمور وامیر جاکو با آنکه بازويء دولت من بودند با من در اندازد ومن این معني را بفراست دریافتم وسخناني که در حــق ایشــان بمن میکفتند نا شنیده مي انکاشتم

وهمچنین جمعي از مـقـربـان من از روي حسد ونفاق سخنان غیــر واقعه از جانب امیر عباس که از امراي کلان معتبــر من بود در خلا وملا بعرض رسانیدند وآتش غضب مرا به باد سخنان دروغ بــر افروختــند تا آنکه در حالت غضب تجربه نا کرده امـر بقتــل وي نمودم ودر آخر حال غدر ایشــانـرا در حق امیر عباس فهمیدم ونادم وپشیمان کـشـتـم

ووزراي مالي که خزانه دار مملکت اند اگر در مالیات تغلب وتـصرف نمایند واکر بمقدار علوفه خود تصرف نموده باشند بانعام وي مقرر دارند اکر

chery will ruin and destroy his loyal and faithful subjects; and by falsehood, and perfidy, and deceit shake and overturn the foundation of his empire.

Thus Ameer Hoossein entered into a treacherous correspondence with one of my Vizzeers. And he administered to his avarice, and he prevailed upon him to sow discord and enmity between me and Eekoo Timour and Ameer Jaukoo, who were the sinews of my power and fortune. And I penetrated into the designs of Ameer Hoossein and my Vizzeer, and I listened not to their accusations against them.

And thus also several of those in whom I confided, from envy and from malice, communicated fictitious tales unto me, both in public and in private, to the prejudice of Ameer Ubbaus, who was one of my most powerful and most faithful chiefs. And they kindled the fire of my resentment by their false reports; and in the moment of anger I ordered him, unheard and unexamined, to be put to death: and in the end I discovered the perfidy of his accusers, and I was ashamed and confounded at my own conduct.

If the Vizzeers superintending the revenues, who hold the riches of the empire, were guilty of peculation therein; and if the sums which they appropriated to their own use, exceeded not the amount of their salaries, I ordered that it should be conferred upon them; that if they had taken sums to twice the amount of

اکر دو مقدار علوفه متصرف شده باشند در علوفه وي حساب نهایند اکر سه برابر علوفه خود کرفته باشند پیشکش کویان از وي تحصیل نهایند

وامر نهودم که از روي اعتبار برنکیرند واعتبار کرده خودرا بي اعتبار نکنند تا آنکه غلط بر سلطنت لازم نیاید

وسخنان ارباب غرض واشرار وحاسدان در حق وزرا نشنوند که این طبقه‌را دشمنان بسیار باشند چه اهل عالم همه دنیا طلب اند اکر وزرا رعایت ایشان نهایند خیانت کرده باشند واکر رعایت نکنند کمر بدشمني بر بندند

چغتاء خان وزیري داشت که ارباب تقریر چندین هزار درست زر بروي نوشته بودند چون آن نوشته‌را بنظر خان در آوردند وزیررا مخاطب ساخت واز روي عتاب کفت که تو مرد پست فطرتي ظاهر شدي چه وزیر مثل من پادشاي باشي واز مملکت من همین قدر قلیل تصرف نهاي وزیر خردمند بهمین احسان ممنون شده هرچه داشت آورده

of their ſubſiſtence, it ſhould be deducted therefrom; and that, if they had defrauded the revenues to three times the amount of their ſalaries, the imperial collectors ſhould levy it upon their fortunes. Book II.

AND I ordered that the collectors ſhould not take more than was due; but that their conduct ſhould be governed by equity and juſtice, that abuſes might not creep into the ordinances of government.

I commanded that the tales of the wicked, the envious, and the malicious againſt my Vizzeers ſhould not be attended to. For miniſters are a claſs of men who have many enemies; and the inhabitants of this world are ſearchers after the things thereof. If a miniſter patronizes and ſupports them, they will deceive and betray him; and if he neglects thoſe people, they will gird up their loins in oppoſition unto him.

CHUGHTAÏ Khaun had a miniſter whom the ſons of calumny accuſed of peculation to the amount of many thouſand pieces of money. When they preſented the impeachment to the king, he commanded the Vizzeer into his preſence, and thus reproached him, "It "is evident that thou art a wretch of a moſt abject diſ"poſition, ſince being the miniſter of a prince rich and "powerful as I am, thou canſt be meanly content with "defrauding thy maſter of ſuch poor and contemptible "ſums as theſe." The ſagacious and good Vizzeer, thus

 honoured

آورده پیشکش خان کرد وعزت واعتبار خودرا نکاهداشت

وسایر سپاه اکر از حد خود تجاوز نموده بر زیر دستي ستمي کنند ویرا بدست آن مظلوم بسپارند که داد خودرا از وي بکیرد

وکلانتران وکدخدایان اکر بر ریزه رعیت ظلمي کرده باشند فراخور ظلم وموافق استطاعت از وي جریمه کیرند حاکم وداروغه اکر از روي تعدي رعیت را خراب ساخته باشد ایشانرا جزا دهند وامر نمودم که بعد از ثبوت کناه اکر از کنه کار جریمه کیرند بشلاق سیاست نکنند واکر بشلاق سیاست کنند جریمه نکیرند

دزدرا امر نمودم در هر جا که باشد وهرکس بیابد بیاسا رسانند

وهر کس مال کسي را بتعدي کرفته باشد مال آن مظلوم را از ظالم کرفته بصاحب مال رسانند

وباقي

honoured by the kindneſs of his prince, brought forth all that he had, and laid it at the feet of his lord; and thus preſerved both his influence and his honour. Book II.

AND I commanded that if any one of my ſoldiers, exceeding the limits preſcribed him, ſhould injure or oppreſs the weak and the helpleſs, he ſhould be delivered into the hands of the injured perſon, that he might retaliate upon him.

AND if the chiefs or the nobles of any tribe or people extorted from the induſtrious huſbandman his ſmall pittance, I commanded that a fine ſhould be levied on the guilty perſon in proportion to the degree of extortion, and to his ability to make retribution: and if the governor or ſuperintendant ſhould cruelly deſtroy the property of a ſubject, that he ſhould be brought to puniſhment: but I ordained that after conviction, if the guilty perſon was fined, in that caſe corporal puniſhment ſhould not be inflicted; and if corporal puniſhment was inflicted, I ordered that he ſhould not be fined.

ROBBERS and thieves, in whatever place they might be found, or by whomſoever detected, I commanded to be put to death.

AND I ordained, that, if any one ſeized by violence the property of another, the value of that property ſhould be taken from the oppreſſor, and be reſtored to the oppreſſed.

وباقي امور از دندان شکستن وچشم
کور کردن وکوش بيني بريدن وشراب خوردن
وزنا کردن اکر از کسی بوقوع آيد در ديوان
قاضي اسلام وقاضي احداث اجلاس نموده انچه
امور شرعي باشند قاضي اسلام در آنها حکم نمايد
وانچه عرفي باشد قاضي احداث تحقيق کرده
بعرض من رسانند

تزوک نکاهداشت وزرا

امر نمودم در وزرا چهار صفت احتياط
نمايند اول اصالت ونجابت دويم عقل وکياست
سيوم سلوک ومعاش با سپاه ورعيت چهارم بردباري
ومسالمت

هرکس باين چهار صفت موصوف باشد
ويرا قابل مرتبه وزارت دانند ووزير ومشير سازند
وعنان امور مملکت وسپاه ورعيت بوي سپارند آنکاه
ويرا بچهار چيز امتياز بخشند اعتماد واعتبار واختيار
واقتدار

کامل

CONCERNING other crimes, the breaking of teeth, and the putting out of eyes, and the slitting and cutting off the ears and nose, and wine-drinking and adultery, I ordained that whoever should be guilty of these, or other crimes, they should be brought into the court of the ecclesiastical and civil judges: that the ecclesiastical magistrate should decide on those causes, which are determinable by the sacred laws; and that those which did not fall under his cognizance, should be investigated, and laid before me by the civil judge.

CONCERNING THE APPOINTMENT OF MINISTERS.

I ordained that in Vizzeers four qualities should be particularly attended to: First, firmness and generosity: Secondly, understanding and sagacity: Thirdly, the power of living in harmony with the soldiers and the subjects: Fourthly, patience under difficulties, and talents for the cultivation of peace and tranquillity:

THAT whoever was endowed with these four qualities should be considered as equal to the office of Vizzeer; should be made both minister and counsellor, and the reins of the concerns of the government, of the army, and the subjects be delivered over to his care; that preeminence should be conferred upon him by four things, confidence, and esteem, and discretionary power, and authority.

كامل الوزارت وزيري باشد كه رتق
وفتق معاملات وامور ملكي ومال را از روي نيكي
ونيكذاتي وحسن سلوك صورت دهد واز جايي كه
نبايد كرفت نكيرد وبجايي نبايد داد ندهد ودر
اوامر ونواهي اثار نجابت واصالت از وي ظاهر كردد
ونغاق ودرانداري از وي ظاهر نشود ونام همه كس از
سپاه ورعيت به نيكي برد وبدي هيچكس نكويد
ونشنود واكر از كسي بدي ديده باشد چنان
سلوك نمايد كه آن شخص از بدي خود باز آيد
وبد كننده خودرا نيكي كند تا بسوي وي باز
كشت نمايد

وهر وزيري كه بد كويد وبد شنود
ودرانداري بكند ومردم نيك را خواهد بواسطه بدي
كه بوي داشته باشد خراب سازد ويرا از وزارت معزول
نمايد

وبد ذاتان وحاسدان وكينه داران واشرار را
وزارت ندهند چه اثاري كه از وزارت اشرار وسغلكان
مترتب كردد همين است كه دولت وسلطنت زود
روي بزوال آورد

چنانچه ملكشاه سلجوقي نظام الملك وزير
خودرا

THAT minister shall be equal to his office, who ordereth and conducteth the affairs and concerns of the government, of land, and of property, with uprightness, and integrity, and moderation; who taketh not where it should not be taken, and remitteth not where it should not be remitted; who in his ordinances and prohibitions giveth proofs of lenity and of firmness; in whom hypocrisy and dissimulation shall not appear; who speaketh well of the soldier and of the subject; and who neither heareth nor sayeth evil of another; who, if he discovereth bad designs in any one, shall so conduct himself towards him, that he shall turn back from his iniquitous intentions; and who shall do good to the man who doeth evil unto him, that he may return into the path of friendship.

LET the Vizzeer who heareth and sayeth evil of others, who soweth contention, and who endeavoureth to ruin a good and virtuous man, from the malice which he beareth unto him, be expelled from his office.

THE office of the Vizzaurut must not be conferred on the wicked, the envious, the revengeful, or the seditious: for the consequence that shall follow from the administration of such men, is the speedy dissolution of the imperial fortune and empire.

THUS it happened to Mullick Shaah Siljokee. He disgraced his Vizzeer Nizzaum ul Moolluk, who

خودرا که بجمع صفات حسنه آراسته بود معزول ساخته وسفله شریری را بجای وی نصب کرد بشامت اعمال وشرارت وبد نفسی وی بنای سلطنتش روی بانهدام آورد.

وهمچنین معتصم بالله عباسی علقمی را که بصفت حسد وکینه موصوف بود وزیرا خود ساخت بواسطه کینه که از خلیفه در خاطر داشت بسخنان منافقانی خلیفه‌را بازی داد وهلاکو خان را ترغیب نموده بر سر خلیفه آورد وویرا کرفتار ساخت ورسید بخلیفه انچه رسید

پس وزیری را اختیار نماید که اصیل ونجیب ونیکذات ونیکو کار باشد که اصل خطا نکند وبد اصل وفا ننماید

وهر وزیری که از راه سلامتی نفس وراستی بامر وزارت قیام نماید وامور ملکی ومالی را از راه صواب ودیانت وامانت پرداخت کند ویرا بمراتب عالیه رسانند

ووزیری

who was adorned with every great and ſhining quality; and appointed an ignoble and worthleſs man in his place. By the ill conduct, viciouſneſs, and villainy of that miniſter the foundation of the power of Mullick Shaah was overturned.

IN this manner Al Kummi, who was noted for his malevolent and revengeful diſpoſition, was raiſed to the dignity of firſt miniſter by Maatuſſim Billau Ubbauſi. Influenced by the ſecret rancour which he harboured in his ſoul againſt the Khulleefeh, that wicked miniſter deceived his maſter with the language of treachery; and exciting the ambition of Hullaukoo Khaun, drew the powerful arms of that prince on the head of the unſuſpecting Khalif: he cauſed his perſon to be ſeized; and that befell the Khalif which did befall him.

THEREFORE the Vizzeer to be choſen is a man of illuſtrious deſcent, and of a noble heart, and of a virtuous diſpoſition, and of prudent conduct. The truly illuſtrious ſwerve not from their duty; but in the baſe and ignoble fidelity and good faith are not to be found.

AND every Vizzeer who conducteth himſelf in his high ſtation with uprightneſs and integrity; who directeth the various departments of government with rectitude, and with fidelity, and with reſpect to the ſacred laws, let him be exalted to the higheſt dignities.

ووزيـري كه از شرارت وبـد نـفسي
معاملات را انجام دهد زود باشد كه خير وبركت از
آن سلطنت برخيزد

ووزيـر دانا وزيري باشد كه بدرشتي
ونرمي كار كند نه بسيار درشت باشد ونه بسيـار
نرم اكر بسيار نرمي بكار برد دنيا طلبان وطماعان
ويرا فرو برند اكر بسيار درشتي نمايد از وي بكريزند
وبوي رجوع ننمايند

پس وزير دانا وزيري باشد كه كارخانه
سلطنت به حسن سلوك وفهميدكي نظام وانـتـظـام
دهـد ودر امـور سلطنت تحـمـل وبردبـاري بكار
برد ومعاملات را بدرشتي ونرمي فيصل دهد

واين قسم وزيري را شريك دولت دانند
چه دولت سلطنت بملك وخـزانه ولشكر قايم باشد
واين هر سه بوزير دانا اصلاح وانجام يابد

ووزير جامع الاخلاق وزيـري باشد كه
بواسطـه نا ملايمه كه بوي رسد كينه ونفاق را در
دل

AND if the miniſter tranſacteth the important concerns of empire by villainy and artifice, it ſhall ſpeedily happen that the power and proſperity of that empire ſhall paſs away.

THAT MINISTER IS A WISE MINISTER, who in his conduct employeth both mildneſs and ſeverity; who is neither immoderately ſevere, nor weakly compliant. For if he acteth with too much mildneſs and compliance, the avaricious and wordly-minded will oppreſs and bear him down: and if his ſeverity be exceſſive, the people will fly from before him, and at all times avoid his preſence.

THEREFORE THAT MINISTER IS A WISE MINISTER, who regulateth and giveth order to the edifice of royalty by a juſt knowledge of mankind, and by an uniform and prudent conduct; who in the execution of his office acteth with patience and forbearance, and conducteth the affairs of government with mildneſs and with ſeverity.

LET ſuch a Vizzeer be conſidered as a friend and companion in the imperial dignity. For the dignity of empire is ſupported by extenſive territories, by a rich treaſury, and by numerous armies: and theſe three things ſhall be obtained and ſecured by a WISE MINISTER.

A PERFECT MINISTER IS THAT MINISTER, who, in conſequence of any harſhneſs that ſhall be offered unto him, permitteth not revenge and enmity to take poſſeſſion

 of

دل خود راه ندهد اگر کینه دار ومنافق باشد از
وي پر حذر باید بود که مبادا بدشمنان دولت
سازکاري نماید وخزانه ولشکر را مختل کرداند

وزیر عاقل وزیري باشد که رعیت را
بیک دست گیرد وسپاه را بیک دست واز جايء که
نباید گرفت نگیرد وبجايء که نباید داد ندهد
وحزم واحتیاط را از دست ندهد وبراستي ودرستي
معامله نماید ونظر بر عواقب امور کند ودر هنگامه
رتق وفتق معاملات خصم را در مقابلهء خود نه
بینند

وزیر کاردان کارگذار وزیري باشد
که معموري مملکت ورفاهت رعیت وجمعیت سپاه
وتوفیر خزانه را در نظر داشته باشد واموري که به
دولت سلطنت نفع رساند در تمشیت آن سعي نماید
واموري که بسلطنت ضرر رساند در دفع آن بمال
وجان ساعي باشد ومهمات سپاه ورعیت را بر وجه
خیر وصلاح فیصل دهد

ووزیر

of his soul. If he be malignant, and harbour revenge, he must be watched with care and with caution; lest he enter into confederacies with the enemies of the imperial power, and involve in confusion the revenues and the army of his prince.

AN INTELLIGENT AND SAGACIOUS MINISTER IS THAT MINISTER, who supporteth the subject with one hand, and with the other hand holdeth up the soldier; who receiveth not whence it should not be received; and who giveth not where it should not be given; who letteth not vigilance and circumspection forth from his hand; who acteth with uprightness and integrity; who looketh forward to the conclusion and consequences of every transaction; and who in negotiating the affairs of the empire seeth not his enemy before him.

THAT MINISTER IS AN EXPERIENCED AND ACTIVE MINISTER, who keepeth in his eye the cultivation and population of the country, and the prosperity of the subjects, and the strength of the army, and the fulness of the treasury; who exerteth himself in promoting those measures which are profitable to government, and hazardeth his fortune and his life in counteracting those, from which evil may follow to the imperial dignity; and who directeth the concerns of the soldier and the subject with prudence and deliberation.

A vir-

وزير نيكو محضر وزيري باشد كه اعمال
خيرش غالب بر انعال شر وي بود

چنين بمسامع من رسيد كه انعال
ذميمه نظام الملك مغلوب اعمال خيرش بوده در آن
وقتي كه وي اراده حج كرد يكي از رجال الله
بوي كفت همين عمل خيري كه در دولت ملكشاه
از تو صادر ميشود كه بندهاي خدا از تو نفع مي
بينند برابر حج است

وبعرض من رسيد كه علي بن لقطي
كه وزير هارون الرشيد بود چون نفع وي بخلق
خدا بسيار ميرسيد روزي كه ارادهء ترك وزارت نمود
يكي از ايمه دين بوي نوشت كه ترا است كه بر
دركاه خليفه ملازم امر وزارت باشي وجدايء اختيار
نكني كه امداد ونفعي كه به بندكان خدا ميرساني
سر آمد جميع اعمال وانعال حسنه تو باشد

وچنين شنيدم كه چون از حضرت
رسول صلي الله عليه وسلم سوال كردند كه اكر
شما به نبوت ورسالت مبعوث نمي شديد بكدام كار
اشتغال

A VIRTUOUS MINISTER IS THAT MINISTER, whoſe good qualities predominate over his failings.

THUS I have heard, that the failings of Nizzaum ul Moolluk were vanquiſhed by his virtues. At that time when he reſolved to perform the holy pilgrimage, one of the men of God ſaid unto him; "Thy "good actions which ſhine forth in the glory and the "power of Mullick Shaah, and the bleſſings which the "people of the Almighty receive from thy hands, are "equal to all the merits of pilgrimage and of ſanctity."

AND it has alſo been related unto me, that on the day when Aali Ben Luckti, who was the miniſter of Hauroon ul Ruſheed, determined to retire from the Vizzaurut; as his adminiſtration had been favourable to the people of God, one of the holy prieſts wrote to him, ſaying; "Thou ſhalt continue to execute thy office in the "palace of the Khalif; thou ſhalt not relinquiſh thy au-"thority: for the comforts and the benefits which thou "conferreſt on the ſervants of the Almighty, are ſuperior "to all the good and glorious actions of thy life."

AND ſo alſo I have heard, that when it was demanded of the holy prophet, (on whom be the protection of God) "If thou hadſt not been ſent forth "the meſſenger and prophet of the Almighty, what oc-"cupation wouldeſt thou have choſen?" He anſwered, ſaying,

اشتغال میفرمودید فرمودند که خدمت سلاطین اختیار میکردم تا بخلق خدا نفع رسانم

از این جهت بود که وزارت وسپهسالاري الیاس خواجه پسر تغلقتیمور خان را قبول کرده بودم که امداد خلق نمایم واز مددکاري خلق خدا بود که الله تعالي مرا بمرتبه سلطنت رسانید

ووزیري که بتدبیر وشمشیر ملکي را مسخر سازد یا نکاهداري ملک نماید آن وزیر را عزیز ومحترم دارند وبر مراتبش بیفزایند ووزیرا صاحب السیف والقلم خطاب دهند

ووزیر خردمند وهوشمند وزیري باشد که براي وتدبیر لشکریرا متفرق سازد وبسازکاري وخوش سلوک لشکریرا متفق کرداند وافواج دشمن را بخود رام کند ونکاهبان ولي نعمت خود باشد وهر مهمي ومشکلي که پادشاه را پیش آید به راي وتدبیر ودور بیني آن مشکل را آسان کرداند اکر بستکي

ſaying, "I would have ſought the ſervice of princes; Book II.
"that I might have been able to do good to the ſervants "of my Creator."

And it was on this account that I conſented to accept the employments of miniſter and general from Ouleaus Khaujeh, the ſon of Tughulluk Timour Khaun; that I might ſuccour and ſupport the people. And from the aſſiſtance and protection which I afforded to his ſervants, it may have come to paſs that Almighty God hath exalted me to the throne of empire.

And if a miniſter by ſkilful meaſures, or by the ſword, conquereth or ſaveth a kingdom, let him be held in honour and reſpect; and let him be exalted and ſtiled, The lord of the sword and the pen.

A skilful and able minister is that minister, who, when neceſſary, can by his counſels and abilities diſperſe and divide the power of armies; and who, when occaſion calleth, can by well-adapted and ſkilful meaſures unite them together; who hath the capacity to ſow diviſions among the forces of the enemy, and to make them ſubſervient to his views, and to be the conſervator of his prince and maſter; who can, by his ſagacity, and wiſdom, and foreſight reſolve and render eaſy the momentous concerns and difficulties which ſurround a king; and who,

 if

بستگي در امور سلطنت بهم رسد آنرا بسر انگشت
عقل وفکر بکشاید

چنانچه در وقتي که علي بيک چون
غرباني مرا در بند انداخت ودر خانه پر از کيک
مقيد ساخت عزيز الدين که از وزراي من بود از
ترمذ ايلغار کرده خودرا بمن رسانيد وعلي بيک را
در خواب کرد وچشم ويرا از من پوشانيد ومرا
قوت داد تا بسبازوي شجاعت ومردي بضرب شمشير
از ميان نگاهبانان بر آمده نجات يافتم چنانچه
نظام الملک سلطان ملکشاه را از بند قيصر خلاص
ساخت

پس اين چنين وزيري را شريک دولت
دانند وعزيز دارند واز گفتار او تجاوز ننمايند که
انچه گويد همه از روي عقل باشد

اگر پادشاه ظالم باشد ووزيرش عادل
بود تدارک ظلم پادشاه ميشود ليکن اگر وزير ظالم
باشد زود باشد که سلسله امور سلطنت بر هم
خورد

تزوک

if the affairs of empire be involved in confusion, can reduce them to order by the hand of understanding and reflection. Book II.

THUS at the time that Aali Beg Choun Ghoorbauni seized on my person, and confined me in a loathsome dungeon, filled with vermin; Aazeez u deen, who was one of my Vizzeers, came to me from Turmuz with speed; and lulling to sleep the attention of Aali Beg, and hiding his eyes from his prisoner, he gave such vigour to my hopes, that with the arm of fortitude and resolution, and by the edge of the sword, I extricated myself from the guards which were stationed over me, and recovered my freedom. In the like manner Nizzaum ul Moolluk delivered Mullick Shaah from the hands of Keesur.

LET therefore such a minister be accounted the companion of the imperial fortune; let him be treated with kindness and affection; and let not his counsels be disregarded: for that which he sayeth, proceedeth from wisdom and understanding.

If a king be oppressive, and his Vizzeer be just, the oppressions of the king are moderated and rectified by the justice of the Vizzeer; but if the Vizzeer be oppressive, the affairs of that government shall be speedily involved in confusion.

تزوک مرتبه امارت وایالت

امر نهودم که به سیصد وسیزده مرد که
نوکران خاص الخاص من بودند امارت بدهند
واین مردم بودند که باصالت ونجابت وعقل وکیاست
وتهور وشجاعت وتدبیر وحزم واحتیاط ودور بیني وعاقبت
اندیشي موصوف بودند

واز براي هریک کوتل* تعین کردم اکر
یکي از ایشان را موت وفوت پیش آید آن کوتل
جانشین وي باشد وآن کوتل را منتظر الامارت نام
نهادم

واین سیصد وسیزده امیر من صاحبان
عقل وهوش وبزم ورزم وصف آراي ولشکر شکني
بودند

وبتجربه من رسیده که لایق امارت
وایالت مردي تواند بود که رموز جنک وشیوه شکست
دادن غنیم را دریابد ووقت جنک دل از دست ندهد
ودست وپا کم نکند وافواج را کار بفرماید واکر
در صفوف لشکر رخنه بظهور رسد آن رخنه را تواند
بربست

وامیر

REGULATIONS CONCERNING THE APPOINTMENT OF SUPERIOR OFFICERS.

I commanded that three hundred and thirteen persons from among my chosen and superior servants should be advanced to exalted dignities. And those were men who were renowned for their high lineage, and for nobleness of mind, and for understanding, and for penetration, and for resolution, and for intrepidity, and for skill, and for vigilance, and for caution, and for foresight, and for deep reflection.

AND to each of them I appointed another person, who on the death of the first should succeed to his rank and dignity; and him I entitled AN EXPECTER OF PREFERMENT.

AND these three hundred and thirteen Ameers were men of judgement and of knowledge; and they were learned in the arts of peace and of war; and they were skilled in the evolutions of armies, and in breaking the lines of the enemy.

FOR by experience it is known unto me, that he only is equal to stations of power and dignity, who is well acquainted with the military art, and with the various modes of breaking and defeating hostile armies; who in the hour of battle giveth not his heart forth from his hand, nor permitteth apprehension and terror to take possession of his soul; who can direct the efforts of his troops; and if their ranks be thrown into confusion, can by his abilities restore them to order.

HE

وامير الامرا او تواند بود كه در بزم ورزم
نايب وقايم مقام من باشد وبشوكت ومهابت تواند
كه لشكريرا كار فرمايد وهركس را كه مخالفت وي
كند تواند كه سياست نهايد

وامر نهودم كه از جهله سيصد وسيزده
نفر چهار كس بيكلر بيكي باشند ويك نفر امير
الامراء مقرر باشد كه حكم وي در يساقها وجنكها بر
امرا وساير سپاه جاري باشد ووي در حضور من نايب
من باشد

دوازده مرد ديكررا كه صاحب غيرت
وناموس بودند بدين ترتيب امارت دادم
امير اول را امارت هزار كس داده بر
ايشان امير كردانيدم وامير دوم را امارت دو هزار كس
دادم وبر آن دو هزار كس امير ساختم همچنين
امير سيوم وچهارم وپنجم را بر سه هزار چهار هزار پنج
هزار كس امير كردانيدم تا دوازده امير بهمين ترتيب
بر شش هزار كس تا دوازده هزار كس امير ساختم
وهريك را بترتيب امارت نايب ديكري مقرر نهودم
چنانچه امير اول نايب امير دوم وامير

He is capable of filling the station of chief of the Omraus, who is worthy of being my lieutenant in peace and in war; who can rule the armies with majesty and with authority; and who hath the vigour to chastize those who rise in opposition to his commands.

I commanded, that of the fore-going three hundred and thirteen Ameers, four should be appointed Beglerbegs; † and that one should be exalted to the dignity of Ameer ul Omrau: whose authority should be over the Ameers and the army, in the field and in action; and who in my presence should act as my deputy.

Twelve other persons, men of reputation and renown, I exalted to high commands, according to this order.

To the first Ameer I gave in charge a thousand men, and appointed him commander over them. And to the second Ameer I gave the command of two thousand men; and appointed him their chief. And, in the same manner, to the third, and the fourth, and the fifth Ameer I gave the command of three, and four, and five thousand men: and thus from the sixth to the twelfth Ameer, from six thousand up to twelve thousand. And each, according to his rank, I appointed the deputy and representative of his superior.

Thus I appointed the first Ameer the deputy of the second, and the second Ameer the deputy of

† i. e. Generals or commanders of the first rank.

دوم نايب سيوم همچنين امير يازدهم را نايب امير دوازدهم ساختم وامير دوازدهم نايب امير الامرا باشد وامير الامرا نايب من باشد تا اكر قضيه پيش آيد نايب قايم مقام وي كردد

واز جمله سيصد وسيزده مرد امر نمودم كه صد مردرا اون باشي نمايند وصد كس را يوز باشي وصد كس را مينك باشي

وامر كردم كه در وقت چار وپلچار* امير الامرا بامرا ومينك باشيان ويوز باشيان واون باشيان خبر رسانند وكار اون باشي را به يوز باشي نفرمايند همچنين كار يوز باشي را به مينك باشي وكار مينك باشي را بامير وكار امير را بامير الامرا نفرمايند

ومهمي كه باون باشي بانجام رسد به يوز باشي محتاج نشوند وهمچنين كاري كه از يوز باشي بر آيد بمينك باشي محتاج نكردانند

وهريك از امرا كه از روي رغبت كار طلب باشد بوي بفرمايند

تزك

the third; thus alſo the eleventh Ameer the deputy of the twelfth Ameer, and the twelfth Ameer the deputy of the Ameer ul Omrau, and the Ameer ul Omrau my deputy: that if an accident ſhould happen, the one might ſupply the place of another. Book II.

I alſo commanded that from amongſt theſe three hundred and thirteen Ameers, a hundred ſhould be ſtiled Ounbauſhees, that one other hundred ſhould be called Euzbauſhees, and that the third hundred ſhould be ſtiled Mingbauſhees.

AND I ordained that in times of ſervice the Ameer ul Omrau ſhould iſſue orders to the Ameers, and the Mingbauſhees, and the Euzbauſhees, and the Ounbauſhees: and that the duty of the Ounbauſhee ſhould not be impoſed on the Euzbauſhee; and in the like manner that the duty of the Euzbauſhee ſhould not be impoſed on the Mingbauſhee; nor the duty of the Mingbauſhee on the Ameer; nor the duty of the Ameer on the Ameer ul Omrau:

AND that on ſuch ſervice as might be executed by an Ounbauſhee, an Euzbauſhee ſhould not be ordered; and that a Mingbauſhee ſhould not be ſent on a ſervice which could be performed by an Euzbauſhee:

AND that every one of the Ameers, who, from a ſpirit of enterpriſe, demanded employment, that his requeſt ſhould be granted.

تزک تربیت سپاه از مرتبهٔ ادني تا

بمرتبه اعلي

امر نمودم که از بهادرانیکه که شمشیر نمایان زده باشد در شمشیر اول اون باشي نمایند ودر شمشیر دوم یوز باشي کنند ودر شمشیر سیوم مینک باشي سازند وتابینان اون باشي را در شمشیر اول اون باشي گردانند

وامر نمودم که شمشیر حفظ را منظور ندارند که گاو هم شاخ میزنند پس نظر بر اصالت ونجابت سپاهي هم باید کرد

ومینک باشي چون بضرب شمشیر فوجي را بشکند امیر اول گردانند وامیر اول چون صف شکني نماید امیر دوم سازند وهمچنین هر امیري که کار نمایان کرده فوج شکني کند از مرتبه وي بالاتر ترقي فرمایند وسایر سپاه چون شمشیر بزنند علوفه ایشان بیفزایند

وهر

REGULATIONS OF PROMOTIONS AND REWARDS TO MY SOLDIERS FROM THE MEANEST TO THE MOST EXALTED.

I ordained, if any one of my ſelect ſoldiers diſtinguiſhed himſelf in battle, that in recompence for the firſt exploit he ſhould be made an Ounbauſhee, and for the ſecond exploit an Euzbauſhee, and for the third exploit a Mingbauſhee; and that the Taubeenaun † of the Ounbauſhee ſhould for the firſt exploit be raiſed to the rank of Ounbauſhee.

I ordained alſo, that an atchievement which ſprung from attention to perſonal ſafety in the moment of peril, ſhould not be regarded: for the ox will ſometimes ſtrike with his horns, and turn upon his purſuers. Therefore the firmneſs and the ſpirit of the ſoldier muſt alſo be conſidered.

I commanded, when a Mingbauſhee vanquiſhed the forces of his antagoniſt by the edge of the ſword, that he ſhould be raiſed to the rank of firſt Ameer: and that the firſt Ameer, on defeating the army of his foe, ſhould be appointed ſecond Ameer: and thus, that every Ameer who ſignalized his valour and abilities, and overthrew the forces of his enemy, ſhould be promoted from his own to a ſuperior ſtation: and that the private ſoldiers who diſtinguiſhed themſelves in battle, ſhould be rewarded by an increaſe of pay.

† i.e. The inferior to the Ounbauſhee.

وهر سپاهي كه در وقت كار روي
گرداند ويرا كورنش ندهند واكر مضطر شده روي
كردان شده باشد معذورش دارند واكر واهمه بر
وي غلبه كرده باشد ويرا باولي* بدهند وهر سپاهي
كه شمشير زند وزخم بردارد ويرا جلدو* بدهند واكر
زخم برداشته رو كردان شده باشد ويرا تحسين
نمايند وزخم خوردن ويرا اعتبار كنند كه اكر وي به
غنيم نرسيده باشد اما غنيم بوي رسيده وزخم وي
كواه حال وي باشد

وحق سپاهي را ضايع نسازند وهر سپاهي
كه به پيري رسد ويرا از علوفه ومرتبه محروم ومعزول
نكردانند وكار سپاه را پوشيده ندارند ومردم سپاهي
كه حيات باقي خودرا بمال فاني ميفروشند مستحق
جلدو* باشند ولايق انعام وتربيت اكر ويرا از انعام
محروم سازند وكارش را پوشيده دارند بي انصافي
كرده باشند

وامر نمودم كه هر اميري ووزيري وسپاهي
كه حق خدمت بر دولت من ثابت كرده باشد

† This word is Mogul, and the meaning unknown.

ولشكري

To every soldier who turned his back in the hour of action, I ordered that Koornish † should not be given; and that if he fled from absolute necessity, he should be pardoned; and that if he should be struck with a panic, and fly in consequence thereof, that he should be pardoned also; ‡ and that to every soldier, who should fight with resolution, and be wounded in action, a compensation should be given; and that if he should be wounded in battle, and then retire from the field, his conduct should be applauded. The wound which he had received should be considered as a proof, that if he reached not to the enemy, yet the arm of the enemy extended unto him: his wound should be a witness in his favour.

I ordained that the right of the warrior should not be injured; and that the soldier who had grown in years should not be deprived of his station or his wages; and that the actions of the soldier should not be suppressed: for those men who sell their permanent happiness for perishable honour, merit compensation, and are worthy of reward and encouragement. If a soldier should be deprived of his reward, and his actions should be hidden from the light, it would be an act of injustice.

I ordained that every chief, minister, and soldier, who by his services had established a claim on my fortune; who had defeated an army, or reduced a king-

‡ The Mogul word is *Bauwulli*, and the sense is doubtful.

ولشكري را شكست داده يا ملكي را مسخر نموده
يا شمشيري زده باشد حق خدمت ويرا منظور دارند
وحق ويرا ادا نمايند

ويپران سپاهرا بعزت بدارند وسخنان از
ايشان بشنوند كه انچه ايشان بكويند از تجربه خواهد
بود وايشانرا مصالح كارخانه سلطنت دانند بعد از
ايشان فرزندان ايشان را قايم مقام ايشان نمايند

وامر نمودم كه هر سپاهي از جانب غنيم
كرفتار كرده ويرا نكشند ومختار كردانند اكر
نوكري قبول كند نوكر سازند والا آزاد كردانند
چنانچه من چهار هزار رومي را آزاد كردم

وهر سپاه كه از جانب غنيم شمشير زند
وحق نمك بجاي آورد خواه از روي اختيار خواه از
روي اضطرار اكر التجا بدركاه من آورد بروي
اعتماد نمايند وعزيز دارند كه وفاداري بصاحب خود
كرده وحق نمك بجاي آورده
چنانچه من به شير بهرام كردم كه وي
در جنك امير حسين بمن در جنك رو بر رو شد
وشمشيرها نمايان زد چون از روي اضطرار بمن پناه
آورد ويرا احترام كردم

ومنكلي

kingdom, or distinguished his valour in the hour of battle; that his claims should be regarded, and that the price of his services should be paid unto him: Book II.

AND that the aged warriors should be treated with honour and attention; and that their counsel and opinion should be heard (for that which they say, must proceed from experience) and that they should be considered as the ornaments of my empire; and that on their demise, their sons should succeed to their stations and dignities.

I ordained that the hostile soldier taken in battle should not be put to death; and that military service and freedom should be offered to his choice; that if he consented to enter into my service, he should be received; if not, that he should be set at liberty. In this manner I once gave freedom to 4000 Roomi. †

I ordered that every soldier who had performed his duty, and fought with valour on the side of my enemy, if, from choice or necessity, he sought shelter under my authority, that he should be received with confidence, and treated with honour and regard: since he had performed his duty, and acted with fidelity to his former master.

THUS I rewarded Share Behraum; who in an action with Ameer Hoossein opposed me face to face, and fought with astonishing valour: when through necessity he fled to me for protection, I received him with honour.

† Turks.

THUS

ومنكلي بوغا در جنك بلخ بر من لشكر كشيد ومن پيش از جنك بوي پيغام داده خواستم بطرف خود بكشم وي نهك تغلقتيمور خان را فراموش نكرد ولشكر آراي كرده با من جنك مرداني كرد وهزيمت يافت

وروزي كه از روي اختيار بمن التجا آورد وزانو زد پايه قدر ومرتبه ويرا بلند ساختم ومشمول عنايت خود كردانيدم وچندان عنايت كردم كه انچه در خاطر داشت فراموش كرد وويرا در هر مجلس آفرين ورحمت ياد ميكفتم

چون مردي بود مردانه در دولت من كارهاء مردانه نهايان كرد ومارا ممنون ساخت ودر جنك اذربايجان كه با قرا يوسف مقابله اتفاق افتاد وقتي كه سپاه من مضطرب شده بودند وي سري از سرهاي سران لشكر قرا يوسف را بر سر نيزه كرده بلند ساخت وسر قرا يوسف نام نهاد ودر لشكر در داد كه قرا يوسف كشته شده ولشكررا دل داد وبر قلب فوج قرا يوسف هجوم آورد وقرا يوسف را هزيمت داد ومن فتح قرا يوسف را بنام وي نوشتم وبر مراتبش افزودم

تزك

THUS alſo Munguli Booghau, in the war of Bullukh, advanced with an army againſt me; and before the engagement commenced, I ſent propoſals unto him, and endeavoured to draw him over to my ſide. But he forgot not his duty to Tughulluk Timour Khaun; and he formed his troops in order of battle, and he charged my forces with undaunted reſolution, and he was defeated.

AND when he afterwards voluntarily came unto me, and kneeled to my authority, I raiſed him to an exalted ſtation, and I included him in the number of my moſt favoured ſervants; and on all occaſions I praiſed and applauded his conduct. And ſuch were the favours which I conferred upon him, that if any reſentment remained in his heart, it was totally obliterated.

AS he was a bold and intrepid warrior, he ſignalized himſelf in my ſervice, and conferred obligations upon me. And in the war of Azzurbauejaun, when I encountered Kurrau Euſoof, in the moment that my troops were diſcouraged and thrown into confuſion, he placed upon the point of his ſpear the head of an hoſtile commander; and he named it the head of Kurrau Euſoof, and called aloud to my forces, that Kurrau Euſoof was ſlain; and he gave courage to my ſoldiers. And he ruſhed on the centre of Kurrau Euſoof's line, and drove him from the field. And this victory over Kurrau Euſoof I imputed to Munguli Booghau; and I exalted him to a ſuperior rank.

 REGULA-

تزک تربیت کردن امرا ووزرا وسپاه
ورعیت بانعام وجلدو*

امر کردم که هر امیري که ملکي را مسخر کرداند یا لشکري را شکست دهد ویرا بسه چیز امتیاز دهند بخطاب وطوغ ونقاره وویرا بهادر لقب کنند وشریک دولت وسلطنت دانند ودر مجلس کنکاش داخل سازند وولایت سرحد بوي حواله نمایند وامرا را تابع وي کردانند وهر امیري که توره را بشکند یا امیر زاده را شکست دهد یا خاني را منهزم اورا بهمان روش بنوازند

چنانچه امیر ایکو تیمور را که بر اروس خان تعین نمودم وویرا شکست داد بوي تومان وطوغ وعلم ونقاره دادم وویرا شریک دولت خود ساختم ووزیر ومشیر خود کردانیدم ودر کنکاش خود داخل کردانیده سرحد ارزاني داشتم وامرا را بوي تابع کردانیدم

وحاسدان درحق وي سخنان کفتند که الوس اوروس خان را غارت کرده واموال واسباب را

† A kind of kettle-drum.

خود،

Book II.

REGULATIONS FOR ENCOURAGING MY AMEERS, AND MY VIZZEERS, AND MY SOLDIERS, AND MY SUBJECTS, BY REWARDS AND BY HONOURS.

I ordained that every Ameer who ſhould reduce a kingdom, or defeat an army, ſhould be exalted by three things, by a title of honour, by the ſtandard, and by the Niccaureh; † and that he ſhould be dignified with the appellation of Bahaudur; ‡ and that he ſhould be conſidered as the aſſociate of the royal power and dignity; and that he ſhould be admitted a member of my imperial council; and that the government of a frontier province ſhould be conferred upon him; and that Ameers ſhould be placed under his command. I alſo ordained that every Ameer who defeated a prince, or the ſon of a prince, or a Khaun, ſhould be exalted after the ſame manner.

THUS I rewarded Ameer Eekoo Timour; whom I had appointed to reduce Auroos Khaun. He conquered that prince; and I conferred upon him a Toumaun, ‖ the ſtandard, the military enſign, and the Niccaureh; I made him the aſſociate of my fortune; and I appointed him my Vizzeer and my adviſer; and I gave him a place in my imperial council; and I conferred upon him the government of a frontier province; and I placed Ameers under his command.

AND the envious uttered inſinuations againſt him, that he had plundered the hord of Auroos Khaun, and that he had taken the ſpoils to himſelf.

‡ The Brave.

‖ The command of 10,000 men.

And

خود متصرف شده وازين سخنان مزاج مرا از وي منحرف ساختند ليکن قصه بهرام جوبين که بمسامع من رسيده بود بتجربه برداشته بودم

که چون خاقان سيصد هزار ترک خونخوار بر هرمز بن نوشروان لشکر کشيد ووي بهرام جوبين را که وزير ومشير وسپه سالار نوشروان بود با سيصد بيست هزار مرد ايراني رو بر رو خاقان فرستاد ووي در مقابله خاقان در آمد وسه شبان روز در قتال وجدال بود تا آنکه خاقانرا شکست داد وحقيقت را بهرمز عرضه داشت نمود وغنايمي که بدست آورده بود بخدمت هرمز فرستاد

وحاسدان وغمازان که در مجلس هرمز راه سخن داشتند غمازي نموده کفتند که بهرام مبلغهاي کلي در ميان نکاهداشت وشمشير وکلاه مرصع وموزه مکلل به جواهر قيمتي خاقان را خود متصرف شده

وهرمز از خام طبعي کار وخدمت بهرام را پوشيده داشت وسخن اهل غرض وارباب افترا را راست دانست وويرا خاين وکنه کار ساخت واز براي وي معجري زنان وطوق وزنجير فرستاد

ويهرام

And my affections were turned aside from Eekoo Timour by their insinuations: but I had heard the history of Behraum Joubeen, and from thence I had acquired experience.

For when the Khaukaun advanced against Hurmuz, the son of Nousharevaun, with an army of three hundred thousand sanguinary Toorks; that prince sent forth Behraum Joubeen (who had been the minister, and the counsellor, and the general of his father) with three hundred and twenty thousand Persians to oppose him. And he engaged that prince; and for three days, and for three nights, the slaughter continued with great fury; till at length he defeated the Khaukaun, and dispatched intelligence of his victory to Hurmuz: and he also sent unto him the spoils which he had taken.

And the envious and the slanderous, who influenced the councils of Hurmuz, forged accusations against him, saying, "Behraum hath secreted the treasures of the enemy; and he hath seized to himself the sword, and the crown, and the buskins of the Khaukaun (ornamented and adorned with jewels of price)."

And Hurmuz, from a mean and contemptible avarice, forgot the services of Behraum; and he credited the accusations of the slanderous and self-interested, and pronounced him a traitor and a criminal; and, *in token of his anger and contempt,* sent a chain unto him, and a collar, and the veil of a woman.

And

وبهرام طوق در کردن وزنجیر در پاء کرده
لباس زنان پوشید وامرا وسران سپاه را طلب نموده
دربار عام داد وچون سرداران وسایر سپاه این حال
مشاهده نمودند هرمزرا مطعون داشته دل خودهارا از
اخلاص هرمز برداشتند

وباتفاق بهرام جوبین بدرگاه هرمز آمده
ویرا از سلطنت خلع نمودند وخسرو پرویزرا بر تخت
سلطنت مملکت عجم نشانیدند

چون این تجربه برداشته بودم بجهت
این که مطعون سپاه نکردم امیر ایکو تیمورا طلب
داشته مجلس آراستم وبار عام دادم واموال واشیایی
که از الوس اروس خان غنیمت شده بود همه را جمع
آورده بامیر ایکو تیمور ودیکر بهادران وسپاهیانی که
همراه وی شمشیرها زده بودند انعام فرمودم

وامر نمودم که هر امیری که در هنکام
جنک خودرا نکاهدارد وفوج مقابل خودرا بشکند در
مرتبه اش بیفزایند

چنانچه

AND Behraum Joubeen placed the collar on his neck, and on his feet he faſtened the chain, and he cloathed himſelf in the female attire. And he called the Ameers and the chiefs of the ſoldiers together, and, thus habited, he gave public audience to his people. And when the chiefs and the forces beheld the ſituation of Behraum, they uttered revilings againſt their prince, and they turned their hearts from their duty to Hurmuz.

AND under the banners of Behraum Joubeen, they proceeded to the palace of the King; and they deprived him of his regal authority; and they ſeated Khiſſuro Purvaze upon the throne of the Perſian empire.

HAVING acquired this experience, that I might not draw upon me the revilings of my people, I ordered Eekoo Timour to appear before me; and I ſeated myſelf on my throne in the midſt of my chiefs; and I gave admiſſion to the people at large. And I commanded the wealth and the effects which had been taken from the tribe of Auroos Khaun to be brought forth; and I conferred the whole of the ſpoils on Ameer Eekoo Timour, and on the warriors and the ſoldiers who had fought under his command.

AND I ordained that every Ameer who acted with firmneſs in the day of battle, and defeated the enemy oppoſed unto him, ſhould be promoted to a ſuperior ſtation.

THUS,

چنانچه تابان بهادر خودرا در جنک توقتمش خان بعلمدار رسانید وعلم ويرا نكون ساخت وزخمها برداشت مدعيان وحاسدان وي خواستند كه كار ويرا بپوشند از انصاف من نكنجيد كه از كار وي چشم پوشم وبوي امارت دادم وتربيت كردم وعلم بوي ارزانی داشتم

وامر نمودم كه چون يكي از اون باشيان ويوز باشيان ومينك باشيان فوج شكني نمايد در جلدوي* اون باشي حكومت شهري بدهند ودر جلدوي يوز باشي حكومت مملكتي ارزاني دارند

چنانچه برلاس بهادر كه يوز باشي بود در جنك توقتمش خان به غنيم خود رو بر رو شد وفوج غنيم را شكست داد حكومت مملكت حصار شادمان را بوي مقرر داشتم

وامر نمودم كه چون مينك باشي فوج غنيم خودرا شكست دهد ويرا والي مملكت كردانند چنانچه محمد ازاد در جنك كتور جماعه سياه پوشانرا كه برهان اغلان را هزيمت داده بودند

شكست

Book II.

THUS, in an engagement with Touktummish Khaun, Taubaun Bahaudur penetrated to the standard-bearer of that prince, and inverted the standard; and he was wounded in many places. And his enemies and the enviers of his renown sought to bury his valour in oblivion: but it was not consistent with my justice that I should shut my eyes to the merits of Taubaun. And I exalted him to a government; and I received him into my favour; and I conferred upon him the standard of honour.

AND I ordained, if an Ounbaushee, or an Euzbaushee, or a Mingbaushee Ameer should vanquish the forces of an enemy; that in reward to an Ounbaushee the government of a city should be given; and that the reward of an Euzbaushee should be the command of a province.

THUS, to Burlaus Bahaudur, who was an Euzbaushee, and who in the war with Touktummish Khaun engaged his enemy and defeated the army of the foe, I gave the command of the province of Hissaur Shaudumaun.

AND I ordained, when a Mingbaushee defeated the forces of his antagonist, that he should be appointed the lord of a principality. Thus, when Mahummud Auzaud, in the war of Kuttour, vanquished the Seah poshaun, † who had defeated Burhaun Aghlaun, I

† *Wearers of black*; so named from the colour of their habits. They inhabited the mountains south of Buddukhshaun.

شکست داده بود ویرا والي مملکت قندز وکولاب
گردانیدم

وامر نمودم که هریک از امرا که
مملکتي را مسخر گردانیده از تصرف غنیم بر آورد
آن مملکت را تا سه سال بانعام وي مقرر دارند

وامر کردم که بهادري که شمشیر زند
کلنک* یا اتاقد* مرصع وکمر وشمشیر واسپ بجلدوي
وي ارزاني دارند وبمرتبه اون باشي امتیاز دهند تا
آنکه در شمشیر دویم وسیوم بمرتبه یوز باشي ومینک
باشي برسد

تزوک عطاي طبل وعلم

امر نمودم که بهریک از امراي دوازدهکانه
یک علم ونقاره بدهند وبامیر الامرا علم ونقاره
وتومان طوغ وچر طوغ ارزاني دارند
ومینک باشي را طوغي ونغیري بدهند
ویوز باشي واون باشي را طبل بدهند وبه امراي

† These words are Mogul, and their significations unknown.
‡ A belt, or girdle.
‖ The Toumaun Toghe and Cher Toghe are also a sort of standards or spears,

اویماق

appointed him to the dominion of the principality of Kunduz and Goulaub. Book II.

AND I ordained, whoever of my Ameers ſubdued and wreſted a kingdom from the hands of the enemy, that for the ſpace of three years the vicegerency of that kingdom ſhould be conferred upon him as a reward.

AND I commanded that the ſelect ſoldier who diſtinguiſhed himſelf in battle, ſhould be rewarded with a Kullung, † or embroidered Autaukeh, † with a horſe, and with a ſword, and with a Kummur; ‡ and that he ſhould be raiſed to the rank of an Ounbauſhee: ſo that for the ſecond, and the third atchievement he might riſe to the ſtations of Euzbauſhee, and of Mingbauſhee.

REGULATIONS FOR CONFERRING THE HONOURS OF THE NICCAUREH AND THE STANDARD.

I ordained that one ſtandard, and one Niccaureh ſhould be conferred on each of the twelve ſelect Ameers; and that the ſtandard, and the Niccaureh, and the Toumaun Toghe, and the Cher Toghe, || ſhould be granted to the Ameer ul Omrau:

AND that a Toghe, and a Nuſſeer § ſhould be allowed to the Mingbauſhee Ameer, and a drum to the Euzbauſhee and Ounbauſhee Ameers; and that to the

ſpears, with certain figures on the ſummit, marking the rank and dignity of thoſe to whom they belong.

§ A ſort of trumpet.

اویماق یرغوی* ارزانی دارند وبچهار بیکلر بیکی
هریک علم ونقاره وچر طوغ ویرغوی بدهند

وهریک از امرا که فوج شکنی نمایند
یا ملکی مسخر سازند اگر امیر اول باشد امیر دویم
سازند واگر امیر دویم باشد بمرتبه امیر سیوم رسانند
واگر امیر سیوم باشد بمرتبه امیر چهارم رسانند
همچنین تا یازدهم که اگر امیر یازدهم باشد
امیر دوازدهم گردانند وعلم وطوغ ونقاره بدهند

چنانچه بامیر اول یک طوغ وبامیر
دوم دو وسیوم سه وبامیر چهارم چهار طوغ ونقاره
بدهند تا آنکه خودرا بمرتبه تومان طوغ وچر طوغ
رسانند

تزوک سامان وسر انجام سپاه

امر نمودم که سایر سپاه در
یساقها هژده نفر یک خیمه بردارند وهریک نفر
دو

Ouyemauk Ameers † an Eurghee ‡ ſhould be granted; Book II.
and that to each of the four Beglerbegs a ſtandard, and a Niccaureh, and a Cher Toghe, and an Eurghee ſhould be allowed.

AND I ordained that every Ameer who vanquiſhed an army, or who conquered a country, if he were a firſt Ameer, that he ſhould be exalted to the rank of ſecond Ameer; and if he were a ſecond Ameer, that he ſhould be raiſed to the rank of third Ameer; and if he were a third Ameer, that he ſhould be exalted to the dignity of fourth Ameer: and thus up to the eleventh Ameer. For if he were eleventh Ameer, I commanded that he ſhould be appointed twelfth Ameer; and that the ſtandard, and the Toghe and the Niccaureh ſhould be conferred upon him.

THUS I ordained that one Toghe ſhould be allowed to the firſt Ameer, and two to the ſecono, and three to the third, and to the fourth Ameer four Toghes, and the Niccaureh: that by their valour and their conduct they might acquire to themſelves the dignity of the Toumaun Toghe and the Cher Toghe.

REGULATIONS CONCERNING THE ARMS AND THE NECESSARIES OF THE SOLDIERS.

FOR the private ſoldiers I ordained, that on an expedition every eighteen men ſhould take one tent;

† Chiefs of tribes.

‡ *Eurghee* is Mogul, and the particular ſignification unknown; but it evidently means ſome mark of diſtinction.

دو اسپ وکماني وترکشي وشمشيري واره ودرفشي
وچوال وچوال دوزي وتبرتيشه وده سوزن ويک
چرم پست بگيرد

وبهادرانيکه هر پنج نفر يک خيمه
بردارند وهريک نفر جوشني وخودي وشمشيري
وترکشي وکماني واسپان خودرا موافق تزوک همراه
بگيرند

واون باشيان هريک خيمه وزرهي
وشمشيري وترکشي وکماني وپنج سر اسپ با خود
داشته باشد

ويوز باشيان هريک خيمه وده سر اسپ
واسلحه از شمشير وترکش وکمان وگرز وکاسکن
وزره وبکتر متعدد بردارد

ومينک باشيان هريک خيمه وسايباني
وسلاح از زره وجوشن وخود ونيزه وشمشير وترکش
وتير هرچه قدر تواند بردارد

امير اول خيمه واتاقي ويک جفت سايبان
بردارد واز اسلحه فراخور امارت خود آن مقدار برد که
تواند بديگران مدد نمايد

وهمچنين

tent; and that each man ſhould be ſupplied with two horſes, and with a bow, and with a quiver of arrows, and with a ſword, and with a ſaw, and with an axe, and with an awl, and with thread, and with ten needles, and with a leathern knapſack; Book II.

AND for the ſelect warriors, that every five men ſhould have one tent; and that each man ſhould take with him a ſkull-cap, and a breaſt-plate, and a ſword, and a bow, and a quiver of arrows, and his horſes agreeably to the regulations;

AND that each of the Ounbauſhees ſhould have with him one tent, and a coat of mail, and a ſword, and a bow, and a quiver, and five horſes;

AND that every Euzbauſhee ſhould have one tent, and ten horſes, and his arms; ſuch as the ſword, and the bow, and the quiver, and the mace, and the club, and the coat of mail, and the breaſt-plate;

AND that each of the Mingbauſhees ſhould have a tent, and a Sauehbaun; † and that of arms and of armour (the coat of mail, and the breaſt-plate, and the helmet, and lances, and the ſword, and quivers, and arrows) he ſhould carry with him as much as he were able;

AND that the firſt Ameer ſhould carry with him a tent, an Autauk, and two Sauehbauns; and correſponding with his rank, ſuch a quantity of arms and of armour, as might enable him to ſupply the deficiencies of others;

† A ſort of upper roof for the tent, which being elevated two or three feet above it, and projecting on all ſides beyond it, defends the owner from the heat of the ſun.

AND

وهمچنین امیر دویم وسیوم وچهارم تا
امیر الامرا نراخور مرتبه خود سامان خودرا از خیمه
واتاق وسایبان واسپان سر انجام نمایند

امیر اول یکصد وده اسپ وامیر دوم
یکصد بیست اسپ وامیر سیوم یکصد وسي اسپ
وچهارم صد وچهل سر اسپ تا امیر الامرا که از سه
صد سر اسپ کمتر همراه نکیرد

وپیادکان هریک شمشیري وکمان وتیر
دسته بردارند وانچه توانند کم وزیاده همراه بکیرند
اما در وقت جنک کمتر از انچه تزوک بسته شده
با ایشان نباشد

تزوک پاتش حضور ومجالس بزم ورزم

امر نمودم که در مجلس بزم سپاهان
وامرا ومینک باشیان ویوز باشیان واون باشیان بي
کلاه وموزه وسر موزه وجامه کریبان دار وبکده
وشمشیر بدیوانخانه حاضر نیایند

ودوازده

And thus alſo, that the ſecond, and the third, and the fourth Ameer, and from him up to the Ameer ul Omrau, each according to his rank and his ſtation, ſhould ſupply and take with him his neceſſaries, his tent, and his Autauk, and his Sauehbauns, and his horſes;

The firſt Ameer a hundred and ten horſes, and the ſecond Ameer a hundred and twenty horſes, and the third Ameer a hundred and thirty horſes, and the fourth Ameer a hundred and forty horſes; and thus up to the Ameer ul Omrau, who was not to take with him a leſs number than three hundred horſes.

And I ordained that every one of the foot-ſoldiers ſhould take with him a ſword, and a bow, and a bundle of arrows; and that he ſhould carry with him as much as he was able, let it be more or let it be leſs; but that in times of war he ſhould not have leſs than was eſtabliſhed.

Regulations of the imperial guards, and rules to be observed in the presence, in peace and in war.

I ordained that in times of peace the ſoldiers, the Ameers, the Mingbauſhees, the Euzbauſhees, and the Ounbauſhees ſhould not appear in the Imperial Deewaun without their Koollauh, † their Mozeh, ‡ and Surmozeh, ‖ their Bukdeh, their Jaumeh § having the collar, and their ſwords.

† Cap. ‡ Boots. ‖ A ſort of leathern clog covering the foot of the boot. § Upper coat.

 And

ودوازده هزار قلچي* شمشير بردار با يراق وصلاح در يمين ويسار وپس وپيش ديوانخانه در كشك* حاضر باشند بدين ترتيب كه هر شب هزار كس از ايشان در پاتش حاضر باشند وبر سر صد قلچي يوز باشي مقرر نمايند وبوقي* بوي بدهند

وامر نمودم كه در معارك رزم هريك از امراء دوازدهكانه ومينك باشيان ويوز باشيان واون باشيان در لشكر ويساقها با دوازده هزار سوار صلاح دار يك شب ويك روز در پاتش خانهاي خود حاضر باشند

واين دوازده هزار سواررا چهار فوج ساخته فوجي در برانغار وفوجي در جرانغار وفوجي در پيش اردو وفوجي در عقب تعين نمايند ونوبت بنوبت بمقدار نيم فرسنك از اردو بر آمده بنشينند وهريك از افواج چهاركانه هراولي از براي خود قرار دهد وهراول قراولي را تعين نموده

سر

AND I ordered that twelve thouſand Kulchee, † men of the ſword, compleatly armed, ſhould be cantoned in the palace; to the right and to the left, and in the front and in the rear of the Imperial Deewaun: thus, that one thouſand of thoſe twelve thouſand ſhould be every night upon guard; and that over each hundred Kulchee an Euzbauſhee ſhould be appointed; and that an Eokee ‡ ſhould be given unto him. Book II.

AND I ordained that in times of war and in the field, each of the twelve ſelect Ameers, alſo the Mingbauſhees, and the Euzbauſhees and the Ounbauſhees ſhould, with twelve thouſand horſemen compleatly armed, for the ſpace of one day and one night, when marching, and when halting, be ready upon guard.

AND I commanded that thoſe twelve thouſand horſe ſhould be divided into four diviſions, and that one diviſion ſhould be poſted to the right of the camp, and one to the left thereof; and one in the front, and one in the rear; and that every watch they ſhould march out to the diſtance of half a Furſung from the camp, and there lie upon their arms;

AND that each of thoſe four diviſions ſhould appoint an advanced guard; and that each of the advanced guards ſhould detach ſcouts in their front; and

† A Mogul word, ſuppoſed to mean Guards.

‡ Mogul — A watch-word.

سر رشته احتياط وهوشياري از دست نداده خبرها رسانند

وامر نمودم كه هر طرف از اطراف لشكر واردو كوتوالي مقرر باشد كه حراست ونگاهباني اردو بديشان متعلق باشد ورسوم از اهالي بازار ميگرفته باشند واگر چيزي از اهل اردو بدزدي رود جواب گويند

وامر نمودم كه چهار فوج چپقونچي تعين نمايند كه تا چهار فرسنگي لشكررا بقيد ضبط در آورند واگر كسي را مقتول ومجروح به بيند از عهده بر آيند واگر مال كسي بدزدي رود جواب گويند

وامر نمودم كه سيوم حصه لشكر خدمت نگاهداشت سرحدها مقرر باشند ودو حصه در خدمت ركاب خاص حاضر باشند

تزوك خدمت وزرا

امر نمودم كه چهار وزير در ديوان حضور مقرر باشند

اول

that they ſhould perform their duty with care and circumſpection, and communicate intelligence of the approach of the enemy.

And I ordained that to each of the four quarters of the camp a Kootwaul ſhould be appointed; and that the police thereof ſhould appertain unto him: that he ſhould collect the cuſtoms from the traders in the markets; and that if any thing ſhould be ſtolen from the camp, he ſhould make it good.

And I ordered alſo that four diviſions of Chupkunchee ſhould be appointed; that they ſhould ſcour, and make themſelves maſters of, the circumjacent country to the diſtance of four Furſung from the camp; and, if any one was murdered or wounded within that diſtance, that they ſhould be accountable; and that they alſo ſhould be anſwerable for whatever was ſtolen.

And I ordained that one third of the imperial forces ſhould be appointed to guard the frontiers of my dominions; and that the remaining two thirds ſhould attend my commands in the preſence.

Regulation of the Departments of Vizzeers.

I ordained that four Vizzeers ſhould be appointed to attend in the Imperial Deewaun.

First,

اول وزیر مملکت ورعیت این وزیر مهمات
ومعاملات مملکت واحوال رعیت وحاصل وواصل وفاصل
ولایات ومداخل ومخارج واباداني ومعموري ونسق
ملک بعرض رساند

دوم وزیر سپاه که علوفه سپاهیان
وتنخواه ایشان را بعرض رساند واز احوال ایشان
آکاه باشد که پریشان نشوند وعرض احوال سپاه را
معروض دارد

سیوم وزیر سایر وهواي که اموال غایبي
ونوتي وفراري وزکوت وباج اموال آیندکان
وروندکان ومواشي ومراعي وآبخور وعلفچرا که
انچه ازین مداخل جمع آید ضبط نموده بطریق
امانت نکاهدارد وانچه اموال غایب واموات باشد
بوارثان ایشان برساند

چهارم

FIRST. THE VIZZEER OF THE COUNTRY AND THE SUBJECT. It was the business of this Vizzeer to superintend, and communicate unto me, the concerns and the affairs of the country; and the state and the situation of the husbandman, of the produce, and of the duties received, and of the deficiencies in the various provinces, of the merchandize brought in and sent out of the land, of the cultivation, and the population, and the police of all my dominions.

SECONDLY. THE VIZZEER OF THE ARMIES. It was his duty to lay before me the accompts of the wages due, and the assignments granted to the troops; and to inform himself of the situations and circumstances of the soldiers (that they might not be distressed or oppressed) and to communicate unto me the state and the strength of my armies.

THIRDLY. THE VIZZEER OF THE SAUIR AND HUVAUEE. It was his duty to take possession of the effects of absentees, † and of the defunct, and of those who had fled their country; and to receive religious donations, and the duties on the merchandize of comers and of goers, and the taxes on the cattle, and on the pasture lands, and on the reservoirs of water. And having taken possession of the produce, he was to retain it as a deposit in his hands, and to restore the effects of the absentees and the defunct to their lawful heirs.

† i.e. Such people as had disappeared suddenly, and whose absence could not be accounted for.

FOURTHLY.

چهارم وزیر کارخانها سلطنت که از مداخل ومخارج وجمیع خرج خزانه ودواب آگاه باشد

وامر نمودم که سه وزیر بر سرحدها ومملکت خالصه تعین نمایند که سر رشته معاملات مالي وولايات نگاهدارند

واين هفت وزير تابع ديوان بيكي باشند که مهمات ومعاملات امور مالي را باتفاق ديوان بيكي انجام داده بعرض رسانند

وامر نمودم که عرض بيكي مقرر باشد که عرض احوال سپاه ورعيت وداد خواهان وخرابي ومعموري ملک وانچه از مهمات فيصل يابد وبانجام رسد بعرض رساند

وامر نمودم که صدر الصدور سيورغالات* سادات وارباب وظايف واوقاف بعرض ميرسانيده باشد وقاضي اسلام امور شريعه وقاضي احداث امور عرفي را معروض دارد

وامر

FOURTHLY. THE VIZZEER OF THE IMPERIAL HOUSEHOLD. It was his duty to ſuperintend the receipts, and the diſburſements, and the general expences. Book II.

AND I ordained that three Vizzeers ſhould be appointed over the frontiers and the domains appertaining unto the crown, and to regulate the concerns thereof.

AND I ordained that theſe ſeven Vizzeers ſhould be ſubject to the controul of the Deewaunbeghee: and that under his inſpection they ſhould regulate and determine the affairs and the concerns of the revenues, and lay them before me.

I commanded that an Erzbeghee † ſhould be appointed; and that he ſhould communicate to me the ſtate of the ſoldiers, and of the ſubjects, and the complaints of my people, and the increaſe or decreaſe of population and cultivation in my dominions, and the concluſion and determination of every momentous concern.

AND I ordained that the Suddur ul Suddoor ſhould lay before me the Sawurghaulaut ‡ of the deſcendants of the prophet, of the ſtipendiaries, and penſioners; and that the eccleſiaſtical judge ſhould communicate unto me all eccleſiaſtical concerns; and that the civil affairs ſhould be laid before me by the civil judge.

† A preſenter of petitions.

‡ *Sawurghaul* is a Mogul word, and ſignifies a grant from the crown of lands or revenues to be enjoyed for ever by the poſſeſſor and his heirs.

وامــر نمودم که در محفل خاص امور ملکي وبند وبست مملکت وتغير وتبديل وتعين سپاه وامرا ومشاورت وتدبـيرات بعرض رسانند

وامر نمودم که منشي محرم که صاحب اسرار تواند بود حاضر باشد که بقلم راستي مخفيات ومشورات را مي نوشته باشد

وامــر نمودم که مجلس نويسان تعين نمايند که نوبت بنوبت در ديوان مجلس حاضر بوده وانچه از مهمات ومعاملات فيصل يابد ومشخص شود صورت واقعه را نوشته نگاهدارند وانچــه بعرض رسد ومن حکم کنم وانچه در مجلس مذکور شود از امور کلي وجزيء همکي را بقلم در آورده داخل وقايــع مــن نـمـايـنـد

وامر نمودم که بهر کارخانه از کارخانهاي سلطنت نويسنده تعين نمايند که اخراجات ومداخل ومخارج يوميه را مي نوشته باشد

تـزوک ايالت امـراي الوسات وتشونات وتـومـانـات

امـر

AND I commanded that all concerns appertaining to the imperial dignity, the regulations of my dominions, and the diſmiſſion, and the changing, and the appointing of armies and of officers, and all conſultations and plans of operation ſhould be communicated unto me in my ſelect council.

AND I commanded that a confidential ſecretary (on whoſe ſecrecy dependence might be placed) ſhould at all times attend, and minute down with the pen of integrity the ſecret tranſactions and deliberations.

AND I ordained that writers of the general council ſhould be appointed, and that they ſhould relieve each other in the hall of the council, and that they ſhould write down and preſerve full and exact accounts of every matter and of every buſineſs which ſhould be ſettled and determined therein: and that all repreſentations made unto me, and all orders iſſued by me, and every matter which was debated in council, ſhould be written and inſerted in the narrative of my tranſactions.

AND I ordained that to every department of the departments of government an accomptant ſhould be appointed; and that he ſhould keep a journal of the daily expences, and of the receipts and diſburſements.

REGULATIONS OF THE GOVERNMENTS OF THE AMEERS OF AULOOSAUT, AND OF KUSHOONAUT, AND OF TOUMAUNAUT.

 I or-

امر نمودم که امیر هر الوسي وتوماني در هنکام یساق از هـر خرکاي* یک سوار واز دواله چوق* یک سوار واز سر خانه یک سوار مقرر کردانند که در سفر همراه بکیرند وآبخور وعلق خور هر سر زمیني که در آن اقامت داشته باشد در وجه علوفه ایشان مقرر باشد بامرا الوسات برغوي وبیرقي* بدهند وایشان فراخور الوسات وتومانات خودها سوار در یساقها حاضر آورنـــد

وامر نمودم که از جملة چهل اویماق که بحـیـط ضبط در آمده دوازده اویـماق را تمغـا نمایند که از جمله نوکران خاصه باشند بـرلاس ترخان ارغون جلایر تولکچي دولدي مغول سلدوز طوغاي قبچاق ارلات تاتار

واز الوس برلاس چهار کس را امـیـر الامرا ساختم امیر خداداد که بوي مملکت بدخشان

ارزاني

I ordained that the Ameer of every Auloos, of every Kushoon, and of every Toumaun should, when called to fulfil his military service in times of war, select and bring with him to the field from each Khirgauh * one horseman, from each Duvvauleh Chouk † one horseman, and from each Khauneh † one horseman; and that the water and the forage on the lands where they should be stationed should be allowed unto them for their subsistence; and that an Eurghee and a Biruck ‡ should be granted to the Ameer of every Auloos; and that those Ameers should attend in the field with forces proportioned to the strength and the numbers of their Auloosaut and their Toumaunaut.

AND I ordained that to twelve of the forty Ouyemauk which had submitted to my government, Tumghau ‖ should be given (that they might be classed amongst my select and superior servants:) to the Ouyemauks of Burlaus, Turkhaun, Aurghoon, Jullauir, Toulkchee, Douldee, Moghool, Suldoze, Toughauee, Kypchauk, Aurlaut, and Tautaur.

AND from among the tribe of Burlaus I selected four Ameer ul Omraus, Ameer Khodaudaud (unto whom I gave the kingdom of Buddukhshaun) and

* Khirgauh is Mogul, and signifies a Tatar tent or hut.

† Duvvauleh Chouk is Mogul, and the meaning unknown. Khauneh signifies a house.

‡ Mogul, a little flag.

‖ i. e. Pay.

Ameer

ارزاني داشتم وامير جاكو وامير ايكو تيمور وامير
سليمان شاه كه بايشان هم سرحد ومملكت ارزاني
داشتم وصد نفر ديكررا از الوس برلاس مينك باشي
ساختم وامير جلال الدين برلاس را امير دهم كردانيدم
وامير ابو سعيد را امير نهم كردم

واز الوس ترخان امير بايزيد را امير
هفتم ساختم وبيست نفر از ايشان را يوز باشي
نمودم

واز الوس ارغون تاش خواجه را امير
هشتم كردم وبيست نفررا مينك باشي وبوز باشي
واون باشي مقرر نمودم

واز الوس جلاير توك تيمور وشير بهرام را
امير هشتم ونهم ساختم وبيست نفررا يوز باشي واون
باشي كردم

واز الوس تولكچي الجايتو بردي را
امارت دادم

واز الوس دولدي تابان بهادر وسان
بهادررا امارت دادم

واز الوس مغول تيمور خواجه اغلان را
بمرتبه امارت رسانيدم

واز الوس سلدوز يلچي بهادررا امارت
دادم

واز

Ameer Jaukoo, and Ameer Eekoo Timour, and Ameer Soolamaun Shaah; on whom I alſo conferred the governments of frontier kingdoms. And a hundred others of the tribe of Burlaus I appointed Mingbauſhees. And I exalted Ameer Jullaul u deen Burlaus to the dignity of tenth Ameer; and Ameer Abou Saeed of the ſame tribe to the rank of ninth Ameer.

AND from amongſt the tribe of Turkhaun I raiſed Ameer Bauezzeed to the ſtation of ſeventh Ameer; and I appointed twenty perſons of the ſame tribe Euzbauſhees.

AND of the tribe of Aurghoon I raiſed Tauſh Khaujeh to the dignity of eighth Ameer; and I gave the appointments of Mingbauſhees, and of Euzbauſhees, and of Ounbauſhees, to twenty people of that tribe.

AND of the tribe of Jullauir I exalted Touk Timour and Share Behraum to the ranks of eighth and of ninth Ameer; and twenty of the ſame tribe I appointed Euzbauſhees and Ounbauſhees.

AND of the tribe of Toulkchee I conferred the dignity of Ameer on Aijauyetoo Burdi.

AND of the tribe of Douldee, I raiſed Taubaun Bahaudur and Saun Bahaudur to the dignity of Ameers.

AND of the tribe of Moghool I exalted Khaujeh Aghlaun to the rank of Ameer.

AND of the tribe of Suldoze I appointed Elchee Bahaudur to the ſtation of Ameer.

AND

واز الوس طوغاي علي درويشرا امارت دادم

واز الوس تپچاق امير سار بوغا را امير ساختم

واز الوس ارلات امير مويد را كه خواهر من درحباله زوجيت وي بود امير الامرا ساختم وسلاچي بهادررا امير كردانيدم

واز الوس تاتار كونك خان را امارت دادم وبيست وهشت اويماق ديكر كه به تمغا نرسيدند ايشانرا امير الوس ساختم كه در وقت يساق در چار وپلچار حاضر شوند وموافق تزوك سواران خودرا حاضر سازند

تزوك سلوك نوكر به صاحب ومعاش صاحب بنوكر

كه نوكر راست بداند كه انچه وي از نوكر خود چشم داشت دارد صاحب وي هم از وي همان چشم داشت دارد پس خودرا در خدمت صاحب معاف ندارد وبداند كه اكر صاحبش اول بوي بر سر عنايت بود وآخر بي عنايت شد تقصير ونقصان بر خود نهد نه بر صاحب خود

ونوكر راست است كه با صاحب اخلاص بورزد وباخلاص كار كند

وهر

AND of the tribe of Toughauee I appoinied Aali Durvaish to the station of Ameer. Book II

AND of the tribe of Kipchauk I raised Ameer Saur Booghau to the dignity of Ameer.

AND of the tribe of Aurlaut I appointed Ameer Muviud (unto whom one of my sisters had been given in marriage) Ameer ul Omrau: and Sullauichee Bahaudur of the same tribe I made an Ameer.

AND of the tribe of Tautaur I raised Kowvung Khaun to the rank of Ameer; and the remaining twenty eight Ouyemauk, unto whom the Tumghau had not been given, I appointed commanders over their own tribes: that in times of war and of service they might attend in the field, and bring with them their horsemen, agreeably to the regulation.

RULES CONCERNING THE CONDUCT OF SERVANTS TOWARDS THEIR PRINCE, AND OF THE PRINCE TOWARDS HIS SERVANTS.

BE it known to every good servant, that that which he expecteth from his own dependant, his prince also expecteth from him. Let him not therefore be backward in his services; but let him know, that if his master be at first well-inclined unto him, and afterwards be ill-inclined unto him, he must lay the fault and the consequence to himself and not to his master.

HE is a good servant who attacheth himself unto his master, and doeth his duty through that attachment.

وهر نوكري كه بي اخلاص وكينه دار باشد از اثر بي اخلاص وكينه وي البته نكبت بوي روي آورد وليكن دولت ونعمت نوكر باخلاص روز بروز در تزايد باشد

راسخ الاعتقاد نوكري باشد كه از اعراض واعتراض صاحب نرنجد وكينه نورزد وتقصيري كه از صاحبش بوقوع آيد آنرا بخود كيرد آن نوكر لايق تربيت باشد

ونوكري كه نظرش بر لقمه وخرقه باشد البته در وقت كار سستي كند

نوكري كه حق خدمت فراموش كند ودر وقت كار روي كردان شود ديكر رويش را نبايد ديد

ونوكري كه در وقت كار بهانه جويد وهنكام يساق رخصت طلبد ونظر بر پشت پا داشته باشد وكار امروز بفردا حواله نمايد چنانچه بولا وتيمور اغلان بمن كردند ومرا بر سر كار كذاشتند نام اين قسم نوكران نبايد برد وايشان را به پروردكار بايد سپرد

وسلاطين

On the servant who is incapable of attachment, and who harboureth resentment, contempt and ignominy shall most certainly fall in consequence of his evil qualities: but the prosperity and the riches of the faithful and affectionate servant shall be daily increasing.

He is a good and faithful servant who taketh not offence at the slights or the reprimands of his prince, who entertaineth not revenge in consequence thereof; but taketh the faults of his master upon himself: such a servant is worthy of the affection and the kindness of his prince.

The servant whose eye is fixed on the morsels and the fragments † which fall from the table of his lord, will undoubtedly be negligent in the moment of trial.

The servant who forgetteth his duty in the hour of action, and turneth his face from the foe of his prince; let the face of that servant be seen no more.

The servant who in the hour of trial searcheth after excuses; and who on the day of enterprise demandeth his dismission, and who keepeth his eye on the means of retreat, and who transfereth till to-morrow the business of to-day, (thus Boulau and Timour Aghlaun acted towards me, and deserted me in the hour of danger) let the names of such servants be held in contempt; and let them be delivered over to the Almighty.

† i. e. A self-interested and avaricious servant.

وسلاطين راست كه هر نوكري را كه عزت دهند زود بيعزت نكردانند وبرداشته خود را نه اندازند وهركس را دانسته وشناخته باشد فراموش نكنند

اكر احيانا بيعزت كنند در عزتش دو برابر افزوده تلافي نمايند وآن نوكررا باخلاص واعتقاد وي حواله سازند كه اكر كينه ونفاق ورزد بالخاصيه نكبت بوي روي خواهد آورد وهر نوكري كه در دل صاحب به نيكي جا كند روز به كردد

وهر نوكري كه باختيار وغير اختيار جدا شود وچون مراجعت نمايد ويرا محترم كردانند كه از جداي خود پشيمان شده ومعاودت نموده

وامر نمودم كه هر نوكري كه از جانب غنيم شمشير از نيام بر آورده ونمك حلال باشد اكر اين چنين مردي در جنك بدست افتد يا از طرف غنيم نا اميد شده بيايد وملازمت اختيار كند ويرا عزيز نمايند وبر مراتبش بيفزايند وويرا وفادار دانند

چنانچه

It behoveth the prince not speedily to degrade the servant whom he hath exalted, not to pull down him whom his own hand hath raised up. Let him not neglect those whom he knoweth or remembereth.

And if it should chance that without cause he put a good servant to shame, let him make amends by conferring two-fold honour upon him: and let him refer that servant to his own affection and fidelity: for if he harboureth hatred and revenge, according to his evil qualities ignominy shall be his reward. But the servant who by good conduct acquireth a place in the heart of his prince, shall prosper in consequence thereof.

If a servant spontaneously, or otherwise, separate himself from his master, and if he afterwards turn back unto him, let that servant be received with honour: since, ashamed of his desertion, he returneth again to his prince.

Every servant who was faithful to his prince, and who drew his sword on the side of my enemy; if such a man became my prisoner in battle, or if, hopeless of reward from the foe, he came in unto me and offered his services, I ordained that he should be received with honour and esteem; and that his fidelity should be acknowledged and relied on; and that dignities superior to those, which he formerly possessed, should be conferred upon him.

چنانچه منكلي بوغا وحيدر اندوخودي
وامير ابو سعيد با شش هزار سوار بر كنار آب بلخ
بمن رو برو شده جنك كردند بعد از آن از تغلقتيمور
خان نا اميد كشته بمن پناه آوردند ايشانرا عزت
داده احترام كردم وولايت حصار شادمان واندجان
وتركستان بديشان دادم

وامر نمودم كه هر نوكري كه در
نزد غنيم معتبر باشد ودر وقت جنك وكارزار سلسله
دوستي بدشمن صاحب خود بجنباند وحق نمك
وصاحبي ونوكري ونعمت را فراموش كند ودشمن
صاحب خود را خواهد كه بر صاحب خود غالب
كرداند اين قسم شخصي را در خدمت راه ندهند روزكار
سزايش را در كنارش خواهد نهاد

وهر نوكري كه در وقت كار از صاحب
خود جدا شده بملازمت آيد اعتماد را شايسته نباشد
اما اكر بعد از خدمت بسيار وفاداري از وي ظاهر
شود نكاهدارند واكر در غير وقت كار ويورش آمده
ملازمت اختيار نمايد ويرا كرامي دارند

واكر

THUS Munguli Booghau, and Hydur Andookhodee, and Ameer Aboo Saeed, on the part of Tughulluk Timour Khaun, opposed and attacked me with six thousand horsemen, on the banks of the water of Bulukh. Afterwards, taking offence at the conduct of Tughulluk Timour, they sought protection from me; and I received them with honour and esteem: and I conferred upon them the provinces of Andijaun, and Hyssaur Shaudumaun, and Toorkistaun.

AND I also ordained that the servant of the foe who was in the confidence of his master, and, who in times of war and of service, vibrated the chain of friendship with the enemy of his prince; and who forgot the sacred ties of lord and of servant, and the fidelity due for the salt and the bread which he had eaten; and who strove to make the enemy of his master the conqueror of his master; I ordained that such a wretch should never be admitted into my service. Time shall hereafter inflict upon him his reward.

THE servant who quitteth his master in times of trial, and offereth his services to another, is not worthy to be admitted: but when by many and long services his fidelity shall be proved, he may then be received into favour. If in times of peace and tranquillity he offereth his services, let him be received with kindness.

IF

واكر وزيري ونوكري از روي راي وتدبير با دشمن رابطه آشنايي درست سازد ودرين لباس خواهد كه كار صاحب خودرا ساخته كردند ويرا عاقلترين دوستان وچاكران بايد دانست وليكن نوكري كه بدشمن بسازد وبا صاحب خود نفاق ورزد اين چنين نوكري را به دشمن ارزاني دارند

واكر نوكري شمشير زند وغنيم را شكست دهد سخن ارباب غرض را در حق وي نشنوند وكار ويرا پوشيده ندارند ويك كار ويرا به ده باز نهايند وبر مرتبه اش بيفزايند تا ديكر نوكرانرا رغبت جان فشاني بهم رسد

وهر فوجي وهر اميري كه روي از راه مرافقت وموافقت بركرداند وبه غنيم پيوند ايشانرا در يورت اورن ندهند چنانچه سرداران لشكر كش از من رو كردان شده باميرحاجي برلاس پيوستند ومن بعد بر ايشان اعتماد نكردم

وهر نوكري را كه حاكم ملكي كرداند ووي از روي بيوفاي به غنيم سازش نموده ملك را بدشمن بدهد ويرا از قيد حيات بر آورند ونوكر ملكدار بمراتب ارجمند بلند مرتبه كردانند

وهر

If a Vizzeer, or other ſervant, through policy and deſign, form an intimacy with his maſters foe; and endeavour, under the garb of that friendſhip, to promote the intereſt of his prince, let him be eſteemed amongſt the wiſeſt and the beſt of ſervants and of friends. But if a ſervant oppoſe his maſters's intereſt, and intrigue with the enemy, preſent ſuch a ſervant as a gift to the foe.

If a ſervant fight valiantly and defeat his foe, let not the inſinuations of the envious be heard to his prejudice; permit not his glory to be concealed, but let it be exhibited in ten-fold ſplendor; and let him be exalted to a ſuperior ſtation, that other ſervants may be inſpired with a thirſt for glory.

If a body of troops, or an Ameer, deſert their prince, and unite with the enemy, let them not again be admitted into his ſervice. Thus the leaders of the forces of Kuſh turned from me their faces, and united themſelves with Ameer Haujee Burlaus; and after that I confided not in them.

Whatever ſervant, unto whom the government of a kingdom ſhall be truſted, who treacherouſly leagueth with the enemy, and delivereth that kingdom into the hands of the foe; let him be put to death. But let the ſervant, who defendeth and preſerveth a kingdom, be raiſed to a diſtinguiſhed and exalted rank.

وهر اميري كه در وقت تنك قدم
اخلاص در ميدان مصاف استوار دارد وطريق مرافقت
بجاي آورد ويرا بمنزله برادر شمارند چنانچه وقتي كه
امرا ولشكر خط كش از من رو كردان شدند بغير
از امير جاكوي برلاس هيچكس در نزد من نماند
وهمراهي نكرد من امير جاكورا برادر عزيز دانسته
شريك دولت خود كردانيدم وامير الامرا ساخته
مملكت بلخ وحصار بوي ارزاني داشتم

تزوك سلوك ومعاش با دوست ودشمن
روزي كه مملكت توران را مسخر ساختم
ودر تختكاه سمرقند بر سرير سلطنت جلوس نمودم
بدوست ودشمن يكسان سلوك كردم امراي بدخشان
وبعضي امراي تشونات از ترك وتاجيك كه بمن
بديها كرده وحيلهها برانكيخته وبر من شمشيرها
كشيده بودند واز كردار نا پسنديده خود متوهم
مي بودند چون بمن آنجا آوردند چندان احسان
كردم كه شرمنده عنايت واحسان من شدند

وهر كسرا رنجانيده بودم باحسان وانعام
تلافي

LET the Ameer, who in the hour of peril and diſtreſs adhereth to his prince, and ſtandeth firm in the field of ſlaughter, be conſidered as a brother. THUS at the time when the forces of Kuſh deſerted my ſtandard, no one remained with me, or conſented to ſhare my fortunes, except Ameer Jaukoo Burlaus; and I afterwards eſteemed Ameer Jaukoo as a beloved brother; and I admitted him to a participation in my fortunes; and I made him an Ameer ul Omrau; and I conferred upon him the kingdoms of Bullukh and of Hiſſaur.

REGULATIONS FOR MY CONDUCT AND BEHAVIOUR BOTH TO FRIENDS AND TO ENEMIES.

ON the day on which I conquered the kingdom of Tooraun, and mounted the throne of empire in the capital city of Summurkund, I conducted myſelf in the ſame manner towards my enemies and my friends. The Ameers of Buddukhſhaun, and other Ameers of Kuſhoonaut, both Toork and Taucheek, who had done me injuries; and who had practiſed deceits upon me; and who had drawn their ſwords in oppoſition unto me; and who were alarmed by the remembrance of their evil conduct; when they ſubmitted to my authority, I received them with ſuch kindneſs and courteſy, that they bluſhed at my generoſity and goodneſs.

AND to every one, whom I had injured or diſtreſſed, I made compenſation; and I balanced the diſ-

تلافي رنجش وي کردم وبمراتب لايق ايشانرا امتياز بخشيدم

ليکن بر امراي سلدوز وجتته نفرين کردم که کابل شاه چنکيزي را که بامارت وخاني برداشته بودند وبوي عهد ودوستي وپيمان اخلاص بربستند چون خبر جلوس من بر تخت سلطنت بمسامع ايشان رسيد نقض عهد کرده ويرا بجهت خوش آمد من بقتل رسانيدند

وکساني را که در مقام شکست من در آمده بر من حسد بردند آن قدر بايشان مروت واحسان کردم که شرمنده احسان من شده غرق عرق خجالت کشتند

ودوستان چون بمن التجا آوردند چون هميشه برضاي من کارکرده بودند ايشانرا شريک دولت دانسته در عطاي مال واسباب مضايقه نکردم

وبتجربه من رسيده که دوست صادق آنست که از دوست نرنجد ودشمن دشمن دوست باشد واکر افتد در دادن جان مضايقه نکند چنانچه بعضي امراي من تا بجان همراهي من کردند ومن هم در هيچ چيز بايشان مضايقه نکردم

وبتجربه

treſſes which he had ſuffered, by kindneſs and by gratuities; and by proper marks of my favour I conferred honour upon him.

But on the Ameers of the tribes of Suldoze and of Jitteh I uttered execrations: for, having exalted Kaubul Shaah of the line of Chungaze to the dignity of Khaun, and ſworn fidelity and friendſhip unto him, when they heard of my exaltation to the throne, they broke their faith and their engagements, and, to flatter and to ſoothe me, put him to death.

And to thoſe who had envied my fortune, and who had endeavoured to ſubvert my power, I conducted myſelf with ſuch kindneſs and generoſity, that they were confounded at my goodneſs, and ſunk under the ſenſe of their own unworthineſs.

And my friends who preſented themſelves before me, thoſe who had ever acted in ſubmiſſion to my will, I conſidered as the partners of my fortune: and I regarded not the riches and the wealth which I conferred upon them.

For by experience it is known unto me, that he is a firm aſſociate, who taketh not offence at the conduct of his friend; and who is the enemy of the enemy of his friend; and who heſitateth not to hazard his life, when occaſion ſhall require. Thus certain of my Ameers followed my fortunes even to death; nor did I with-hold from them aught which I had.

And

وبتجربه من رسيد که دشمن عاقل بهتر
از دوست جاهل باشد چنانچه امیر حسین نبیره امیر
قزغن از دوستان جاهل بود وانچه در دوستی بمن
کرد هیچ دشمن در دشمني نکند

امیر خداداد بمن کفت که دشمن را
چون لعل وجواهر نکاهدار وچون بسنک لاخي
برسي چنانش بر سنک زن که اثري از وي نماند

ونیز کفت که چون دشمن پناه آورد
وزانو زند بر وي رحم کن ومروت نما چنانچه من
به توقتمش خان کردم چون بمن پناه آورد مروت
کردم

اکر دشمن مروت واحسان دیده دیکر
باره بر سر دشمني رود ویرا بپروردکار بسپار

ودوست آنست که از دوست نرنجد
واکر برنجد عذر پزیر باشد

تزوک اجلاس واورن

امر نمودم که فرزندان ونبایر وخویشان
موافق

AND by experience it was known unto me, that a wiſe enemy is preferable to a fooliſh friend. THUS Ameer Hooſſein, the grandſon of Ameer Kurghun, was one of thoſe fooliſh friends: and the miſchiefs which in his friendſhip he did unto me, were ſuch as no enemy would do in the exceſs of his enmity.

AMEER Khodaudaud once ſaid unto me, "Watch thou thy enemy, as thou wouldſt guard a ruby "of luſtre, or a jewel of high price: but when thou "meeteſt with a ſtone of Laukh, cruſh him thereon un-"til not one particle of him remain."

HE alſo ſaid, "When an enemy fleeth "unto thee for protection, and kneeleth before thee, "have compaſſion upon him, and receive him with kind-"neſs." THUS I acted towards Touktummiſh Khaun. When he fled to me for ſhelter, I treated him with tenderneſs and humanity.

IF an enemy, after taſting of thy generoſity and bounty, return again to enmity, deliver him over to the juſtice of the Almighty.

HE is a true friend who taketh not offence at the conduct of his friend; or if he doth, is willing to receive his acknowledgements.

REGULATIONS OF PRECEDENCY AND OF ADMISSION TO THE IMPERIAL PRESENCE.

I ordained that my ſons, and my grandſons, and my relations, ſhould, according to their different

موافق مراتب خود هاله وار صف زده بر دور سریر
سلطنت بنشینند

وسادات وقضات وعلما وفضلا ومشایخ
واکابر واشراف بر طرف دست راست جلوس
نمایند

وامیر الامرا وبیکلر بیکیان وامرا ونونیان
وسرداران وامیران الوس وتومانات وتشونات ومینک
باشیان ویوز باشیان واون باشیان مطابق مراتب خودها
طرف دست چپ جلوس نمایند

وبراي دیوان بیکي ووزرا در مقابل
تخت جاي نشستن مقرر کردم وکلانتران وکدخدایان
مهالک در عقب وزرا صف زده نشسته باشند

وبهادرانیکه که خطاب بهادري یافته
باشند وجوانان شمشیر زن در عقب سریر سلطنت
طرف دست راست بنشینند وقراول بیکیان را طرف
دست چپ عقب تخت حکم نشستن کردم

وامیر هراول در پیش روي اورن بکیرد
ومحرم یساول بر در خرکاه پیش پایه تخت ایستاده
باشد

ferent ranks encircle and ſit round the throne in regular order. Book II.

And that the deſcendants of the prophet, and the judges, and the theologians, and the learned men, and the prelates, and the grandees, and the nobles ſhould ſit on the right hand of the throne.

And that the Ameer ul Omrau, and the Beglerbegs, and the Ameers, and the Nouniaun, and the chiefs, and the leaders of tribes, and of Toumaunaut and of Kuſhoonaut, and the Mingbauſhee, and the Euzbauſhee, and the Ounbauſhee-Ameers ſhould take their places ſuitably to their ranks and their ſtations, on the left hand of the throne.

And I appointed a place oppoſite to the throne for the Deewaunbeghi and for the Vizzeers. And I ordered that the leading men and the magiſtrates of the empire, ſhould form a line and ſeat themſelves behind the Vizzeers;

And that the ſelect ſoldiers, who had obtained the title of Bahaudur, and the mighty men of prowess ſhould ſit on the right hand in the rear of the throne. And the leaders of the light troops I ordered to be ſeated in the rear of the throne on the left hand.

And I commanded that that the Ameer of the Hurrauwul ſhould take his ſtation in the front; and that the chief of the Yuſſauwul † ſhould ſtand at the door of the imperial pavilion, oppoſite the foot of the throne;

† The chief of the meſſengers. *Mogul.*

باشد وداد خواه در چپ وراست بایستند
وسایر سپاه وخدم وحشم بمراتب خود
صف زده ایستاده شوند وجاي خودرا نکاهدارند
وامر نمودم که چهار میر تزک دست
راست ودست چپ وپیش وپس مجلس را تزک
دهند

وحکم کردم که چون مجلس بر
تزوک در آید هزار طبق آش وهزار نان در مجلس
عام شیلان بکشند وهزار طبق در محفل خاصش حاضر
آورند از این جمله پانصد طبق به الوس امرا وسرداران
نام بنام بفرستند

تزوک ملک کیري

در هر ملکي که ظلم وجور وفسق
بسیار شود سلاطین را است که به نیت عدالت
عزیمت دفع ورفع فسق وظلم بسته بر آن ملک ترکتاز
آورند که تنکري تعالي بهمین نیت آن ملک را از ظالم
بکیرد وبه عادل بسپارد چنانچه من ولایت ماورالنهر
از

throne; and the receivers of petitions on the right and on the left;

And that the soldiers in general, and the imperial domestics, should stand in lines according to their degrees, and be attentive to keep in their proper stations.

And I commanded, that four Meer Toozzuk † should establish and preserve order in the imperial assembly; before, and behind, and on the right, and on the left of the throne.

And I commanded, when the assembly was formed and regulated, that among the inferior people a thousand dishes of meat, and a thousand loaves, should be distributed; and that a thousand dishes of meat and a thousand loaves should be brought into the imperial assembly; and that five hundred of that thousand should be sent to the Ameers of tribes, and to the chiefs; to each by his name, and by his title.

Regulations concerning the reduction of kingdoms.

If in any kingdom tyranny, and oppression, and iniquity shall be predominant, it is the duty of a prince, from a regard to justice and the law, to resolve on the expulsion and extirpation of the authors of that oppression and iniquity; and to assault that kingdom. For Almighty God from the same motives will wrest that

† Regulators, masters of the ceremonies.

از دست ظالمان اوزبکیه بنیت عدالت انتزاع نمودم

ودر هر ملکي که شریعت ضعیف باشد وبزرک کردهاي خدارا عزیز ندارند وبندها خاص خداي تعالي را آزرده کرداند سلطان ملک کیر را است که نیت رواج دین وشریعت محمدي صلي الله علیه وسلم کرده بدآن ملک در آید که رسول خدا ویرا تایید خواهد نمود چنانچه من دار الملک هندوستان را از سلطان محمود نبیره فروز شاه وملوخان وسارنک انتزاع نمودم ودین وشریعت را رواج دادم بتخانهاي آن دیاررا خراب ساختم

وهر مملکتي که متوطنان وساکنان آن مملکت از حاکم ووالي خود در آزار باشند ودلهاي اهل آن دیار از والي خود منصرف کردد ملک ستان را است که آن ملک را بحیطه تصرف در آورد وبمجرد توجه سلطان نیکو سیر آن ملک مسخر کردد

چنانچه من ممالک خراسان را از سلاطین کرت انتزاع نمودم وبمجرد توجه من بعزیمت تسخیر

kingdom from the hand of the tyrant, and deliver it over to the upright aſſailant. THUS, from a regard to juſtice and the law, I delivered the country of Mauwur u Nuhur from the hands of the Ouzbuk tyrants. Book II.

AND in whatever country the holy laws are diſregarded; where they neglect thoſe to whom the Almighty hath given dignity; where they injure and oppreſs his choſen ſervants; it is the duty of a conqueror, with a firm determination to ſupport the faith and the laws of Mahummud (on whom be the bleſſing of God) to invade that country: for the prophet of the Lord ſhall aſſiſt him in all his undertakings. THUS I wreſted from Sooltaun Muhmood (the grandſon of Feeroze Shaah) from Mulloo Khaun, and from Saurung, the capital of the empire of Hindoſtaun; and I re-eſtabliſhed the true faith; and I overturned the habitations of the idols in that country.

IT is the duty of a victorious king to bring under his authority every empire or kingdom, where the inhabitants thereof are oppreſſed by their prince and ruler, and where the hearts of the people are turned aſide from their governor. No ſooner ſhall the upright prince approach, than that kingdom ſhall fall into his hands.

THUS I delivered the kingdom of Khorauſaun from the princes of the houſe of Kurroot. As ſoon as I advanced, with the reſolution to reduce the capital of

دار الملک خراسان سلطان غیاث الدین آمده مملکت
خراسان را با خزاین ودفاین پیشکش کرد

ودر هر ملکي که الحاد وزندقه بسیار
شود واهل آن دیار از سپاه ورعیت بطوایف متنوعه
متفرق شوند زوال آن مملکت نزدیک رسیده باشد
جهان ستان را است که بر آن مملکت ترکتاز آورد
چنانچه من ممالک عراق عجم وفارس را از وجود
ملاعین ملاحده پاک ساختم وملوک طوایف را بر
انداختم وبندهاي خدا را از ظلم ایشان که هریک در
ناحیه علم سلطنت بر افراخته بودند نجات دادم

ودر هر ملکي که عقاید اهالي آن ملک
از عقاید خاندان حضرت سید المرسلین صلوات الله
علیه تغییر یابد سلاطین را واجب است که آن
ولایت را مسخر کردانند واهالي آن ملک را از اعتقاد
بد ایشان باز آورند چنانچه من بمملکت شام در آمده
جماعت که بد اعتقاد بودند ایشانرا بسزا رسانیدم

وچون شروع در ملک کیري کردم چهار
امر را پیش نهاد خاطر خود ساختم

اول در امور ملک کیري تدبیر
وکنکاش درست بکار بردم

دوم

of Khoraufaun, Sooltaun Gheeaus u deen came forth unto me, and he delivered the treafures, and the wealth, and the kingdom into my hands.

AND in every kingdom, where herefy and fchifm fhall abound, and where the inhabitants of that country, both foldiers and fubjects, fhall be divided into different parties and factions, the deftruction of that kingdom is at hand; and it is the duty of a victorious monarch to invade that country. THUS I purified the kingdoms of Fauris and Erauk a Ajjum from the exiftence of the accurfed heretics; and I overturned the leaders of the factions, who had each of them elevated the ftandard of power, throughout thofe territories, and I delivered the fervants of God from their tyranny and oppreffions.

AND in every kingdom, where the articles of the faith of the inhabitants thereof fhall be altered from thofe of the defcendants of the prince of the prophets, (on whom be the bleffing of Almighty God) it is the duty of an Emperor to reduce that Kingdom, and to bring back the inhabitants thereof from their evil tenets. THUS I entered the kingdom of Shaum, and punifhed all thofe who held pernicious doctrines.

WHEN I firft entered upon the reduction of kingdoms, I firmly adhered to four certain maxims.

FIRST, in thofe things which appertain to the acquifition of dominions, I acted from deep deliberation, and from mature counfel.

SECONDLY,

دوم اندیشه وحزم واحتیاط بسیار نمودم تا آنکه در کارها غلط نکردم وبتایید آلهي هر تدبیري که کردم راست ودرست افتاد ومزاج وطبایع اهل هر ملکي را بخاطر آوردم وموافق طبیعت ایشان سلوک کرده حاکم تعین نمودم

سیوم سیصد وسیزده مردم مردانه اصیل وشجاع وفرزانه بخود متفق ساختم وایشان در اتفاق بمرتبه بودند که گویا همکي ایشان یک تن بودند وعزیمت وراي وگفتار وکردار ایشان همي یک بود چون میگفتند که این کار میکنم بر نمي گشتند وتا آن کاررا باتمام نمي رسانیدند دست از آن باز نمیداشتند

چهارم کار امروزرا بفردا نینداختم ودر هنگام نرمي نرمي بکار بردم ودر وقت درشتي درشتي کردم ودر زمان تاني شتاب نکردم ودر کار شتاب درنگ ننمودم وکاري که بتدبیر سر انجام یافتي بشمشیر نمیکشادم

ورزوها

SECONDLY, I used reflection, and caution, and circumspection, that I might not err in execution. And such was the favour of the Almighty, that every determination which I formed, proved in the end judicious and successful. I informed myself of the dispositions and genius of the natives of every country; and I accommodated myself to their prejudices in the appointment of their governors.

THIRDLY, I united unto myself three hundred and thirteen resolute men, of nobility, of bravery, and of wisdom; and so firmly were they united, that the whole, it might be said, were as one person: and their resolutions, and their actions, and their declarations were the same. When they said, "We will do thus," they did it: for until they had concluded the enterprise on which they had determined, they withdrew not their hands therefrom.

FOURTHLY, I postponed not till to-morrow the business of to-day. When lenity was necessary, I acted with lenity; and in the hour of severity I was severe. At the time when delay was policy, I acted not with precipitation; and when expedition was necessary, I was not guilty of delay: and the business which could be concluded by address and negotiation, I committed not to the sword.

وروزها با ارباب تجربه وهوشمندان
شطرنج ملک کیري مي باختم وشبها که در خوابکاه
تکیه میزدم در تمشیت امور مملکت تفکر میکردم
وصورت انجام آنرا بخود تصویر مینمودم

وطریق ملک کیري را خود بخود اندیش
میکردم که از کدام راه در آیم وکدام طرف بدر
آیم ودر معاملات سپاه فکر میکردم که کدام یکي را
تربیت نمایم وچه کسرا کار فرمایم تا غلط نکنم وپیش
بیني در هر کار مینمودم وهر کس از اعیان سپاه
که بمن دوستي کردند بایشان احسان نمودم وهر
کس بمن دشمني کرد بوي مدارا کردم

وکساني که بآنها نیکي کردم وآنها
بمن بدي کردند ایشانرا حرام زاده دانستم که قول
رسول رب العالمین است که ولد الزنا از دنیا بیرون
نرود تا بمحسن خود بدي نکند

پیر من بمن نوشت که ترا است
که بحکم خدا ورسول خدا عمل نماي، وآل
وذریات

THE day I past in examining the difficulties of conquest with wise and experienced men; and in the night when I laid myself down in the chamber of repose, I deliberated on the execution of my resolutions, and I formed the plan on which they were to be conducted.

AND I myself reflected on the measures I should pursue in the reduction of kingdoms; how I should advance, and which way I should retreat. And I also considered those things which concerned my soldiers, whom I should encourage and reward, and whom I should order upon service; that I might not err in my resolves. And I exerted foresight and circumspection in every transaction. And the leaders of my soldiers who attached themselves unto me, I treated with kindness and distinction; and I conducted myself with seeming attention towards those who were my enemies.

AND I considered as base-born those on whom I had conferred favours, and who, for the good which they had received, returned evil. For it is the proverb of the prophet of the Creator of men and angels, 'That the base-born will not depart from the world, 'until he hath deceived and injured his patron, and benefactor.'

MY venerable PEER wrote unto me, saying, "It is thy duty to act in obedience to the commands of "thy God and the prophet of thy God, and to protect "and

وذريات آنحضرت را نصرت دهي

وسلاطين را كه نعمتهاي خدا ميخورند وبخدا ورسول وي باغي شده اند از ملك خدا اخراج نماي، ودر ملك خدا عدالت بكار بري كه كفته اند ملك بكفر باقي ماند وبظلم باقي نماند

وترا است كه افعال قبيحه واعمال شنيعه از ملك خدا براندازي كه افعال بد در عالم آن اثر ميكند كه غذاي بد در بدن واثار ظلم را محو نماي،

وطول بقاي ظالم را در عالم حمل بر نيكي ظالم نكني وسبب طول بقاي ظالمان وفاسقان آنست كه ظلم وفسقي كه در نهاد ايشان نهاده اند از قوت بفعل آورند آنكاه بسخط وغضب آلهي كرفتار كردند

كاه باشد كه قدرت آلهي ظلمه وفسقه وفجره را به بند وزندان وتاراج وقحط وكرسنكي ووباء عام وموت فجاء بيك مرتبه كرفتار كرداند

وكاه

" and assist the descendants and posterity of that holy " messenger.

" And those princes who feed on the bounties of the Creator, and yet rebel against their God and " his prophet, thou shalt drive out from the kingdoms of " the Lord. And thou shalt act with justice in the land " of thy Creator: for it is said, That dominion may be " continued to the infidel; but that to the tyrant it shall " not be continued.

" And it is thy duty to root out from the " country of God all pollutions and abominations; for " evil practices have that effect on the world, which per- " nicious aliment hath on the human body. Obliterate " every vestige of cruelty and oppression.

" And ascribe not the continued prospe- " rity of the tyrant in this world to the merits of the " tyrant: for the cause of the long duration of the power " of the wicked and the oppressors is this, that they may " bring forth into action all the wickedness and all the " crimes which they have treasured up in their hearts, " and then be overtaken by the wrath and indignation of " Almighty God.

" It shall sometimes come to pass, that " the omnipotence of the Creator shall at once chastize " the cruel, and the wicked, and the impious, with a " variety of punishments; by chains, and by prisons; " and by desolation, and by famine, and by hunger; by " an universal pestilence, and by sudden death; and by " unforeseen destruction.

وگاه باشد که صلحا واتقیا ونیکو کاران وبیگناهان بشامت افعال واعمال بدان در بلا افتند وگرفتار شوند چه آتش که در نیستان افتد تر وخشک آنرا بسوزد

واز ترقیات واستدراجات کفار وفجار وظلمه وفساق تعجب نکني وبغلط نروي وبا خود نگوي، که ظالمان وفاسقان وفاجران هرچند ظلم وفسق وفجور بیشتر میکنند نعمت ایشان بیشتر میشود

پس سبب بسیاري نعمت ایشان را باید دانست چه سببش اینست که شاید نظر بر عنایت منعم حقیقي کرده از ظلم وفسق باز آیند وشکر نعمت بجاي آورند

چون از اداي شکر الهي غافل شوند وبدرگاه سبحاني باز گشت ننمایند ونعمت خدا ورسول خدا فراموش کنند در آخر بغضب وسخط ایزدي گرفتار گردند

چون نامه پیر من بمن رسید ملک خدا را از چنگ ظالمان وکافران وملاحدان ومنافقان وفاسقان

"AND it ſhall ſometimes come to paſs, "that the juſt, and the religious, and the virtuous, and "the innocent ſhall be overtaken and involved in the ca-"lamities of the evil doers. For the fire, which falleth "in the wilderneſs of reeds, conſumeth both the green "and the dry.

"AND be not ſurprized at the proſperity "and the ſucceſs of the impious, and the wicked, and "the infidel, and the tyrant. And err not in thy conclu-"ſions, and ſay not unto thyſelf, The good things of "the wicked, and of the impious men, and of the tyrant "are increaſed unto them; although in wickedneſs, and "in tyranny, and in impiety they daily increaſe.

"THOU oughteſt firſt to underſtand the "cauſe of their increaſing proſperity. For the cauſe is, "that perhaps (reflecting on the bounties of their true "benefactor) they may turn back from their wickedneſs "and oppreſſions, and be grateful for the favours which "they receive.

"BUT if they neglect to pay the tribute "of gratitude to their God, and return not back to the "holy gate, and if they forget the bounties of their "Creator, and the prophet of their Creator, they ſhall in "the end be overtaken by the anger and the vengance of "the omnipotent chaſtiſer."

WHEN the letter of my venerable PEER came to my hands, I wreſted from the graſp of the op-

preſſors

وفاسقان وفاجران بر آوردم ودر دفع ورفع ايشان كمر همت بر بستم

تزوك ملك داري

هر ملك را كه مسخر ساختم عزيزان آن ملك را عزيز داشتم وسادات وعلما وفضلا ومشايخ را تعظيم واحترام نمودم وسيورغال ووظيفه ومرسوم بايشان مقرر ساختم وكلانتران آن ولايت را بمنزله برادر وخوردان واطفال را بجاي فرزند دانستم

وسپاه آن ملك را بدركاه خود راه دادم ورعايا را مستمال كردانيدم وهمه را در ميانه اميد وبيم نكاهداشتم وبه نيكان هر ملك نيكي كردم وبدان واشرار وبد نفسان را از مملكت اخراج نمودم

واداني واراذل را در مرتبه ايشان نكاهداشتم ونكذاشتم كه قدم از حد خود فراتر كذارند واكابر واشراف را بمراتب عاليه امتياز دادم وابواب عدالت در هر ملك مفتوح داشتم وطريق ظلم وستم را مسدود كردانيدم

وحاكم

pressors and the infidels, and from the seditious, and the wicked, and the impious, the lands of the Lord: and I girded up my loins to extirpate and destroy them. Book II.

REGULATIONS CONCERNING THE GOVERNMENT OF CONQUERED KINGDOMS.

In every kingdom which I conquered, I respected those who were worthy of respect, and I venerated and honoured the posterity of the prophet, and the theologians, and the learned, and the holy men; and I conferred upon them estates, and pensions, and appointments. And I considered the powerful and the opulent of that country as my brethren; and as my children, the poor and the helpless infants thereof.

And the soldiers of that kingdom I admitted to my presence; and I soothed and encouraged the subjects; and I kept both the one and the other suspended between hope and fear. And to the good of every country I did good; and I expelled from my kingdoms the vicious, and the wicked, and the seditious.

The base and the abject I confined within their proper bounds; and I permitted them not to exceed the limits prescribed them. And on the nobles and the grandees I conferred preeminence by exalted dignities; and I threw open the portals of equity and justice in every country; and I closed up the avenues to cruelty and oppression.

وحاكم هر ملكي را كه مسخر من شد
حكومت آن ولايت را باز بوي ارزاني داشتم وويرا بقيد
احسان در آورده مطيع ومنقاد خود ساختم وهر كه
بمن در نيامد ويرا بكردار وي كرفتار كردانيدم وحاكم
عادل وعاقل وعامل بر ايشان تعين نمودم

وامر كردم كه دزدان وقطاع الطريق
هر ملك را بياسا رسانند ومفسدان واشرار وبد نفسان را
از ملك اخراج نمايند وهرزه كاران را در شهر وملك
نكذارند
وكوتوالي بهر شهر وقصبه تعين كنند
كه نكاهبان رعيت وسپاه باشد وانچه از هر كس
بدزدي رود در عهدهء كوتوال باشد

وامر نمودم كه بر سر راهها ضابطان
تعين نمايند كه حارث وپاسپان راهها بوده اموال
واسباب وامتعه متردين تجار ومسافران را منزل بمنزل
برسانند واكر فوتي ونرو كذاشتي در آن بشود از
عهدهء جواب آن بر آيند

وامر

AND every kingdom which I reduced, I gave back the government of that kingdom to the prince thereof; and I bound him in the chains of kindness and generosity; and I drew unto me his obedience and submission. The refractory I overcame by their own devices; and I appointed over them a vigorous, and sagacious, and upright governor.

AND I commanded that the thieves and the high-way robbers of every country should be put to death; and that the seditious, and the vicious, and the profligate should be banished from the realm; and that vagrants and buffoons should not be permitted to reside in the cities or in the country;

AND that a magistrate should be appointed in every city and in every town, who should watch over the conduct of the soldier and the subject; and that he should be accountable for every thing that was stolen.

AND I ordered that guards should be stationed at the entrance of the roads; and that they should watch and defend the roads and the stages; and conduct in safety from stage to stage the merchandize, and the effects, and the property of the merchant and the traveller; and that if any loss or deficiency should be found therein, that they should be answerable for the value thereof.

وامر نمودم که حکام به تهمت وسخنان
ارباب غرض وبد کویان وبد نفسان بر هیچ فردي از
افراد متوطنان وساکنان بلاد وامصار جریمت نکنند
بعد از ثبوت کناه از احداث اربعه جریمت فراخور کناه
از مجرم بکیرند

وامر نمودم که سر شماري وخانه شماري
از هیچ شهري وقصبه نکیرند وهیچکس از سپاه در
خانه رعیت بزور نزول نکنند وچهارپایان واولاغ* رعایا
نکیرند
ودر جمع امور رعایاء هر مملکتي
در سلوک ومعاش حد اعتدال نکاهدارند وامر نمودم
که کدایان هر ملک را وظیفه مقرر کردانند تا رسم
کداي‌ء بر افتد

تزوک خبر داري وآکاهي از احوال
ملک ومملکت ورعیت وسپاه

امر نمودم که در هر سرحدي وولایتي
وشهري ولشکري خبر نویسي تعین نمایند که از
اعمال

AND I commanded that the governors ſhould not preſume to puniſh or oppreſs any one of the inhabitants of the towns or the cities under their juriſdiction, on the accuſation (or information) of the malevolent, and the profligate and the ſelf-intereſted; but that after conviction, according to the FOUR INSTITUTIONS, a fine ſhould be levied on the guilty perſon in proportion to the miſdemeanour.

AND I ordained that the poll-tax and the houſe-tax ſhould not be levied on any town, or on any city whatever; and that no one of the ſoldiers ſhould preſume to enter by force the dwelling of a civil inhabitant, or to ſeize on the cattle, or the property, of the ſubject;

AND that in every concern of the inhabitants of every country, the governors thereof ſhould in their conduct keep within the limits of equity and juſtice. And I ordained that ſubſiſtence ſhould be allowed to the mendicants of every kingdom, that the practice of begging might be aboliſhed.

REGULATIONS FOR THE OBTAINING INTELLIGENCE AND INFORMATION OF THE STATE OF THE EMPIRE, AND OF THE PROVINCES, AND OF THE SOLDIERS, AND OF THE SUBJECTS.

I ordained that on every frontier, and in every country, and in every city, and in every camp a writer of intelligence ſhould be eſtabliſhed; and that each

اعمال وافعال حكام ورعيت وسپاه ولشكر خود ولشكر
بيكانه ومداخل ومخارج مال ومنال ودر آمدن وبر
آمدن مردم بيكانه وقوافل از اهل هر مملكت واخبار
ممالك وسلاطين همسايه واعمال وافعال ايشان وجماعه
علما وافاضل كه از بلاد بعيده روي بدركاه من
آورده باشند بتفصيل از روي راستي ودرستي بدركاه
مينوشته باشند

واكر خلاف نمايند واز قرار واقع ننويسند
انكشتان اخبار نويسان قطع نمايند واكر اخبار نويسي
كار سپاهي را پوشيده دارد ودر لباس ديكر بنويسد
دست ويرا قطع كنند واكر دروغي را بنابر تهمت
وغرضي نوشته باشد اورا بقتل رسانند وامر نمودم كه
اخبار مذكور روز بروز وهفته بهفته وماه بماه بعرض
برسد

وامر نمودم كه يك هزار نفر جمازه سوار
واسپ سوار چپقونچي* رونده دونده وهزار نفر پياده
جلد تعين نمايند كه اخبار ممالك وسرحد واراده
ومقاصد

each ſhould write to the imperial preſence, with truth and perſpicuity, full accounts of the conduct and the behaviour of the governors, and of the officers; and of the ſoldiers, and of the ſubjects; and of the ſtate of my own armies, and of thoſe of foreign powers; and of the bringing in, and the carrying out of all merchandize and commodities; and of the entrance, and the departure of all ſtrangers, and of all Kauruvvauns of every country; and of the tranſactions of the neighbouring kingdoms and princes, and of their conduct and behaviour; and alſo of the learned and ſkilful men of diſtant countries, who might turn their faces towards my dominions:

AND that if the writer of intelligence was guilty of falſehood, and wrote not the true ſtate of the facts, his fingers ſhould be cut off: and that if he ſuppreſſed the laudable actions of a ſoldier, or wrote an unjuſt account thereof he ſhould be deprived of his right hand: and that if he wrote a falſe account from enmity and from malice, he ſhould be put to death. And I commanded that theſe accounts ſhould be tranſmitted unto me day by day, and week by week, and month by month.

AND I ordained, that a thouſand ſwift camel-men, and a thouſand ſwift horſe-men, and a thouſand expeditious foot-men ſhould be ſelected; and that they ſhould inform themſelves of the occurrences of the countries, and of the frontiers; and of the intentions and the

ومقاصد سلاطين جواررا تحقيق نموده وبحضور آمده
خبر رسانند تا آنكه پيش از وقوع واقع اعلاج نمايم
چنانچه خبر شكست يافتن توقتمش
خان از اروس خان بمن رسيد دانستم كه وي بمن
پناه خواهد آورد واستعداد جنك اروس خان وامداد
توقتمش خان نمودم

چنانچه در وقتي كه بر تسخير ممالك
هندوستان عازم شدم بمن خبر رسانيدند كه در هر
نواحي هندوستان حاكمي ووالي بر تخت سلطنت
نشست
چنانچه سارنك برادر ملو خان در سر
زمين ملتان علم حكومت بر افراخته ودر دهلي سلطان
محمود خان علم سلطنت بر افراخته ودر ناحيه لاهور
ملو خان لشكر جمع آورده ومبارك خان در نواحي
قنوج بدعوي سلطنت بر خاسته ودر هر ولايتي از
ولايت هندوستان شخصي كردن بدعوي سلطنه
برافراخته
چون اين خبر بمسامع من رسيد تسخير
آن ملك در نظر من آسان نمود ليكن در نظر سپاه
مشكل بود

چنانچه

the designs of the neighbouring princes; and that they should return unto the presence, and give me information thereof, that I might provide the remedy before the evil arrived. Book II.

Thus I received intelligence of the defeat of Touktummish Khaun by Auroos Khaun. I knew that Touktummish Khaun would fly for protection unto me; and I made the necessary preparations to support Touktummish, and to wage war with Auroos.

Thus at the time that I was about to undertake the reduction of the empire of Hindostaun, information was brought unto me, that independent princes and chiefs were seated on the throne of government in every quarter of those dominions;

Thus, that Saurung, the brother of Mulloo Khaun, had elevated the standard of power in the land of Mooltaun; and that in Dehli Sooltaun Muhmood Khaun had erected the ensign of authority; and that in the territories of Lauhore Mulloo Khaun had drawn together a numerous army; and that Mubbauruk Khaun had aspired to the regal title in the kingdom of Kunnouj; and that in every province of the provinces of Hindostaun some one had assumed the regal dignity.

When I received this information, the conquest of that empire appeared easy in my sight; but in the eyes of my soldiers it was an undertaking of difficulty.

چنانچه در وقت که مملکت هندرا مسخر ساختم خبر بمن رسید که قیصر روم بر بعضي مملکت من ترکتاز آورده وکرجیان از حد خود تجاوز نموده به بعضي قلاع که لشکرهاي من آنرا محاصره داشتند آمده مدد اهالي قلعه کرده اند

وخود بخود کنکاش کردم اکر در هند توقف نمایم در مملکت ایران خللي روي خواهد داد نسق دار الملک هند نموده ایلغار کردم وروزي چند در ماورالنهر توقف نمودم واز آنجا متوجه روم وکرجستان شدم وجمیع آن ممالک مسخر ساختم

تزوک سلوک ومعاش بمتوطنان وساکنان بلاد ونسق مزارات اولیا وبزرکان دین واوقاف ونذارات

امر نمودم که هر مملکتي که مسخر کردد سپاهي که در آن مملکت باشد وپناه آورد نوکر سازند وجاي دهند ورعایا ومتوطنان آن دیاررا از حوادث وقتل وغارت واسیري محافظت نمایند

واموال

Thus, when I had ſubdued the empire of Hind, I received intelligence that the Keeſur of Room had ravaged certain of my provinces; and that the natives of Goorjiſtaun, exceeding their proper limits, had advanced to certain caſtles which were beſieged by my forces; and that they had given ſuccour to the inhabitants of thoſe caſtles. Book II.

And I reflected with myſelf, that if I tarried longer in the empire of Hindoſtaun, diſorders would ariſe in the kingdom of Eraun. Having ſettled the affairs of the empire of Hind, I returned from thence with ſpeed. And I halted for a few days in Mauwur u Nuhur; and from thence I proceeded towards Room and Goorjiſtaun; and I conquered the whole of that extenſive empire.

Regulations concerning the conduct to be observed towards the natives, and the inhabitants, of every country. And of the establishments of the shrines of the saints, and of the fathers of the holy religion. And of the gifts and pious donations.

I ordained, in every kingdom which ſhould be ſubdued, that the warrior of that kingdom who ſubmitted unto me ſhould be received into my ſervice; and that the ſubjects and the inhabitants of that country ſhould be protected from injuries, and from ſlaughter, and from rapine, and from ſlavery;

 And

واموال واسباب ایشان را از تاراج وبغما
نکاهدارند وغنایمي را که از آن ملک بدست آید
بقید ضبط در آورند

وسادات وعلما ومشایخ وفضلا واکابر
واشراف را اعزاز نمایند وکدخدیان وکلانتران
ودهقانان ومزارعان را استمالت دهند

ورعایا را در میانهء امید وبیم نکاهدارند
ومقدار کناه واستعداد او جریمت بکیرند

وامر نمودم که بسادات وعلما ومشایخ
وفضلا ودرویشان وکوشه نشینان هر مملکي که
بتسخیر در آید سیورغالات ووظیفه ومرسوم بدهند وبفقرا
وعجزه مساکین مدد ومعاش مقرر دارند وبمدرسین
ومشایخ وظیفه معین نمایند

وبروضات ومزارات اولیاي واکابر دین

مواضع

AND that their effects and their property ſhould be protected from ravage and from plunder; and that the ſpoils which had been gathered from that country ſhould be taken from the ſpoilers;

AND that the poſterity of the prophet, and the theologians, and the holy and the learned men, and the nobles and the grandees ſhould be treated with honour and reſpect; and that the chiefs, and the leading men, and the principal men of the towns and the villages, and thoſe who followed agriculture, ſhould be protected and encouraged;

AND that the ſubjects in general ſhould be kept ſuſpended between hope and fear; and that when guilty of a crime, they ſhould be fined in proportion to the offence, and to their ability.

AND I ordained that to the poſterity of the prophet, and to the theologians, and to the learned, and to the holy men, and to the religious, and to the recluſe in every country which ſhould come under my dominion, lands, and penſions, and appointments ſhould be granted; and that ſubſiſtence and ſupport ſhould be allowed to the poor, and to the helpleſs, and to the indigent; and that to the teachers, and to the learned in religion ſalaries ſhould be granted;

AND that for the ſupport of the ſhrines and the ſepulchres of the ſaints, and the fathers of the holy

مواضع وقف كنند وفرش وآش وروشناي مقرر نمايند

واول بروضه مقدسه امير المومنين شاه مردان علي ابن ابي طالب كرم الله وجه محال نجف وجله را وقف نمايند

وبروضه منوره امام حسين رضي الله عنه وبروضه قدوة الاوليا شيخ عبد القادر ومقبره امام اعظم ابو حنيفه رحمت الله عليه ومزارات ديكر مشايخ واكابر وبزركان دين كه در بغداد آسوده اند از براي هريك علي قدرهم مواضع ودهات كربلا وبغداد وغيره وقف نمايند

وبراي روضه منوره امام موسي كاظم وامام محمد نقي وسليمان فارسي محال مزروعه از جزاير وغيره حاصلات مداين وقف كنند

وبجهت روضه متبركه امام علي ابن موسي ناحيه كته بست ومحال شهر طوس را وقف نمايند وفرش وروشناي وآش يوميه مقرر سازند وبجهت مزارات

holy religion, lands ſhould be appointed; and that carpets, and food, and lamps ſhould be allowed to thoſe who reſided therein: Book II.

AND firſt, that for the holy ſhrine of the commander of the faithful, the king of men, Aali † the the ſon of Aboo Taulib (on whom be the favour of God) the diſtricts of Bukhf and Jilleh ſhould be aſſigned;

AND that for the pure ſhrine of the Imaum Hooſſein (whom the Almighty reward) and for the ſhrine of the mirror of the ſaints, Sheikh Abdulkaudir: and for the ſhrine of the great Imaum Aboo Khunneefeh (the mercy of God be upon him) and for the ſepulchres of the other ſaints, and fathers, and diſtinguiſhed men of the holy religion, who reſted from their labours in the city of Bughdaud; that for each of them, according to their dignities, the lands and the villages of Kurbullau and of Bughdaud, and other diſtricts ſhould be aſſigned;

AND that for the ſupport of the holy ſhrines of Imaum Mooſi Kauzim, and Imaum Mahummud Nukki, and Soolamaun Faurſi, the fertile lands of Juzzauir and other cities ſhould be granted;

AND that for the ſupport of the ſacred ſepulchres of Imaum Aali, the ſon of Mooſi, the lands of Kutteh Buſt, and the environs of the city of Toos ſhould be aſſigned; and that carpets, and lamps, and

† The fourth Khalif, and ſon-in-law to the Mahummudan lawgiver.

daily

مـزارات ومقابر مشايخ ايران وتوران نام بنام نذورات
واوقـاف معين نمايند

وامر نمودم كه هر مملكتي كه مسخر
كردد كدايان آن ملك را جمع ساخته يوميه ووظيفه
مقرر نمايند وايشان را تمغا* كنند كه ديكر كداي‌ء را
بـر طرف سازند واكر بعد از تمغا كداي‌ء نمايند
ايشانرا به بلاد بعيده بفروشند يا سر دهند تا كدازان
از مملكت من كم شود

تـزوك تحصيل مال وخـراج از رعيت
ونـسـق وروتق مـلـك ومعموري واباداني وضبط
وحـراسـت مملكت

امـر نمودم كه مال وخراج از رعيت
بنهجي بكيرند كه موجب خرابـي رعيت وويـراني
مملكت نشود كه خرابي رعيت موجب كمي خزانه
است وكمي خزانه باعث تـفرقه سپاه است وتـفرقه
سپاه موجب اختلال مرتبه سلطنت است

وامر

daily bread ſhould be allowed to the religious; and that benefactions and gifts ſhould be granted for the ſepulchres and the Mauſoleums of each of the ſaints of Eraun and of Tooraun.

And I ordained that, in every kingdom which ſhould be conquered, the mendicants of that country ſhould be gathered together; and that ſubſiſtence and daily bread ſhould be allowed unto them; and that they ſhould be made penſioners and beg no more. And if after they were made penſioners they continued the practice of aſking alms, I commanded that they ſhould be ſold into foreign countries, or expelled from the realm: that the race of beggars might become extinct in my dominions.

Regulations concerning the collection of the revenues and the taxes from the subjects; and the order and the arrangement of the provinces; and the cultivation, and the population, and the government, and the police of the empire.

I ordained that the revenues and the taxes ſhould be collected in ſuch a manner, as might not be productive of ruin to the ſubject, or of depopulation to the country. For the ruin of the ſubject cauſeth a diminution of the imperial treaſures; and a diminution of the imperial treaſures effecteth the diſperſion of the troops; and the diſperſion of the troops produceth the extinction of the imperial power.

وامر نمودم که هر مملکتي که مسخر
کرده واز حوادث در امن وامان در آيد حاصل
وواصل آن ملک را ملاحظه نمايند

اکر رعايا بجمع قديم راضي باشند
برضاي ايشان عمل نمايند والا موافق تزوک جمع
بربندند

وامر نمودم که خراج موافق حاصل
زراعت بکيرند وجمع بر حاصل زمين بر بندند

چنانچه اول اراضي مزروعه رعيت را که
بآب کاريز وچشمه ونهر وورود خانه زراعت کرده
باشند وآن آبها دوام واستمرار داشته باشد ضبط
نمايند وانچه حاصل آن آراضي باشد دو حصه برعيت
کذارند ويک حصه بسرکار اعلي تحصيل نمايند

واکر رعايا آداي اراضي مضبوطه بنقدي
راضي باشد انچه غله حصه سرکار را موافق نرخ وقت
نقدي بر رعيت قرار دهند وموافق نرخ نقد
بسپاهي برسانند

واکر

AND I ordained that, in every country that ſhould be ſubdued (to the inhabitants of which charters of ſafety and ſecurity from dangers ſhould be granted) the produce and the revenue of that country ſhould be inſpected;

IF the ſubjects were ſatisfied with the old and eſtabliſhed taxes, that thoſe taxes ſhould be confirmed, agreeably to the wiſhes of the ſubjects; or if not, that they ſhould be determined according to the REGULATION.

AND I ordained that the duties ſhould be determined in proportion to the produce of the cultivated lands; and that the taxes on the produce of thoſe lands ſhould be affixed and aſcertained:

THUS firſt, that the cultivated grounds of the ſubject, which ſhould be made fertile by the water of canals, or by ſprings, or rivulets, or rivers (if thoſe waters flowed perpetually and continually) ſhould be ſuperintended by the officers of the crown; and that of the amount of the produce of thoſe grounds, two thirds ſhould be allowed to the poſſeſſor thereof, and one third be paid into the royal treaſury;

AND if the ſubject ſhould conſent to pay the tax for the reſtricted lands in ſpecie, that for the grain due to the treaſury the ſum ſhould be fixed on the ſubject according to the current price of the grain; and that correſponding to the current price of the grain, the money ſhould be paid to the ſoldiers; †

† If the price of grain was low the ſoldiers pay was leſs, if high, it was more: that is to ſay, it was always exactly proportioned to the value of the neceſſaries of life.

واكر رعيت بحاصل وقسمت سه توده راضي نشوند اراضي مضبوط را اول ودوم وسيوم جريب نهايند وجريب اول را سه خروار وجريب دوم را دو خروار وجريب سيوم را يک خروار جمع بربندند ونصف را کندم ونصفي را جو اعتبار کنند وانچه جمع شود دو يک مال بکيرند

واكر رعيت با وجود اين هم بدادن مال راضي نشود خرواري کندم را پنج مثقال نقره وخرواري جورا دو نيم مثقال نقره نرخ نهايند وساوري قلعه بر آن اضافه کنند وديکر بهيچ اسم ورسم چيزي از رعايا مطالبه ننهايند

وباقي زراعت خريف وربيع وزمستاني وتابستاني رعيت را وزراعتي که بآب باران مزروع شده باشد جريب نهايند وانچه بتحرير در آيد به ثلث وربع عمل کنند

† A *Jurreeb* is a certain land-measure, as our acre.

وسر

And if the subject should not be satisfied with the mode of collection, and with the partition of the general produce into three parts, that the restricted lands should be divided into first, and second, and third Jurreeb; † that the produce of the first Jurreeb should be estimated at three loads, and the produce of the second Jurreeb at two loads, and the produce of the third Jurreeb at one load; and that half thereof should be estimated as wheat, and half thereof as barley; and that of the total amount one half of the produce should be collected;

And if the subject, notwithstanding this, should be unwilling to pay the tax in kind, that the value of a load of wheat should be fixed at five Miskauls of silver, and the value of a load of barley at two and a half Miskauls of silver; and that the duty of the Kellaah ‡ should be exacted over and above: but that nought else should be demanded of the subject under any pretext or denomination whatever;

And that the rest of the lands of the husbandman, those which produced in the autumn, and in the spring, and in the summer, and in the winter; and the lands which depended on the rain for fertility, should be divided into Jurreebs; and that of the produce of those which were numbered, a third or a fourth should be collected;

‡ What this duty is, is unknown to the translator.

And

وسر سهار ومخترفه وساير جهات بلدان

ومواضع وآبخور وعلف چرا ومراعي موافق دستور

العمل تديم بعمل آوردند واگر رعيت راضي نشود

به هست وبود عمل نمايند

وامر نمودم كه پيش از رسيدن محصول

بر رعيت مال وجهات اطلاق نمايند وچون محصول

برسد بسه دفعه مال تحصيل كنند

واگر رعيت بي تحصيلدار مال گذاري

نمايد تحصيلدار تعين ننمايند واگر بتحصيلدار

محتاج شوند بحكم وسخن مال بگيرند كار

بچوب وريسمان وشلاق نرسانند ورعيت را به بند

وزنجير مقيد نكردانند

وامر نمودم كه هركس صحراي اباد

كند ويا كاريزي احداث نمايد يا باغي سبز كند

يا موضع ويراني را نو اباد سازد در سال اول چيزي

نگيرند ودر دوم انچه رعيت برضاي خود بدهد

بگيرند ودر سال سيوم موافق تزك مال بگيرند

وامر

AND that the duties on the herbs, and on the fruits, and on all the other productions of the country, and on the reservoirs of water, and on the commons, and on the pasture lands should be fixed and determined according to the ancient and established practices: and if the subject should not be content therewith, that the collections should be settled according to the Hust and Bood. †

AND I ordained that, before the time of the gathering in the grain, the taxes should not be demanded; and, when the period of the harvest arrived, that they should be collected at three different times;

AND if the subject paid the royal dues spontaneously, that a tax-gatherer should not be appointed over him; and if there should be occasion for a tax-gatherer, that he should levy the duties by threats and by authority; but that he should not make use of the cudgel, and the cord, and the scourge; nor presume to confine the subject in fetters and in chains.

AND I ordained, whoever undertook the cultivation of waste lands, or built an aqueduct, or made a canal, or planted a grove, or restored to culture a deserted district, that in the first year nothing should be taken from him, and that in the second year whatever the subject voluntarily offered should be received, and that in the third year the duties should be collected according to the REGULATION.

† This regulation is not understood by the translator.

وامر نهودم که اکر ارباب وکلانتر
بر ریزه رعیت تعدي نهاید وموجب خرابي ریزه رعیت
باشد مقدار خرابي که بر ریزه رعیت رسیده باشد
از ارباب وکلانتر کرفته بایشان برساند که بحال
خود باز آیند

ومواضع خراب اکر صاحب نداشته
باشند در خالصه معهور نهایند واکر صاحب داشته
باشند واکر پریشان باشد مصالح الاملاک بوي دهند
که موضع خودرا اباد سازد

وامر نهودم که در زمین خراب کاریزها
جاري سازند وپلهاي خراب را عمارت نهایند وبر نهرآبها
ورود خانها پلها بنا کنند ودر راهها بمقدار یک منزل
رباطي تعمیر نهایند وراهداران ومستحفظان در راهها
مقرر دارند ودر هر رباطي جمعي را متوطن سازند
که راهداري ونکاهباني بدیشان متعلق باشد ومال
که از اهل غفلت در راهها بدزدي برود راهداران
از عهده بر آیند

وامر نهودم که در هر شهري وبلدي
مسجدي

AND I ordained, that if the rich and the powerful ſhould oppreſs the poorer ſubject, and injure or deſtroy his property, an equivalent for the damage ſuſtained ſhould be levied on the rich oppreſſor, and be delivered to the injured perſon; that he might be reſtored to his former eſtate:

AND that all ruined lands which lay uncultivated (if there were no owners to thoſe lands) ſhould be annexed to the crown. And if there were owners, and thoſe owners were reduced to diſtreſs, I ordained that the neceſſary ſupplies ſhould be granted unto them, that they might cultivate their lands anew.

AND I commanded that the ruined bridges ſhould be repaired; and that bridges ſhould be conſtructed over the rivulets and over the rivers; and that on the roads, at the diſtance of one ſtage from each other, Kauruvvaunſurai † ſhould be erected; and that guards and watchmen ſhould be ſtationed on the road, and that in every Kauruvvaunſurai people ſhould be appointed to reſide; and that the watching and the guarding of the roads ſhould appertain unto them: and that thoſe guards ſhould be anſwerable for whatever ſhould be ſtolen on the roads from the unwary traveller.

AND I ordained that in every town and in every city a moſque, and a ſchool, and a monaſtery,

† Buildings for the reception of travellers.

مسجدي ومدرسه وخانقاهي بنا كنند ولنكر خانه
بجهت فقرا ومساكين ودار الشفاي بجهت مرضان
مقرر دارند وطبيبي را موظف ساخته بر دار الشفا
موكل دارند ودر هر شهري دار الاماره ودار العداله
تعمير كنند وقورچيان* بجهت نكاهباني زراعت ورعيت
مقرر نمايند

وامر نمودم كه در هر ملكي سه وزير
تعين نمايند يكي براي رعيت كه انچه از رعيت
تحصيل شود واصلات آنرا سر رشته نكاهدارد كه چه
مبلغ وچه مقدار از رعيت بهر اسم ورسم بر آمده جمع
آنرا نكاهدارد

ووزير دوم از براي سپاه كه بسپاهيان
چه مبلغ رسيده وچه مبلغ طلب دارند

ووزيـر سيوم از بـراي ضبط اموال غايب
وآينده ورونده وحاصل بادي وهـواي وضبط اموال
مجانين ومواريث واثام كه باستصواب قاضي وشيخ
الاسلام جمع سازد

وامر

and an alms houſe for the poor and the indigent, and an hoſpital for the ſick and infirm ſhould be founded; and that a phyſician ſhould receive a ſalary, and ſhould be appointed to attend the hoſpital: and that in every city a governtment-houſe, and a court for the adminiſtration of juſtice ſhould be built: and that ſuperintendants ſhould be appointed to watch over the cultivated lands, and over the huſbandmen.

AND I ordained that in every country three Vizzeers ſhould be ſtationed. The FIRST for the ſubject, To keep a regular account of the taxes and the duties received, and what ſums, and to what amount, were paid in by the ſubject, and under what denomination, and on what account; and to preſerve an exact ſtatement of the whole.

THE SECOND for the ſoldier, To take account of the ſums paid to the troops, and of the ſums remaining due unto them.

THE THIRD, To take poſſeſſion of the Amwaul a Ghauibi,† and of the cuſtoms on the comers and on the goers; and of the revenues of the Baudi and the Huvvaui; and to take poſſeſſion of the effects of thoſe who ſhould become inſane, and of thoſe who died inteſtate, and of thoſe who ſuffered by the laws. And he was to take poſſeſſion of thoſe effects with the approbation of the magiſtrate and of the eccleſiaſtical judge.

† The effects of people loſt, or abſconded.

وامر نهودم که اموال اموات را بوارث
رسانند واکر وارث نباشد در ابواب الخیر صرف
نمایند یا بمکه معظمه بفرستند

تزوک جنک وجدل ودر آمد وبر آمد
معرکه وصف آرایء وفوج شکني

امر نهودم که اکر غنیم از دوازده
هزار سوار کم باشد درین جنک امیر الامرا سردار
باشد ودوازده هزار سوار از اویماق وتومانات بوي همراه
نمایند واز مینک باشیان ویوز باشیان واون باشیان
نیز همراه کردانند

وبمسافت یک منزل بجانب غنیم پیش
رفته به غنیم رو برو شود وخبر بمن بفرستند

وامر نهودم که این دوازده هزار سوار
نه فوج مرتب سازند برین ترتیب قول یک فوج وبرانغار
سه فوج وجرانغار سه فوج وهراول یک فوج وقراول یک
فوج

وفوج برانغار مشتمل باشد بر هراولي
وچپاولي وشغاولي وهمچنین فوج جرانغار متضمن سه
فوج هراول وچپاول وشغاول باشد

وامر

And I commanded that the property of the deceaſed ſhould be reſtored to the lawful heir; and if there ſhould be no heir, that it ſhould be expended in pious uſes, or be ſent to the holy city of Mecca.

REGULATIONS OF WAR: FOR ENTERING INTO AND RETIRING FROM THE FIELD OF BATTLE; AND FOR FORMING THE LINE; AND FOR DEFEATING ARMIES.

I ordained, if the enemy exceeded not twelve thouſand cavalry, that an Ameer ul Omrau ſhould command the oppoſing army: and that twelve thouſand horſemen of the Ouyemauk, and the Toumaun; alſo Mingbauſhee, and Euzbauſhee, and Ounbauſhee Ameers ſhould be placed under his command:

And that he ſhould advance to within the diſtance of one day's march from the enemy, and that he ſhould halt oppoſite unto them, and ſend me information thereof.

And I commanded that thoſe twelve thouſand horſe ſhould be formed in nine diviſions after this manner: The main body one diviſion, and the right wing three diviſions, and the left wing three diviſions, and the advanced guard one diviſion, and the advanced guard of the advanced guard one diviſion:

And that the right wing ſhould conſiſt of its own advanced guard, and its right and its left diviſions; and that the left wing ſhould alſo conſiſt of its own advanced guard, and of its right and its left diviſions.

And

وامر نمودم که امیر الامرا در زمین
جنگ گاه چهار چیز ملاحظه نماید اول آب آن
سر زمین دوم زمینی که سپاه را نگاهدارد سیوم
که بر غنیم مشرف باشد وآفتاب رو برو نباشد تا
شعاع آفتاب چشم سپاه را خیره نگرداند چهارم پیش
روی جنگ گاه کشاده ووا باشد

وامر نمودم که پیش از جنگ یک روز
صف آرایء نمایند وتزک افواج نموده قدم پیش
گذارند وسمتی که میرفته باشند سر اسپان خود
از آن سمت بر نگردانند وبچپ وراست میل نکنند
وامر نمودم که چون نظر سپاه بر افواج غنیم افتد
باوازه بلند تکبیر گفته سورن اندازند

واگر عارض لشکر ببینند که
سردار خطا کند آن عارض دیگری را بجا وی
بنشاند ویرلیغ فتح که من بوی سپرده ام بامرا
وسپاه نمودار گرداند

† *Ullab ackbur*, God is great.

وامر

AND I ordered that the general ſhould attend to four particulars in his choice of the field of battle.—FIRST, the water thereof.—And SECONDLY, the ſtrength of the ground, that his flanks and his rear might be covered.—And THIRDLY, that his ſituation be more elevated than the ſituation of the enemy; and that the ſun be not in his front, that the glare thereof dazzle not the eyes of his troops.--FOURTHLY, that the ground before his lines be extenſive and open.

AND I commanded that the army ſhould be marſhalled, and the line be formed on the day preceding the action; and that (the forces being ranged in order of battle) they ſhould march towards the enemy; and that they ſhould not turn the heads of their horſes from the direction in which they were advancing; that they ſhould neither incline to the left nor to the right. And when the eyes of the army fell upon the forces of the enemy, I ordered that they ſhould utter a great ſhout, and repeat the Tuckbeer † with a loud voice.

AND I commanded, if the Auriz ‡ of the army ſaw that the leader thereof was deficient in his duty, that he ſhould deprive him of his command, and appoint another in his place; and that he ſhould open and communicate to the Ameers and to the ſoldiers the order which I had delivered unto him for that purpoſe.

‡ A ſort of field-deputy, appointed to obſerve the conduct of the commander in chief.

AND

وامر نهودم که سردار لشکر باتغاق عارض
کهي وبسياري لشکر غنيم را ملاحظه نهايند وسرداران
طرف خود وطرف غنيم را مقابله نهايند ودر کهي
وبسياري تلاني وتدارک کنند واسلحه سپاه خود وسپاه
دشهن بخاطر آورند ورفتار غنيم را به بينند که
باهستکي وپيوستکي بجنک مي در آيند يا باضطراب

وروش جنک غنيم را بخاطر آورند که
بيک مرتبه ترکتاز مي آورند يا فوج فوج متعاقب
يکديکر حهله مي آورند وبه بينند که در هنکام
تاختن خودرا غنيم ميرساند وبر مي کردد وباز حهله
آورد يا بهمان حهله اول اکتفاي نهايند اکر چنين
باشد سپاه را است که صدمه تاخت ايشانرا بردارد
وصبر نهايد که شجاعت صبر يک ساعت است

وامر نهودم که تا غنيم بجنک مبادرت
ننهايد بر وي سبغت نکيرند وامر نهودم که چون
غنيم

AND I ordained that the general of the army ſhould, in conjunction with the Auriz, reconnoitre the numbers of the foe; and that he ſhould compare his chiefs with thoſe of the enemy, and confront them to each other accordingly; and that he ſhould take the neceſſary precautions to ſupply all deficiencies; and that he ſhould conſider well the different kinds of arms uſed by the ſoldiers of the enemy and by his own; and that he ſhould obſerve the motions of his foes, whether they advanced into the field ſlowly and in good order, or whether they ruſhed forward in confuſion;

AND that he ſhould conſider and comprehend the movements and the order of the enemy's battle, whether they charged at once and in an united body, or by detachments, the one ſucceeding the other; and that he ſhould obſerve, in the moment of aſſault, whether the enemy advanced and retired, and prepared to charge again, or whether they appeared ſatisfied with their firſt attempt. When the latter is the caſe, it is the duty of the ſoldier to bear lightly the ſhock of the enemy's attack, and to ſtand firm and patient. For bravery is but patience and firmneſs for an hour.

AND I ordained that until the foe advanced to the attack, he ſhould not be attacked. And I ordered, when the enemy entered the field of battle, that the at-

غنیم بمیدان در آید سردار را نظر بر فرمایش وکار فرمودن افواج نهکانه باشد

چه کار سردار همین است که افواج را کار فرماید وسردار را است که در وقت کار دل خودرا پاي ندهد ودست وپا کم نکند وهر فوجي را بمنزله سلاحي از اسلحه فرا گیرد از تیر وتبر وشمشیر وگرز وکارد وخنجر وهر فوج را بوقت کار فرماید

وسردار را است که نه فوج را وخودرا بمنزله شخص کشتي گیر فرا گیرد که به هر عضو خود از دست وپا وسر وسینه وغیره بجنک در آمده وامید است که چون نه ضرب شمشیر دفعه دفعه بر فوج غنیم برسد البته در ضرب نهم شکست یابد

وسردار را است که اول فوج هراول را بر غنیم بدواند وهراول برانغار متعاقب آن بمدد بفرستد واز عقب هراول برانغار هراول جرانغار را براند تا آنکه سه ضرب بر افواج غنیم آید اگر درین وقت هراولان زبوني نمایند فوج اول برانغار را براند واز عقب

tention of the general ſhould be turned to the conducting and the directing of the efforts of his troops. Book II.

FOR the duty of the commander is to govern and to guide the movements of his forces; and to be cool, and firm, and collected within himſelf in the hour of trial; and to conſider each diviſion of his army as a particular inſtrument of the inſtruments of war; as the arrow, and the battle-axe, and the ſword, and the mace, and the poniard, and the dagger; and to direct the edge or the point of each in the moment of neceſſity.

AND it is the duty of a general to conſider himſelf and the nine diviſions of his army as a wreſtler who entereth into action, and fighteth with every part of his body — with his arms and with his feet, and with his breaſt, and with his head. And there is ground for expectation, when eight aſſaults ſhall have been ſucceſſively made on the line of the enemy, that in the ninth ſhock they will certainly be defeated.

AND it is the buſineſs of a ſkilful general firſt to charge the foe with his advanced guard. And let him then ſend forward the advanced guard of his right wing to ſupport them; and after them the advanced guard of the left wing: that three ſucceſſive ſhocks may be given to the force of the enemy. And if at this juncture the advanced guards ſhould ſhrink back from before the foe, let him direct the firſt diviſion of the right wing to

عقب وي فوج دوم جرانغاررا براند اكر فتح نشود فوج دوم برانغار براند ومتعاقب وي فوج اول جرانغاررا براند وخبر بمن فرستند

ومنتظر رايات من باشد وتكيه بر عنايات الهي كرده سردار خود بجنك در آيد ومرا در معرك حاضر داند كه بتوفيق الله چون هشت ضرب بر غنيم واقع آيد در ضرب نهم غنيم شكست خورد وفتح روزي شود

وسرداررا است كه تيز جلوي نكند ولشكررا كار فرمايد وبعد از آنكه كار بسوي رسد تا تواند خودرا بكشتن ندهد كه كشته شدن سردار بد نامي آرد وموجب خيركي غنيم مي كردد

پس سرداررا است كه براي وتدبير كار كند وتعجيل نكند كه تعجيل از شيطان است وبجاي در نيآيد كه از آن نتواند بر آمد

ترتيب صف آراي،

charge, and after them the ſecond diviſion of the left wing: and if victory proceedeth not from them, let him order the ſecond diviſion of the right wing into action, and let them be followed by the firſt diviſion of the left wing. And in this ſtate of the conflict let the commander diſpatch information unto me. Book II.

AND let him depend upon the arrival of my ſtandard, and reſting on the favour of Almighty God, advance himſelf upon the foe, and conſider me as preſent in the action. For when (by the favour of God) eight ſucceſſive ſhocks have been given to the ſtrength of the enemy, they muſt ſink under the ninth, and the victory be obtained.

AND it is the buſineſs of a general neither to be raſh nor precipitate; but to direct the operations of his troops *with firmneſs and preſence of mind.* And when he himſelf ſhall be obliged to enter into action, he muſt not, whilſt he can avoid it, give himſelf up to death: for the death of the general bringeth diſgrace upon the army, and encreaſeth the obſtinacy of the enemy.

THEREFORE it is the duty of a commander to ſhun temerity, and to act with deliberation and prudence: for temerity is the offspring of the devil. And let him alſo be careful that he venture not into a ſituation, out of which he cannot extricate himſelf and his army.

فـوج قراول

فوج هراول

فوج هراول برانغار   فوج هراول جرانغار

اول فوج برانغار * دويم فوج برانغار   اول فوج جرانغار * دويم فوج جرانغار

قـول

See PLATE I.

تـزوك صف اراي‌ء افواج قاهره را چنين بر بسـتـم

امر نمودم كه اگر لشكر غنيم از دوازده هزار سوار زياده باشد ليكن بچهل هزار نرسد يكي از فرزندان كامكار سردار باشد ودو بيگلر بيگي در ركاب وي با امراي وقشونات وتومانات والوسات كه از چهل هزار سوار كمتر نباشند حاضر باشند

وافواج قاهره بايد كه مرا حاضر دانسته سر رشته تدبـير ومردي ومردانگي از دست ندهند

وامر نمودم كه چون پيشخانه اقبال مرا بـر آورند دوازده فوج معين نمايند وبر هـريـك اميـري از امراي الوسات مقرر باشد وتـزك نمايند تا دوازده تـزكي كه در روش صف اراي‌ء وافـواج شكني ودر آمد وبر آمد كه بر بسته ام در نظر داشته بـاشـد

† *Paiſhkhauneh* is the tent, or ſet of tents, of the prince; which on a march are ſent forward and erected againſt his arrival at every ſtage: i. e. there are two ſets of tents, and thoſe at the firſt ſtage, when ſtruck and ſent forward, are not unloaded at the ſecond, but proceed on to the third ſtage, and

وسردار

THUS I FORMED REGULATIONS FOR THE ARRANGEMENT OF MY SUPERIOR ARMIES.

IF the forces of the enemy exceeded in number twelve thousand horsemen, and were inferior in number to forty thousand, I ordained that one of my fortunate sons should command against them; and that two Beglerbegs, and the Ameers, with the Toumaunaut, and the Kushoonaut, and the Auloosaut, in number not inferior to forty thousand men, should attend his command:

AND that the troops and the officers, who composed this victorious army, should consider me as present in the field, and give not forth from their hands their discipline, and their courage and their conduct.

AND I commanded, when my Paishkhauneh † was brought forth, that twelve bodies of troops should be ordered out; and that an Ameer of the Ameers of the Auloosaut should be appointed to each, and that they should cause them to perform their exercises and evolutions; that they might keep before their eyes the TWELVE MILITARY REGULATIONS, ‡ which I had established for forming, and for breaking the line of battle, and for advancing, and for retreating.

and are there pitched. And thus the tents at the second stage are, when the prince departs, sent on to the fourth stage, so that the two sets are inhabited alternately.

‡ These regulations are not in the MS, and therefore are supposed to have been omitted by the transcribers through ignorance or inattention.

وسردار آن است که سرداران سپاه
غنیم را بشمار در آورده در مقابل ایشان سرداران
تعین نماید وسپاه جنکي غنیم را از اوقچي* وشمشیري
ونیزه دار بنظر اعتبار در آورد ورفتار سپاه غنیم را
ببیند که پیوسته وآهسته فوج فوج بمیدان جنک
مي در آیند یا مغلوبه مي تازند وراه در آمدن وبر
آمدن خودرا بمیدان جنک ملاحظه نماید وشیوه
وروش جنک غنیم را در یابند

که کاه باشد که خودرا کم نمودار کنند
وخودرا کریزان وا نمایند پس بمکر وکریز پاي ایشان
فریفته نباید شد

وسردار جنک دیده وکار کرده آنست
که بند وبست جنک را بفهمد که کدام فوج را کشاد
باید داد وکدام رخنه را بتدبیر باید بر بست وچکونه
باید جنک انداخت سردار آنست که اراده غنیم را
بفهمد که بکدام روش بجنک مي در آید وراه
همان شیوه ویرا بروي مسدود کرداند

سردارا را است که بدین ترتیب چهل
هزار سوارا را چهارده فوج مرتب نماید

اول

He is a commander, who, numbering the chiefs of the forces of the enemy, appointeth proper chiefs in oppoſition unto them; and who conſidereth with the eye of attention the veteran ſoldiers of the foe, the bow-men, and the ſword-men, and the ſpear-men; and who obſerveth the motions of the enemy, whether they advance into the field of battle ſlowly and in juſt order, ſquadron by ſquadron, or whether they ruſh forward in confuſion; who pre-examineth the approach to the field, and alſo the avenue of retreat; and who penetrateth the order of the enemy's battle.

For it ſhall ſometimes come to paſs, that they will cauſe their numbers to appear ſmall, and put on the ſemblance of flight and diſmay. A general therefore muſt not permit himſelf to be deceived, and drawn into danger, by their pretended flight.

He is an able and experienced commander, who underſtandeth the diſcipline and the ſcience of war, and who knoweth what diviſion to ſend forward to the charge, and what evil to remedy by his ſkill, and what meaſures to follow in attacking the enemy. He is a general who comprehendeth the intentions of the foe, and who obſerveth their mode of attack, and counteracteth their motions and deſigns.

The general who commands forty thouſand horſe, muſt form them into fourteen ſquadrons after this manner.

اول صف خودرا آراسته ساخته قول نام نهد آنگاه سه فوج برانغار مرتب سازد ویکي از آن سه فوج را هراول برانغار نام کند وسه فوج دیکر جرنغار آراسته ساخته یک فوج را هراول جرانغار نام کذارد

وهمچنین سه فوج دیکر در پیش افواج برانغار مرتب ساخته چپاول نام نهد ویکي از آن سه فوج را هراول چپاول کرداند

وهمین قسم سه فوج دیکر آراسته در پیش افواج جرانغار مقرر داشته شقاول نام کند ویکي از آن سه فوج را به هراولي شقاول تعین نماید

بعد از آن هراول بزرک را که در مقابل قول مي باشد از اوقچیان وشمشیر داران ونیزه داران وبهادران ازموده کار کرده را بوجه پسندیده استحکام دهد که الغ* سورن انداخته همین افواج هراول لشکر غنیم را شکست دهد

1 *Koul*; the main body.

2 *Burraunghaur*; the rear line of the right wing.

3 *Hurrauwul a Burraunghaur*; the advanced guard of the rear line of the right wing.

4 *Jurraunghaur*; the rear line of the left wing.

5 *Hurrauwul a Jurraunghaur*; the advanced guard of the rear line of the left wing.

وسردار

FIRST, let him arrange his own line, and call it the Koul.[1] Let him afterwards form the Burraunghaur[2] with three ſquadrons; and let one of thoſe three ſquadrons be called the Hurrauwul a Burraunghaur.[3] And with three other ſquadrons let him form the Jurraunghaur;[4] and let him name one of thoſe ſquadrons the Hurrauwul a Jurraunghaur.[5]

AND thus alſo let him form, and ſtation, three other ſquadrons in the front of the Burraunghaur, and call them the Chuppauwul.[6] And let him appoint one of thoſe ſquadrons the Hurrauwul a Chuppauwul.[7]

AND in the ſame manner let him arrange three other ſquadrons, and form them in the front of the Jurraunghaur, and call them the Shuckauwul;[8] and let him nominate one of thoſe ſquadrons the Hurrauwul a Shuckauwul.[9]

AND let him afterwards form in perfect order the grand Hurrauwul,[10] which ſhall be poſted in the front of the Koul, from the bow-men, and the ſword-men, and the ſpear-men, and the warriors of proof: that theſe troops charging with loud ſhouts, may diſperſe and defeat the advanced guards of the enemy.

6 *Chuppauwul*; the front line of the right wing.

7 *Hurrauwul a Chuppauwul*; the advanced guard of the front line of the right wing.

8 *Shuckauwul*; the front line of the left wing.

9 *Hurrauwul a Shuckauwul*; the advanced guard of the front line of the left wing.

10 *Grand Hurrauwul*; grand vanguard.

AND

وسردار را است که نظر بر رفتار غنیم
داشته باشد وهر امیر که بي حکم حرکت وتیز جلوي
کند اورا تنبه نهاید

وسردار را است که نظر بر در آمد وبر
آمد غنیم داشته باشد ودر جنک انداختن اضطراب
نکند تا آنکه غنیم بجنک مبادرت نهاید وچون غنیم
بجنک در آید سردار را است که روش جنک ایشانرا
به بیند که بر چه کیفیت بمیدان جنک مي در
آیند ومي بر آیند وچکونه بر ایشان حمله آرد اکر
حمله آورده باز میکردند وتابو دیده رو بکریز میآورند
وتابو دیده بر میکردند

وسردار را است که بدنبال غنیمي که
خود بخود شکست خورده نرود که این چنین غنیم
پشت کرم کومک خود باشد
وسردار را است که به بیند که اکر
غنیم بمیدان مبادرت غنچه شده ترکتاز مي آرد
ویا افواج چپ وراست خودرا کشاده است سردار را
باید که اول هراول را بایشان رو برو کرداند وبجنک
اندازد
ومتعاقب آن هراول چپاول وهراول
شغاول را بمدد هراول کلان بفرستند واز عقب
ایشان

AND it is the duty of the general to keep his eye on the motions of the foe, and to chaſtize thoſe officers under his command, who, without orders, preſume to advance upon the enemy.

AND it is the duty of the general to attend to the onſet of the enemy, and not to venture to attack them, until they advance to the charge. And when they advance, it is the duty of the general to examine their order of battle, in what manner they come into action, and in what manner they retire therefrom, and after what manner he ſhall engage them; whether they charge and retire, and, ſeeking advantage therein, put on the ſemblance of flight; and then, ſeizing a favourable criſis, rally and charge again.

AND it is the duty of a commander not to purſue the enemy who without cauſe flieth from the field: for ſuch an enemy may be well prepared for his defence.

AND it is the duty of the general to obſerve whether the enemy advance into the field of battle, and charge in an united body; or whether they commence the attack with the ſquadrons of their right and their left wings. Let the commander firſt oppoſe his Hurrauwul unto them, and puſh them on to the charge.

AND after them let him ſend forward the Hurrauwul a Chuppauwul and the Hurrauwul a Shuckauwul to ſupport the grand Hurrauwul. And in the

ایشان فوج اول چپاول وفوج دوم شغاول را بجنگ اندازد واز عقب ایشان فوج دوم چپاول وفوج اول شغاول را براند

اگر باین هفت ضرب که بر غنیم آید فتح نشود درین وقت هراول برانغار وهراول جرانغار را بدواند تا آنکه نه ضرب بر غنیم وارد شود

واگر ازین نه ضرب فتح میسر نشود فوج اول برانغار وفوج دوم جرانغار را بدواند

اگر باین یازده ضرب هم فتح روی ننماید فوج دوم برانغار وفوج اول جرانغار را بجنگ بفرستد امید چنانست که باین سیزده ضرب افواج غنیم شکسته شود وفتح میسر گردد

واگر احیانا باین سیزده ضرب فتح حاصل نشود در این وقت سردار را است که افواج قول را تزوک کرده روان شود وخودرا بمثال کوهی در نظر غنیم نمودار گرداند وبآهستگی وپیوستی روان گردد

وبهادران جنگی را بفرماید که بشمشیر در آمده هجوم آورند واوچیان شپه تیر نمایند واگر فتح

the rear of them, let him order into action the first squadron of the Chuppauwul and the second squadron of the Shuckauwul, and after them the second squadron of the Chuppauwul and the first of the Shuckauwul.

If from these seven shocks which the enemy shall have received, the victory be not obtained, let him at this period send forth the Hurrauwul a Burraunghaur and the Hurrauwul a Jurraunghaur, until nine charges be made on the enemy's line.

And if victory followeth not from these nine shocks, let him send into battle the first squadron of the Burraunghaur and the second squadron of the Jurraunghaur.

If by these eleven efforts also the victory be not decided, let him order to the charge the second squadron of the Burraunghaur and the first of the Jurraunghaur. Thus it may be expected that by these thirteen successive charges the lines of the enemy may be broken, and the glory of the day be acquired.

But if it should come to pass that the victory should not be won by these thirteen attacks, it is at this crisis the duty of the general to form his Koul in exact order, and put them in motion. Let him shew himself as a lofty mountain to the eyes of the enemy, and move forward with slowness and regularity.

And let him direct his veteran bands to rush on the foe sword in hand, and command his archers to gall the enemy with their arrows. And if the fate of the

فتح نشود سردار خود بجنگ قدم پیش گذارد ومنظر
رایات من باشد   ترتیب آراستن چهار ده فوج

هراول

هراول چپاول   هراول شغاول

فوج اول چپاول* فوج دویم چپاول]

فوج اول شغاول* فوج دویم شغاول]

هراول برانغار   هراول جرانغار

فوج اول برانغار* فوج دویم برانغار]

فوج اول جرانغار* فوج دویم جرانغار]

قول

See Plate II; pag. 383.

وچنین

the day ſhould ſtill remain in ſuſpence, let the general himſelf advance into action and depend on the appearance of my victorious ſtandards. † Book II.

وچنین تزوک بر بستم که اگر غنیم از چهل هزار سوار زیاده باشد بیکلر بیکان وامرا ومینک باشیان ویوز باشیان واون باشیان وبهادران وسایر سپاه نظر بر رایات ظفر ایات من داشته باشند

وامر نمودم که به امیر هر فوج که یرلیغ فرستم مطابق حکم یرلیغ عمل نمایند واز آن تخلف نورزند وهر کس از بیکلر بیکان وامرا از حکم تخلف وتجاوز نماید ویرا بشمشیر بگذرانند وکوتل ویرا که منتظر الامارت باشد بجاي وي نصب کنند

وامر نمودم که از جملهء چهل اویماق الوسات وقشونات وتومانات دوازده اویماق که بتمغا رسیده اند بچهل فوج قسمت نمایند وامراي بیست وهشت اویماق را که به تمغا نرسیده اند در عقب فوج قول صف بر بندند وفرزندان ونبیرکان پیش دست راست قول افواج خودرا آراسته کردانند وخیشاوندان وقرابتان پیش دست چپ قول افواج خودرا

THUS also I ordained, that if the enemy should in number exceed forty thousand horse-men, that the eyes of the Beglerbegs, and the Ameers, and the Mingbaushees, and the Euzbaushees, and the Ounbaushees, and the select warriors, and the soldiers in general should be fixed on my victorious standards. † Book II.

AND I commanded, that the chief of every squadron to whom I issued my orders, should act conformably to the tenour of those orders, and presume not to deviate therefrom; and that every one of the Beglerbegs, and the Ameers, who was tardy in performing, or disobeyed, the orders which I sent unto him, should be instantly put to death; and that his Kotul, who is the expecter of promotion, should be appointed to his command.

AND I ordained, that from among the forty Ouyemauk of the Aloosaut, the Kushoonaut, and Toumaunaut, that the twelve Ouyemauk who had obtained the Tumghau, ‡ should be divided into forty squadrons; and that the Ameers of the twenty eight Ouyemauk who had not obtained the Tumghau, should form their line in the rear of the Koul; and that my sons and my grandsons should draw up their forces before the right of the Koul; and that my relations and my kindred, with the troops under their command, should take their station

† i. e. That he would lead them in person.

‡ Those who received military pay.

before

خودرا مراتب دارند که افواج ایشان طرح باشد که بهر جا مدد باید رسانید کومک نمایند

ودر برانغار شش فوج مقرر نمایند ویک فوج دیگر هراول برانغار مقرر باشد وهمچنین در جرانغار شش فوج آراسته یک فوج دیگر بهراولي جرانغار مقرر دارند

وهمچنین امر نمودم که شش فوج در پیش افواج برانغار مقرر گردانند وآنرا چپاول نام گذارند ویک فوج دیگررا آراسته هراول چپاول کنند

وهمچنین در پیش افواج جرانغار شش فوج معین نمایند وشغاول نام نهند یک فوج آراسته دیگر هراول شغاول گردانند

ودر پیش افواج چپاول وشغاول شش فوج از امراي کار کرده وبهادران ازموده آراسته ساخته هراول بزورک مقرر گردانند

ویک فوج سواي این شش فوج هراول مقرر کرده پیشتر معین دارند وهراول هراول نام کنند

ودو

before the left of the Koul; and that those troops should be bodies of reserve, and that they should dispatch succour to every quarter, where re-inforcement should be wanted:

AND that six squadrons should constitute the Burraunghaur, and that one other squadron should be appointed the Hurrauwul a Burraunghaur: and thus also, that six squadrons should form the Jurraunghaur; and that one other squadron should be nominated the Hurrauwul a Jurraunghaur.

AND thus also I ordained, that six squadrons should be posted in the front of the Burraunghaur, and that they should be denominated the Chuppauwul; and that one other squadron should be formed, and appointed the Hurrauwul a Chuppauwul:

AND that in the same manner six other squadrons should be stationed in the front of the Jurraunghaur; and that they should be called the Shuckauwul; and that one other chosen squadron should be appointed the Hurrauwul a Shuckauwul.

AND I ordained that six other squadrons, headed by distinguished Ameers, and composed of warriors of proof and experience, should be advanced before the Chuppauwul and the Shuckauwul; and that they should be called the grand Hurrauwul:

AND that one other squadron, over and above those six squadrons, should be posted in their front; and be denominated the Hurrauwul a Hurrauwul:

AND

ودو قــراول بــيكي را با جماعه برادران بر دست راست وچپ هراول مقرر نمايند كه ديدبان لشكر غنيم باشند

وامر نمودم كه امراي افــواج چهلكانه ما دام كه يرليغ من بايشان نرسد بجنك در نيآيند وتا نوبت جنك بايشان نرسد دست برد ننمايند ليكن مستعد وآماده جنك باشند

وچــون حكم جنك بايشان برسد روش غنيم را ديده بجنك در آيند كه غنيم از كدام راه بجنك مي درآيد آن راه را بر ايشان بر بندند وهر راهي كه غنيم بر بندد آنرا به تدبــير بكشايند

وامر نمودم كه چون هــراول هــراول بجنك مبادرت نمايد امير هــراول افــواج ششكانه خودرا متعاقب يكديكر بجنك اندازد كه چون شش ضرب

And that two Kurrauwul Beghs, † with detachments of their brotherhood, ſhould be poſted to the right and to the left of the Hurrauwul a Hurrauwul; and that they ſhould be the Deedbaun ‡ on the army of the enemy.

And I ordained that no one of the commanders of the forty ſquadrons, until he received orders from me, ſhould preſume to enter into battle; and that until the moment of his ſervice arrived, he ſhould not move from his ſtation; and that he ſhould ſtand ready and prepared for action:

And when he received orders to engage, that he ſhould accommodate his mode of attack to that of the enemy; and that he ſhould obſerve in what manner the foe advanced into battle, and counteract his deſigns; and that he ſhould, by ſkilful and judicious diſpoſitions, carry into effect ſuch of his own movements as had been traverſed by the enemy.

And I ordained, when the Hurrauwul a Hurrauwul-began the action, that the leader of the grand Hurrauwul ſhould order his ſix ſquadrons to charge ſucceſſively; that by ſix ſhocks, repeatedly given, the enemy may be broken and thrown into confuſion. It

† *Kurrauwul Beghs*; chiefs of the light troops or ſcouts.

‡ *Deedbaun*; obſervers, people appointed to reconoitre the motions of the enemy.

 is

ضرب مرتبه بمرتبه بر غنیم زده شود بهم بر آیند وشکسته شوند دربن وقت امیر چپاول را است که شش فوج خودرا دفعه بدفعه بکومک فرستد وخود هم ترکتاز آورد

وهمچنین امیر افواج شغاول فوجهاي ششکانه خودرا بمدد افواج پیش روانه سازد وخودرا هم برساند که بحول الله وقوته چون هژده ضرب بر غنیم زده آید شکسته وگسیخته گردند

واگر با وجود خوردن این ضربها غنیم خیرگي نماید امیر برانغاررا باید که هراول خودرا براند وامیر جرانغار نیز هراول خودرا بدواند

چون این هر دو هراول از چپ وراست در آیند لشکر غنیم البته بي تاب ونا توان گردد

واگر غنیم خیره باشد امیر برانغار وامیر جرانغار افواج خودرا مرتبه بمرتبه بر غنیم برانند واگر بیند که افواج غنیم را از افواج قاهره شکستي نرسیده امیران برانغار وجرانغار خودها متوجه دفع ورفع دشمنان شوند

واگر

till his wounds are healed, 49. de-
parts from Kurrumseer with 40 horse-
men, and proceeds towards the moun-
tains of Bullukh, *ibid.* is joined by
Suddeuk Burlaus with 15 horse-men,
ibid. also by Kurraunchee Bahaudur
with 100 horse-men, 51. encamps
in the valley of Arsuff, *ibid.* is joined
by 70 warriors, 53. collects his people
together, and makes a feast, 55. his
forces increase to 313 horse-men, *ib.*
determines to reduce the castle of
Aulaujou, *ibid.* is joined by 300
men of the tribe of Doulaun Jau-
wun, who desert from the castle, 57.
arrives at the defile of Souf, *ibid.* is
joined by Umlis with 200 horse-men,
ibid. receives intelligence of the army
of Jitteh, 59. marches to the streights
of Guz, *ibid.* encamps in the plain
of Ilchee Booghau, *ibid.* receives
intelligence that several Ameers of
Jitteh are coming to join him with
1000 horse-men, 61. encamps on
the banks of the river, opposite the
army of Jitteh, *ibid.* forms his troops
1362 in order of battle, 63. engages the
forces of Jitteh, and drives back the
squadrons of Ameer Aboo Saeed, *ibid.*
opposes Hydur Andookhodee and
Munguli Booghau face to face, and
defeats them and the whole army of
Jitteh, *ibid.* crosses the Jihoon at
Turmuz, 65. is attacked by sur-
prise by the army of Ouleaus Khau-
jeh, *ibid.* defends himself in a pen-
insula, 67. encamps opposite the
Jetes for the space of a month, *ibid.*
sends forces to pursue the Jetes, *ibid.*
encamps at Khullum, *ibid.* arrives
at Kunduz, and is joined by the
people of Yeurldaiee, 69. marches
to Taulkhaun, and is joined by many
of the soldiers of Buddukhshaun, *ibid.*
arrives in the kingdom of Khuttulaun,
ibid. sojourns in the Dusht of Kou-
lauk, 71. receives intelligence that
the Jetes, consisting of 20,000 horse-
men, are encamped at the bridge of
Sungheen, *ibid.* receives an ambas-
sador from the Jetes, shews him his
army twice and dismisses him, *ibid.*
receives intelligence that 6000 horse-
men are coming upon him, 73. his
army seized with a panic, *ibid.* at-
attacks the advanced guard of the
Jetes, and drives them back to the
bridge of Sungheen, 77. stations
2000 men at the bridge opposite the
Jetes, *ibid.* swims over the river
with 5000 men, 79. and encamps
on a hill above the enemy, *ibid.* the
Jetes pretend a flight, he penetrates
their design, *ibid.* is attacked by
them, 81. defeats Ouleaus Khau-
jeh, and drives him beyond the Si-
hoon, 83. returns in triumph to 1363
Mauwur u Nuhur, *ibid.*

He meditates how he may attain
the sovereign power, 85. admits
Ameer Hoossein partner of his for-
tune, *ibid.* is always opposed by
him, *ibid.* make him swear friend-
ship, *ibid.* gains over to his interest
Sheikh Mahummud with seven Ku-
shoons, *ibid.* gives to each Ameer of
those Kushoons the command of a
province, *ibid.* confers a province
on Share Behraum, 87. gains over
several Ameers by his kindness to
Ameer Hoossein, *ibid.* several of his
Ameers consider themselves as his e-
quals, *ibid.* he determines to reduce
them all to subjection, 89. gains
over to his interest Ameer Haujee
Burlaus, *ibid.* wins Ameer Bauez-
zeed Jullauir to his interest by
kindness, 91. takes possession of
the lands of Sheikh Mahummud,
deceased, 89. opposes Ameer Hoos-
sein to Ameer Ilchee Booghau Sul-
doze, 91. gains over Mahummud
Khaujeh Erudee by giving him a pro-
vince, *ibid.* sows division amongst
the princes of Buddukhshaun, and
gains them severally to his interest,
ibid. assists Ki Khissero against Al-
jauitoo Burdi, *ibid.* reconciles them
together, and sends them against A-
meer Khizzur Yessooree, 93.

1365 INVITED by Ameer Hoossein to
a conference at the pass of Chuck-
chuck, 101. secretes a number of
warriors about the pass, for fear of
treachery, *ibid.* is informed of Hoos-
sein's perfidy by Share Behraum, 103.
defeats the army sent by Hoossein to
circumvent him, and marches to
Kurshee, *ibid.* upbraids Hoossein with
his treachery, 105. loses the castle
of Kurshee, 93. crosses the Jihoon
under pretence of going to Khorau-
saun, 95. meets a Kauruvvaun go-
ing to Kurshee, *ibid.* sends a spy
with them to discover the situation of
the enemy, *ibid.* tarries on the banks
of the Jihoon till the spy returns, 97.
re-crosses the river with 243 warriors,
and arrives at Sharekund by forced
marches, *ibid.* halts at the distance
of 3 miles from Kurshee, *ibid.* com-
mands scaling ladders to be prepared,
and goes by night, accompanied by
2 persons only, to reconnoitre the
castle, 99. discovers the guards asleep.
ibid. brings up his warriors, and
takes possession of the castle, *ibid.*
He marches towards Bullukh, and en-
camps on the frontiers, 109. Ameer
Hoossein comes forth to fight with
him, *ibid.* he defeats him and be-
sieges him in the castle, *ibid.* takes
1369 the castle. *ibid.* Hoossein slain, *ibid.*
1375 Receives an ambassador from Auroos
Khaun, 115. attacks Auroos Khaun
and puts him to flight, 117.
1380 Pretends to return from Bullukh
to Summurkund, 111. turns back,
and takes Mullik Gheaus u deen in
1381 Hurraut, 113. subdues the whole
country of Khorausaun, *ibid.*
Receives the submission of Aali,
governor of Mauzinduraun, 117.
1383 Summons the rulers of Seistaun,
Kundahaur, and of the Afghauns, to
submit to him, 115. is obeyed, *ibid.*
1387 Sends armies against the countries
of Kilaun and Jurjaun, 119. con-
quers the city of Isfahaun, and sta-
tions 3000 men there, *ibid.* com-
mands a general slaughter to be made
of the people of Isfahaun for their
rebellion and cruelty, *ibid.* Pursues
Touktummish Khaun 5 months in the
Dusht of Kipchauk, 121. his army 1392
reduced to great straits for want of
provision, *ibid.* is opposed by Touk-
tummishKhaun with a very numerous
army, 123. his Ameers disheartned, *ib.*
he plots secretly with the standard-
bearer of Touktummish, *ibid.* his
Ameers take courage from the intre-
pidity of his sons and grandsons, 125.
appoints the prince Aboo Bukkur,
with 8000 men, the advanced guard,
ibid. commands his troops in the
heat of battle to pitch their tents and
prepare victuals, *ibid.* obtains the
victory through his intrigue with the
standard-bearer of Touktummish, *ib.*
Marches into Erauk a second time,
and collects an army of 80,000 men, 1393
121. is attacked in person by Shaah
Munsoor, *ibid.* sends an ambassador
to Sooltaun Ahmud Jullauir, to
inform himself of his abilities, 125.
receives his account, 127. arrives sud-
denly at Bughdaud, and conquers it, *ib.*
Marches a second time into the Dusht 1395
of Kipchauk, and, having conquered
the countries of the 5th and 6th cli-
mates, returns victorious to Summur-
kund, 129 Demands counsel of his sons 1398
and Ameers concerning the reduction
of Hindostaun, *ibid.* seeks an omen
in the Koraun, 133. pitches his
tents towards Hindostaun, *ibid.* com-
mands the prince Peer Mahummud
Jehaungheer, with 30,000 horse-men,
to subdue Mooltaun, *ibid.* orders
Sooltaun Muhmood Khaun, &c.
with 30,000 men, to go against Lau-
hore, 135. he himself, with 32,000
horse-men, forms the main body, *ib.*
his whole army consists of 92,000
horse-men, *ibid.* proceeds to Hin-
dostaun, *ibid.* is informed that the
Oughauns infest the road to Hindo-
staun, and plunder therein, *ibid.* is
requested by Mullik Mahummud to
revenge

revenge the murder of his brother
Lushkur Shaah upon Moosi his mur-
derer, 137. seeks to get Mullik into
his power by policy, *ibid.* is shot at
by an arrow, *ibid.* is opposed by
Sooltaun Muhmood, and Mulloo
Khaun, with 50,000 men, and 120
elephants in Dehli, 139. pretends
fear, in order to draw them out of
1399 Dehli, *ibid.* defeats Sooltaun Muh-
mood, and gains immense spoils, *ibid.*
conquers Dehli in the space of one
year, and returns to Summurkund, *ib.*
receives information of the encroach-
ments of the people of Goorjistaun,
141. summons his armies to join him
at Isfahaun, *ibid.* arms himself, 143.
1400 subdues the castles of Seewaus and
Goorjistaun, and divides the spoils
amongst his soldiers, *ibid.* punishes
the seditious of Azzurbauejaun, *ibid.*
subdues Mulluteah and the neigh-
bourhood thereof, *ibid.* subdues Hul-
lub and Humsau, 145. determines
on the reduction of Missur and Shaum,
ibid. is opposed by Keesur, at the in-
stigation of Kurrau Eusoof, with a
mighty army, *ibid.* writes a letter to
Keesur, 147. reduces the city of
Dummishk, 149. receives by his
ambassador a letter of defiance from
Keesur, *ibid.* marches towards Bugh-
daud by the way of Moosul, *ibid.*
turns back by the way of Tubbu-
1401 raze, and arrives at Bughdaud, 151.
subdues the castle and city of Bugh-
daud, after a siege of 2 months and
some days, *ibid.* commands it to be
razed to the ground, *ibid.* sojourns
some time in the kingdom of Azzur-
bauejaun, *ibid.* collects his forces
together from all quarters to oppose
1402 Keesur, 153. departs from Azzur-
bauejaun to wage war with Keesur,
ibid. is opposed by Keesur, with
400,000 men, *ibid.* assaults Keesur
and takes him prisoner, and obtains a
compleat victory, *ibid.* returns tri-
umphant to Summurkund, after a war
of 7 years, *ibid.*

ABULGHAZI KHAUN, 27, N.

AFGHAUN. See OUGHAUN.

ALCHOUN BAHAUDUR, brother of Beghchuck, marches against Timour, 65.

ALJAIE TURKAUN AUGHAU, sister of Ameer Hoossein, and wife of Timour, 35, 43. carried behind him on his horse in the desart of Khauruzm, 35. secured in a house of the Toorkummauns, 39. secreted by Timour in the environs of Bokhaura, 43.

ALJAUITO (or ALJAUETOO) BURDI, flees to Timour for shelter, 91. is reconciled to Ki Khissero, 93.

——— SOOLTAUN, son of Arghoon Khaun, supporter of the Mahummudan faith in the 7th century of the Hij. 189. on the death of his brother, assembles the Siuds and Theologians in the imperial Musjid, and asks their consent to his ascending the throne, *ib.* and 193. obtains it, 195. ordains that the names of all the successors of the prophet shall be recited in the Khutbeh, and impressed on the coins of the empire, *ib.*

ALKUMMI, a man noted for his malevolent and revengeful disposition, 257. raised to the dignity of prime minister by Maatussim Billau Ubbausi, *ibid.* betrays the Khalif into the hands of Hullaukoo Khaun, *ibid.*

ALLUGH TUKTIMOUR, one of Tughulluk Timour Khaun's generals, sent to invade Mauwur u Nuhur, 19.

AMEER UL OMRAU, of Ameer Hoossein, submits to Timour, 111.

AMEER AALI, ruler of Mauzinduraun, seeks protection from Timour, 117.

——— ABOO SAEED, of the tribe of Burlaus, 311. made general of the Jetes, 61. his squadrons defeated by Timour, 63. taking offence at the conduct of Tughulluk Timour Khaun, flees to Timour, and is appointed by him ninth Ameer and governor of a province, 319, 311.

——— BAUEZZEED, of the tribe of Turkhaun, made seventh Ameer, 311.

AMEER BAUEZZEED JULLAUIR, ruler of the province of Khujjund, 91. asks counsel of Timour, 15. retires into Khorausaun, 17. forced to submit to Timour, 91.

——— BIAUN SULDOZE, father of Sheikh Mahummud, 85, 89.

——— GOOLAUL, a devout man consulted by Timour, 33. advises Timour to go to Khauruzm, *ibid.* is promised the revenue of Sumurkund for one year, if Timour proves victorious, *ibid.*

——— HAUJEE BURLAUS, uncle of Timour, 15, N. asks counsel of Timour, *ibid.* the troops of Kush desert Timour and join him, 321. unites himself with Timour, 89.

——— HINDOOKEH deserts the army of Jitteh, and joins Timour, 59.

——— HOOSSEIN. See HOOSSEIN.

——— ILCHEE BOOGHAU SULDOZE lays claim to the city of Bullukh, 91. is opposed by Ameer Hoossein through the policy of Timour, *ibid.*

——— JAUKOO, of the tribe of Burlaus, 311. one of the chief supporters of Timour's power, 247. alone remains with him after the desertion of the forces of Kush, 323. Ameer Hoossein endeavours in vain to set Timour at variance with him, 247. is made Ameer ul Omrau, 323. and governor of a frontier kingdom, 311. appointed to the government of Bullukh and Hissaur, 323.

——— JULLAUL U DEEN deserts the army of Jitteh, and joins Timour, 59.

——— KHIZZUR YESSOOREE takes possession of Taushkund, 93. is reduced low, and flees to Timour, *ib.*

——— KHODADAUD, of the tribe of Burlaus, made Ameer ul Omrau and governor of Buddukhshaun, 309. his advice to Timour, 327.

——— KURGUN, or Cazagan, grandfather of Ameer Hoossein, 67, 85, 327.

——— KURRAUCHAUR NOOYAUN, fifth ancestor of Timour, and Vizzeer of Chughtauee Khaun (son of Chungaze Khaun) 23, N. Toumaun of, restored to Timour by Tughulluk Timour Khaun, *ibid.*

AMEER MOOSI, stationed at the bridge of Sungheen opposite Ouleaus Khaujeh, 77. and in Kurshee against Timour, 93. surrounds Timour therein with twelve thousand horsemen, 9. is defeated, *ibid.*

——— MUVIUD AURLAUT, stationed at the bridge of Sungheen opposite Ouleaus Khaujeh, 77. made Ameer ul Omrau, 313.

——— SAUHIBA KURRAUN, *Lord of the fortunate Conjunction.* Timour so called, 181, 183, 195, 197.

——— SAUR BOOGHAU, of the tribe of Kipchauk, made Ameer, 313.

——— SIFE U DEEN joins Timour, 53. is honourably received by him, 55.

——— SHEIKH MAHUMMUD, son of Biaun Suldoze, joins Timour, 85. destroyed by drinking wine, 89.

——— SOOLAMAUN BURLAUS deserts the army of Jitteh, and joins Timour, 59. one of the commanders of the left wing in Timour's engagement with Keesur, 405. *m.* 73.

——— TIMOUR, TAMERLANE so called, 31, 39, 53, 57, 97, 111.

——— UBBAUS, one of Timour's most faithful chiefs, 247. put to death by him unjustly, *ibid.*

——— ZAUDEH ABOO BUKKUR, *grandson of* Timour, appointed commander of the advanced guard, in the engagement with Touktummish Khaun, 125. leads the reserve of the right wing in Timour's engagement with Keesur, 407.

——— ——— MEERAUN SHAAH, commander of the right wing of Timour's forces in his engagement with Keesur, 405.

——— ———SOOLTAUN MUHMOOD KHAUN, *nominal emperor of* Chughtauee, sent by Timour to attack Lauhore, with 30,000 horse-men, 135. one of the commanders of the left wing in Timour's engagement with Keesur, 405.

AMUVEAH (or AMU) *the* Jihoon, *so called from*

from the city situate near it. Lat. about 39°. *Long.* 62°. 10′. *E. from London.* Timour crosses it, 95.

ANDIJAUN, *a city of* Toorkistaun, *Lat. about* 42°. 10′. *Long.* 69°. 0′. *E. from Lond.* the government of, given by Timour to Munguli Booghau, 319.

ANDURAUB, *a city of the province of* Bullukh, *situate at the foot of the mountains which divide the dominions of the* Great Mogul *and* Persia *from* Great Bukharia; *Lat.* 36°. 20′. *L.* 69°. 0′. *E. from Lond.* Timour encamps there, 35.

ANGOOREAH, *a city of* Anatolia *on the river* Melus, 150 *miles E. of* Constantinople (*remarkable for the victories of* Pompey *and* Timour *over* Mithridates *and* Bajazet). *Lat. about* 39°. 50′. *Long. about* 33°. 0′. *E. from London.* Timour marches by the way of, to attack Bajazet, 153.

ARABIA, cities of, *m.* 217.

ARGHOON KHAUN, father of Ghauzaun Khaun, 187.

ARHUNG, [supposed to be the same as Arhungserai] *a city of* Tookhuristaun *on the river* Jihoon, *Lat.* 37°. *Long.* 66°. *from London.* Country of, seized by Ki Khissero and Aljauitoo Burdi, 91.

ARKUNUT, tribe, Haujee Beg of, 19.

ARSUFF, valley of, Timour encamps there, 51.

ATCHEGHI, *a hilly country, lying near the* Jihoon. Timour encamps there, 45.

AULAUJOU, castle of, reduced by Timour, 57.

AURGHOON, tribe of, appointed to receive Tumghau, 309. Taush Khaujeh of, made eighth Ameer, 311. twenty persons of, promoted, *ibid.*

AURLAUT, tribe of, receive Tumghau, 309. Ameer Muviud of, made Ameer ul Omrau, 313. Sullauichee Bahaudur of, made Ameer, *ibid.*

AUROOS KHAUN sends an ambassador to Timour after the defeat of Touktummish Khaun, 115. is attacked unprepared, and vanquished by Timour, 117. *m.* 283.

AURUFFAUT, mount of, 30,000 pilgrims martyred there, 185.

AZZUD U DOWLA DELUMI supporter of the Mahummudan faith in the 4th century of the Hij. 185. deposes Muttei Laumrilla Ubbausi from the Khillaufut, and places Taulaa Billau, his son, on the throne, 187.

AZZURBAUEJAUN, *a province of* Persia, *part of the antient* Media. *It is bounded on the N. by the province of* Shurwaun, *on the S. by the provinces of* Erauk a Ajjum *and* Kurdistaun (*the ancient* Assyria), *on the E. by the province of* Kilaun *and the* Caspian *sea, and on the West by* Turkomania. Touktummish Khaun sends a mighty army upon it, 127. the seditious of, chastised by Timour, 143. Timour sojourns there, 151. departs thence, 153.

B.

BAUBAU AALI SHAAH, a dervise, his advice to Timour, 89.

BAUKHTUR ZEMEEN, subdued by Timour, 45, 163.

BEGCHUCK, one of the Ameers of Jitteh, appointed by Tughulluk Timour Khaun to ravage Mauwur u Nuhur, 19.

BEHRAUM JOUBEEN, general to Hurmuz, with 320,000 Persians engages the Khaukaun, and after a battle of three days and three nights, defeats him, 285. unjustly accused to Hurmuz of having secreted the enemy's treasures, *ibid.* pronounced a traitor, and treated with contempt by Hurmuz, *ibid.* deposes Hurmuz, 287.

BEHRAUM JULLAUIR joins Timour, 45.

BOKHAURA, *the capital of a province of that part of* Mauwur u Nuhur *now called* Bucharia Proper, *situate in about* 39°. 0′. *of Latitude, Long.* 63°. 0′. *E. from London.* Environs of, two hundred persons, dispersed in, 43. Aljaiè Turkaun Aughau, secreted there by Timour, *ibid. m.* 45.

BOULAU deserts Timour in time of danger, 315.

BOULAUD BOOGHAU [supposed to be the same as the preceding] separates from Timour, 69.

BUDDUKHSHAUN, *a city of the province of* Bullukh, *situate at the foot of the mountains which separate* Hindostaun *from* Great Tartary, *on the N. side of the* Jihoon, *about* 100 *miles from its source, and* 230 *from* Bullukh. *Lat.* 37°. 10′. *Long.* 69°. 30′. *E. from Lond.* Princes of, prepare for war, 69. soldiers of, join Timour, *ibid.* princes of, submit to his authority, *ibid.* after their treachery to Timour, received by him with kindness, 323. *m.* 33, 67, 91, 111, 135.

BUGHDAUD, *the capital of the province of* Erauk a Arrub, *situate on the Tigris. Lat.* 33°. 30′. *Long.* 44°. 20′. *E. from London.* Conquered by Timour, 127. surrounded by an army under Timour's sons, 151. besieged by Timour himself, and taken after a siege of two months, *ibid.* razed to the ground, *ibid. m.* 125, 149. revenues of, assigned for supporting the sepulchres and shrines of the saints, 359.

BUKHF and JILLEH, districts of, assigned for supporting the shrine of Imaum Aali, son of Moosi, 359.

BULLUKH, *the capital of a province of that name, situate towards the borders of* Persia, *about* 50 *miles S. of* Turmuz *on the river* Dehash, *Lat.* 37°. 0′. *Long.* 64°. 30′. *E. from London.*

——— PROVINCE OF, *lies to the S. of* Summurkund, *and E. of that division of* Mauwur u Nuhur, *called* Proper Bucharia. *Its length, according to modern geographers, is about* 360 *miles, and its breadth about* 250. Kingdom of, Timour sojourns there, 49. hunts in the mountains of, 51. taken from Timour by Ameer Hoossein, 87. claimed by Ameer Ilchee Booghau, 91. given to Ameer Hoossein by Timour, 107. Timour encamps there, 109. *m.* 111, 113. given to Ameer Jaukoo Burlaus, 323.

BURHAUN AGHLAUN, 289.

BURLAUS, tribe of, *m.* 29, 93. appointed to receive Tumghau, 309. four Ameer ul Omraus selected from it, *ibid.* two Ameers of, promoted, 311. a hundred Mingbaushees appointed therefrom, *ibid.*

BURLAUS BAHAUDUR (one of Timour's Euzbaushees) engages Touktummish Khaun, and defeats him, 289. is appointed governor of Hissaur Shaudumaun, *ibid.*

BURTUN KHAUN, 25, N.

C.

CHEEN, kingdom of, its prince called Fughfoor, 131.

CHUCKCHUCK, pass of, Timour and Ameer Hoossein agree to meet there, 101.

CHUGHTAUEE KHAUN, *son of* Chungaze Khaun, 23, N. his conduct towards a minister accused of peculation, 249.

CHUGHTAUEE, *the countries of* Transoxiana, *&c. which were given to* Chughtauee Khaun. The Toumaunaut and Kushoonaut of, become celebrated on account of Timour's exploits, 93.

CHUNGAZE KHAUN, (or Ghengis Can) 23, N.

D.

DAUOOD, armour of, Timour cloaths himself in it, 143.

DAURAU, name given to the king of Hindostaun, 131.

DEAUR A BUKKUR, *the capital of a province of the same name, situate on the* Tigris, *near its source,* 212 *miles E. of* Hullub, *and* 261 *N. of* Bughdaud. *Lat.* 37°. 42′. *Long.* 40°. 17. *E. from London.* Bajazet sends his forces against it, 153.

DEHLI, *the capital of* Hindostaun, *situated on the river* Jumna, 142 *miles N. of of* Agra, *and* 339 *S. of* Lauhore, *Lat.* 28°. 20′. *Long.* 87°. 20′. *E. from Lond.* Castle of, fortified by Sooltaun Muhmood, 139. subdued by Timour, *ibid.*

DOULAUN JAUWUN, three hundred men of the tribe of, join Timour, 57.

DOULDEE, tribe of, appointed to receive Tumghau, 309. two persons of, made Ameers, 311.

DUMMISHK, *the capital of the South part of* Shaum, *ninety five miles N.E. of* Jerusalem, *and two hundred and ten S. of* Hullub. *Lat.* 33°. 23′. *Long.* 36°. 20′. *E. from London.* Mullik Furruj arrives there, 149. reduced by Timour, *ibid.*

DURBUND, *a city of* Daughestaun, *on the W. coast of the* Caspian Sea. *Lat.* 42°. 0′. *Long.* 50°. 0′. *E. from London.* Timour passes by it in his way to the Dusht of Kipchauk, 127. Touktummish Khaun sends a mighty army that way against Azzurbauejaun, *ibid.*

E.

EEKOO TIMOUR, conquers Auroos Khaun, 283. is promoted by Timour, *ibid.* is accused to Timour of having appropriated to his own use the spoils taken from Auroos Khaun, *ib.* commanded to appear before Timour, 287. the whole of the spoils taken from Auroos Khaun, conferred on him and his soldiers, *ibid.*

ERAUK A AJJUM, *or* Persian Erauk, *the chief province of* Persia, *lying in the centre of that kingdom, bounded by* Kilaun *and* Azzurbauejaun *on the N.* Khoozistaun *and* Fauristaun *on the S. by* Khorausaun *and* Kurdistaun *on the W. Its capital* Isfahaun. Cleared from heretics by Timour, 335. *m.* 125.

ERAUK A ARRUB, *or* Babylonian Erauk, *comprises the districts which lie on each side of the* Tigris, *having* Deaur a Bukkur *on the West, and* Koohistaun *on the East. Its capital* Bughdaud, *m.* 125.

ERAUK, people of, petition Timour on account of the oppressions of the race of Muzuffur, 117. Timour draws his army into it, 119. attacks it a second time, 121.

ERAUKS, THE TWO, the governors of, petition Timour to punish the infidels of Goorjistaun, 141.

ERAUN, *all the country lying between the* Jihoon *and the* Tigris, *i. e.* Persia *and the neighbouring countries. m.* 131, 355.

F.

FAURIS, *or* Persis, *a province of* Persia, *bounded by* Erauk a Ajjum *on the N. by* Kurmaun *on the E. by the* Persian Gulf *on the S. by* Khoozistaun *on the W. Its capital* Shauraze. *m.* 141, 355.

FUGHFOOR, a title given to the king of Khuttun, Cheen and Maucheen, 131.

FURRUKH, left governor of Bughdaud by Sooltaun Ahmud Jullauir, 151. drowned in the Tigris, *ibid.*

G.

GHAUZAUN KHAUN, (son of Arghoon Khaun and grandson of Hullaukoo Khaun) promoter of the faith in the 6th century of the Hij. 187. converted, with 100,000 Toorks, to the Mahummudan faith by Sheikh Ibraheem Hummuee in the plain of Laur, 189.

GHIZNEIN, 225.

GHIZNI, *the capital of a province separated by mountains from the North West parts of* Hindostaun, *situate near* Kundahaur, *and lying to the South of* Gaur. *Lat.* 33°. 30′. *Long.* 66°. 0′. *E. from Lond.* Emperor of, will not suffer a stone to be removed, which he had placed at the entrance of the plain of Ghiznein, 225.

GOOLAUB, Mahummud Auzaud appointed governor of, 291.

GOORJISTAUN, *a province of* Asia, *bounded by* Circassia *on the North, by the* Caspian Sea *on the East, by* Armenia *on the South, and by* Mingrelia *on the West. Its capital* Teflis. *Lat.* 43°. 30′. *Long.* 47°. 24′. *E. from Lond.* Its inhabitants complained of by the governors of the two Erauks, 141. subdued by Timour, 143. *m.* 155.

GURKUS, tribe of, governed by Moosi, 135.

GUZ, streights of, Timour arrives there, 59.

H.

HAUJEE MAHUMMUD, a Toorkummaun, 39. recollecting Timour, commands the people to desist from attacking him, and joins him himself, *ibid.*

——— MUHMOOD SHAAH YESSOOREE succeeds to the command of the armies of Jitteh, 21.

HIND, king of, called Daurau, 131. *m.* 355. See HINDOSTAUN.

HINDOSTAUN, *a large country lying between* 7°. *and* 37°. *Lat. and between* 64°. *and* 93°. *E. Long. from London. Bounded by* Ouzbuk Tartary *and little* Thibet *on the North, by* Thibet, *the kingdom of* Asem, Ava *and* Pegu *on the East, the bay of* Bengal *and the* Indian *ocean on the South, the* Indian *ocean and* Persia *on the West; being about* 2043 *miles in length from N. to S. and* 1412 *in breadth from E. to W.* Fortified with many ramparts, 129. always governed by the Shaahinshaah, or king of Eraun and Tooraun, 131. road of, infested by the Oughauns, 135. cleared by Timour, 137. its chief city, conquered by Timour, 139. the reduction of, *m.* 353.

HIREMUN, *river, takes its rise in a range of mountains in Lat. about* 30°. 40′. *Long.* 64°. 0′. *from Lond. passing by* Seistaun, *a branch of it falls into the lake* Zare, 231 *miles S. W. of* Kundahaur, *in Lat.* 33°. 0′. *Long.* 60°. 0′. *E. of Lond.* Timour sojourns near it, 45.

HISSAUR, or HISSAUR SHAUDUMAUN, kingdom of, given to Ameer Jaukoo Burlaus, 323. *m.* 319.

HOOSSEIN, (Ameer HOOSSEIN) grandson of Ameer Kurgun, joins Timour in the desarts of Khauruzm, 35. his sister wife to Timour, *ibid.* comes to Timour, 67. his ill conduct occasions the desertion of Timour's officers, 69. wants to establish himself on the throne of Mauwur u Nuhur, 85. always envies and opposes Timour, *ibid.* is forced to swear friendship to him, *ibid.* seeks to overthrow Timour, *ibid.* takes the country of Bullukh and the castle of Shaudumaun from Timour, *ibid.* is opposed in his claims by Ilchee Booghau Suldoze, 91. breaks his oaths with Timour, 93. takes the castle of Kurshee from Timour by fraud, and places a strong garrison in it, *ibid.* sends a Koraun to Timour, swearing friendship upon it, 101. desires to have a personal conference with Timour at the pass of Chuckchuck, *ibid.* slays Share Behraum, 103. his treachery to Timour, *ibid.* receives a letter from Timour, and is confounded, 105. is presented with the country of Bullukh and the castle of Shaudumaun by Timour, 107. seeks to take Mauwur u Nuhur from Timour, *ibid.* fights several times with Timour, and is always defeated, *ibid.* slays Humoochee the brother of Ki Khissero, ruler of Khuttulaun, *ibid.* comes forth to fight with Timour, 109. is defeated and slain, *ibid.*

——— lost his dominions through the oppressions of a wicked and cruel minister, 203.

——— bribed one of Timour's Vizzeers to raise enmity betwixt Timour and Ameer Jaukoo and Eekoo Timour, 247. his design discovered, *ibid.* his friendship more hurtful to Timour

is at this crisis the duty of the leader of the Chuppauwul to detach his six squadrons one after the other to support the grand Hurrauwul; and afterwards to advance, himself, to the charge. Book II.

And in the same manner also, let the commander of the Shuckauwul push forward successively his six squadrons to reinforce those who are engaged; and lastly let the commander himself advance into action. Thus, by the power and assistance of Almighty God, when eighteen charges shall have been made on the line of the enemy, they will break and disperse.

But if notwithstanding those shocks received by the foe, they should continue resolute and firm, it is then the duty of the chief of the Burraunghaur to dispatch forward his Hurrauwul, and of the leader of the Jurraunghaur to send forth his Hurrauwul also.

When those two Hurrauwuls advance and charge on the right and on the left of the enemy, their order and their strength shall certainly be broken.

But if it should come to pass that the foe still continues firm, let the leaders of the Burraunghaur and the Jurraunghaur order their squadrons successively on to the charge. And if they see that the enemy give not way to the efforts of the imperial forces, the leaders of the Burraunghaur and the Jurraunghaur must themselves advance, and rush upon the foe.

واكر در اين وقت اميران برانغار وجرانغار زبوني نمايند امير زادكاني كه طرح برانغار اند وخويشاوندان كه طرح جرانغار اند بر غنيم تركتاز آورند

وبايد كه نظر ايشان بر سردار وعلم سردار باشد وبشجاعت ومردي صف شكن غنيم كردند وقصد كرفتن سردار نمايند وكوشش كنند كه علم مخالفانرا نكونسار كردانند

واكر با وجود اين ضربها غنيم قايم بوده باشد در اين وقت بايد كه افواج متفرقه وبهادران قول وافواج الوساتي كه در عقب قول آراسته شده بودند بيك مرتبه هجوم آورده تركتاز نمايند

واكر در اين وقت فتح نشود سلطان را است كه خود با دل قوي وهمت بلند در حركت آيد

چنانچه من در جنك قيصر كردم كه بامير زاده ميران شاه كه سردار دست راست بود امر نمودم كه از دست چپ قيصر سركن پركن در آيد وبامير زاده سلطان محمود خان وامير سليمان كه اميران دست چپ بودند يرليغ فرستادم كه بر دست راست قيصر هجوم آورند

وبامير

AND if at this period the commanders of the Burraunghaur and the Jurraunghaur ſhew themſelves deficient in their duty, the royal princes, and thoſe related to the imperial family, who are the reſerves of the Burraunghaur and of the Jurraunghaur, muſt advance to the aſſault.

AND they muſt keep their eyes on the commander and the ſtandard of the commander, and preſs upon the foe with valour and intrepidity. They muſt endeavour to ſeize the general of the hoſtile army; and they muſt ſtrive to invert the ſtandard of the ſoe.

AND if, notwithſtanding theſe ſhocks, the enemy ſtill remain firm and unmoved, the royal guards, and the ſelect warriors of the Koul, and the forces of the Ouyemauk, which were formed in the rear of the Koul, muſt ruſh forward, together and at once, to the charge.

AND if at this period the victory be not decided, it is the duty of the emperor, with fortitude of heart and with exalted reſolution, to put himſelf and the Koul of his army into motion.

THUS I acted in my engagement with Keeſur. I commanded the Ameer Zaudeh Meeraun Shaah, who was the leader of the right wing of my forces, to charge headlong on the left of Keeſur. And I ſent orders to Ameer Zaudeh Sooltaun Muhmood Khaun, and to Ameer Soolamaun, who commanded my left wing, to attack the right of Keeſur.

AND

وبامیر زاده ابو بکر که امیر فوج طرح دست راست بود حکم کردم که بر تول ایلدرم بایزید که بر پشته ایستاده بود ترکتاز آورد ومن خود با افواج قول ولشکرهای اویماق روی همت بطرف قیصر آوردم

ودر حمله اول شکست بر افواج قیصر افتاد وسلطان محمود خان بتعاقب قیصر شتافته ویرا دست گیر کرده بدرگاه حاضر آورد وتوقتمش خان را نیز بهمین تزوکات شکست دادم وفرمودم که علم ویرا نکونسار گردانیدند

واگر غنیم قزاقی * کرده افواج چپاول وشغاول وبرانغار وجرانغاررا بر هم زند وخودرا بفوج قول رساند سلطان را واجب است که پای شجاعت در رکاب صبر مستحکم گردانیده متوجه دفع ورفع غنیم شود

وچنانچه من در جنگ شاه منصور کردم که خودرا بهن رسانید بذات خود رو برو شدم تا آنکه بر خاک هلاک افتاد

ترتیب آراستن چهل فوج از لشکر دوازده ویماقی که به تمغا رسیده اند

AND I issued directions to the Ameer Zaudeh Aboo Bukkur, who led the reserve of the right, to advance upon the Koul of Yeldurrum Bauezeed, † who was posted on an eminence: and lastly I myself, with the forces of the Koul and the Ouyemauk, turned the face of resolution toward mine enemy.

THE armies of Keesur were defeated, and put to flight at the first onset. And Sooltaun Muhmood pursued the vanquished Keesur; and he made him my prisoner, and he brought him to the royal tent. By this disposition also I conquered Touktummish Khaun, and caused his standard to be inverted.

IF the enemy should become formidable, and throw into disorder the Chuppauwul, and the Shuckauwul, and the Burraunghaur, and the Jurraunghaur, and should advance to charge the Koul; it is then the duty of the emperor to conduct himself with courage and with fortitude, and to proceed to repel and disperse the foe.

THUS I acted in the engagement with Shaah Munsoor, who penetrated even to the Koul of my army. I opposed him in my own person, face to face, until he fell lifeless on the plain.

THE PLAN OF THE ARRANGEMENT OF FORTY SQUADRONS, FORMED FROM THE TWELVE OUYEMAUK WHO HAD OBTAINED THE TUMGHAU.

† Bajazet.

قراول دست راست　　قراول دست چپ

هراول

فوج اول دویم سیوم چهارم پنجم ششم

هراول چپاول　　هراول شغاول

چپاول　　شغاول

اول دویم سیوم چهارم پنجم ششم]　　اول دویم سیوم چهارم پنجم ششم]

هراول برانغار　　هراول جرانغار

برانغار　　جرانغار

اول دویم سیوم چهارم پنجم ششم]　　اول دویم سیوم چهارم پنجم ششم]

فوج امیرزاده ها　　فوج خویشاوندان

قول

بیست وهشت اویماق که بتمغا

نرسیده اند

تم

FINIS.

INDEX

OF

PERSONS AND PLACES.

N.B. *m.* signifies *mentioned.*

AALI, first successor of Mahummud, 193. one of the orthodox Khalifs, 31, N. commander of the faithful, 183. son of Aboo Taulib, 359. the districts of Bukhf and Jilleh, assigned for supporting his shrine, *ibid.*

AALI, son of Moosi Jaufir, 185.

——— BEG CHOUN GHOORBAUNI takes Timour prisoner, 37. is ashamed of his conduct, *ibid.* commands Timour's arms to be delivered to him, and dismisses him with marks of disrespect, *ibid.*

——— BEN LUCKTI, minister of Hauroon ul Rusheed, dissuaded from resigning his office, 263.

——— DURVAISH, of the tribe of Toughauee, made Ameer, 313.

——— YEZZUDI, his relation differs from Timour's, 23, N. his history inferior to that of Timour, written by himself, 27, N. 123, N. ignorant of the plot between Timour and the standard-bearer of Touktummish Khaun, *ibid.*

AAZEEZ U DEEN, one of Timour's Vizzeers, assists Timour in extricating himself from prison, 267.

ABDULLAH, a servant of Timour, who accompanied him in recònnoitring the castle of Kurshee, 99.

ABOO (OR ABAU) BUKKUR. See AMEER ZAUDEH.

——— TAUHIR heads the sect of Kuraumuteh, 185. seizes the city of Mecca, *ibid.* martyrs 30,000 pilgrims on mount Auruffaut, *ibid.* takes away the black stone from the temple of Mecca, *ibid.* is totally defeated by Mocktaudir Billau, *ibid.*

ABU'L MUNSOOR TIMOUR, or TAMERLANE, descended in a right line from Kaujooli Bahaudur, son of Toumuneh Khaun, 25, N. of the same lineage with Chungaze Khaun (Ghengis Can), *ibid.* begins his enterprises at 12 years of age, 163. Upon Tughulluk Timour Khaun's first invasion of Mauwur u Nuhur, is doubtful whether he shall flee into Khorausaun, or submit to Tughulluk Timour, 17. asks counsel of his

PEER, is advised to submit, *ibid.* goes to the Ameers of Jitteh, and diverts them by presents from ravaging Mauwur u Nuhur, 19, 21. departs from the Ameers, and goes to Tughulluk Timour, 21. Tughulluk restores to him the Toumaun of Ameer Kurrauchaur Nooyaun, and appoints him governor of Mauwur u Nuhur, 23. he loses the government of Mauwur u Nuhur, and accepts the post of counsellor and general to Ouleaus Khaujeh, 25. is accused of rebellion, 27. ordered to be put to death by Tughulluk Timour, *ibid.* the order falls into his hands, *ibid.* he gathers together the youth of the tribe of Burlaus for his defence, 29. resolves to oppose the Ouzbuks, *ib.* the people of Mauwur u Nuhur unite themselves with him, *ibid.* is nominated to the empire by the people of Mauwur u Nuhur, 31. is desirous of attacking the Ouzbuks, *ibid.* the worthless reveal his intention, *ibid.* he deliberates concerning attacking the Ouzbuks in Summurkund, *ibid.* fears the people of Mauwur u Nuhur will shrink back from their engagements, 33. quits Summurkund, and retires to the neighbouring hills, *ibid.* waits seven days, expecting to be joined by the people of Mauwur u Nuhur, *ibid.* no one joining him, he proceeds to Buddukhshaun, *ibid.* goes to Ameer Goolaul, who directs him to proceed towards Khauruzm, *ibid.* promises Ameer Goolaul the revenue of Summurkund for one year, if he defeats the Ouzbuks, *ibid.* is attacked by Tukkul Bahaudur with 1000 horsemen, whom he opposes with 60 warriors, 35. slays 950 of them, with the loss of 50 of his own, *ibid.* is called a wonderful man by Ouleaus Khaujeh and the Ameers of Jitteh, *ibid.* his fortune reduced very low, *ibid.* wanders in the desart of Khauruzm, with his wife behind him on horse-back. *ib.* & 37. of his ten associates, three (natives of Khoraufaun) desert him, *ibid.* is taken prisoner by Aali Beg Choun Ghoorbauni, and confined in a dungeon 62 days, *ibid.* wrests a sword from one of the guards, and forces his way into the presence of Aali Beg, *ibid.* is dismissed by Aali Beg with marks of disrespect, *ibid.* proceeds to the desart of Khauruzm, 39. is joined by twelve horsemen, *ibid.* is attacked by the Toorkummauns, *ibid.* and recognized by Haujee Mahummud, one of the Toorkummauns, who joins him, *ibid.* his troops increase to 60 horse-men, *ibid.* journeys towards Khoraufaun, 41. is joined in the way by Mubauruk Shaah Sunjuri, governor of Maukhaun, with 100 soldiers, and by many others, *ibid.* disperses his people in the environs of Bokhaura, and advances towards Summurkund, 43. is joined in the way by Tumookeh Kouchein with 15 horse-men, whom he sends to Mubauruk Shaah, *ibid.* enters Summurkund by night, *ibid.* and passes 48 days undiscovered in the house of his sister Kuttulugh Turkaun Aughau, *ibid.* narrowly escapes being discovered, *ibid.* flees from Summurkund by night with 50 horse-men, and proceeds towards Khauruzm, *ibid.* encamps at Atcheghi, 45. his family, and several others, join him, *ibid.* his army increases to near 1000 horsemen, *ibid.* departs thence, and subdues the countries of Baukhtur Zemeen and Kundahaur, *ibid.* arrives at the river Hiremun and sojourns there, *ibid.* is joined by near 1000 horsemen, and Kurrumseer submits to his authority, *ibid.* determines to invade the kingdom of Seistaun, 47. receives rich presents from the governor of Seistaun, and joins him against his enemies, *ibid.* is attacked by the soldiers and people of Seistaun, *ibid.* wounded in his arm and foot by an arrow, *ibid.* obtains the victory, *ibid.* sojourns in Kurrumseer till

Timour than the malice of his greatest enemies, 327.

HOOSSEIN, the Khalif, 183.

HUKKEEM SUNNAI, cotemporary with, and preceptor to, Sooltaun Sunjuri, 187.

HULLAUKOO KHAUN, father of Arghoon Khaun, 187. excited by Alkummi to attack Maatussim Billau Ubbausi, 257.

HULLUB, *the present metropolis of* Shaum, *Lat.* 36°. 12′. *Long.* 37°. 40′. *E. from London.* Subdued by Timour, 145. Timour arrives there in his march against Keesur, 149. Keesur sends troops against it, 153.

HUMOOCHEE, brother of Ki Khissero, slain by Ameer Hoossein, 107.

HUMS, Keesur sends troops against it, 153. See HUMSAU.

HUMSAU, *a town of* Shaum *near* Hama, *Lat.* 34°. 30′. *Long.* 38°. 10′. *E. from Lond.* Subdued by Timour, 145.

HURMUZ, son of Nousharevaun, sends Behraum Joubeen, with 320,000 Persians, to oppose the Khaukaun, 285. forgetting the services of Behraum, pronounces him a traitor, and treats him with contempt, *ibid.* is deposed, 287.

HURRAUT, *a city of* Khorausaun, 171 *miles S. E. of* Toos, *Lat.* 34°. 0′. *Long.* 59°. 20′. *E. from Lond.* Prince of, Mullik Gheaus u deen, 113. conquered by Timour, *ibid.*

HYDUR ANDOOKHODEE advances to fight with Timour,, and is defeated, 63. taking offence at the conduct of Tughulluk Timour Khaun, flees to Timour, and is appointed by him governor of a province, 319.

HYSSAUR. See HISSAUR.

I.

IMMAUM A AAZUM, his opinion, 191.

——— HOOSSEIN, revenues assigned for supporting his sepulchre, 359.

——— MAHUMMUD NUKKI, *ibid.*

——— MOOSI KAUZI, *m. ibid.*

——— SHAUFEI, 191.

ISFAHAUN, *the capital of the province of* Erauk a Ajjum *and of all* Persia *in* Asia, *lying about* 223 *miles N. of the* Persian Gulph, *and* 321 *S. of the* Caspian Sea. *Lat.* 32°. 40′. *Long.* 51°. 40′. *E. from* London. Conquered by Timour, 119. people of, rebel and slay the governor with the whole garrison, *ibid.* all commanded to be put to the sword, *ibid.* appointed a place of rendevouz for Timour's forces, 141.

JIHOON, *the ancient* Oxus, *a river rising in mount* Imaus *in the Northern parts of* India *in* Asia, *Lat.* 39°. 30′. *and running N. W. through* Ouzbuk Tartary, *divides it from* Persia. *Forty leagues from its mouth, it divides into two branches; one falling into the* Caspian Sea, *Lat.* 44. *the other into the lake* Aral, *Lat.* 42°. 0′. *Long.* 59°. 50′. *E. from London.* Timour halts there some days, 65. crosses it, 67. *m.* 23, N.

JILLEH. See BUKHF.

JITTEH, *a kingdom having* Toorkistaun *on the E. the river* Sihoon *on the S.* Kipchauk *on the W. and part of* Toorkistaun *on the N. m.* 19, 23, &c. &c.

JOUJI, tribe of, abandoned by Touktummish Khaun, 125. *m.* 129.

JULLAUIR, tribe of, appointed to receive Tumghau, 309. two Ameers of, promoted, 311. twenty people of, promoted, *ibid.*

JURJAUN, country of, *m.* 117.

JUZZAUIR, lands of, assigned for supporting the shrines of Immaum Moosi Kauzim, Immaum Mahummud Nukki, and Soolamaun Faursi, 359.

K.

KAUBOOLISTAUN, *the province of* Kaubul, 163.

KAUBUL, *capital of* Kauboolistaun, *N. W. of* Hindostaun, *and about* 110 *miles E. of* Kundahaur. *Lat. about* 34°. 30′. *Long.* 69°. 12′. *E. from London.* Peer Mahummud Jehaungheer stationed there with 30,000 men, 1??.

KAUBUL SHAAH, of the line of Chungaze, slain by his Ameers, to ingratiate themselves with Timour, 325.

KAUJOOLI BAHAUDUR, brother of Kubbul Khaun, eighth ancestor of Timour, and great grandfather of Kurrauchaur Nooyaun, 25, N.

KEESUR, or BAJAZET, supposed to be descended from a Toorkummaun sailor, 147, N. resolves on a war with Timour, at the instigation of Kurrau Eusoof, 145. comes down with a mighty army, and calls the forces of Missur and Shaum to his aid, *ibid.* receives a letter of advice from Timour, 147. marches to oppose Timour, with 400,000 men, 153. is defeated, and brought prisoner to Timour, A. D. 1402, *ibid.* *m.* 355, 405, 407.

KEHULKEH, castle of, Timour sends his Kurrauvul against it, 65.

KHAUJEH AGHLAUN, of the tribe of Moghool, made Ameer, 311.

——— SHUMS U DEEN, sepulchre of, Ameer Hoossein swears friendship to Timour there, 85.

KHAUKAUN, THE, advances against Hurmuz with 300,000 Toorks, 285. is defeated by Behraum Joubeen, after an engagement of three days and three nights, *ibid.*

KHAURUZM, *a kingdom situate on the Eastern shore of the* Caspian Sea, *near the mouth of the* Jihoon, *having* Mauwur u Nuhur *on the E.* Khorausaun *on the S. and great* Tartary *on the N. it extends from* 37°. *to* 42°. *of Lat. and from* 52°. *to* 62°. *of Long. from Lond.* TIMOUR advised to go thither, 33. Tukkul Bahaudur engages with him there, 35.

——— desart of, Timour wanders in it with his associates, and is taken prisoner, 37.

KHILLAUTEE, *a town of* Mauwur u Nuhur *lying near the* Jihoon. The Ameers of Jitteh encamp there with 20,000 horse-men, 71.

KHIOOK, *a town of* Khorausaun, *situate near the* Jihoon, *W. of* Bokhaura. *Lat. about* 39°. 40′. *Long.* 62°. 30′. *E. from London.* Tukkul Bahaudur its governor, 35.

KHISSURO PURVAZE, advanced to the throne of Persia, in the place of Hurmuz deposed, 287.

KHORAUSAUN, *a province of* Persia, *bounded by the mountains of* Bullukh (*which separate it from* Mauwur u Nuhur) *and the province of* Kundahaur *on the E. by* Seistaun *on the S. by the provinces of* Erauk a Ajjum *and* Mauzinduraun *on the W. and by the province of* Asterabad *and the river* Jihoon (*which separate it from* Khauruzm) *on the N. Its capital* Hurraut. Ameer Haujee Burlaus and Ameer Bauezzeed Jullauir retire thither upon Tughulluk Timour Khaun's first invasion of Mauwur u Nuhur, 17. *m.* 15, 113, 141, 333.

KHUJJUND, *a city of* Mauwur u Nuhur *situate on the river* Sihoon, *about* 7 *days journey N. E. of* Summurkund. *At this place is a famous passage over the river, Lat.* 41°. 15′. *Long.* 67°. 30′. *E. from London.* Waters of, crossed by Tughulluk Timour Khaun with intention to invade Mauwur u Nuhur, 15. crossed by Ouleaus Khaujeh in his flight from Timour, 83.

KHULLUM, *a town of* Tookhauristaun, *Lat.* 36°. 40′. *Long.* 65°. 50′. *E. from London.* Timour encamps there, 67.

KHUTTULAUN, *a province situate between the rivers* Vakhsh *and* Hurraut, *and bounded by* Tartary, Buddukhshaun, *and the territory of* Bullukh. Timour arrives there, 69. seized by Ki Khisseio and Aljauitoo Burdi, 91.

KHUTTUN, the country of, *m.* 131, 163.

KHUZZAUR, *a town of* Mauwur u Nuhur *situate S. of* Kush, *in Lat.* 38°. 30′. *Long. about* 65°. The armies of Tughulluk Timour Khaun arrive there, 19.

KILAUN, *a province of* Persia *bounded by the* Caspian Sea *on the N. by* Khorausaun

ſaun *on the E. by* Erauk a Ajjum *on the S. and by* Azzurbauejaun *on the W. m.* 141.

Kipchauk, (*called by Europeans* Grand Tartary) *contains all the country ſituate between the* Leſſer, *or* Crim Tartary *and* Toorkiſtaun. Tribe of, appointed to receive Tumghau, 309. Ameer Saur Booghau of, made Ameer, 313.

——— Duſht of, the Ameers of Tughulluk Timour Khaun rebel there, 23. Timour enters it, 129. ſubdued by Timour, 117.

Kooch Timour, (ſon of Begchuck) an Ameer of Jitteh, 71.

Koottub ul Aktaub, Timour's Peer, 125. See Peer.

Koulauk, Duſht of, Timour ſojourns there, 71.

Kowvung Khaun, of the tribe of Tautaur, made Ameer, 313.

Kubbul Khaun, (twin-brother of Kaujooli Bahaudur, and ſon of Toumuneh Khaun) great grandfather of Chungaze Khaun, *m.* 25, N.

Kundahaur, *Capital of a territory of the ſame name, ſituate on the confines of* Perſia *and the dominions of the* Great Mogul, 436 *miles N. W. of* Lauhore, *Lat.* 33°. 10′. *Long.* 67°. 10′. *E. from London.* Subdued by Timour, 45, *m.* 141.

Kunduz, *a town of* Tookhauriſtaun, *ſituate in Lat.* 36°. 36′. *Long.* 66°. 0′. *E. from London.* Timour arrives there, 69. and appoints Mahummud Auzaud governor of it for his bravery againſt the Seah Poſhaun, 291.

Kunnouj, *a town and kingdom ſituate between the two arms of the* Ganges, 282 *miles E. of* Mooltaun. *Its Capital* Kunnouj *is in Lat.* 26°. 45′. *Long.* 80°. 10′. *E. from London.* Mubbauruk Khaun aſpires to the ſovereignty of, 353.

Kurbullau, *a town of* Erauk a Arrub *on the W. ſide of the* Euphrates. *Lat.* 32°. 40′. *Long.* 44°. 10′. *E. from London.* Lands and villages of aſſigned to ſupport the ſepulchres and ſhrines of the ſaints, 359.

Kurmaun, *a province of* Perſia *ſituate between* Fauris *and* Seiſtaun, *extending from the frontiers of* Erauk a Ajjum *to the ſtreights of* Hormuz, *m.* 141.

Kurrau Eusoof, the Toorkummaun, defeated by Timour, 281. ſtirs up Keeſur to make war upon him, 145. Timour demands him of Keeſur, 147. he moleſts the Kauruvvauns going to the ſacred cities, 153.

Kurraunchee Bahaudur, joins Timour with a hundred horſe-men, whom he had ſeparated from the armies of Jitteh, 51.

Kurroot, houſe of, Timour delivers Khorauſaun from its princes, 333.

Kurrumseer ſubmits to Timour, 45. Timour ſojourns there for two months, 49.

Kurshee, *a town of* Mauwur u Nuhur, *at ſome diſtance to the North of the* Jihoon. *Lat.* 38°. 35′. *Long.* 64°. 0′. *E. from London.* Taken by fraud from Timour, 93. Timour attacks it with 243 warriors, 7. taken by Timour, *ibid.* and 99. Timour ſurrounded therein by Ameer Mooſi and Mullik Bahaudur, 9.

Kush, *a city of* Mauwur u Nuhur, *a few miles to the E. of* Kurſhee, *and S. of* Summurkund. Principality of, *m.* 45, N. its forces deſert Timour, and join Ameer Haujee Burlaus, 321.

Kushmeer, *a kingdom ſituate on the W. ſide of the* Ganges, *and on the E. ſide of the* Indus. Part of Timour's troops march that way againſt Lauhore, 135.

Kutteh Bust, lands of, aſſigned to ſupport the Shrine of Immaum Aali, ſon of Mooſi, 359.

Kuttoor, *a mountain of* Buddukhſhaun. The Seah Poſhaun vanquiſhed near it, 289.

Kut-

KUTTULUG TURKAUN AUGHAU, eldest sister of Timour, secretes him in her house forty days, 43.

KYLANAUT, *m.* 163. See KILAUN.

KYPCHAUK. See KIPCHAUK.

L.

LAUHORE, *capital of the province of* Punjaub *in* Hindostaun, 322 *miles W. of* Dehli. *Lat.* 31°. 53′. *Long.* 73°. 30′. *from London.* Part of Timour's forces march against it, 135. territories of, a numerous army drawn together in by Mulloo Khaun, 353.

LAUR, *a city of* Fauris, 372 *miles S. of* Isfahaun. *Lat.* 27°. 20′. *Long.* 53°. 35′. *E. from London.* Plain of, a hundred thousand Toorks converted at once there by Sheikh Ibraheem Hummuee, 189.

LUSHKUR SHAAH, brother of Mullik Mahummud, killed by Moosi, 137.

M.

MAATUSSIM BILLAU UBBAUSI makes Alkummi his prime minister, 257. is betrayed by him into the hands of Hullaukoo Khaun, and put to death, *ibid.*

MAHUMMUD, the Arabian Law-giver, 9. number of his Attributes ninety two, 135. prayers due to him, and his descendants, 189. a proverb of his, 339.

——— posterity of, exalted above other men, 203. pensions and salaries ordained them by Timour, 235.

MAHUMMUD AUZAUD, one of Timour's Mingbaushees, vanquishes the Seah Poshaun in the war of Kuttoor, 289. is appointed governor of Kunduz and Goolaub, 291.

——— JEHAUNGHEER, Timour's eldest son, the subsistence of twelve thousand horse-men allowed him for his support, 241.

MAHUMMUD KHAUJEH ERUDEE, of the Hord of Tauemun, having seized the country of Shereghaunaut, opposes Timour, 91. submits to Timour, on his presenting him with another province, *ibid.*

——— MEHDI, the last of the 12 successors of Mahummud, 193.

MAUKHAUN, *a city of Khoraushaun, Lat.* 37°. 30′. *Long.* 60°. 0′. *from Lond.* Its governor Mubbauruk Shaah Sunjuri, 41.

MAUMOON UL RUSHEED, supporter of the Mahummudan Faith in the 2d century of the Hij. 185. abrogated seventy two unorthodox tenets, and established the true rites according to the Sunna, *ibid.* took possession of the government by the consent of Aali, the son of Moosi Jaufir, *ibid.* who was appointed by him successor to the Immaumut, *ibid.*

MAUWUR U NUHUR, *or* Transoxiana, *comprehends in general the whole country situate between the* Jihoon *and* Sihoon. *Its capital* Summurkund. (N. B. *Some modern geographers apply the name of* Mauwur u Nuhur *to a part of* Transoxiana, *called the province of* Summurkund, *about* 540 *miles long from W. to E. and* 500 *broad from S. to N.*) People of, unite themselves with Timour, 29. make a written engagement to support him with their lives and fortunes, *ibid.*

——— country of, is oppressed by the Ouzbuks, 27. delivered by Timour, *ibid.* is cleared from the abominations of the Ouzbuks, 87. from discord and anarchy, 93. being delivered from oppression, submits to Timour's government, 107. Timour halted there a few days in his march from Hindostaun to Room and Goorjistaun, 355. *m.* 333.

MAUZINDURAUN, *a province S. of the* Caspian Sea. Governor of, Ameer Aali, seeks protection of Timour, 117. *m.* 118, 141.

MECCA, *capital of a territory bearing its name, and of all* Arabia Felix *in* Asia, *the birth-place of* Mahummud. *It lies* 200 *miles* S. *of* Medina. *Lat.* 21°.30′. *Long.* 38°.50′. *E. from Lond.* Seized by Aboo Tauhir in the third century of the Hij. 185. *m.* 373.

MEER SIUD SHURREEF (one of the most respectable doctors of the eighth century of the Hij.) a letter of his to Timour, 181, 183, &c. *m.* 195.

——— ZEAU U DEEN, (*probably the same as* Siud Zeau u deen) a holy man noted for the efficacy of his prayers, 207. prays for Timour's success during his engagement with Touktummish Khaun, *ibid.*

MEERAUN SHAAH, Timour's third son, the subsistence of nine thousand horse-men allowed him for his support, 241. See AMEER ZAUDEH MEERAUN SHAAH.

MISSUR (or Egypt), forces of, called to the aid of Keesur, 145. defeated by Timour, 149. *m.* 143.

MOCKTAUDIR BILLAU UBBAUSI, promoter of the Mahummudan Faith in the third century of the Hij. 185. totally defeats Aboo Tauhir, and his associates, *ibid.*

MOGHOOL, tribe of, appointed to receive Tumghau, 309. Khaujeh Aghlaun of, made Ameer, 311.

MOOLTAUN, *a city of* Hindostaun (*capital of a province of the same name*) 414 *miles W. of* Dehli. *Lat.* 29°.40′. *Long.* 71°. 10′. *E. from London.* The prince Peer Mahummud Jehaungheer ordered to go against it, 133. *m.*353.

MOOSI, the Oughaun, head of the tribe of Gurkus, attacks Lushkur Shaah the Oughaun, 135. kills him, 137. is slain himself, *ibid.*

MOOSI JAUFIR, father of Aali, 185.

MOOSUL, *a city of* Deaur a Bukkur, *situate on the W. shore of the* Tigris. *Lat.* 36°.30′. *Long.* 43°.30′. *E. from Lond.* Timour marches by the way of, to invade Azzurbauejaun, 149.

MOSCOW, Timour penetrates as far as, 129, N.

MUBBAURUK KHAUN aspires to the sovereignty of Kunnouj, 353.

MUBBAURUK SHAAH SUNJURI, governor of Maukhaun, joins Timour with an hundred soldiers, 41. advises him to quit the desart, *ibid.* joins him at Atcheghi, 45.

MUGHRIB, kingdom of, *m.* 163.

MULLIK BAHAUDUR and AMEER MOOSI sit down in Kurshee with 12,000 horse-men, 7.

——— BURKOOK, 149.

——— FURRUJ, king of Missur and Shaum, departs to Dummishk, 149. is pursued by Timour, *ibid.* defeated, *ibid.*

——— GHEAUS U DEEN, ruler of Khorausaun, is in great fear of Timour, 111. hearing of Timour's departure, remits of his diligence and caution, 113. is surprized and taken by Timour, *ibid.*

——— MAHUMMUD, brother of Lushkur Shaah, solicits Timour to revenge his brother's death, 137. is confined by Timour, *ibid.*

——— SHAAH SILJOKEE loses his kingdom, by disgracing a worthy minister, and appointing a worthless man in his place, 255, 257.

MULLOO KHAUN, Vizzeer of Sooltaun Muhmood, on Timour's invasion of Hindostaun, gathers together a numerous army in Lauhore, 353. in conjunction with Sooltaun Muhmood, opposes him in Dehli with 50,000 horse-men, and 120 elephants, 139. their troops defeated, *ibid.* he is deprived of his power by Timour, 333.

MULLUTEAH, *a town of* Room, *capital of* Little Armenia. *Lat.* 38°. 0′. *Long.* 39°. 0′. *from Lond.* Subdued by Timour, 145.

MUNGULI BOOGHAU SULDOZE, governor of the castle of Aulaujou under Ouleaus Khaujeh, 55. refuses to hearken to Timour's proposals, 57. leaves the castle, and flees from Timour, *ibid.* in the war of Bullukh advances with an army against Timour, 281. Timour attempts in vain to corrupt him, *ibid.* he charges Timour with undaunted valour, and is defeated, *ibid.* taking offence at the conduct of Tughul. Timour Khaun, he flees to Timour, and is by him appointed governor of a province, 281, 319. signalizes himself in Timour's service, 281. rallies Timour's troops, when thrown into confusion, and decides the victory, *ibid.* is promoted by Timour, *ibid.*

MUTTEI LAUMRILLA UBBAUSI, deposed from the Khillaufut, 187.

MUZUFFUR, race of, accused to Timour of oppression, 117.

N.

NIZZAUM UL MOOLLUK, Vizzeer to Mullik Siljokee, 257. unjustly disgraced by him, *ibid.* his failings exceeded by his virtues, 263. is dissuaded from his intention of going on pilgrimage, *ibid.* he delivered Mullik Shaah from the hands of Keesur, 267.

NOUSHAREVAUN, father of Hurmuz, *m.* 285.

O.

OMUR ABDUL AZEEZ, the supporter of the Mahummudan faith in the first century of the Hij. 183. abolished the profane practice of execrating Aali from the pulpits, 183.

——— SHEIKH, second son of Timour, 241. the subsistence of ten thousand horse-men allowed for his support, *ibid.*

OUGHAUNS, *inhabitants of the mountains S. of* Kundahaur. Certain of, infest the road to Hindostaun, 135. are extirpated by Timour, 137.

OUJ KURRAU BAHAUDUR stationed at the bridge of Sungheen, opposite Ouleaus Khaujeh, 77.

OUZBUKS, *probably in this work the same as the* Jetes. *At present the* Ouzbuks, *or* Uzbecs, *possess all the country between the* Caspian Sea *and the dominions of the* Great Mogul. Are guilty of cruelty and oppression in the kingdom of Mauwur u Nuhur, 27. are attacked by Timour, *ibid.* extirpation of, authorized by the Siuds, 29. extirpated from Mauwur u Nuhur, 87. from Tooraun, 105. garrisons of, in certain castles of Mauwur u Nuhur, *ibid.* are drawn out by the policy of Timour, and flee, 107. *m.* 333.

P.

PEER MAHUMMUD JEHAUNGHEER, *son of* Mahummud Jehaungheer. His opinion concerning the conquest of Hindostaun, 129. ordered by Timour to march from Kaubul with 30,000 horse against Mooltaun, 133.

R.

ROOM, (Anatolia, *or* Asia Minor) *is terminated on the N. by the* Euxine Sea; *on the E. by* Georgia, Armenia, *and* Turcomania; *on the S. by* Shaum *and the* Levant; *and on the W. by the* Archipelago, Hellespont, *and* Propontis. King of, called Keesur, 131. country of, Timour sends an army to ravage it, 153. entirely conquered by Timour, 355.

ROOMI, Turks, inhabitants of Room, 279.

S.

SAUN BAHAUDUR, of the tribe of Douldee, made Ameer, 311.

SAUREEK BAHAUDUR, an Ameer of Jitteh, 71.

SAURUNG, brother of Mulloo Khaun, assumes

aſſumes the ſovereignty of Mooltaun, 353. diſpoſſeſſed by Timour, 333.
SEAH POSHAUN, *inhabitants of the mountains S. of* Buddukhſhaun, 289. and *N.* defeat Burhaun Aghlaun, *ibid.* are vanquiſhed by Mahummud Auzaud, *ibid.*
SEEWAUS, *a city of* Room, *Lat.* 39°. 6′. *Long.* 38°. 40′. *E. from London.* Subdued by Timour, 143.
SEISTAUN, *a province of* Perſia. *Its capital* Zurunge *is ſituate in Lat.* 32°. 25′. *Long.* 61°. 0′. *E. from London.* Governor of, ſends preſents to Timour, and requeſts his protection, 47. joins with his enemies againſt Timour, *ibid.* is conquered by Timour, *ibid.*
——— armies of, ordered to make ready for war, 141.
SHAAH MUNSOOR oppoſes Timour face to face, and is ſlain, 407.
SHAAHROKH, Timour's fourth ſon, the ſubſiſtence of nine thouſand horſe-men allowed him, 241. his opinion concerning the war of Hindoſtaun, 129.
SHARE BEHRAUM, of the tribe of Jullauir, 311. had ſeparated from Timour to go to Hindoſtaun, 55. returns to him, *ibid.* attempts to corrupt the governor of the caſtle of Aulaujou, 57. ſeparates from Timour, 69. returns to him, 87. informs him of the deſigns of Ameer Hooſſein, 103. is ſlain by Ameer Hooſſein, *ib.*—he had deſerted Timour and united with his enemies, 171. was pardoned by Timour in conſideration of his valour, *ibid.* was made ninth Ameer, 311. fought againſt Timour with aſtoniſhing valour, 279. fled to him for protection, and was honourably received, *ibid.*
SHARAUZE, *capital of* Fauris, *about* 176 *miles S. of* Isfahaun. *Lat.* 29°. 50′. *Long.* 53°. 10′. *E. from London.* Inhabitants of, rebel, 121. are reduced by Timour, *ibid.*
SHAREKUND, *a town of* Mauwur u Nuhur *N. of* Kurſhee. *Lat.* 38°. 40′. *Long.* 64°. 0′. *E. from London.* Timour halts there, 97.
SHAREVAUN. See SHURWAUN.
SHAUDUMAUN, or HISSAUR SHAUDUMAUN, *a town of* Saganian. *Lat.* 38°. *Long. about* 65°. 0′. Taken from Timour by Ameer Hooſſein, 87. given to Ameer Hooſſein by Timour, 107. *m.* 319.
SHAUM (or Syria) *a country in* Aſia *bounded on the W. by the* Mediterranean, *on the N. by mount* Armenus, *on the E. by the* Euphrates, *and on the S. by* Arabia Petræa. *Its capital* Dummiſhk. Forces of, called to the aid of Bajazet, 145. conquered by Timour, 149. *m.* 163. Heretics of, puniſhed by Timour, 335.
SHEIKH ABDUL KAUDIR, lands allowed for ſupporting his ſhrine, 359.
——— AHMUD JAUMI, contemporary with, and preceptor to, Sooltaun Sunjur, 187.
——— IBRAHEEM HUMMUEE converts a hundred thouſand Toorks at once in the plain of Laur, 189.
SHUNGOOM, an Ameer of Jitteh, 71.
SHURWAUN, *a province of* Perſia *ſituate on the* Caſpian Sea. *Its capital* Shamaki *is in Lat.* 40°. 50′. *Long.* 60°. 0′. *E. from London.* Touktummiſh Khaun's army marches by it, to invade Azzurbauejaun, 127. *m.* 117.
SHURWAUNAUT, *m.* 163.
SIHOON, *or the* Jaxartes, *bounds* Mauwur u Nuhur *on the N. m.* 23, N.
SIND, *or the* Indus, *riſes in the mountains which divide* Tartary *from* India, *and paſſing through* Kuſhmeer *and* Mooltaun, *empties itſelf in the* Indian Sea. Croſſed by the armies of Timour, in their way to Mooltaun and Lauhore, 133, 135.
SIUD HOOSSUN adviſes Timour to quit the deſart of Khauruzm, 41. joins him, 45.

SIUD ZEAU U DEEN, 41. See MEER ZEAU U DEEN.
SOOLAMAUN, mountain of, *m.* 133, 247, 248.
——— FAURSI, a revenue assigned for supporting his Shrine, 359.
SOOLTAUN AHMUD JULLAUIR, governor of Bughdaud, receives an Ambassador from Timour, 127. treated contemptuously by the Ambassador in a letter to Timour, *ibid.* flees towards Kurbullau, *ibid.* departs from Bughdaud leaving one of his officers to defend it, 151.
——— GHEAUS U DEEN, *m.* 113, 335. See MULLIK GHEAUS U DEEN.
——— HOOSSEIN, *son of* Timour's *daughter named* Akia Beghi, his opinion concerning the war of Hindostaun, 131.
——— MAHUMMŬD (*or* MUHMOOD) KHAUN *nominal emperor of* Chugtauee. See AMEER ZAUDEH.
——— MUHMOOD, *emperor of* Ghizni, an instance of his determined resolution in enforcing his commands, 225. deposed by his ministers, *ibid.*
——— MUHMOOD KHAUN, *ruler of* Dehli, 353. opposes Timour with 50,000 men, 139. is defeated, and flees to the mountains, *ibid.*
——— SUNJUR, son of Sooltaun Mullik Shaah, promoter of the faith in the fifth century of the Hij. 187. contemporary with, and disciple of, Sheikh Ahmud Jaumi and Hukkeem Sunnai, *ibid.*
SUBZVAUR, *m.* 207.
SUDDEUK BURLAUS, of the race of Yeldurreen Kurrauchaur Nooyaun, joins Timour with 15 horse-men, 49.
SULDOZE, tribe of, appointed to receive Tumghau, 309. Ilchee Bahaudur of, made Ameer, 311.
——— Ameers of, swear fidelity to Kaubul Shaah, 325. hearing of Timour's exaltation to the throne break their faith, and put him to death, *ibid.* execrated for it by Timour, *ibid.*
SULLAUICHEE Bahaudur, of the tribe of Aurlaut, made Ameer, 313.
SUMMURKUND, *capital of* Mauwur u Nuhur, *situate in the valley of* Sogd, *about 7 days journey N. E. of* Bokhaura. *Lat.* 39°. 40′. *Long. about* 65°. 0′. *E. from London.* Timour returns thither after the conquest of Hindostaun, 139. after the defeat of Bajazet, 153. *m.* 31, 323.
SUNGHEEN, bridge of, 71. station of Ouleaus Khaujeh, 77.

T.

TAUBAUN BAHAUDUR, of the tribe of Douldee, 311. in an engagement with Touktummish Khaun, penetrates to the standard-bearer, and inverts the standard, 289. his enemies seek in vain to obscure his renown, *ibid.* received into favour, and promoted by Timour, *ibid.* made Ameer, 311.
TAULAA BILLAU, son of Mutteilaumrilla Ubbausi, appointed to the Khillaufut, in the room of his father, by Azzud u dowla, 187.
TAULKHAUN, *a town of* Tookhauristaun. *Lat.* 36°. 50′. *Long.* 67°. *E. from London.* Timour arrives there, 69.
TAUSH KHAUJEH, of the tribe of Aurghoon, made eighth Ameer, 311.
TAUSHKUND, a *town of* Toorkistaun *situate near the* Sihoon. *Lat.* 42°. *Long. about* 63°. *E. from London.*
TAUTAUR, tribe of, appointed to receive Tumghau, 309. Kowvung Khaun of, made Ameer, 313.
TIGRIS, river, Furrukh drowned in it, 151.
TIMOUR, or TAMERLANE. See ABUL MUNSOOR TIMOUR.
TIMOUR, river, crossed by Timour, 129.
TIMOUR AGHLAUN, *m.* 315.

TIMOUR KHAUJEH AGHLAUN, with his forces, joins Timour, 45.

——— NOUBUKAUN, second Ameer of Jitteh, 71.

TOORAUN, *all the countries situate beyond the* Jihoon. Timour becomes lord of it, 87. clears it of the Ouzbuks, 105. certain of the seditious of Khorausaun, sent thither, 143.

——— Saints of, benefactions and gifts granted for their sepulchres and mausoleums, 361, *m.* 163.

TOORKISTAUN, infidels of, almost annihilate the Mahummudan religion by their conquests, 187. a hundred thousand of them converted at one time by Sheikh Ibraheem Hummuee, 189. *m.* 319.

——— king of, called Khaukaun, 131.

TOOS, *a city of* Khorausaun 123 *miles S. E. of the* Caspian Sea, *and* 604 *S. W. of* Bokhaura. The revenues of its environs, assigned for supporting the sepulchre of Immaum Aali, son of Moosi, 359.

TOUBUK BAHAUDUR joins Timour, 53.

TOUGHAUEE, tribe of, appointed to receive Tumghau, 309. Aali Durvaish of, made Ameer, 311.

TOUK TIMOUR, of the tribe of Jullauir, made eighth Ameer, 311.

TOUKTUMMISH BUDDAU KHAUN, defeated by Auroos Khaun, 115.

——— KHAUN, 289. his standard inverted by Taubaun Bahaudur, *ibid.* his army defeated by Burlaus Bahaudur, 289. fleeing to Timour, is treated by him with kindness, 327. defeated by Auroos Khaun, 353.

TOULAUN BOOGHAU, sent to Timour by the Ameers who deserted from the army of Jitteh, 59.

TOULKCHEE, tribe of, appointed to receive Tumghau, 309. Aljauitoo Burdi of, made Ameer, 311.

TOUMUNEH KHAUN, father of Kubbul Khaun and Kaujooli Bahaudur, and fourth ancestor of Chungaze Khaun, 25, N.

TUBBURAUZE, *a city of* Azzurbauejaun, 396 *miles N. of* Isfahaun. *Lat.* 38°. 25′. *Long.* 47°. 0′. *E. from London.* Timour marches towards it, 151. turns back by the way of, *ibid.*

TUBBURISTAUN, *a province of* Persia, *having the* Caspian Sea *on the N.* Kilaun *on the W.* Erauk a Ajjum *on the S. and* Khorausaun *on the E.* Armies of, ordered to make ready for war, 141.

TUGHULLUK KHAUJEH, brother of Khaujeh Beg, Ameer of Jitteh, 71.

——— KHAUJEH BURLAUS (*probably the same as the preceeding*) joins Timour, 53. and is received by him with marks of joy and respect, 55.

——— SULDOZE, overpowered by Timour, 75 and 77.

——— TIMOUR KHAUN, of the line of Chungaze, 15. his Ameers rebel in the Dusht of Jitteh, 11. follows the advice of Timour, *ibid.* crosses the Sihoon at Khujjund, 15. determines to reduce Mauwur u Nuhur, *ibid.* issues mandates of summons to Timour, Ameer Haujee Burlaus and Ameer Bauezzeed Jullauir, *ibid.* rejoiced at the coming of Timour, 21. follows his counsel, *ibid.* hears that the Ameers of his three Armies had received presents from the inhabitants of Mauwur u Nuhur, *ibid.* turns them out of their commands, and appoints Haujee Muhmood Shaah Yessooree to supply their place, *ibid.* disturbed at the rebellion of his chiefs, asks counsel of Timour, 23. returns back to the Dusht of Jitteh, *ibid.* gives Timour the government of Mauwur u Nuhur, *ibid.* restores him the Toumaun of Ameer Kurrauchaur Nooyaun, *ibid.* breaks his engagements with Timour, and brings an army a ſecond time againſt Mauwur u Nuhur, 25. gives the government of it to Ouleaus Khaujeh his ſon, *ibid.* and appoints Timour miniſter and general to Ouleaus Khaujeh, *ibid.*

TUKKUL BAHAUDUR, governor of Khiook, falls upon Timour with a thouſand men, 35.

TUMOOKEH BAHAUDUR, ſent over the river at Turmuz with three horſemen to gain intelligence of the Jetes, 59. returns after four days, *ibid.*

——— KOUCHEIN joins Timour with 15 horſe-men, 43. is ſent by him to Mubbauruk Shaah, *ibid.*

TURKHAUN, tribe of, appointed to receive Tumghau, 309. Ameer Bauezzeed of, made ſeventh Ameer, *ibid.* twenty perſons of, made Euzbauſhees, *ibid.*

TURMUZ, *a city of* Mauwur u Nuhur *ſituate on the* Jihoon, *about* 50 *miles N. of* Bullukh, *being a famous paſſage over the river. Lat. about* 37°. *Long.* 66°. 0′. *E. from London.* Waters of, croſſed by Tumookeh Bahaudur, 59. by Timour, 65. land of, the armies of Jitteh plunder there. 59.

——— OLD, the Ameers who deſerted the army of Jitteh arrive there, 59.

U.

UBBAUS, one of the three Orthodox Khalifs, 183.

UMLIS, ſon of Toumun Bahaudur, coming into the neighbourhood of Bullukh to plunder, joins Timour with 200 horſe-men, 57.

Y.

YELDURRUM BAUEZZEED, or Bajazet, 149, 407. See KEESUR.

YESSOOR, tribe of, aſſiſt Ameer Khizzur Yeſſooree, 93. are pillaged by Ki Khiſſero and Aljauitoo Burdi, *ib.*

YEURLDAIEE, people of, join Timour, 69.

INDEX

INDEX

OF THE

PRINCIPAL MATTERS.

ACCOMPTANT, one, appointed by Timour to every department of government, to keep a journal of the daily receipts and disbursements, 307.

Alous. See Auloos.

Alms-house, one, ordered by Timour to be built in every city for the poor, 219.

Ameer, a *prince* or *leader*; a title given to all the nobility of the first rank in the Mogul empire, 15, N.

Ameers, divided into twelve ranks, of which the Ameer ul Omrau is chief. (See Ameer ul Omrau.) The First to be made Second on his signalizing himself; the Second, Third; the Third, Fourth; &c. 275,293. One Toghe allowed to the First, two to the Second, three to the Third, four and the Niccaureh to the Fourth, &c. up to the Ameer ul Omrau. (See 291.) The First to bring with him into the field a hundred and ten horses, the Second a hundred and twenty, &c. 297. revenues of the frontier provinces assigned for their payment, 237. are enjoined, in collecting the revenues, not to exact more than the accustomed dues on any pretence, 239. are to hold a Jaugheer for three years; and longer, if the inhabitants are satisfied with their conduct, 241. to be degraded from their commands, if they disobey orders in time of action, 245. to be exalted by a title of honour, the standard, the Niccaureh, the appellation of Bahaudur, and other dignities, on their defeating an army, or reducing a kingdom, 283. to be appointed to the vice-gerency of a kingdom for three years, upon their conquering it, 291. if tardy in executing, or disobedient to, commands, to be instantly put to death, 397.

Ameers, Three hundred and thirteen, of wisdom and judgment, selected from Timour's chosen and superior servants, and advanced to exalted dignities, 269. who were as firmly united together, and to Timour, as if one soul had animated them all, 337. never desisted from an undertaking till they had brought it to a conclusion, *ibid.* an *expecter of preferment* appointed to succeed on the death of each, *ibid.* a hundred stiled Ounbaushees; a hundred, Euzbaushees; and a hundred, Mingbaushees, 273.

273. Four of these appointed Beglerbegs; and one, Ameer ul Omrau, 271.

Ameers, Twelve of reputation and renown exalted to high commands by Timour, each commanding a squadron proportionate to his rank, 271. and each being deputy to his next superior, *ibid.* the Twelfth Ameer, a commander of twelve thousand horse, and deputy to the Ameer ul Omrau, 273.

Ameer ul Omrau, *Chief of the Ameers or Nobles*, 233, N. his office to issue orders to the Ameers, 273. and to superintend the payment of the Mingbaushees, 233. his pay ten times as much as that of the officer subordinate to him, 235. receives it under the inspection of the Deewaunbeghee and Vizzeers, *ibid.* a stipend granted him from the revenues of a frontier province, 237. is not to perform the duty of an Ameer, 273. not to take less than three hundred horses with him into the field, 297. insignia of his office, the Standard, Niccaureh, Toumaun Toghe and Cher Toghe, 291. his place in the Deewaun on the left side of the throne, 329.

Ameers of Auloosaut, their orders for entering the field, 309. an Eurghee and Birruck granted to each of them, *ibid.*

——— of Hurrauwul, their place in the Deewaun, in the front of the throne, 329.

——— of Kushoonaut, what they were to bring into the field and what should be allowed them, 309.

——— of Toumaunaut, the same. *ibid.*

Ameer Zaudeh, *a son or grandson of a King or Emperor*, 405.

Amwaul a Ghauibi, *the effects of people lost or absconded*, 371.

Arabic, sentences quoted in it, 74, 88, 118, 132, 180, 188.

Arrub or Ajjum, *Arabian or Persian*, *m.* 217, 323.

Artificers, of every sort, of Timour's XI. Class, 215. admitted into his palace and camp, *ibid.* those of the tribes which submitted to him, employed in his service, 217. Architects employed by Timour in raising magnificent buildings, 213.

Astrologers, of Timour's VIII. Class, 213. essential to the dignity of empire, *ibid.* assist him in ascertaining the benign or malignant aspects of the stars, *ibid.*

Audience, hall of, the infantry &c. paid there, 237. assignments for the payment of the Ameers and Mingbaushees delivered there, 239.

Auloos, *a tribe or hord.* Plural, Auloosaut.

Auriz, *a sort of field-deputy*, 375, 377.

Autaukeh, an embroidered one, a military reward, *m.* 291.

Authority, Timour's, so secured by order and regulation that none had power to interpose in his government, 199.

B.

Bahaudur, *the brave*, an appellation given to those who signalized themselves in battle, 283, N.

Baudi and Huvvaui, revenues of, 371. See Huvvaui.

Bauwulli, a Mogul word, its meaning unknown, 277.

Begging not allowed by Timour, 349, 361. See Mendicants.

Beglerbegs, *generals or commanders of the first rank*, *m.* 271. if tardy in executing, or disobedient to commands, to be instantly put to death, 397.

Birruck, (Mogul) *a little flag*, 309.

Buffoons and vagrants, not to be suffered in city or country, 347.

Bukdeh, part of the dress of ceremony of the Ameers, &c. 297.

Burraunghaur, *the rear line of the right wing*, 389. consists of 3 squadrons in an army of 12,000, *ibid.* of 6 in an army of 40,000, p.399. when to enter into action, 393, 403. *m.* 405, 407.

C.

Caaba, the black stone torn from its corner, 185.

Cavalry, their accompts made up half-yearly, 237. paid from the treasury, *ibid.*

Cher Toghe, *a sort of standard or spear*, a military distinction granted to the Ameer ul Omrau, 291.

Chupkunchee, four divisions of, appointed to scour the country round the camp, 301.

Chuppauwul, *the front line of the right wing*, 389. when to enter into action, 393. consists of six squadrons, when the army exceeds 40,000, *ibid.* their order of entering into action, 403. *m.* 407.

Classes,

Timour divides his people into XII. 205. and considers them as the 12 months, and as the 12 signs of the Zodiac, predominating over the concerns of his empire, *ibid.*

Class I. The descendants of the Prophet, theologians, doctors learned in the law, and holy men, *ibid.*

II. Persons of wisdom, deliberation, vigilance, circumspection, and aged men, *ibid.*

III. Devout and pious men (supposed to be a selection from the first class), 215, and N.

IV. Ameers, chiefs, and commanders of forces, 207.

V. Soldiers and subjects, 209.

VI. A selected number from amongst the wise and prudent, to whom secrets and the most hidden transactions were entrusted, 211.

VII. Vizzeers, secretaries and scribes, *ibid.*

VIII. Physicians, surgeons, astrologers, and geometricians, 213.

IX. Historians, and men of knowledge, *ibid.*

X. Holy and pious men, possessed of wisdom (supposed to be Hermits or Monks), 215, and N.

XI. Artificers of all sorts, *ibid.*

XII. Travellers, voyagers, merchants, and chiefs of Kaurruvvauns, *ibid.*

Conduct, an account of Timour's, left by him as an example to his sons and descendants, for the attaining and preserving of dominion, 158, 159. He promoted the worship of Almighty God, and always supported the Mahummudan faith, 159. ranked his people under different classes (see Classes) 159, 201. always complied with times and occasions, 161. conducted the affairs of his empire with generosity, patience, and policy, *ibid.* so regulated his government by order and discipline, that none of his subjects could aspire beyond their respective degrees, *ibid.* encouraged his officers and soldiers by his liberality, *ibid.* shared with them in all their labours and hardships, *ibid.* on his accession to the throne, abandoned ease and safety, to establish the glory of his name, 163. gained the affections of his people by justice and clemency, *ibid.* by rewards and punishments kept his subjects divided between hope and fear, 165. compassionated the lower ranks of his people, *ibid.* always gave sentence agreeably to the sacred law, *ibid.* received with kindness all who submitted to him, *ibid.* treated with esteem and veneration all persons distinguished for religion or learning, *ibid.* associated with good and learned men, intreated their support, and sought success from their prayers, 167. loved the poor, and neither oppressed nor excluded them his favour, *ibid.* attended not to malevolent insinuations, *ibid.*

ibid. made one undertaking the ſole object of his attention, until it was brought to a concluſion, *ibid.* dealt not with ſeverity towards any, nor was oppreſſive in any of his actions, *ibid.* enquired into the laws and regulations of ancient princes, and therefrom ſelected models for his own imitation, *ibid.* eſteemed the great as his brethren, and the poor as his children, 169. made himſelf acquainted with the diſpoſitions and wiſhes of the inhabitants and nobles of every country, and appointed over them governors adapted thereto, *ibid.* puniſhed all who were guilty of oppreſſion or cruelty, *ibid.* received all officers, of what tribe, country, or nation ſoever, with particular reſpect, 171. always repaid the value of ſervices, *ibid.* and 199. received his enemy with kindneſs and liberality when he ſubmitted, and pardoned diſloyalty in conſideration of valour, *ib.* peculiarly diſtinguiſhed in his proſperity all thoſe with whom he had been connected in the days of diſtreſs, 173, 199. ſhewed clemency to his relations, ever ſubſtituting pardon in the place of puniſhment, *ibid.* and N. dealt with every one according to his opinion of the perſon's worth, *ib.* conducted himſelf with caution and policy towards friends and enemies, *ibid.* honourably treated the captive who had behaved with fidelity to his maſter, *ibid.* and conſidered the ſoldier of the foe who deſerted in the time of action, as the moſt deteſtable of men, 175. ſo ſecured his authority by regulations and order, that none had power to interpoſe in his government, 199. either overlooked, or bore with patience, the faults of thoſe about him, *ibid.* buried in oblivion all paſt evil actions, *ibid.* never gave way to revenge, 201. ordered that all repreſentations ſent to him, all orders iſſued by him, and every matter debated in council to be inſerted in the narrative of his tranſactions, 307. expelled from his preſence the wicked and ſeditious, *ibid.* obtained the obedience of his ſubjects by complacency, mercy and indulgence, *ibid.* commanded that every perſon who came before him, and attracted his notice, ſhould receive honours proportionate to his rank, *ibid.* regulated his conduct by certain maxims and rules (ſee Maxims and rules), 221 and 335. thoſe admitted not into his ſervice who had been faithleſs to his enemies, 319. on his attaining ſupreme power, he conducted himſelf in the ſame manner both to friends and enemies, 323. and received his enemies who had injured and practiſed deceit upon him with ſuch kindneſs that they bluſhed at their own unworthineſs, *ibid.* and 325. made compenſation to every one whom he had injured or diſtreſſed, and balanced his diſtreſſes by kindneſs and gratuities, *ibid.* and 325. conſidered his friends who had always adhered to him, as the partners of his fortune; and regarded not the riches and wealth he conferred upon them, 325. overcame the refractory by their own devices, 347. confined the baſe and abject within their proper bounds, 345. gave back the government of every country to its reſpective prince, and ſecured his obedience by kindneſs, 347. protected the inhabitants of every conquered kingdom from injuries, 355. and ordered the ſpoils taken thence to be re-taken from the ſpoiler, 357.

Council, general, writers of, appointed to keep a full account of all matters debated there, which were ordered to be inſerted in the narrative of Timour's tranſactions, 307. the malevolent and evil not ſuffered to enter therein, 167. Timour's Ameers, chiefs, and commanders of forces admitted thereto, 207.

Council, private, persons of wisdom, deliberation, vigilance and circumspection, and aged men admitted thereto, 205. several members thereof, treacherous to Timour, 229. all matters appertaining to the imperial dignity, the appointment of officers, plans of operation &c. communicated to Timour therein, 307. secretary appointed to attend it, *ib.* See Secretary.

Counsel, one of the chief supports of empire, 7. used by Timour in all his enterprises, 9, 15. two sorts of, of the tongue, and of the heart, 13. that of the heart alone attended to by Timour, *ibid.* that rejected which caused disunion amongst his soldiers, 15. that only regarded, which was given with firmness and judgment, *ibid.*

Counsellors, those only worthy who steadfastly adhere to their determinations, 13.

Criminals, pardoned by Timour for their first offence, 219. adequately punished if they offend afterwards, *ibid.* not to be fined and corporally punished at the same time, 251.

D.

Deedbaun, *observers, people appointed to reconnoitre the motions of the enemy*, 401.

Deewaun, none to appear there in time of peace without the dress of ceremony, 297. the dress of ceremony described, *ibid.*

Deewaunbeghi, *president of the council.* 23, N. his place in the Deewaun opposite the throne, 329. his subsistence ten times as much as that of an Ameer, 235. superintends the payment of the Ameer ul Omrau, *ibid.* his office to lay before the emperor the statement of the salaries of the people, and to pay them agreeably thereto, *ibid. m.* 305.

Dervaish, *a hermit or monk*, Timour's grand-children to be reduced to this state when they rebel, 243. people of this profession, loved by Timour, 167. *m.* 89.

Designs, formed by Timour for the reduction of kingdoms, and for his conduct towards friends and enemies, &c. 3.

I. When Tughulluk Timour Khaun first invaded Mauwur u Nuhur, 19.

II. When Tughulluk invaded Mauwur u Nuhur a second time, 25.

III. When Aali Begh Choun Ghoorbauni had imprisoned him, 35.

IV. When he had escaped from Aali Begh, and was sojourning in the desart of Khauruzm, 39.

V. When he had gathered together an army, and was meditating the invasion of Mauwur u Nuhur, 45.

VI. When Kurrumseer had submitted to him, and he was collecting an army to subdue Mauwur u Nuhur, 49.

VII. When his army was increased to 313 horse-men, and he was meditating the reduction of Aulaujou, 55.

VIII. When he was opposed by the army of Jitteh, 61.

IX. When he had defeated the army of Jitteh, and was endeavouring to establish his regal power, 65.

X. When he departed to subdue the countries of Buddukhshaun, 67.

XI. When Buddukhshaun had submitmitted to him, and he was meditating the conquest of Khuttulaun, 69.

XII. When some of his chiefs were dissatisfied, and he was endeavouring to reconcile them, 73.

XIII. When he was opposed by Ouleaus Khaujeh at the bridge of Sungheen, 77.

Designs, Timour's, for subduing Hurraut, 111. for conquering the countries of Seistaun, Kundahaur, and the land of the Oughauns, 113. for vanquishing Auroos Khaun, 115. for subduing Kilaun, Jurjaun, Mauzinduraun, Azzurbauejaun, Shurwaun, Fauris and Erauk, 117. for reducing Touktummish Khaun, 121. for conquering Bughdaud and Erauk a Arrub,

rub, 125. for extirpating Touktummish Khaun, 127. for reducing the empire of Hindostaun, 129. for clearing the road to Hindostaun of the Oughauns, 135. for vanquishing Sooltaun Muhmood, the ruler of Dehli, and Mulloo Khaun, 137. for reducing the country of Goorjistaun, 141. for conquering Missur and Shaum, 145. for subduing the cities of Room, and defeating the armies of Keesur, 149.

Drum, one, allowed to the Euzbaushee and Ounbaushee Ameers, as a military distinction, 291.

Dusht, *a large plain, or champain country.*

Duvvauleh Chouk, one horse-man to be brought from each by the Ameer of every Auloos, 309 and N.

E.

Empire, without religion, likened to a naked man, 175. and to a house without a roof, gates, or defences, *ibid.* the offices in an earthly one, symbols of those in the heavenly, 201. it's concerns necessary to be divided amongst many, lest too much being entrusted to one, he become too powerful, 225. will decay, unless established in morality and religion, 175. it's chief support deliberation, counsel, and provident measures, 7. physicians, surgeons, and geometricians essential to it's dignity, 213.

Eookee (Mogul) supposed to signify a watch-word, 299.

Erzbeghee, *a presenter of petitions*, 305, N.

Eusoof, *Joseph*, chap. of, *m.* 19. the Koraun opened by Timour at that place, on his seeking an omen, *ibid.*

Euzbaushee, *commander of a hundred*, 229. the manner of his appointment, *ibid.* has power to appoint an Ounbaushee, 231. may be appointed by a Mingbaushee, *ibid.* his subsistence double that of the Ounbaushee, 233. receives his subsistence under the inspection of the Mingbaushee, *ibid.* his duty not to be imposed on the Mingbaushee, 273. to be appointed Mingbaushee on his signalizing himself, 275. the command of a province to be given him on his conquering an enemy, 289. his accoutrements of war, 295. his dress of ceremony in times of peace, 297. his place in the Deewaun on the left side of the throne, 329. *m.* 397.

F.

Friend, useful in all places, 103. a firm, is the enemy of his friend's enemy, and fears not to hazard his life, when necessary, 325. a foolish, is worse than a wise enemy, 327. a true, is not offended at the conduct of his friend, *ibid.* and 325.

Furraushaun, *people employed to erect tents*, 235. subsistence of, fixed at from 100 to 1000, *ibid.*

Fursung, *a league of about six thousand yards*, 9, N.

G.

General (or Commander), of Timour's IV. Class, 207. his place in the Deewaun on the right side of the throne, 329. admitted to Timour's private councils, 207. questions concerning the art of war &c. proposed to him by Timour, 209. to be deprived of his command, if found insufficient, 375. his duty, to reconnoitre the enemy, and compare his chiefs with those of the foe, and carefully to examine the enemy's weapons and mode of attack, 377. not to begin the engagement, till first attacked by the enemy, *ibid.* to govern the movements of his forces, and to be cool, firm, and collected within

within himself, 379. to consider himself and his army as a wrestler, who fighteth with every part of his body, *ibid.* the manner in which he ought to attack the enemy, *ibid.* and 381. he must not be rash and precipitate, nor expose himself unnecessarily to danger, 381. his death bringeth disgrace upon the army, *idid.* A good one numbereth the chiefs of the forces of the enemy, and appointeth proper chiefs in opposition to them, 387. pre-examineth the field of battle and order of the enemy, *ibid.* understandeth the science and discipline of war, and what measures to pursue in attacking the enemy, *ib.* comprehendeth their intentions, and counteracteth their motions and designs, *ibid.* and 269.—of 40,000 horse directions for, 387, 389. his duty to watch continually the motions of the foe, and to chastize those officers, who, without orders, advance on the enemy, 391. not to pursue an enemy, who, without cause, fleeth from the field, *ibid.* Directions for his attacking the enemy, 391, 393. a treacherous, to be put to death, 321.

Geometricians, of Timour's VIII. Class, 213. esteemed by him as essential to the dignity of Empire, *ibid.* assisted him in planning and constructing magnificent buildings, *ib.*

Governors, those not fit to govern, whose authority is inferior to the power of the scourge, 241. their duty to levy fines on the guilty proportionate to their misdemeanours, 349.

Guards stationed at the entrance of roads, to defend the merchants and travellers, 347, 369. accountable for the value of every thing lost therein, *ib.*

H.

Hermits, (or Monks) supposed to be the holy, pious men of Timour's X. Class, 215, N. knowledge of a future state acquired from them, *ibid.* delight and satisfaction reaped from their conversation and working of miracles, *ibid.*

Hijrut, or Hijreh, *the Mahummudan Æra, commencing A. D.* 622, *m.* 153.

Historians, of Timour's IX. Class, 213. treated with esteem and veneration by him, 165. his knowledge of history and geography acquired from them, *ibid.*

Hoorrum Surrai, *Seraglio*, a lady of Timour's, receives the donation of 12 years of life from 12 Siuds, 207.

Hospital, Timour orders one for the sick to be built in every town and city, 371. a physician appointed to attend it, *ibid.*

Hunter Dr, his MS. fragment of *the Life of Timour written by himself*, refutes an assertion of Ibn Arabshaah, 25, N.

Hurrauwul, *the advanced Guard*, 77. in an army of 12,000 consists of one squadron, 373. first opposed to the enemy, 391.

——— Grand, *the Grand Vanguard*, 389. in an army of 40,000 consists of six squadrons, 399. their order of entering into action, 401. supported by the Chuppauwul, 403.

——— a Burraunghaur, *the advanced guard of the rear line of the right wing*, 389. consists of one squadron, *ibid.* and 399. when to enter into action, 393, 403.

——— a Jurraunghaur, *the advanced guard of the rear line of the right wing*, 389. consists of one squadron, *ibid.* and 399. when to enter into action, 393, 403.

——— a Chuppauwul, *the advanced guard of the front line of the rigth wing*, 389. consists of one squadron, *ibid.* and 399. when to enter into action, 391.

——— a Shuckauwul, *the advanced guard of the front line of the left wing*, 389. consists of one squadron, *ibid.*

ibid. and 399. when to enter into action, 391.

——— a Hurrauwul, *the advanced guard of the advanced guard*, 399. consists of one squadron, *ibid.* begin the action, 401.

Husband-man, The, not possessed of the implements of agriculture, to be furnished therewith, 219. supplies to be granted to the distressed, that he may be enabled to cultivate his ruined lands, 369. superintendants appointed to watch over him and the cultivated lands, 371.

Hust and Bood, *some regulation for collecting certain duties*, 367.

Huvvaui and Baudi, the third Vizzeer in every country to take possession of their revenues, 371. See Sauir.

I.

Immaum, *a priest or prelate.*

Immaumut, *the office of* Immaum. Aali appointed successor to it, 185.

Intelligence, concerning foreign princes and countries, transmitted to Timour by 1000 swift camel-men, 1000 horse-men and 1000 foot-men whom he selected for that purpose, *ibid.* also by travellers, whom he encouraged for the same, 215. and by merchants and chiefs of Kauruvvauns, 217.

——— writer of, an officer appointed by Timour in every place, to send him a full account of all things transacted therein, 349, 351. how punished for giving false accounts, 351.

Islaum, religion of, *the same as the Mahummudan, m.* 175, 177, 179, 183, 189, 193, 197. See Religion.

J.

Jaugheer, *a royal grant of certain lands; or more properly, an assignment of the crown-revenues of a certain district to any one, and revocable at the pleasure of the prince*, 239, N.

Jaugheerdaur, *the holder of a Jaugheer*, 239, N. his conduct inspected by two supervisors, *ibid.* the state of his province to be inspected after three years, *ibid.* to be deprived of it, and his subsistence, for 3 years, if the inhabitants are dissatisfied, 241.

Jaumeh, *an upper coat*, a part of the dress of ceremony of the Ameers, &c. 297.

Judge, one, appointed in every city and town, 177.

——— one, established for the army, 177.

——— one, for the subjects, *ibid.*

——— one, in equity, appointed by Timour, to transmit to him all matters of litigation, 179.

——— ecclesiastical, (and the Suddur) ordered to lay before Timour, from time to time, all the ecclesiastical affairs of the empire, 179. and to decide on cases determinable by the sacred law, 253.

——— civil, his office to lay before Timour those cases which were not determinable by the sacred law, *ibid.*

Judges, their place in the Deewaun on the right side of the throne, 329.

Jurraunghaur, *the rear line of the left wing*, 389. consists of 3 squadrons in an army of 12,000, *ibid.* of six squadrons in an army of 40,000, p. 399. when to enter into action, 393, 403. reserves of, those related to the imperial family, 405. who when the commander of the Jurraunghaur fails in his duty, must advance to the assault, *ibid.*

Jurreeb, *a certain land-measure.* Restricted lands, divided into first, second and third Jurreebs, when the subject was dissatisfied with the mode of collection, 365.

——— the estimation of the produce of the first, second, and third, *ibid.* lands depending on rain, divided into, *ibid.*

Jussauwullaun, *probably some particular order of soldiers*, *m.* 235. subsistence of, established at from 1000 to 10,000, *ibid.* were payed yearly together with the infantry &c. in the hall of audience, 237.

K.

Kauruvvauns, *m.* 95,97,153. their departure and arrival, registered by Timour's writers of intelligence, 351.
——— Chiefs of, appointed by Timour to travel into different countries, to bring back merchandize, and to inform him of the situation, manners, and customs of the inhabitants, 215, 217.
Kauruvvaunsurai, *buildings for the reception of travellers*, ordered to be built in every road at the distance of a stage from each other, and people appointed to reside there, 369.
Keesur, *title of the* Turkish *emperors*, 131.
Khaun, *a prince or emperor*, 283.
Khaukaun, *title of the King of Toorkistaun*, 131.
Khauneh, *a house*, 309.
Khillausut, *the office of Khalif*, *m.* 187.
Khirgauh, a Tartar tent or hut, 309.
Khulleesch, *a successor of* Mahummud, *m.* 257. the Fourth Khulleesch, a question proposed to him, 17. his answer, *ibid.* *N.B. This Fourth is* Aali, *who is elsewhere stiled first successor of* Mahummud. *His being called both first and fourth, is occasioned by the different sects of* Mahummudans, *some holding that* Aali *was the first, others that* Aboo Bukkur, Omur, *and* Osmaun *preceded him.* Timour *was of this latter sect, who are called* Sunnites.
Khutbeh, *a discourse read by the* Mullas *on fridays in the Mosques, in which the prince then reigning is prayed for.* Aljauitoo Sooltaun orders the names of the successors of Mahummud to be recited therein, 195.
King, A, ought not speedily to degrade the servant whom he hath exalted, nor to neglect those whom he knoweth or remembreth, 317. but if he chance unjustly to disgrace a faithful servant, he ought to confer double honour upon him, *ibid.* his duty to extirpate the authors of tyranny and oppression from every kingdom, 331, 333. ought to establish the true faith, by invading those countries wherein it is neglected, *ibid.* his duty to invade a kingdom divided by factions, and heresies, 335.
—— twelve Maxims necessary for every one to adhere to, 221. See Maxims.
Kings, nothing more worthy their valour than conquering kingdoms and empires, and waging holy war with infidels, 141. Timour obtained the Thrones of twenty seven, 163.
Koollauh, *a cap*, part of the dress of ceremony, 297.
Koornish, not to be given to the soldiers who turn their backs in battle, 277.
Kootwaul, one appointed in each quarter of Timour's camp, 301. his office, *ibid.*
Koraun, Timour seeks an omen in it concerning his submitting to Tughulluk Timour Khaun, 19. concerning his attacking the army of the Jetes, 75. concerning his taking the absolute command, 89. concerning his invading Hindostaun, 133, *m.* 101.
Kotul, a person appointed to succeed on the death or dismission of an officer, 75.
Koul, *the main body*, 389. when to enter into action, 393, 403. order of the troops near it, 397, 399.
—— of Yeldurrum Bauezzeed, attacked by Aboo Bukkur, 407.
—— of Timour, penetrated to by Shaah Munsoor, *ibid.*
Kulkchee, twelve thousand men of the sword, cantoned in and about the palace, 299.

Kulluck.

Kulluckcheaun, *probably some particular order of soldiers*, m. 235. subsistence of, established at from 1000 to 10,000, *ibid.* payed yearly, together with the infantry, &c. in the hall of audience, 237.

Kullung, *a military mark of distinction*, 291.

Kummur, *a belt or girdle*, 291.

Kuraumuteh, *a sect founded by* Kuramut *in the third century of the Hij.* They seize the city of Mecca under Aboo Tauhir, 185.

Kurrauwul, plur. Kurrauwulaun, *light troops, or scouts*, 65, 401. negligence of, occasions Timour's being surprized by Ouleaus Khaujeh, 65. bring intelligence to him of the army of Ameer Hoossein, 103. are stationed on each side of the Hurrauwul a Hurrauwul, 401.

——— Beghs, *commanders of the* Kurrawulaun, *ibid.*

Kushoon, *a body of military men something less than the Toumaun*, 29, N. Plur. Kushoons, and Kushoonaut, *m.* 85, 323.

M.

Maulaumauni, *imposts*, or duties, 237, and N.

Maxims XII; necessary for every prince to adhere to, 221.

I. To make it evident to all his subjects, that his words and actions are his own, and that none else hath influence therein, *ibid.* to hear the counsel of all, but not to be so far guided thereby, as to make them his equals in the concerns of government, *ibid.*

II. To adhere steadfastly to justice in all his actions, and to employ virtuous and just ministers, *ibid.*

III. To act with such resolution and firmness in his commands, that none may presume to violate them, 223.

IV. To persist invariably in his determinations, till they are brought to a conclusion, *ibid.*

V. To enforce obedience to his commands, whatever be the result, *ibid.*

VI. Not to trust the concerns of government, or his authority, to any one, 225.

VII. To attend to the opinions of his servants, and to select what is good therefrom, 227.

VIII. To be cautious and circumspect in forming his determinations; not suffering himself to be influenced by the information of his officers concerning any one, until the truth be proved, *ibid.*

IX. To so impress the majesty of his dominion on the hearts of his subjects, that none may presume to disobey his commands, *ibid.*

X. To adhere to that which he sayeth; his word being the most valuable of all things, *ibid.*

XI. To consider himself as single and sole governor; not allowing any one to become his associate, 229.

XII. To make himself acquainted with the manners and dispositions of his courtiers and favourites, and to be very cautious in whom he reposeth confidence, *ibid.*

Maxims IV. steadfastly adhered to by Timour in his reduction of kingdoms, 335.

I. To enter upon every enterprize with deep deliberation, and mature counsel, *ibid.*

II. To use policy and circumspection in executing his designs, 337. to inform himself of the dispositions and genius of the natives of every country; and to accommodate himself to their prejudices in the appointment of their governors, *ibid.*

III. To gain the affections and attachment of a select part of his Nobility, *ibid.* See Ameers.

IV. Always to act with expedition, except when delay was policy; and with severity or lenity, as occasion required. Never to commit to the sword what might otherwise be effected.

fected. To spend the day in examining the difficulties of conquest with wise and experienced men, and the night in deliberating, and forming the plan for the execution of his resolutions, 339.

Mendicants, subsistence allowed them by Timour, 349, 361. to be sold, or expelled his dominions, if, after receiving this subsistence, they continued to ask alms, 361.

Meer Toozzuk, *regulators*, *masters of the ceremonies*, 331, and N.

Mingbaushee, *leader of a thousand*, the manner of his appointment, 231. appoints the Euzbaushee, *ib.* his subsistence three times as much as that of the Euzbaushee, 233. receives his pay under the inspection of the Ameer ul Omrau, *ibid.* the interior districts allotted for his subsistence, 237. to be appointed Ameer on his signalizing himself, 275. to be appointed lord of a principality on his defeating the forces of his antagonist, 289. his accoutrements of war, 295. his dress of ceremony, 297. his place in the Deewaun, on the left side of the throne, 329. *m.* 273, 397.

Minister. See Vizzeer.

Miskaul, *an arabic drachm, the 12th. part of an ounce*, *m.* 365.

Mogul words, distinguished from the Persian by an asterisk in this edition, 3, N.

Monastery, one, ordered by Timour to be built in every city, 179.

Mosque, one, ordered to be built in every town by Timour, 371.

Mozeh, *boots*, part of the dress of ceremony of the Ameers, 291,

Musjid (or Mosque) the imperial, the theologians assembled there by Aljauitoo Sooltaun, 189. *m.* 193.

N.

Niccaureh, *a kind of kettle-drum*, 283, and N.

Nooyaun, *a prince or descendant of a prince*, 23, N.

Nouniaun, *of the same signification as the preceeding*, 329.

Nuffeer, *a sort of trumpet*, a military distinction allowed to the Mingbaushee Ameer, 291.

O.

Omens, sought for by Timour previous to all his undertakings, 19. one, drawn from the Koraun, concerning his submission to Tughulluk Timour Khaun, *ibid.* concerning his attacking the Jetes, 75. concerning his taking the absolute sovereignty, 89. concerning his expedition against Hindostaun, 183.

Ounbaushee, *commander of ten*, 229 the manner of his appointment *ib.* upon the death of a soldier has power to appoint another in his place, 231. may be appointed by the Euzbaushee, *ibid.* his subsistence ten times as much as that of the common soldier, 233. receives it under the inspection of the Euzbaushee, *ibid.* his duty not to be imposed on the Euzbaushee, 273. to be appointed Euzbaushee on his signalizing himself, 275. the government of a city to be conferred upon him on his vanquishing an enemy, 289. his accoutrements of war, 295. his dress of ceremony, in time of peace, 297. his place in the Deewaun on the left side of the throne, 329. *m.* 397.

Ouyemauk, *a Tartar hord, or tribe*, 309, &c.

P.

Paishkhauneh, *the tent, or set of tents, of a prince; which on a march are sent forward, and erected against his arrival at every stage*, 385, N.

Peer, *a kind of ghostly father*, 5, N. Timour's Peer, his name and character, *ibid.* his letters to Timour; concerning

concerning government, 5. concerning his seeking protection from Tughulluk Timour Khaun, 17. concerning his being appointed by the theologians Supporter of the Mahummudan faith, 197. concerning the proper administration of empire, 201. concerning the prosperity of wicked men and tyrants; their certain destruction; and why the just sometimes suffer calamities, 341, 343. concerning Mullik Gheaus u deen, 113. concerning Timour's invasion of Erauk, 125.

Philosophers, treated with esteem and veneration by Timour, 165.

Physicians, of Timour's VIII. Class, 213. essential to the dignity of empire, *ibid.* salaries appointed by Timour for those who attended the hospitals, 371.

Plan, Timour rejected every one in which the hazard was two-fold, and chose that where the peril was single, 11. always acted on one which was uniform and good, *ibid.*

Poor, accommodated by Timour agreeably to their situations, 219. almshouses ordered to be built for them in every town and city, 369.

R.

Rebellion, punished, in Timour's sons, by imprisonment, 233. in his relations, by confiscation of their estates, *ibid.* in others, sometimes by death; but not hastily inflicted, 245.

Region, or Climate, the fifth and sixth conquered by Timour, 129. m. 131.

Regulation, Timour's, concerning the division of his people into Classes, 205. concerning those tribes which submitted to him, 217. for the forming his army, 229. the payment of his forces, 231. the distribution of provinces and districts, 237. the maintenance of his children and descendants, 241. the punishments of his children, grand-children, relations, chiefs and ministers, 243, 245. the payment of his ministers and superior officers, 253, 269. the promoting and rewarding his soldiers, 275. the conferring honours and rewards on his Ameers, soldiers, and subjects, 283. concerning the arms and necessaries of soldiers, 293. the honours of the Niccaureh and Standard, 291. concerning the imperial guards, with rules to be observed in the Presence, in times of war and peace, 297. the departments of Vizzeers, 301. the governments of the Ameers of Auloosaut, Kushoonaut, and Toumaunaut, 307. the behaviour of servants towards their prince, and of the prince towards his servants, 313. concerning his own conduct towards friends and enemies, 323. precedency and admission to the imperial presence, 327. the reduction of kingdoms, 331. the obtaining of intelligence and information of the state of all his dominions and subjects, 349. the conduct to be observed towards the people of every country, 355. the shrines of saints and fathers, and concerning gifts and pious donations, *ibid.* taxes, the cultivation, population, and police of the empire, 361. war, 373. the arrangement of Timour's superior armies, 385. twelve military regulations mentioned, *ibid.*

Religion, adherence to, and encouragement of, the chief support of empire, 159. the basis of all grandeur and power in an empire, 175. Mahummudan, the established religion of Timour's empire, *ibid.* its promulgation and support, Timour's first regulation, 177. Timour proclaimed its Restorer and Supporter by the theologians, and declared to be so appointed by God, 183. a propagator of, sent in every century by the Almighty, *ibid.* the foundation of Timour's power kept firm by it, 197. teachers

teachers of, appointed by Timour in every city, 179. and salaries granted them, 357.
Robbers, wherever found, or by whomsoever detected, to be put to death, 251.
Rujjub, *the 7th month of the Mahummudan year*, 153.
Rules, Twelve, established by Timour for the support of his glory and empire, 159.
I. To promote the worship of God, and to propagate the Mahummudan faith throughout the world, *ibid.*
II. To consider his people as divided into XII. different classes, and to assign them suitable stations, *ibid.*
III. To use counsel, deliberation, and provident measures; and to comply with times and occasions, 161.
IV. To regulate the concerns of his empire by order and discipline, *ibid.*
V. To reward liberally his officers and soldiers, *ibid.*
VI. To gain by justice and equity the affections of his people, *ibid.*
VII. To treat with profound respect men of learning and religion, 165.
VIII. To make one business the sole object of his attention, till accomplished; and to regulate his conduct by the good example and institutions of former princes, 167.
IX. To make himself perfectly acquainted with the circumstances and situations of all his subjects, and to appoint over them governors adapted to their manners and wishes, 169.
X. To receive all who submitted to him with distinction and respect, and to honour them according to their different degrees, stations, and merits, 171.
XI. To treat with distinguished favour his relations, and those whom he had known in the days of his adversity, 173.
XII. To hold in high esteem his soldiers; and to honour those of the enemy who had behaved with bravery and fidelity to their prince, *ibid.*

S.

Sauhebaun, *a sort of upper roof for the tent* &c. 295 and N, 297.
Sauir and Huvvauee, the Vizzeer of, his office, 297.
Sawurghaul, pl. Sawurghaulaut, *a grant from the crown of lands or revenues to be enjoyed for ever by the possessor and his heirs*, 305, and N.
School, one, ordered by Timour to be built in every city, 369.
Secretary, confidential, appointed by Timour to minute down all secret transactions and deliberations, 307.
Shuckauwul, *the front line of the right wing*, 389. consists of 3 squadrons in an army of 12,000, *ibid.* of 6 in an army of 40,000, p. 399. when to enter into action, 393, 403.
Siuds, *descendants of Mahummud*, of Timour's III. Class, 205. seventy, massacred by the Ouzbuks, 27. prayers of, implored by Timour, 205. their blessings, supplicated by him on his actions, *ibid.* the greatest advantage reaped from their mediation, 207. victories obtained through their prayers, *ibid.* an instance thereof, *ibid.* twelve holy, restore one of Timour's wives to health for 12 years, each giving her a year of his own existence, *ibid.*
Slander, many people lovers of it, 229.
Soldiers, equally regarded as the subjects by Timour, 209. kept in readiness, and their wages advanced to them before they were due, *ibid.* confined to their respective stations, *ibid.* those rewarded who signalized themselves, *ib.* those of the enemy, incorporated with Timour's troops on their submission, 217. descendants of, enrolled amongst the imperial forces, and promoted according to their conduct, 219. ten distinguished, appoint the Ounbaushee, 229. subsistence

tence of, fixed at the value of their horses, 233. subsistence of the foot, fixed at from 100 to 1000, *ibid.* a written order for their subsistence to be delivered to each, 235. the foot, paid yearly, and the horse, half-yearly, *ibid.* on their being guilty of oppression, to be delivered into the hands of the oppressed, 251. to be promoted to the rank of Ounbaushee, on their first signalizing themselves, 275. their firmness and spirit to be considered, *ibid.* Koornish not to be given to those who turn their backs in battle, 277. those to be pardoned, who flee from absolute necessity, or who are struck with a panic, *ibid.* their wounds to be considered as proofs of their valour, and they to be rewarded accordingly, *ibid.* their rights not to be invaded, *ibid.* not to be deprived of their rank and pay, when advanced in years, *ibid.* the aged warriors to be treated with honour, their counsel to be regarded, and themselves to be considered as the ornaments of the empire, 279. their sons to succeed to their dignity and station, *ibid.* those taken in battle, not put to death by Timour, *ibid.* received into his service, if they consented; if not, were set at liberty, *ibid.* those treated by Timour with honour and confidence, who after behaving faithfully to their Prince, left him through necessity, *ibid.* and 317. their habiliments of war, 293, 295, 297. character of the good and faithful, 313, 315, 317, 319. any one quitting his master in time of peace, may be received by another, 319. the glory of him who defeateth his enemy, to be exhibited in a ten-fold light, and himself to be promoted for the encouragement of others, 321. he to be presented as a gift to the foe, who opposeth his master's interest, and leagueth with the enemy, *ibid.* his duty to bear lightly the shock of the enemy's attack, and to stand firm and patient, 377. to be rewarded with a Kullung, or embroidered Autaukeh, with a horse, sword, and belt, on his distinguishing himself, 291. the insinuations of the envious not to be heard against a valiant one, 321. one of tried magnanimity more valuable than a thousand who want discretion, 7. those prohibited Timour's service, who had been faithless to his enemies, 319. to be received with honour, on their spontaneous return to their master after desertion, 317.

Subordination, neglect of, causeth corruption and violence, 203.

Suddur, or Sedr, his authority, 177, N. appointed by Timour to watch over the conduct of others, to regulate the manners of the times, to appoint superiors in holy offices, and to ordain pensions &c, *ibid.* ordered to lay before Timour all ecclesiastical affairs, 179, 305.

Sunna, *the traditions of* Mahummud, *which by the orthodox* Moslems *are considered as a supplement to the* Koraun, *and of equal authority*, 185.

Supervisors, two appointed by Timour to every province on which a royal assignment was granted, 239. their office, *ibid.*

——— one appointed by the Suddur to inspect the weights and measures, 177.

Surgeons, of Timour's VII. Class, 213. essential to the dignity of empire, *ibid.*

Surmozeh, *a sort of leathern clog covering the foot of the boot*, a part of the dress of ceremony of the Ameers &c. 297.

Sword, one tenth of the requisites for conducting the affairs of dominion, 7. far inferior to policy, *ibid.* nothing to be committed to it, which can otherwise be effected, 339.

Taxes,

T.

Taxes, the poll and house, not to be levied on any town, 349. old ones, to be continued, if agreeable to the subjects of any reduced kingdom, 363. to be determined according to the fertility and quantity of cultivated lands, *ibid.* equal to $\frac{1}{3}$ of the produce, if the lands were watered by perpetual springs, *ibid.* value always fixed according to the value of the necessaries of life, *ibid.* equal to half the produce of the land, divided into Jurreebs, 365. equal to $\frac{1}{3}$ or $\frac{1}{4}$ of the lands depending on rain, *ibid.* not to be collected before the gathering in of the grain, 367. may be collected by threats, but not by actual punishment, 241. a gatherer of, not to be appointed, if the subject pay spontaneously, 367.

—— on herbs &c. determined according to the ancient practice, 367. to be settled according to the Hust and Bood, when the subjects are dissatisfied, *ibid.* collected at three different times after harvest, *ibid.* not settled till three years after the first cultivation of waste lands, and then determined according to the Regulations, *ibid.*

Theologians, of Timour's I. Class, 205. their place in the Deewaun on the right side of the throne, 329. treated by Timour with esteem and veneration, 165. access to him granted them at all times, *ibid.* questions proposed to them by him concerning things lawful and forbidden, 205. those of the enemy received with reverence, on their submission, 217, 357. pensions, salaries, and subsistence allowed them by Timour, 235, 357. they decree Timour to be the Restorer and Promoter of the Mahummudan faith, 181. selections from the works of former ones, 183, 185, 187, 189, 191, 193, 195. were assembled by Aljauitoo Sooltaun, 189. decreed that prayers were due to the descendants of Mahummud, *ibid.* their decree concerning Aljauitoo Sooltaun, 195. concerning Timour, *ibid.*

Toghe, one, to be allowed to the Mingbaushee Ameer, 291. See Cher Toghe.

Toork or Taucheek, explained in N, 217. *m.* 171, 323.

Toorki language (or Mogul) Timour writes in it to Ameer Hoossein, 103.

Toumaun, *a military fief capable of sending forth* 10,000 *fighting men; it also signifies that number of men collected together*, 23, N.

Travellers, of Timour's XII. Class, 215. structures built for them in every road, 179. encouraged by Timour to bring intelligence concerning foreign nations, 215.

Tumghau, *Soldier's pay*, 309, N.

Tyrant, his prosperity not to be ascribed to his merit, 341. the causes of the long duration of his power, *ibid.* dominion rather continued to an infidel than to him, *ibid.* the cause of his increasing prosperity, 343.

U.

Universe, The, preserved from confusion by the deity's being absolute alone, 89.

V.

Victory obtained by the divine favour, not by greatness of armies, 7. Timour's ascribed by him to the aid of the Almighty, 7, 35, 39, 127. obtained by the prayers of devout and pious men, 207. foretold to Timour by a voice from heaven, 79. hidden by the curtain of fate, 145.

Vizzeers, of Timours VII. Class, 211. the most respectable and confidential of the servants of royalty, 245. their place in the Deewaun opposite the throne, 329. their subsistence ten times as much as that of the Ameers, 235. their office to lay before the emperor the affairs of his whole government, 211. to keep the treasury rich, *ibid.* to inspect the revenues and expences of government, *ibid.* not to be hastily punished, when accused of treachery, 245. their punishment, when guilty of peculation, 247, 249. are a class of men who have many enemies, 249. are betrayed by those they patronize, and opposed by those they neglect, *ibid.*

Four qualities necessary for Vizzeers,
I. Firmness and generosity.
II. Understanding and sagacity,
III. A capacity of conciliating mens affections.
IV. Patience under difficulties.

Pre-eminence to be conferred on such ministers by confidence, esteem, discretionary power, and authority, 253, 257.—to be stiled *Lords of the sword and pen*, upon their conquering or preserving a kingdom, 265. to be expelled from their office, if they say evil of others, and endeavour to ruin the good and virtuous, 255. their office not to be conferred on the wicked and revengeful, *ibid.* nor on persons of mean birth, 257.

Vizzeer, a bad, causeth the destruction of his master's power, 223, 259, 267.
——— a wise, he who useth mildness and severity in moderation, 259.
——— a perfect, who never giveth way to revenge, *ibid.*
——— an intelligent and sagacious, who acteth with circumspection and policy, 261.
——— an experienced and active, who attendeth to the population and cultivation of the country, and hazardeth his fortune and life in the service of his master, *ibid.*
——— a virtuous, whose good qualities exceed his failings, 263.
——— a skilful and able, who hath capacity to divide or unite the power of armies, and to sow divisions amongst the enemies of his master, 265. four appointed to attend the imperial Deewaun, subordinate to the Deewaunbeghee, 301, 307.
——— I. of the country and the subject, his office, 303.
——— II. of the armies, his office, *ibid.*
——— III. of the Sauir and Huvvaui, his office, *ibid.*
——— IV. of the imperial house-hold, his office, 305.
——— Three, appointed over the frontiers, and the demesnes of the crown, *ibid.* subordinate to the Deewaunbeghee, *ibid.*
——— Three, to be stationed in every country, 371. their offices, &c. *ibid.*

W.

Wicked and seditious, expelled by Timour from his presence, 201.

Word, nothing so valuable to princes as having a just veneration for it, 227. equal to a family of princes and a rich treasury, *ibid.* maketh numerous subjects and powerful armies, *ibid.*

Y.

Yettool, *a royal grant.* See Jaugheer.

Yole Bolishun, a Mogul expression, used by Timour to Ouleaus Khaujeh, 83.

Yussauwullaun, *a sort of guards or messengers*, their subsistence established at from 1000, to 10,000, p. 235. paid yearly, together with the infantry &c. in the hall of audience, 237.
——— chief of, stationed at the door of the imperial pavilion, 329.

The Names of the principal Perſons and Places mentioned in this Work, according to the different Orthography of Mr. DAVY, and Monſ. PETIS DE LA CROIX; accommodated to the Uſe of thoſe who wiſh to compare the different Accounts.

LA CROIX.		MR. DAVY.
	A.	
Abbas	—	Ubbaus.
Aboubecre	—	Aboo Bukkur.
Akitimur	—	Eekoo Timour.
Aleppo	—	Hullub.
Ali	—	Aali.
Anatolia	—	Room.
Azad	—	Auzaud.
Azerbijane	—	Azzurbauejaun.
	B.	
Bagdad	—	Bughdaud.
Bajazet	—	Keeſur.
Balc	—	Bullukh.
Barcoc	—	Burkook.
Bedakchan	—	Buddukſhaun.
Bei	—	Begh.
Berlas	—	Burlaus.
Bocara	—	Bokhaura.
	C.	
Cabul	—	Kaubul.
Cabulchah	—	Kaubul Shaah.
Cachmir	—	Kuſhmeer.
Can	—	Khaun.
Candahar	—	Kundahaur.
Cannoudge	—	Kunnouj.
Capchac	—	Kipjauk.
Cara	—	Kurrau.
Carezm	—	Khauruzm.
Carſchi	—	Kurſhee.
Caratchar	—	Kurrauchaur.
Catlan	—	Khuttulaun.
Cazagan	—	Kurgun.
Cazanchi	—	Kurraunchee.
Cayaſeddin	—	Gheaus u deen.
Chahmanſour	—	Shaah Munſoor.
Charoc	—	Shaarokh.
Cheik	—	Sheikh.
Chekidgek	—	Chuckchuck.
Chir	—	Share.
Chiras	—	Sharauze.
Chirkunt	—	Sharekund.
Chirouan	—	Shurwaun.
Cogende	—	Khojjund.
Coja	—	Khaujeh.
Condoz	—	Kunduz.
Coraſſane	—	Khorauſaun.
Cotan	—	Khuttun.
Cotluc	—	Kuttulug.
	D.	
Damaſcus	—	Dummiſhk.

Deli

La Croix.		Mr. Davy.
Deli	——	Dehli.
Diarbekir	——	Deaur a Bukkur.

E.

La Croix.		Mr. Davy.
Egypt	——	Miſſur.
Elias	——	Ouleaus.
Emeſa	——	Hums.
Emir	——	Ameer.
Enderabe	——	Anduraub.
Erlat	——	Aurlaut.

F.

La Croix.		Mr. Davy.
Fars	——	Fauris.

G.

La Croix.		Mr. Davy.
Gehanghir	——	Jehaungheer.
Gelair	——	Jullauir.
Georgia	——	Goorjiſtaun.
Gete	——	Jitteh.
Ghengis Can	——	Chungauze Khaun.
Gihon	——	Jihoon.

H.

La Croix.		Mr. Davy.
Hadgi	——	Haujee.
Herat	——	Hurraut.
Houlacou Can	——	Hullaukoo Khaun
Huſſein	——	Hooſſein.

I.

La Croix.		Mr. Davy.
Irac Agemi	——	Erauk a Ajjum.
Irac Arabi	——	Erauk a Arrub
Iſpahan	——	Isfahaun.

K.

La Croix.		Mr. Davy.
Kech	——	Kuſh.
Kei Coſru	——	Ki Khiſſero.
Kerbela	——	Kurbullau.
Ketuer	——	Kuttoor.
Kirman	——	Kurmaun.
Kivac	——	Khiook.

M.

La Croix.		Mr. Davy.
Macan	——	Maukhaun.
Mahmoud	——	Muhmud.
Mahomet	——	Mahummud.
Malatia	——	Mulluteah.
Malek	——	Mullik.
Mazenderan	——	Mauzinduraun.
Mellou Can	——	Mulloo Khaun.
Mir	——	Ameer.
Miranchah	——	Meeraun Shaah.
Mirza	——	Ameer Zaudeh.
Mobarekchah	——	Mubbauruk Shaah
Mouſſa	——	Mooſi.
Muaid	——	Muviud.

N.

La Croix.		Mr. Davy.
Nevian	——	Nooyaun.

O.

La Croix.		Mr. Davy.
Oladgia Itou	——	Aljauitoo.
Olagiai	——	Aljaiè.
Olatchou	——	Aulaujou.
Oluc	——	Allugh.
Oughanian	——	Afghaun, and Oughaun.
Ourous Can	——	Auroos Khaun.
Oxus	——	Jihoon.

P.

La Croix.		Mr. Davy.
Poulad	——	Boulau.

S.

La Croix.		Mr. Davy.
Saddic	——	Suddeuk.

Samarcande

La Croix.		Mr. Davy.
Samarcande	—	Summurkund.
Sebaste	—	Seewaus.
Sultan	—	Sooltaun.
Syria	—	Shaum.
	T.	
Tauris	—	Tubburaze.
Tekil	—	Tukkul.
Termed	—	Turmuz.
Timur	—	Timour.
Timur Bec	—	Abu'l Munsoor Timour, and Ameer Timour.
Tocatmich	—	Touktummish.
Tocluc	—	Tughulluk.
Touchi	—	Jouji.
Transoxiane	—	Mauwur u Nuhur.

La Croix.		Mr. Davy.
	U.	
Uzbec	—	Ouzbuk.
	V.	
Veli	—	Aali.
	Y.	
Yakou	—	Jaukoo.
Yousef	—	Eusoof.
	Z.	
Zagataie	—	Chugtauee.

SPECIMENS

OF

COMPOSITION

IN THE

PERSIAN LANGUAGE

See the PREFACE.

The Exordium of JAUMI's Poem, entitled, *Eusoof* and *Zoolleikha*.

IN the name of him whose name is the refuge of the Souls *of the faithful*;
Whose praise is the ornament of eloquent tongues.
The most high, the only God, the eternal, the omniscient;
He who bestoweth strength and *power* on the feeble *and the helpless.*
The heavens he illumines with multitudes of constellations;
And with the human race he decorateth the earth, as with stars.
He who prepared the vaulted roof of the revolving sphere,
Who raised up the quadruple fold of the elements.
He who gives fragrance to the bosom of the rose-bud,
And ornamenteth the parent-shrub with wreaths of flowers.
He weaveth the garment for the brides of the spring,
And teacheth the graceful cypress to erect his head on the border *of the lake.*
He crowneth with success the virtuous intention,
And humbleth the pride of the self-conceited.
He accompanies the solitude of those who watch the midnight *taper*;
He passeth the day with the children of affliction.
From the sea of his bounty issues the vernal cloud,
Which waters alike the thorn and the jessamine.

From

From the repoſitory of his beneficence proceeds the autumnal
gale,
Which beſpangles with gold the carpet of the garden.
It is his preſence that enflameth the orb of day,
From whence every atom derives its light.
Should he hide his countenance from the two great luminaries
of the world,
Their *mighty* ſpheres would deſcend quick into the area of an-
nihilation.
From the vault of heaven to the centre of the earth,
Which ever way we direct our thought and imagination;
Whether we deſcend, or haſten upwards,
We ſhall not diſcover one atom uninfluenced by his power.
Wiſdom is confounded in the contemplation of his eſſence;
The inveſtigation of his ways exceeds the powers of man.
The angels bluſh at their want of comprehenſion;
And the heavens are aſtoniſhed at their own motion.

A PRAYER directed by the BRAHMINS to be offered up to the Supreme Being; written originally in the *Shanscrit* Language, and translated by C. W. BOUGHTON ROUSE, Esq; from a Persic Version of *Dara Shekoo*, a Son of *Shah Jehan*, Emperor of Hindostan.

O RUDER, I reverence thee in thy Majesty and in thy Displeasure. I reverence thy Arrows, which convey destruction; and thy bow, thy quiver, and thy arms, which are the givers of victory. Look toward me with that countenance of benignity, mild like the face of the moon, by which thou bestowest joy, and doest away all sins.

O THOU, who art the Lord of mighty mountains, dispel the pains of all mankind; make them joyful and defend them from harm: and grant that I may remain secure under thy guardianship and protection. Thou art the great Physician of Physicians! heal thou my infirmities; disperse my vicious and malevolent inclinations, which lead me into the road of evil.

I REVE-

I REVERENCE thee in the Sun, which is thy Image, whilst it ſcatters a hundred thouſand vivifying rays over the univerſe whilſt in meridian brightneſs it diffuſes gladneſs; nor leſs when at morn or eve its flaming countenance denotes thy anger. Turn away that anger from me. I reverence him who is the ſource of joy to living creatures, whoſe nature is exempt from decay, and knows not the increaſe of age. — To Him and all that ſprings from Him I owe reverence and honour.

O RUDER, ſtring thy bow to defend me from all my open or ſecret enemies. Shoot the arrows of thy quiver to deſtroy them. When thou haſt deſtroyed my enemies and unſtrung thy bow, and taken off the points of thy arrows, and art rejoiced; then grant that I likewiſe may rejoice. But thy bow is not like other bows, nor thy arrows like other arrows. Thou neededſt not to ſtring the bow, nor to ſharpen the points of arrows. Thou neededſt not the ſword like other ſwords, to accompliſh thy purpoſes. O thou who canſt fulfil deſires, whoſe deſigns no enemy can baffle, guard and protect me on every ſide, and drive my enemies far from me.

O RUDER, thy arm is like ſhining gold. Thou art the Lord of all armies. All cauſes of things have their origin in thee. Thou art the cauſe of cauſes. Thou art ſpace. The verdure of the fields is thine. Thou art Lord of all the beaſts, and the birds, and other living creatures. Thou art the Guide. Every light that ſhines is thy light. Thou entereſt into all: thou ſuſtaineſt all.

O PUNISHER of thoſe who go aſtray, O Lord of life, O pureſt of Beings! terrify not thy creatures, ſtrike them not, deſtroy them not: nor let even one of them ſuffer pain from thee. O thou, who giveſt ſtrength to the feeble, and medicines to the ſick; grant me thy ſupport, that I may enjoy health and

live.

live. O RUDER, turn my underſtanding toward thee, for thou art the Lord of power. I beſeech thee to keep all creatures which belong to me, whether man or beaſt, in quiet and ſecurity. Preſerve all the inhabitants of this city. Afflict them not with ſickneſs: do thou, RUDER, give them health, and drive diſeaſes far from them. We all come before thee in ſupplication. Grant unto us all thoſe bleſſings, which our fathers aſked of thee for us, when they were deſirous of bringing us into exiſtence. Old men, and young children, and infants yet unborn, all join in ſacrifice and prayer unto thee. O thou, who art ever young and mighty, thou ſource of joy, be gracious toward me. O thou, who wanteſt nothing, who art worthy of adoration, I reverence thee. O thou, who employeſt thy arms for my ſecurity, who haſt thouſands of thouſands of weapons; ſcatter my enemies, and deſtroy them: for thou, RUDER, art ſupreme in every part of nature. Exert for my protection thy powers, which are over the earth, the air, and the heavens, and under the earth: which ſhew themſelves in the plains, in the vegetation of the trees, in the various ſpecies of living creatures, in the waters, and in food provided for the ſupport of life. Thou, who deſtroyeſt all which eat the food and drink the waters; who art amidſt the guardians of the highways and in the places of worſhip; in all thou art the infinite RUDER: in every one I implore thee to protect me, and to diſarm my enemies. To thee, and all thy other various powers and attributes not here enumerated, I offer reverence. Ten times toward the Eaſt, ten times toward the South, ten times toward the Weſt, and ten times toward the North, I bow myſelf before thy earthly powers, and invoke their aid that I may enjoy health and ſee the deſtruction of my enemies. Ten times toward the Eaſt, ten times toward the South, ten times toward the Weſt, ten times toward the North, and ten times with my eyes on Heaven above, I bow myſelf before thy aerial and heavenly powers, whoſe arrows are the wind and rain: I invoke their aid, that

I may

I may enjoy health, and ſee the deſtruction of my enemies. Every one of theſe is RUDER; whoſe infinite power I reverence: RUDER, whoſe fullneſs is in all. All that has been, it is He. All that is, it is He. All that ſhall be, it is He.

The foregoing Prayer is extracted from the Judger Bede: *to which it may be curious to ſubjoin a Deſcription of* RUDER, *to whom it is addreſſed, as contained in another ſacred Book, intitled the* Atherbun Bede.

THE Angels having aſſembled themſelves in Heaven before RUDER, made obeiſance and aſked him, O RUDER, what art thou? RUDER replied, were there any other, I would deſcribe myſelf by ſimilitude. I always was, I always am, and always ſhall be. There is no other, ſo that I can ſay to you, I am like Him. In this Me is the inward eſſence, and the exterior ſubſtance of all things. I am the primitive cauſe of all. All things that exiſt in the Eaſt, or Weſt, or North, or South, above or below, it is I. I am all. I am older than all. I am King of Kings. My attributes are tranſcendent. I am truth. I am the ſpirit of creation; I am the Creator. I am the knowledge of the four BEDES.* I am Almighty. I am purity. I am the firſt, and the middle, and the end. I am the light. And for this purpoſe do I exiſt, that whoſoever knows Me, may know all the angels, and all books, and all their ordinances. And whoſoever knows the learning of the Bedes, from thence he will learn the duties of life, he will underſtand truth, and his actions will be virtuous. And to thoſe who practiſe virtue, will I give fullneſs and tranquillity.

RUDER having pronounced theſe words to the Angels, was abſorbed in his own brightneſs.

* The ſacred Writings of the Hindoos in the *Shanſcrit* language.

THE foregoing Specimens I intended to have introduced by an Essay of some extent on the great importance and utility of the Persian *Language, and by a Proposal for establishing a* Persian *Professorship in the University of Oxford. But having since met with a pamphlet of much merit, written some years ago by Governor* HASTINGS, *directed to the same object, I have thought it unnecessary to prosecute my design.*

Whilst I was engaged in writing the intended Essay *and* Proposal, *I received from Mr.* DAVY, *in answer to my repeated enquiries, the following* LETTER: *which places the importance of the* Persian *Language for transacting the Company's affairs in* India, *in so clear and just a light; is founded throughout on such striking facts; and supported and illustrated with so many judicious observations and remarks; that I conceived it to be highly worthy the attention of the* East India Company, *and of the Gentlemen in their service. Impressed with this idea, notwithstanding I afterwards relinquished my original design, I determined, if possible, to lay the Letter before the Public: but as it was communicated for my private use only, Mr.* DAVY'S *approbation was necessary for the purpose; which, at my particular solicitation, he has been pleased to grant.*

Gloucester, Sept. 24. 1779.

MY GOOD FRIEND,

IN compliance with your repeated applications, I have at length taken up my pen, with a determination to reply as fully as possible to all your Enquiries.

"I CANNOT communicate any "important facts of times or places, when and where a want of knowledge of the Persian in the servants of the Company has been attended with particular disadvantage to their affairs *in a political point of view*:" one only, supported by proof, occurs to my memory, of which I shall shortly take notice. Such facts, in their full extent at least, have not lately existed; because, for some years past, a a few gentlemen have been found tolerably well qualified to act as Persian interpreters in the transaction of the Company's more important concerns with the native Powers. That such facts did formerly exist, is certain; and that the want of such knowledge now would be attended with still worse effects is as certain. To prove which, I think, you will meet with little difficulty. The same reasons which will establish the authority of the fore-going observations, will moreover be sufficient to prove the positive necessity of a still more extensive and general knowledge of the Persian, than has hitherto been acquired by the gentlemen in India.

WE

"We are to consider, that the territories now under the dominion of the East India Company, the provinces of *Bengal* and *Bahar*, with part of *Orissa*, the coast of *Coromandel*, and the settlements on that of *Malabar*, are together twice as extensive as Great Britain and Ireland. In a word, such is their extent, and such their importance, that it has been deemed necessary to keep on foot an army of fifty thousand disciplined men for their defence and protection: for that is the amount of the forces of the three establishments, *Bengal*, *Madrass*, and *Bombay*. These rich and fertile territories, except where embraced by the ocean, are separated and surrounded by native independent Princes and Powers, some of them exceedingly formidable. It follows, that dominions so extensive and so situated, must be secured and protected as much by policy as by arms: a vast political system must be established; an exact and perfect balance of power must be preserved; the weak must be supported, the too powerful must be circumscribed and depressed. For these purposes Friendships, Alliances, and Treaties, must be formed with some in opposition to others; and these Alliances, Treaties, and Friendships, must again be dissolved, and give way to others, as the strength, influence, and resources of the different independent Princes of the Empire may be diminished or increased. Hence the everlasting train of conferences, correspondences, and negotiations, with the native Powers. Hence the necessity of watching their motions, discovering their hidden strength and resources, and diving into their secret councils, connections, and alliances. These are all businesses of the first importance; they require the strictest integrity, and the most profound secrecy in the negotiators: and finally, these businesses are all to be transacted in, and by the assistance of, the Persian tongue.

"Mr. Orme, a very accurate and able historian, whose long residence in India enabled him to acquire a perfect knowledge of the ſubject, gives a very ſtriking inſtance of the fatal conſequences that may enſue from employing native interpreters in our tranſactions with the princes of Hindoſtan; and judiciouſly points out the poſitive neceſſity of entruſting the execution of ſuch important concerns to European gentlemen only *. Nothing indeed can be more abſurd or dangerous, than for the government in India to rely on the honour and integrity of natives for the tranſaction of ſuch weighty, political matters, as I have pointed out; and more eſpecially to confide in that inferior claſs of them, who are content to bear the yoke of ſervitude under a foreign power from neceſſity, or pecuniary motives. Such are all the native ſervants to Europeans. But that natives of a ſuperior rank are not altogether proof againſt the influence of gold, I have met with ſeveral inſtances. A very ſtrong evidence of the above aſſertion I have now in my poſſeſſion; namely, exact copies of all the Letters wrote by the reigning Mogul, *Shaab Aulum*, in the years 71, 72, 73, to the ſeveral independent Princes of the Empire. Theſe copies were regularly tranſmitted by one of the King's confidential ſecretaries, and often came into my poſſeſſion, before the perſons to whom they were ſent could receive the originals. By this means the councils, negotiations, and intrigues of the court of Dehli, and of others, the native Powers and Princes of Hindoſtan, were entirely laid open to our inſpection. This happened during the period that I had the honour to fill the poſt of Perſian Secretary to SIR ROBERT BARKER, the then commander in chief of the forces of *Bengal*. The above, I think, is a ſtrong and pointed proof: and it follows, that European gentlemen only can, in prudence and in policy, be entruſted with this important buſineſs; and that a partial knowledge of the Perſian Language is by no means ſufficient to qualify even them to be truſted. To be able ſimply to converſe in the Perſian, is a very inade-

* Vide Hiſt. of the Military Tranſactions of the Britiſh Nation in Hindoſtan. Vol. I. p. 350, &c.

quate

quate degree of knowledge. A Persian interpreter should not only be able to speak fluently in the Language, but to read all such Letters as he may receive; not only to read all such Letters, but to answer them with his own hand, if the importance of the subject, of which they treat, should render it necessary. Otherwise the secret negotiations and correspondence of government are liable to be made public through the medium of the native *Munchees*, or Writers, whom he will be obliged to employ and trust. Some natives he must have, to assist in the ordinary business, from its great multiplicity; but even this, by a proper encouragement of the study of the Language, might be obviated. Junior servants, when qualified, might be appointed to act under their Seniors, and the natives be totally excluded. And such a Plan, I am convinced, would be productive of much advantage.

"FROM the foregoing hints, I dare say, you will be able to prove, that the study of the Persian, in a political point of view, is highly worthy of encouragement.

"THE general study of this valuable Language, abstracted from all political views, is a matter of very great importance to the East India Company. How it is possible that their civil servants should be able to do their duty effectually in the various posts and offices to which they are appointed, without any knowledge of it, is difficult to conceive. That by far the greater number of them do perform the businesses allotted to them without a knowledge of any of the country Languages, is certain; but that the manner in which they perform them must be exceedingly defective, every one will be convinced, by reflecting on the nature of the offices which they fill. Servants of all ranks * are detached from the presidency, and spread

* By these are meant Writers, Factors, junior and senior Merchants, and in the more important departments, often members of the Council: but these last are generally assisted by European Interpreters.

abroad

abroad throughout the provinces and districts of the Company's territories, for the purposes of superintending the cultivation and regulation of the countries, the administration of justice in the *Kucheries*, or native courts of Judicature, and the collection of the Revenues *. Many also are appointed to the different Factories, to superintend the fabrication and making up of the Investments for the European market.

"HAVING given this detail of the employments, to which the senior and junior civil servants of the Company are in rotation appointed, I think it will be needless to dwell on the great utility, and indeed absolute necessity of a knowledge of some language or other, understood in the country, to gentlemen so employed †; or to shew how much more effectually they would be able, with such knowledge, to do their duty, than they can now through the medium of their *Surcors*, or native Clerks ‡, to whom, from an ignorance of the language, they are obliged, in a great measure, to delegate their authority, to pay an implicit attention to their advice and opinions, and, what is still worse, from the above deficiency, to receive through them every complaint and grievance of the subject; though the complaints are frequently levelled against those very Agents,

* It may be necessary to observe, that this arrangement took place but a very few years ago; and therefore the importance of the Persian in the point of view now under consideration, is to be dated from that period only.

† It is true, that *in Bengal*, but in Bengal only, an acquaintance with the dialect of that province, might be made to answer the purposes of gentlemen employed as above-mentioned: but as that dialect would be of very little use to them, even in the neighbouring province of Bahar, much less in any other part of Hindostan; as the Persian, on the contrary, is the polite language throughout the Empire; and as it is impossible to acquire a knowledge of that, without forming, at the same time, a familiar acquaintance with the *Moors*, from the intimate connection between them; and as the *Moors* is the vulgar tongue of all the Mahummudan natives, and is as well known to the generality of the Aborigines or Hindoos, as to the Mahummudans themselves; for these reasons it is evident, that the Persian is most worthy the attention of Europeans.

‡ The *Surcors* are all Hindoos; and by some little knowledge of the English, which they are careful to acquire, are enabled to act as Interpreters to the gentlemen who employ them.

and

and the grievances complained of generally originate from their knavery, avarice, and extortion.

"True it is, that in *Bengal*, the Dialect bearing that name is now most frequently used in the transacting of mercantile concerns; but it does not follow, that the Persian language, and that of Hindostan (vulgarly called the *Moors*) are therefore entirely superfluous: on the contrary, I conceive it to be easy to prove, that if the Company's civil servants were generally acquainted with the Persian, they would find themselves enabled to fill every department in which they could possibly be placed, without the assistance of any medium whatever.

"In a *private commercial light* also, I think, much may be said in its favour. Individuals, such as could find leisure to study the language, would reap a singular advantage from the knowledge of it. In the western provinces of Hindostan, though not so universally in Bengal, the Persian is used in all mercantile transactions: and if the study of it was generally followed, and applied to practice, hundreds of *Surcors* and *Banians*, who now eat up two thirds of the merchants profits, oppress the country under the name of English *Gomausbtehs*, and brand the character of their masters with infamy, might be discarded and turned adrift; or at least meet with such checks, as would, in a great measure, put a stop to their rogueries.

"It may be further observed, that the study of the Persian is by no means unworthy the attention of the *Military*, for this plain reason; because it is the best, and indeed the only road to a perfect acquaintance with the language of Hindostan; without which, no officer, however great his military abilities, can be esteemed properly qualified to command a battalion of our native troops. The loss of more than one detachment from that very deficiency, has proved this beyond dispute. It may be added, that an officer on a detached command, must always have

have occaſion to correſpond, ſometimes to negotiate with the chief men of the diſtricts and provinces, where he may be, or through which he may have occaſion to paſs: and theſe negotiations, however trifling they may at firſt appear, have been frequently known to lead to matters of vaſt importance. This is another, and, I think, no bad reaſon, why an officer ought to be acquainted with the Perſian and Hindoſtan languages.

“ In oppoſition to the foregoing it may be aſſerted, that the difficulties attending the ſtudy and acquiſition of a copious and elegant language, differing totally from our own in phraſe and idiom, and cloathed in unknown, complex, and obſcure characters, would be inſurmountable to many; and that the various occupations and buſineſſes, in which the Company's ſervants in India are employed, cannot afford them leiſure and opportunity to engage in ſo troubleſome and arduous an undertaking; and therefore, as heretofore, the acquiſition of this valuable knowledge muſt be left to thoſe young men, who, from curioſity, ambition, or ſuperior abilities, are inclined to devote themſelves to ſuch difficult ſtudies. In reply to the *firſt* of the above objections, I can, from perſonal knowledge, venture to affirm, That a very moderate ſhare of abilities and of memory, ſupported by a common proportion of perſeverance and attention, are ſufficient to overcome the ideal difficulties, ariſing from the copiouſneſs of the language itſelf, from the difference of the idiom, and from the obſcurity of the character.

“ In anſwer to the *ſecond*, I will allow that the occupations and employments of the Company's junior ſervants are many and various; and that if pleaſure and diſſipation be admitted of the number, they have not a moment to ſpare. But ſuppoſing it practicable for them to curtail their attendance on the laſt mentioned important buſineſſes but for two ſhort hours in the day, I do aſſert, that they may with eaſe make themſelves

maſters

mafters of the language, and that in a very moderate fpace of time.

"The advantages arifing from a knowledge of the Perfian to gentlemen in India have not, till within thefe few years, been perfectly underftood. In fact, its *general* utility has not exifted but from that period, when the Company found it neceffary to place the entire adminiftration of the provinces of *Bengal* and *Bahar* in the hands of their own proper fervants. It is therefore reafonable to fuppofe, that a circumftance which did not immediately ftrike many of the ableft of their fuperior officers abroad, could not fuddenly engage the attention of their adminiftration at home. And hence we muft account for the little encouragement hitherto given to the ftudy of the Perfian language.

"But I conceive it is now evident, that the Court of Directors, from the information which they have from time to time received, are fully convinced of its great utility; and that they are determined to promote the cultivation of it to the utmoft of their power. For to this intention we muft afcribe the very neceffary encouragement which they have given to the learned Author of the Perfian and Arabic Dictionary; the firft volume of which has been already publifhed. Of this valuable work, as appears by the printed propofals, they have engaged to take one hundred and fifty copies: which, it is reafonable to fuppofe, they intend to diftribute among their fervants abroad, and thereby to facilitate the ftudy of the language, now rendered infinitely more eafy than it was formerly, by the labours of the foregoing and another learned Author; whofe Grammar, added to this Dictionary, has entirely removed every poffible impediment. Indeed, all that appears wanting at prefent to promote a general application to the Perfian in India, is a proper encouragement on the part of the Eaft India Company, fupported by their orders and authority; and a confequent conviction in their junior ſervants, that a knowledge of that language is neceſſary to their promotion. If they were taught to know, that an acquaintance with the Perſian was the principal avenue, through which they were to expect to arrive at ſuperior rank, and that that knowledge for the future would be ſo far ſubſtituted in the place of ſeniority, as to render ſeniority of no avail without it, it would then become the principal object of the junior claſſes of their ſervants; and the language of courſe would be generally ſtudied.

"It may be added, that the above ſcheme, though a partial, would be no bad ſcale, by which to meaſure the abilities of their younger ſervants: for though a knowledge of that language in the perſons who poſſeſſed it, could not point out the extent of their abilities; yet the want of that knowledge in thoſe who could not acquire it, would certainly diſcover thoſe who had no abilities at all. For a man who, ſo circumſtanced, wanted talents, memory, or perſeverance to form a moderate acquaintance with any language whatever; although he might make a tolerable ſmith, or carpenter, or bricklayer, would certainly turn out a very bad merchant, a very indifferent inſpector of a province, or military officer.

"In my ideas of the utility and importance of a knowledge of the Perſian in the ſervants of the Company, I am ſupported by the opinions of ſeveral of the firſt Characters who have appeared in India; amongſt whom, Mr. Hastings, now Preſident of the ſupreme Council in *Bengal*, and the late Governor Vansittart, are particularly diſtinguiſhed. Thoſe gentlemen did not think the Perſian unworthy their attention; they found leiſure to acquire a knowledge of that, and, conſequently, of the language of Hindoſtan; in which they doubtleſs found their advantage. And I have been credibly informed, that both Mr. Vansittart and Mr. Hastings had in contemplation the eſtabliſhment of an Academy in England, in order

order to promote the ſtudy of the Perſian language; and to enable ſuch young men, as were intended for the India ſervice, to acquire the rudiments of that uſeful knowledge at home. The return of theſe gentlemen to India rendered their intentions abortive: but thoſe intentions, neverthelеſs, tend to prove the high idea they entertained of its importance and utility.

"In a word, the neceſſity of a knowledge of the Perſian, to gentlemen reſiding in India, may, I think, be placed in a very clear point of view, by the following conciſe and ſimple Query, or Compariſon. If an inhabitant of France, a Spaniard, a Swede, or a Dane, were to viſit England with a view of improving his fortunes, would it not be neceſſary for him to learn the language of this country, in order to render himſelf capable of filling any employment whatever, either Civil or Military?

"The general ſtudy of the Perſian language would be productive of one other advantage to the Eaſt India Company, well worthy their attention. From the ſmallneſs of the number of thoſe who have acquired a practical knowledge of the Perſian language, and the ſtill ſmaller number who have returned to England poſſeſſed of that knowledge, I have been led to believe, that a Department, which I ſhould conſider of much importance to the Company, has not hitherto been eſtabliſhed. If the ſtudy of the Perſian ſhould meet with the encouragement it merits, and, in conſequence thereof, the application to that ſtudy ſhould become general, many gentlemen might return from India well qualified for the purpoſe, and with ſuch moderate fortunes, as might not place them above the acceptance of the office I am about to point out. It is well known, that the Court of Directors annually receive from their ſettlements in India, Letters, Memorials, Treaties, and other important papers, in the Perſian language, tranſmitted to them as vouchers by their officers abroad. It is true, that tranſlations of ſuch Papers are uſually ſent with the originals. But it muſt be well known to gentlemen converſant in India affairs, that from *many circumstances*, accurate translations of such Letters, Memorials, and Treaties, by a gentleman unbiassed by party, faction, or interest, and under their own immediate protection, must be highly acceptable and advantageous to the India Government at home. Such a person would also be able to translate into the Persian language all such Treaties and Letters, as they might have occasion to send or write to the native Powers of Hindostan; which might be transmitted to India under their proper Seal, and consequently not be liable to an erroneous translation abroad.

"I HAVE been informed from good authority, that several gentlemen in the Direction, a very few years ago, were sufficiently convinced of the utility of such an establishment. The arrangement and expences of a regular Persian Secretary's Office at the India House, by some who are advocates for œconomy, might be esteemed an objection: but this, I conceive, may be easily obviated. For such a person as I have pointed out, might be induced, for a moderate salary to undertake the Office: he might reside in, or at any distance from the Capital; the necessary papers might be transmitted to him by their proper Secretary for the time being, and might be returned by him to the same Secretary, with their translations.

"THE foregoing Observations contain all that occurs to me on the subject, and I sincerely wish, that they may afford you some little assistance, in proving the high importance of Persian literature; and that you will be enabled to point out the propriety of promoting in this country the study of a language, so necessary to the servants of the Company, so advantageous to the Company themselves; and, from the extent and wealth of their Territories and Commerce, not an unimportant object to the British Nation.

I am, &c.

WILLIAM DAVY"

FINIS.

آورده است می گوید که ازروی همین یادداشتها و بکمك آنها تیمور بعدها تاریخ زندگانی خود و طرحها و تعبیه‌های خویش‌را شخصاً نگاشت ولی چون تاریخ خصوصی بود نسخهٔ آن منتشر نشد، و شرف‌الدّین علی یزدی و میرخواند صاحب روضة‌الصّفا آن‌را ندیدند و فقط بدست مورخین دورتر و متأخرتر (= ابوطالب حسینی!) رسید.

چون این گفتار مستر دیوی مبتنی بر دلیل و مدرکی نیست و بطلان این انتساب امروز مسلم است ارزش آن‌را ندارد که بتفصیل باز گفته شود.

جوزف هوایت در انتهای مقدّمهٔ خود فهرستی از گفتارهای حکیمانهٔ امیرتیمور که‌درضمن این کتاب آمده‌است چاپ کرده‌است. این فهرست‌را که بانگلیسی است شخصی از دوستان وی بنام‌هندرسن Hendersen از روی همین ترجمه ترتیب داده، و عبارات استخراج شده ازان‌را درتحت چهارعنوان: گفتارهای سیاسی، گفتارهای‌نظامی، وقایع‌مهم، گفتارهای دینی، تدوین کرده است.

خردادماه ۱۳۴۲

مجتبی مینوی

است اطلاع داده‌است که : نسخه‌ای که متن از روی آن چاپ و با ترجمه‌منتشر شده‌است در کتبخانهٔ دکترویلیام‌هنتر Dr. W. Hunter محفوظ است*. ترجمهٔ فصلی از این نسخه‌را نمونه‌وار در ۱۷۸۰ من منتشر کردم و بسیارمورد توجه شد؛ و خواستم تمام‌را ترجمه کنم در نقل اصطلاحات نظامی‌و تعبیرات مأخوذ اززبان تاتاری چنان‌اشکالاتی پیش راه من آمد که ناچارکار ترجمه‌را به مستر دیوی محوّل کردم که هم‌ازلحاظ آشنائی بفنّ نظام ، وهم از جهت علم به‌زبان،شایستگی بیشتر دارد . ترجمه‌را تمام کردو بهندوستان رفت و کار نشر کتاب بعهدهٔ من افتادو در مراقبت نشرمتن‌و طبع ترجمه‌و تهیّهٔ فهرست به وظیفه‌ای که داشتم عمل کردم. طبع این‌متن‌و ترجمه علاوه براینکه خواننده‌را با محصول فکر تیمور آشنا می کندو از اعمال اوآگاه می سازد وسیلهٔ خوبیست از برای تعلّم زبان فارسی که امروز در مستملکات ما درهندوستان بجهت انگلیسیهائی که آنجا مانده‌اند وکار می کنند کمال لزوم را داردو موجب امتیازو مزیت‌است .

سپس‌نامه‌ای‌را نقل می کند که‌مستر دیوی راجع به اصیل‌بودن یا حقیقت نداشتن نسبت این تزوکات به‌شخص امیرتیمور نوشته‌است . وی دلایل و براهینی بر صحّت این انتساب اقامه کرده‌است که کلیهٔ آنها استحسانی‌است‌و خود او اقرار کرده‌است که هیچ برهان تاریخی بر صحیح بودن این نسبت بدست نیاورده است . بعد از آنکه ملخّص اقوال شرف‌الدّین علی یزدی‌را (که سابقاً گذشت) ترجمه کرده و

---

* بنده نمی‌داندآن نسخه فعلاکجاست و آن کتابخانه یاموزهٔ دکترهنتر چه شده‌است .

عمایم از سادات و علماءو فقهاءو اهل فضل‌و دانش از بخشیان ایغور و دبیران فرس ملازم می‌بوده‌اند و همواره جمعی ازیشان بر حسب فرمان هرچه وقوع می‌یافت از صادرات افعال و اقوال آن حضرت‌و واردات‌احوال ملك و ملّت‌و ارکان دولت همه‌را تحقیق نموده‌باهتمامی تمام قلمی می کردند ، وحکم چنان بود که هر قضیّه چنانچه درواقع بوده باز نموده‌شود بی تصرّفی‌دران بزیادتی و نقصان ... وهم‌به‌اشارت علیّهٔ آن حضرت اصحاب‌بلاغت‌و براعت آن‌را کسوت‌عبارت پوشانیده بنظم‌و نثردر سلك تألیف می کشیدندبهمان شرط که در ضبط آن‌رفته بود ، و بکرّات در مجلس عالی بسمع مبارك می رسانیدنـد تا وثوق تمام بصحّت آن حاصل می‌شدو بدین نمط منظومه‌ای ترکی و مؤلفی فارسی هریك ازان مشتمل بر معظّمات احوال و اوضاع آن حضـرت رقم زدهٔ‌کلك نظم‌و تألیف شده بود ... حضرت سلطنت پناهی (یعنـی شاهرخ) مجموع نسخ مذکوررا از منظوم‌و منثور ترکی‌و فارسی از تمام ممالك طلب داشته جمع آمده بودو آماده نهاده ... الی آخر .

با وجود این نسبت کتاب ابوطالب حسینی به امیرتیمورامروز مورد قبول محققین نیست ، و اگرچه متنی ترکی وجود داشته است او آن‌را در دست نداشته ، و بهرحال آن‌هم انشای خود تیمور نبوده است ، و مسلماً بعضی از اشارات تاریخی آن با آنچه در ظفرنامه‌های شامی‌و یزدی‌و تواریخ دیگرآمده‌است اختلاف فاحش دارد . مع‌هذا کتاب بخواندن می‌ارزد ، و مخصوصاًاز این‌حیث که‌فارسی وانگلیسی آن باهم‌است از برای دانش‌آموزان و دانشجویان سودمنداست .

در مقدّمه‌ای که جوزف‌هوایت‌بر متن‌و ترجمهٔ چاپ خودنوشته

افزوده‌است حذف کند و کتاب‌را از نو بصورتی مفصّلتر انشا و تحریر نماید ـ و او این‌کار را کرد.

در اینکه درعهدامیر تیموریادداشتهائی دربارهٔ واقعات‌زندگانی او نوشته می‌شده‌است (نه توسط شخص او بلکه بقلم وقایع نگاران) گویا تردیدی نباشد ، زیرا که غیاث‌الدّین علی‌یزدی آن‌را بدست داشته،و نظام‌الدّین شامی‌وشرف‌الدّین علی‌یزدی هردو ازآنها استفاده کرده‌اند. در ظفرنامهٔ شامی (چاپ فلیکس تاور ، ۱۹۵٦ ، ج ۱ ، ص ۱۰ تا ۱۱) اشاره‌ای باین خبر آمده‌است که ملخّص آن اینست: در سال‌هشتصدو چهار امیر صاحبقران باحضار بندهٔ کمینه نظام شامی‌مثال داد، واشارت عالی نفاذ یافت تاتاریخی که‌جهت‌آن حضرت و صادرات افعال ایشان از مبدأ ظهور این دولت ابد پیوند الی یومنا نوشته‌اندو ترتیب‌آن کما ینبغی بتقدیم نرسیده این بنده به تنقیح‌و ترتیب آن مشغول گردد ، امّا بشرطی که از حلیهٔ تکلّف و پیرایهٔ تصلّف مصون‌و محروس‌باشد ... علما درحقّ سخن پسندیده گفته‌اند ما تُدرکه العامة ولا تُنکره الخاصة ... التزام کردم که سوانح حالات و وقایع‌صادرات ایام این‌دولت چنانچه تاغایت ضابطانی که حاضر بوده‌اند و ملازمانی که در سفرو حضر وقایع و حوادث‌را ناظر ، ثبت کرده باشند لباس عبارتی پاك بی‌تکلّف پوشاند.

و شرف‌الدّین علی یزدی بتفصیل بیشتر در باب این‌مطلب بحث می کند و خلاصهٔ سخنان او اینست (ظفرنامه ، چاپ‌کلکته ، ج ۱ ، ص۲٤ وما بعد) :

حضرت صاحب قران‌را در سفر و حضر پیوسته اعاظم ارباب

استیوارت Major Ch. Stewart در ۱۸۳۰ در لندن بچاپ رسیده است . قسم تزوکات بفرانسه هم ترجمه شده و مقالهٔ مفصّلی نیز به آلمانی در بارهٔ تمام کتاب تحریر شده‌است . رجوع شود به «ادبیّات ایران» تألیف استوری ج ۱ ص ۲۸۰ تا ۲۸۲ . عنوان تزوکات تیموری گاهی نیز بر هردو قسمت کتاب اطلاق شده‌است ، ولی آنچه در این دو قسم آمده‌است گویا اصل ترکی نداشته‌و از انشای امیر تیمور نبوده است . ابوطالب حسینی تربتی که خویشتن‌را مترجم این کتاب از ترکی بفارسی معرّفی می کند در مقدّمه‌ای که بران نوشته‌است دعوی می کند که در حرمین اشرفین در کتبخانهٔ جعفر پاشا حاکم یمن کتابی ترکی دیدم از ملفوظات عالی حضرت جنت مکانی فردوس آشیانی صاحبقرانی ... آن‌را از ترکی بفارسی نقل نمودم .

ظنّ اینکه این مطلب را ابوطالب حسینی راست نگفته باشد و تمام کتاب اختراع خود او و تلفیق و تحریر اخباری باشد که از کتابهای تاریخی مثل ظفرنامهٔ نظام‌الدّین شامی و ظفرنامهٔ شرف‌الدّین علی‌یزدی وغیره برداشته‌است بسیار قوی است ، مخصوصاً که دارای اغلاط تاریخی متعدّد است . از مقدّمهٔ کتاب دیگری بنام **ملفوظات صاحبقرانی** تألیف افضل بخاری برمی‌آید که در ۱۰۴۷ وقتی که‌این کتاب ابوطالب حسینی تقدیم شاه جهان گردید و بر وی خوانده شد آن پادشاه متوجه خطاهای تاریخی آن واختلافاتی که بین مندرجات این کتاب‌و مضامین‌ظفرنامهٔ یزدی موجوداست گردید و به محمّدافضل پسر تربیت خان بخاری امر کرد آن را با کتب تاریخ مقابله کرده اغلاط آن‌را مرتفع سازد و عباراتی‌را که ابوطالب حسینی از خود

دیباچه

آنچه بنام **واقعات تیموری** یا **ملفوظات تیموری** شناخته می‌شود کتابیست بفارسی که حاوی بعضی مطالب تاریخی استو بقلم شخصی بنام ابوطالب‌حسینی تربتی‌تحریر یافته و او دعوی کرده‌است که اصل کتاب بزبان ترکی جغتائی و بانشای امیرتیمور گورکان بوده است و یادداشتهای شخصی او بوده‌است از وقایع زندگانیو سلطنت خودش . این کتاب دوقسمت دارد ، یکی ملفوظات و دیگری تُزوك یا تُزوكات (بمعنی بنیانها و تأسیسات و طرحها و تعبیه‌ها) . همین‌قسم اخیر است که باراوّل‌در ۱۷۷۳در اکسفرد باترجمهٔ انگلیسیو مقدّمهٔ مفصّلی به انگلیسی انتشار یافت و خواننده اینك چاپ مجدّد آن را در دست دارد . مترجم کتاب به انگلیسی شخصی بنام میجر ویلیام دیوی Major W. Davy بوده‌استو مهیّا کنندهٔ متن فارسی از برای چاپو ناشر مجموع متنو ترجمه شخصی بنام جوزف هوایت Joseph White که در آن زمان در اکسفرد مدرس زبان عربی بوده است . مصحّح و ناشر بعضی از عبارات متن‌را حذف کرده بوده‌و ترجمهٔ آنهارا هم نیاورده‌است ، مع‌هذا این متنو ترجمه‌خالی از ارزش نیست واقدام به تجدید طبع آن مفید می‌نمود . متن فارسی همین قسمت یعنی تزوکات در ایران بچاپ سنگی همراه قابوس نامه باهتمام رضاقلی‌خان هدایت لله باشی در۱۲۸۵ هجری منتشر شده ، و ترجمهٔ انگلیسی قسم نخستین یعنی ملفوظات نیز توسّط میجر چارلز

انتشارات کتابفروشی اسدی شماره ۶

تزوکات تیموری

تحریر ابوطالب حسینی تربتی بفارسی

با ترجمهٔ انگلیسی آن

از روی چاپ ۱۷۸۳ شهر اکسفرد

بطریق افست نقل شد

باهتمام کتابفروشی اسدی

طهران - میدان بهارستان

۱۳۴۲